Contents

*Addresses, telephone numb_____ _____ _____ this guide are
accurate at the time of pub_____ _____ ____nces resulting
from outdated information, ____ ____ ___ suggestions that may
assist us in preparing the next edition. Send us your comments:*
Michelin Travel Publications, PO Box 19001, Greenville, SC 29602-9001.

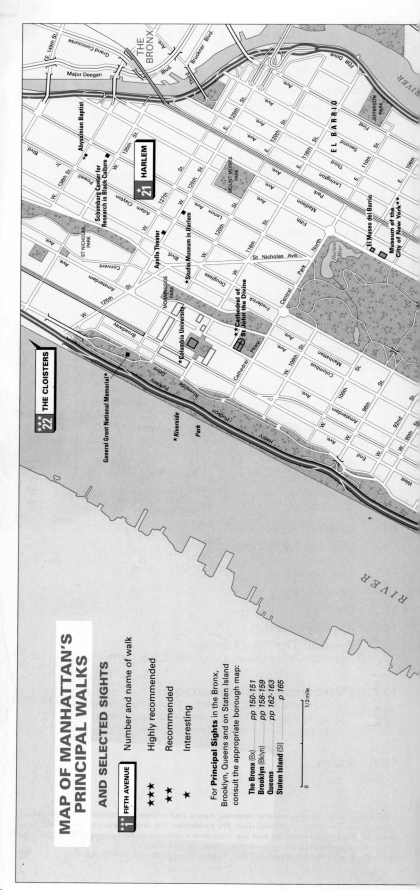

MAP OF MANHATTAN'S PRINCIPAL WALKS

AND SELECTED SIGHTS

★★★ **1 FIFTH AVENUE**   Number and name of walk

★★★   Highly recommended

★★   Recommended

★   Interesting

For **Principal Sights** in the Bronx, Brooklyn, Queens and on Staten Island consult the appropriate borough map:

The Bronx (Bx) ———— *pp 150-151*
Brooklyn (Bklyn) ———— *pp 158-159*
Queens ———— *pp 162-163*
Staten Island (SI) ———— *p 165*

0   1/2 mile

★★ **22** THE CLOISTERS

General Grant National Memorial ★

★ Riverside Park

★ Columbia University

★★ **21** HARLEM

Abyssinian Baptist

Schomburg Center for Research in Black Culture

Apollo Theater

★ Studio Museum in Harlem

★★ Cathedral of St John the Divine

THE BRONX

Major Deegan

Grand Concourse

Bruckner Blvd.

FDR Drive

EL BARRIO

JEFFERSON PARK

El Museo del Barrio

Museum of the City of New York ★★

MOUNT MORRIS PARK

ST NICHOLAS PARK

MORNINGSIDE PARK

Harlem Meer

RIVER

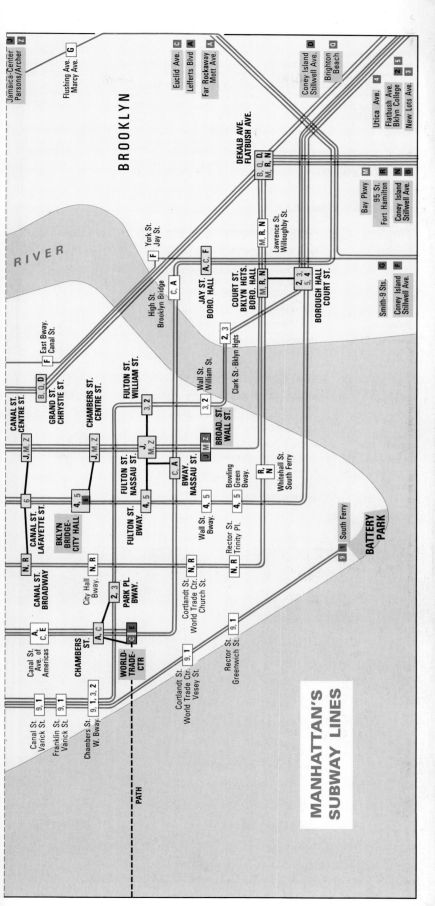

MANHATTAN'S SUBWAY LINES

TWO- AND FOUR-DAY ITINERARIES

Planning Hints. – The suggested itineraries described below are designed for visitors pressed for time and are best suited to the period from April to September, when daylight is more plentiful. For historical and practical information on the various sights and museums, consult the sight description *(page reference given in parentheses)*.
For additional information on organized sightseeing tours, see p 184. For ticket information for Broadway shows or Lincoln Center performances, see p 185. A list of Broadway theaters can be found on p 53.

Eating. – On-site eating facilities are indicated under the individual sight description by means of the symbol ⍟. Snacks, such as hot dogs, pretzels and shish-kebabs, are available from street vendors located on the main avenues and cross streets. A variety of delis, coffee shops and pizzerias offer light fare, some 24hrs/day. For additional restaurant information, see p 186 or consult the *Big Apple Guide (p 179).*

TWO-DAY ITINERARY

First Day	Getting Acquainted with New York
Morning	Gray Line Grand Tour (tour no. 3) *Departs daily 9, 11am & noon (mid-Jun–mid-Oct additional tour 2pm) from 900 Eighth Ave at 53rd St. Duration 4-5hrs. Commentary. $27.* ☎ *397-2600.*
Lunch	In midtown
Afternoon	The Metropolitan Museum of Art *(p 120)*
Evening	Broadway – Times Square★★ *(p 51)* or Lincoln Center★★ *(p 95)*

Second Day	From Rockefeller Center to SoHo and Greenwich Village
Morning	Rockefeller Center★★★ *(p 37)* Fifth Avenue★★★ *(p 30)* Empire State Building★★★ *(p 31)* Financial District★★★ *(p 58)*
Lunch	In lower Manhattan
Afternoon	Statue of Liberty★★★ *(p 55)* Ellis Island★★ *(p 57)*
Evening	SoHo★★ *(p 75)* or Greenwich Village★★ *(p 77)*

Aerial view of Manhattan

Stefan Schulhof

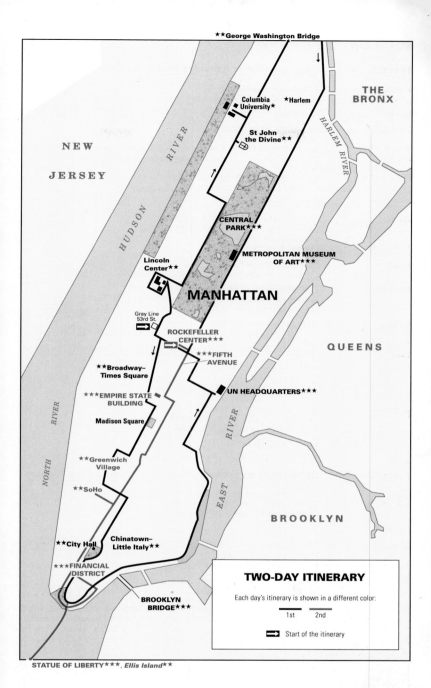

★★George Washington Bridge

↓

THE
BRONX

Columbia
University ★   ★ Harlem

St John
the Divine ★★

NEW

JERSEY

HUDSON RIVER

HARLEM RIVER

↑

CENTRAL
PARK★★★

METROPOLITAN MUSEUM
OF ART★★★

Lincoln
Center★★

MANHATTAN

QUEENS

Gray Line
53rd St.

ROCKEFELLER
CENTER★★★

★★★FIFTH
AVENUE

↓

★★Broadway–
Times Square

UN HEADQUARTERS★★★

★★★EMPIRE STATE
BUILDING

Madison Square

↑

EAST RIVER

NORTH RIVER

★★Greenwich
Village

★★SoHo

BROOKLYN

★★City Hall

Chinatown–
Little Italy★★

★★★FINANCIAL
DISTRICT

TWO-DAY ITINERARY

Each day's itinerary is shown in a different color:

1st   2nd

⇒ Start of the itinerary

BROOKLYN
BRIDGE★★★

STATUE OF LIBERTY★★★, *Ellis Island*★★

When in New York, take the time to:

- *get a facial at Bloomingdale's (p 94)*
- *go food shopping at Dean and DeLuca's (p 76) or at Zabar's (p 95)*
- *have tea at the Rainbow Room (p 39)*
- *walk across the Brooklyn Bridge (p 71)*
- *visit the Fulton fish market (p 67) at dawn*
- *have a drink at the Oak Bar at the Plaza Hotel (p 91)*
- *go Sunday bargain hunting on Orchard Street (p 75)*
- *have Sunday brunch at Tavern on the Green (p 90)*
- *enjoy ethnic cuisine in Chinatown (p 72), Little India (p 84)
  or Little Italy (p 73)*
- *shop for fresh produce at the Greenmarket at Union Square (p 109)
  on Saturday morning*
- *go gallery hopping in SoHo (p 75) on Saturday afternoon*

FOUR-DAY ITINERARY

First Day	**From Rockefeller Center to Broadway**
Morning	Rockefeller Center★★★ *(p 37)* The Museum of Modern Art★★★ *(p 140)*
Lunch	In midtown
Afternoon	Circle Line Boat Tour *(p 184)* *Departs mid-Mar–mid-Dec daily from Pier 83,* *W. 42nd St at Hudson River. Round-trip 3hrs. $18.* *Commentary. ✖ ♿ For sailing schedule ☏ 563-3200.*
Evening	Broadway – Times Square★★ *(p 51)*

Second Day	**From the Empire State Building to Lincoln Center**
Morning	Empire State Building★★★ *(p 31)* Stroll along Fifth Avenue★★★ *(p 30)* and 57th Street★ *(p 41)* Central Park★★★ *(p 87)*
Lunch	Picnic in Central Park *(numerous delis are located around Columbus Circle)*
Afternoon	The Metropolitan Museum of Art★★★ *(p 120)* or Solomon R. Guggenheim Museum★★ *(p 117)* Upper East Side★★ *(p 91)*
Evening	Lincoln Center★★ *(p 95)*

Third Day	**From the Statue of Liberty to SoHo and Greenwich Village**
Morning	Statue of Liberty★★★ *(p 55)* Ellis Island★★ *(p 57)*
Lunch	Ellis Island
Afternoon	Financial District★★★ *(p 58)* Civic Center – Brooklyn Bridge★★ *(p 68)* Chinatown – Little Italy★★ *(p 72)*
Evening	SoHo★★ *(p 75)* or Greenwich Village★★ *(p 77)*

Fourth Day	**United Nations Headquarters, The Cloisters, Park Avenue**
Morning	United Nations Headquarters★★★ *(p 48)* Stroll along East 42nd Street★★ *(p 45)* Grand Central Terminal★★ *(p 46)*
Lunch	In midtown
Afternoon	The Cloisters★★★ *(p 101)* Fort Tryon Park★★ *(p 106)* Stroll along Park Avenue★★ *(p 42)*
Evening	Dine in one of the elegant hotels surrounding Grand Army Plaza *(p 91)*

For visitors with additional time, or for those who wish to substitute certain sights along the above itineraries in Manhattan, we recommend consulting the museum section *(pp 110–146; see also p 14)* or the section on New York City's other four boroughs *(pp 147–175)*. Turn to p 11 for ideas on fun things to do while in New York City.

Ken Druse/The New York Botanical Garden, The Bronx

Peggy Rockefeller Rose Garden, New York Botanical Garden, The Bronx

FOUR-DAY ITINERARY

Each day's itinerary is shown in a different color:

1st   2nd   3rd   4th

➡ Start of the itinerary

THE CLOISTERS★★★

Fort Tryon Park★★

George Washington Bridge

HARLEM RIVER

HUDSON RIVER

NEW JERSEY

THE BRONX

MANHATTAN

CENTRAL PARK★★★

METROPOLITAN MUSEUM OF ART★★★

Guggenheim Museum★★

Lincoln Center★★

Upper East Side★★

Columbus Circle

★57th St.

Grand Army Plaza

Circle Line Pier 83

★★★ROCKEFELLER CENTER

42nd St.

★★Broadway– Times Square

FIFTH AVENUE★★★

Park Ave.★★

QUEENS

42nd St.★★

UN HEADQUARTERS★★★

EMPIRE STATE BUILDING★★★

EAST RIVER

Greenwich Village★★

SoHo★★

NORTH RIVER

★Civic Center

Chinatown– Little Italy★★

FINANCIAL DISTRICT★★★

BROOKLYN

BROOKLYN BRIDGE★★★

STATUE OF LIBERTY★★★, Ellis Island★★

13

Manhattan's Museums: What to See Where
(see index p 189 for page reference of sight descriptions):

20C Art	Alternative Museum
	Solomon R. Guggenheim Museum
	The New Museum of Contemporary Art
	The Museum of Modern Art
	Whitney Museum of American Art
African Art	The Metropolitan Museum of Art
	Museum for African Art
African-American Art and History	Schomburg Center for Research in Black Culture
	The Studio Museum in Harlem
American Art	American Wing at The Metropolitan Museum of Art
	National Academy of Design
	Whitney Museum of American Art
Asian Art and History	The Asia Society
	Chinatown History Museum
	Japan House
	The Metropolitan Museum of Art
Coins and Medals	American Numismatic Society
Decorative Arts	American Craft Museum
	Cooper-Hewitt National Museum of Design
	The Metropolitan Museum of Art
Old Masters	The Frick Collection
	The Metropolitan Museum of Art
Fire Trucks and Memorabilia	New York City Fire Museum
Folk Art	Museum of American Folk Art
Hispanic Art and History	El Museo del Barrio
	Hispanic Society of America
House Museums	Abigail Adams Smith Museum
	Fraunces Tavern
	The Frick Collection
	Gracie Mansion
	Morris-Jumel Mansion
	Old Merchant's House
Immigration	Ellis Island Immigration Museum
	Lower East Side Tenement Museum
Manuscripts	New York Public Library
	Pierpont Morgan Library
	Grolier Club
Maritime	Intrepid Sea-Air-Space Museum
	South Street Seaport
Media	Museum of Television and Radio
New York City History	Federal Hall National Memorial
	Fraunces Tavern
	Museum of the City of New York
	The New-York Historical Society
Photography	International Center of Photography
	The Metropolitan Museum of Art
	The Museum of Modern Art
Natural History	American Museum of Natural History
	Hayden Planetarium

Introduction

D & J Heaton/First Light

THE CITY OF NEW YORK

By far the most populous city in the United States, New York is a world unto itself by virtue of its size, the density and diversity of its population, its dynamic economic activity and its vibrant cultural life.

Location. – On the east coast of the United States at 40° north latitude and 74° west longitude, New York City is bathed by the Atlantic Ocean. The city occupies the western end of Long Island, all of two smaller islands (Manhattan and Staten Island) and a piece of the mainland to the north, adjacent to the Hudson River. The islands provide protection for one of the largest and safest harbors in the world, ideal for ocean-going vessels *(p 22)*. Access to the ocean is through the Narrows, a passage between Staten Island and Long Island. The city is rimmed by over 578 miles of coastline, which include some 14 miles of beaches.

In addition to its major islands, New York City also encompasses several small islands, notably Liberty Island, home of the STATUE OF LIBERTY; ELLIS ISLAND, once the nation's leading immigration center; Riker's Island (located north of LaGuardia airport), site of a large municipal prison; GOVERNOR'S ISLAND, a major US Coast Guard site; and ROOSEVELT ISLAND, once home to public health institutions and now a fashionable residential location.

The total area of the five boroughs *(below)* that make up New York City is about 320sq mi; the longest distance between its boundaries, from the northeast to the southwest, is about 35mi. New York City's height above sea level varies from 5ft (BATTERY PARK at the southern tip of Manhattan) to 400ft (Washington Heights in northern Manhattan). Its climate is continental, with predominating western winds and frequent refreshing sea breezes *(see details on the seasons p 179)*.

The Five Boroughs. – New York City as it exists today was created in 1898 when, under State Charter, the original city was expanded from its original confines of Manhattan to incorporate Brooklyn (Kings County), Queens (Queens County), the Bronx (Bronx County) and Staten Island (Richmond County). The counties correspond to the original colonial administrative divisions, and the names still persist to designate judicial districts. The five boroughs are not developed to the same extent: a few open spaces exist on the fringes of Brooklyn and Queens, and Staten Island, despite the construction of many new dwellings in the last decades, is still somewhat countrified.

Brooklyn, situated on the southwest tip of Long Island, is today the most populous of the five boroughs. Queens, to the northeast of Brooklyn, is the largest and fastest growing. The heavily developed Bronx, the only borough which is part of the mainland, forms the gateway to the city from the affluent suburbs to the north. Although it remains the least populated borough, Staten Island has been growing since the completion of the VERRAZANO-NARROWS BRIDGE from Brooklyn in 1964. Manhattan, the smallest of the boroughs with an area of 22sq mi, constitutes the heart of the city. With a population of 1,487,500, it is the most densely populated county in the US. This tongue-shaped island is the center for much of New York's cultural, financial, business and trade activity.

Although the consolidation of the five boroughs took place nearly a century ago, residents of the so-called "outer boroughs" traveling to Manhattan still say they are "going to the city."

Metropolitan Area. – The city's vast metropolitan area encompasses 22 counties and planning regions extending over 7,000sq mi and including about 18,087,000 residents. Seven of these counties are in New York State, nine in New Jersey and six in Connecticut. In addition to New York City, the area includes Newark, New Jersey (pop 275,200) and ten other cities of over 100,000 people.

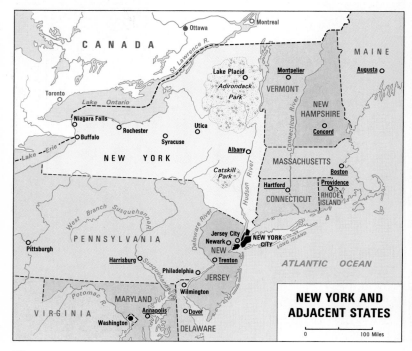

NEW YORK AND ADJACENT STATES

0   100 Miles

Among the organizations responsible for the operation and expansion of regional transportation facilities are the Port Authority of New York and New Jersey, which plans for the 17-county area in those two states, and the Triborough Bridge and Tunnel Authority.

The State of New York. – The city gave its name to the state, the 11th of the original 13 states of the Union, which by virtue of its economic expansion and political influence became known as the "Empire State." New York State extends from east of the Hudson River to the Great Lakes and Niagara Falls, and borders Canada on the north. The state is divided into counties and its capital is Albany (New York City was the capital from 1784 to 1797).

The flag of New York City, with its blue, white and orange vertical stripes, was inspired by the flag of the Netherlands in the 17C.

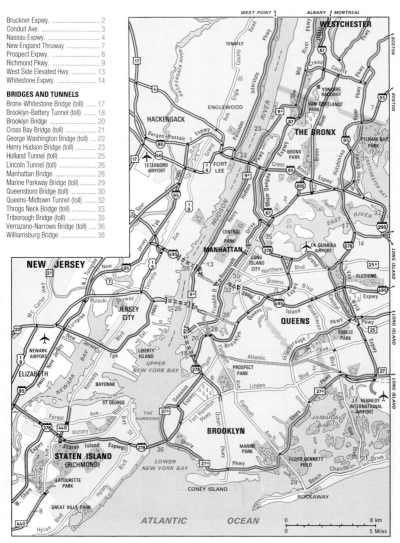

From Nieuw Amsterdam to New York

Before the arrival of Europeans, the island of Manhattan was inhabited by Algonquian- and Iroquoian-speaking Indians. The Algonquin tribe is credited for naming the island *Manhattan*, meaning "island of the hills."

1524   **Giovanni da Verrazano**, an Italian explorer in the service of the French king, François I, is the first European to land on the island of Manhattan *(p 157)*.

1609   **Henry Hudson** sails up the river (now bearing his name) in his ship, the *Half Moon,* while on a voyage for the Dutch East India Company.

1614   The name New Netherland, given to the newly founded Dutch colony, designates the area around present-day New York City. The term New England is given to the territory north of New York.

1625   First permanent European settlement is established on Manhattan. The trading post is named **Nieuw Amsterdam**.

1626   **Peter Minuit** of the Dutch West India Company buys Manhattan from the Algonquin Indians for the equivalent of $24.

1628   With the arrival of a regular minister, a member of the Reformed Dutch Church, the island's first church is established.

1639   The Dane, Johannes Bronck, settles beyond the Harlem River in the area now known as the Bronx.

1642   A settlement is founded at Maspeth (Queens), but first permanent settlement in Queens is not established until 1643, at Flushing.

1647   **Peter Stuyvesant** is appointed Director General of New Netherland.

1653   The city of Nieuw Amsterdam receives a charter and municipal rule. Stuyvesant has a protective wall built on the present location of WALL STREET.

1654   First permanent Jewish colonial settlement is established in Nieuw Amsterdam.

1661   First permanent settlement on Staten Island is established at Oude Dorp, near the site of present-day Fort Wadsworth.

1664   As a repercussion of the English and Dutch trading rivalries in Europe, the English take Nieuw Amsterdam without a struggle and rename it **New York** after the Duke of York, brother of the English king, Charles II.

British Rule

1667   The Treaty of Breda, ending the second Anglo-Dutch war, confirms English control over the province of New Netherland. The town of New York passes under the English system of municipal government. English replaces Dutch as the official language.

1673   The Dutch retake New York without a fight and rename it New Orange.

1674   By the Treaty of Westminster the province of New Netherland becomes permanently English.

1686   The Dongan Charter—the second English charter—is granted, carrying the city seal *(p 17)*.

1725   New York's first newspaper, *The New-York Gazette,* is founded by **William Bradford**.

1729   New York's first synagogue is established on Beaver Street, in lower Manhattan.

1733-34   **John Peter Zenger** founds *The New-York Weekly Journal,* in which he attacks the governor. A year later Zenger is imprisoned for slander. His acquittal marks the beginning of a free press.

1754   The first college, **King's College,** now COLUMBIA UNIVERSITY, opens.

1763   The Treaty of Paris marks the end of the French and Indian War, or Seven Years' War (1756-1763), and confirms English control on the North American continent.

1765   Meeting of the Stamp Act Congress in New York, where representatives from nine colonies denounce the English colonial policy of taxation without representation.

1766   Repeal of the Stamp Act. A statue is erected to **William Pitt**, the British statesman who did most to obtain the repeal.

1767   Parliament passes the **Townshend Acts**, a series of four acts that increased taxation and threatened the already established traditions of colonial self-government. The repeal three years later coincided with the Boston Massacre.

1775-83   The War of Independence, also known as the **American Revolution**.

View of New York c.1850

Eno Collection, New York Public Library

1776	The **Declaration of Independence** (July 4) is adopted. On November 17, Fort Washington in northern Manhattan falls and the British occupy all of the present New York City until 1783.
1783	The **Treaty of Paris** (September 3) ends the American Revolution and England recognizes the independence of the 13 colonies. The last British troops evacuate New York and Washington returns to the city in triumph before bidding farewell to his troops at FRAUNCES TAVERN on December 4.
1784	New York City becomes the capital of New York State and a year later, is named US capital under the Articles of Confederation.
1788	The **US Constitution** is ratified.
1789	**George Washington,** elected first president, takes the oath of office at FEDERAL HALL in New York City.

A Century of Growth

1790	First official census of the population of Manhattan: 33,000. Federal capital moves to Philadelphia.
1792	Founding of the forerunner to the New York Stock Exchange by the buttonwood tree *(p 63)* on Wall Street .
1797	Albany becomes the permanent capital of New York State.
1807	**Robert Fulton** launches his steamboat, the *Clermont,* on the Hudson. The first demonstration had been made on the Collect Pond by John Fitch in 1796 *(p 68).*
1812	**War of 1812**: the United States declares war on Britain and the port of New York suffers from the ensuing blockade. Present CITY HALL opens.
1814	The Treaty of Ghent ends the War of 1812.
1825	Opening of the **Erie Canal.** New York becomes the gateway to the Great Lakes and the West. Growing overseas trade makes New York a leading port.
1828	The SOUTH STREET SEAPORT becomes the center of New York's port activities.
1834	City of Brooklyn is incorporated.
1835	The Great Fire destroys an extensive area in the business district *(p 59).*
1853	World's Fair at the Crystal Palace *(p 32).*
1857	Construction of CENTRAL PARK begins; the park is officially completed in 1876.
1861	Outbreak of the **Civil War** with New York, one of the 23 Northern States.
1865	End of the Civil War. Assassination of President Abraham Lincoln *(p 69).*
1868	Opening of **the El**, first experimental elevated railway in lower Manhattan.
1869	On September 24, financier Jay Gould, who had tried to corner the gold market with his associate James Fisk, sold out and brought about the financial panic known as "Black Friday" *(p 59).*
1882	Electricity is offered for general use by Thomas Edison's plant in lower Manhattan.
1883	Opening of the **Brooklyn Bridge** *(p 71).*
1886	Inauguration of the **Statue of Liberty** *(p 55).*
1891	**Carnegie Hall** *(p 42)* is inaugurated with Tchaikovsky's American conducting debut.
1892	Inauguration of the immigration facility at **Ellis Island** *(p 57);* until the mid-1920s, over 12 million immigrants are processed here.
1898	**Greater New York City** is created comprising five boroughs: Manhattan, Brooklyn, the Bronx, Queens and Staten Island. With a population of more than 3 million, New York is the world's largest city.

Twentieth Century

1902	Completion of one of the first skyscrapers in New York, the FLATIRON BUILDING.
1904	Opening of the first underground line of the subway.
1913	**Armory Show** *(p 26)*, an international exhibit introducing modern art to America. Completion of GRAND CENTRAL TERMINAL and the WOOLWORTH BUILDING.
1914-18	**World War I.**
1916	First zoning resolution *(p 25)* pertaining to construction of skyscrapers using setbacks.
1920s	Harlem *(p 99)* experiences its heyday as an entertainment center, with jazz clubs featuring such names as Duke Ellington and Cab Calloway.
1929	Stock market crash (financial panic of October) signals the start of the Great Depression.
1931	The **Empire State Building** is completed after two years work *(p 31).*
1934-45	Fiorello H. La Guardia *(p 162)* is mayor of New York City.
1939-40	World's Fair at Flushing Meadow attracts over 44 million visitors.
1939-45	**World War II.**
1940	The 12 core buildings of the **Rockefeller Center** *(p 37)* are completed.
1945	**United Nations** charter is drafted in San Francisco.
1948	The JOHN F. KENNEDY AIRPORT (originally Idlewild) opens in Queens.
1952	The General Assembly of the UNITED NATIONS meets for the first time in its New York headquarters overlooking the East River.
1959	Construction of **Lincoln Center** *(p 95)* begins.
1964	Inauguration of the VERRAZANO-NARROWS BRIDGE, the longest suspension bridge in the US, which links Brooklyn to Staten Island.
1964-65	World's Fair on the same site as the 1939-40 Fair *(above).*
1965	Assassination of Malcolm X at the Audubon Ballroom in Harlem.
1969	Ticker Tape Parade: New York gives a triumphal welcome to the crew of Apollo 11, the first astronauts to land on the moon.
1973	Opening of the WORLD TRADE CENTER in Manhattan.
1975-76	American Bicentennial celebrations (New York City: May 1975–Nov 1976).
1980	John Lennon is assassinated in front of his New York residence, the DAKOTA.
1986	**Statue of Liberty Centennial** celebrations (New York City: July, Liberty Weekend '86).
1989	Election of New York City's first African-American mayor, David Dinkins.
1990	Opening of the ELLIS ISLAND IMMIGRATION MUSEUM.
1993	Terrorist bomb rocks the World Trade Center, injuring hundreds.

POPULATION

New York City is the most populous city in the United States and was one of the few cities of the industrial Northeast to increase its population between 1980 and 1990. Its growth was attributable to the acceleration of immigration during the 1980s. Population expanded from 7,071,639 in 1980 to 7,322,600 in 1990. Of those 7.3 million people, more than 28 percent (2,082,931) were born abroad.

The surge in immigration continues a pattern begun in the mid-19C. New York has long been known for its diversity, traceable to the successive waves of immigration that arrived through the major port of entry into the New World. It has often been described as the "largest Irish city" or the "largest Jewish community" or the "second largest Italian community" in the world. The influx of immigrants, which slowed following the restrictive immigration laws of the early 1920s, began again in the 1960s, with new arrivals coming from Latin America, Asia and the Middle East. It is a tribute to the city that New Yorkers have come to share a common outlook and way of life, retaining their ethnic identity and the pride of their cultural heritage.

The growth of newcomers during the 1980s transformed many neighborhoods in New York City. Expanding population in Manhattan's CHINATOWN, for example, has dislodged residents of LITTLE ITALY to the north. Similar developments have occurred in Sheepshead Bay in Brooklyn, where Russian immigration has been heavy, or in Washington Heights *(above West 155th St, flanking the Hudson River)* in northern Manhattan, where immigrants from the Dominican Republic have settled in large numbers.

Population from 1626 to 1990

Year	No. of Inhabitants	
1626	200	The first boatload of settlers brought by the Dutch to Nieuw Amsterdam consists primarily of French Huguenots.
1656	1,000	The first immigrants are followed by English, Scots, Germans and Scandinavians.
1756	16,000	
1790	33,000	
1800	60,000	Half of New York's population is of English origin.
1850s	630,000	Germans and Irish arrive in large numbers.
1880	1,911,700	Eastern Europeans and Southern Italians immigrate in great waves. This influx continues until 1924.
1900	3,437,200	This figure includes residents of the five boroughs, which were incorporated in 1898.
1920	5,620,000	After World War I, black migration increases both from the American south and from the West Indies.
1924		Immigration laws limit foreign immigration.
1930	6,930,500	Decline in growth rate.
1950	7,892 000	After World War II, a large Puerto Rican colony settles in New York.
1960	7,782,000	From 1950 to 1960, the city loses more than 100,000 inhabitants as many New Yorkers move to the suburbs.
1970	7,896,000	Out-migration of New York's population from the city to the suburbs continues, mirroring the overall trend of cities in the northeast.
1980	7,072,000	
1990	7,322,600	New York's foreign–born population of 2 million persons reflects the great influx of immigrants from Asia, Latin America and the Caribbean since 1965.

A Cosmopolitan Mix

In the 19C and at the beginning of the 20C, recent immigrants, referred to as "hyphenated citizens" (Irish-Americans, Italian-Americans, German-Americans and so on), were often denied social status by the "aristocracy" of British and Dutch origin. However, the pyramid of New York society was unable to withstand the forces of change, and today these multi-cultural strands together with the more recent waves of immigrants, make up the very fabric of New York's population.

The Irish. – Irish immigration dates back to the 17C, but it was the outbreak of the Irish potato famine, in 1846, that touched off the mass exodus from Ireland. In 1890, one fourth of all New Yorkers were Irish. From the beginning, the Irish were drawn to public affairs and actively participated in city government. Carrying on the religious tradition of their homeland, they have largely contributed to the influence of the Roman Catholic Church in the United States. Still a quite homogeneous group, Irish-Americans are famous for their exuberant celebration of St Patrick's Day, March 17, to honor their patron saint.

Italians. – Large-scale immigration, mainly of laborers and peasants from southern Italy and Sicily, started only after 1870. Some returned to the old country with their first savings, but the vast majority brought their families to settle in America. Many Italian immigrants started out in the building industry where they worked under the heavy hand of "padroni" (construction bosses); however, over the years, hard work and enterprise often combined to establish a small family business, especially in the restaurant, contracting and trucking trades. After generations of economic and social rewards in the New World, Italian-Americans remain deeply attached to the traditions of their family and community life. The colorful atmosphere of their homeland is still reflected in LITTLE ITALY.

Germans and Austrians. – This was probably the most rapidly assimilated group, although one of the largest. Composed of conservatives and liberals, craftsmen, laborers, businessmen and intellectuals, the German-speaking immigrants no longer form a very unified group. Leaving behind them in most cases the language of the "old country," they still share a few national traditions. Germans arrived in great numbers during the 19C, particularly after the failed 1848-1849 revolution in Germany. They settled mostly around TOMPKINS SQUARE from where they later moved further uptown. Some German atmosphere can still be found in YORKVILLE.

The Chinese. – Coming to America after the Civil War to work on railway lines and in mines, Chinese immigrants hailed mainly from Canton. The most recent newcomers, primarily from Hong Kong, Shanghai and Taiwan, have swelled their numbers to an estimated 360,000, with the great-

Italian Family en route to Ellis Island (c.1905), by Lewis W. Hine

Lewis W. Hine Collection, New York Public Library

est concentration living in steadily expanding CHINATOWN. Many second-generation Chinese make their home in boroughs other than Manhattan, particularly in Queens. The overall Asian population in the city doubled during the 1980s to 512,000.

Eastern Europeans. – The massive waves of pre-World War I emigration from the old Russian Empire were not made up of Russians, but mostly of members of various minority nationalities—Ukrainians, Poles, Lithuanians and others. Like most newly arrived immigrants they tended to congregate in the same neighborhoods as their countrymen. The 1917 Revolution brought only a trickle of so-called White Russians to New York as compared to the large numbers who emigrated to European capitals. Many Ukrainians and Russians, however, were among the displaced persons who settled in New York in the wake of World War II. During the 1980s and 1990s, migration from Russia grew sharply with many of the new residents settling in Brooklyn.

Jews. – Sephardic Jews, originally from Spain and Portugal, had come to New York in the 17C, mostly via Holland and Latin America. Today, however, the majority of the New York Jews are of Eastern and Central European descent (Ashkenazi). Manhattan's LOWER EAST SIDE was the first home for 1.5 million Jews who entered America between 1880 and 1910; a great number also settled in Brooklyn communities. The New York Jewish population has actively participated in economic and cultural endeavors, and the names of many Jewish individuals and institutions are woven into the history of New York.

African-Americans. – Although there were blacks among the early inhabitants of New York, it was only in the 20C that blacks migrated to the city in large numbers. Today, African-Americans number about 1,757,000 or roughly one-fourth of the New York population. Initial black migration came from the American south. In the past two decades, migration from the Caribbean has resulted in a new Caribbean community in Upper Manhattan and Brooklyn.
The black community has richly contributed to the character of the city. It has produced distinguished writers, playwrights and performers, and the influence of "rhythm and blues" and jazz is deeply felt on the American musical scene *(p 100)*. During recent decades many blacks have availed themselves of the great educational and economic opportunities offered in New York, thus increasing their numbers in the professions as well as politics, government and private business. Particularly notable was the 1989 election of David Dinkins, the first African-American to serve as mayor of New York City. Yet, despite the progress of some, many more black New Yorkers have yet to escape the effects of a heritage that includes centuries of slavery and discrimination. Many African-American neighborhoods in the city, including parts of HARLEM in Manhattan, Bedford-Stuyvesant in Brooklyn and South Jamaica in Queens, show the effects of poverty—abandoned buildings, trash-strewn lots, shuttered stores. On many of the city's indices—unemployment, homelessness, infant mortality, school drop-out ratio— African-Americans continue to suffer disproportionately.

Latinos. – The rapid growth of the Puerto Rican population has brought their number from less than a thousand in 1910 to almost 900,000 in 1984. Puerto Ricans are American citizens and as such are free to travel between Puerto Rico and the continental United States without a visa or regard to quotas. The Latino population, which includes Puerto Ricans together with the latest newcomers from the south—Cubans, Dominicans, Colombians, Ecuadorians and other Latin Americans—now forms about one-fifth of the city's population, numbering 1,783,000 in 1990, and representing its largest foreign language group. The major concentration of the Puerto Rican population in the city is in the Bronx, but the heart of New York's Puerto Rican community is East Harlem, better known as EL BARRIO. Parts of the UPPER WEST SIDE, the Bronx, Brooklyn and Queens are also host to significant numbers of Latin Americans. Mindful of their culture, Latinos have emerged as a vital community, lending a distinctive flavor to the life of the city.

Additional Ethnic Groups. – A sizable Greek community lives in Astoria, Queens, and a number of Armenians have settled in the Bronx. The liberalization of the immigration regulations has brought an influx of such diverse ethnic groups as Koreans, Indians, Vietnamese, Haitians, Arabs and Senegalese, making New York City home to more than 100 different nationalities.

ECONOMY

Despite periodic hand-wringing about its economy, New York City boasts a powerful lineup of economic assets. First is its sheer size: the New York area has the largest concentration of people, income, finance, industry and transportation of any urban area in the US. Some 7.3 million people live in New York City, twice as many as in any other American city. The economy provides over 3.5 million jobs, most in an agglomeration of 200,000 businesses notable for their diversity. The city is home to 41 of the *Fortune 500* industrial companies and 59 of the *Fortune 500* service companies.

New York streets have long been synonymous with some of the city's key industries: Wall Street with finance, Broadway with entertainment, Madison Avenue with advertising and Seventh Avenue with fashion.

The Port. – New York's sheltered, ice-free harbor, and 750mi of shoreline easily accessible to the Atlantic yet safe from its buffeting, contributed to the city's early ascendancy. Ships anchored in safety and, as industry built berths in lower Manhattan along the East and Hudson rivers, the city became a center of young America's trade with the world. The port is still the nation's largest, although the advent of containership technology has forced most active piers from crowded Manhattan to roomier sites in Brooklyn, Staten Island and New Jersey, where the world's largest container terminal is at Port Newark/Elizabeth. Some 100 shipping lines serve about 300 ports in 120 countries. In 1990, the harbor handled $50 billion worth of cargo.

Most port services are managed by the powerful Port Authority of New York and New Jersey. The Authority operates: the harbor's general cargo and containership terminals; six tunnels and bridges connecting the city with New Jersey; the region's major bus terminal on West 42nd Street; the Port Authority TransHudson (PATH) rail rapid transit system; three major airports; two heliports; the World Trade Center complex in lower Manhattan; and a passenger ship terminal on the Hudson River, home port for the world's largest and most luxurious cruise ships.

Finance. – New York's eminence as a seaport led to its leadership in banking. The city now holds 21 percent of the world's banking assets, and its five largest commercial banks—Citicorp, Chase Manhattan, Morgan, Chemical and Bankers Trust—boast cumulative assets of about half a trillion dollars. All major financial institutions, domes-

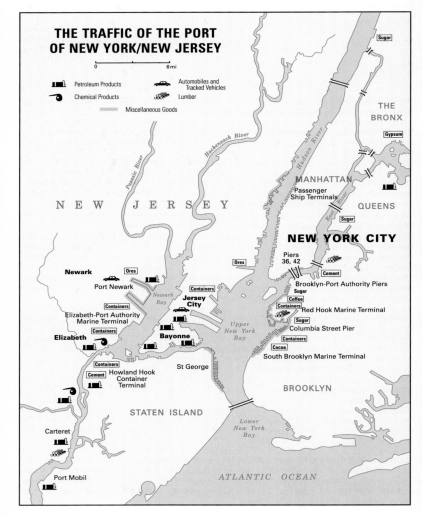

tic and foreign, maintain a presence in New York; among them are 400 foreign banks, far more than in any other US city. Nearly 100,000 of the city's banking jobs are tied to exports. Much of the industry is crowded into the downtown FINANCIAL DISTRICT, but it has expanded onto major midtown avenues, including Park, Madison and Fifth, and its operations are now spreading to Queens and Brooklyn.

New York is also the place where the nation buys and sells its stock. Some 73 percent of US-based stock trades are conducted here, notably on Wall Street's NEW YORK STOCK EXCHANGE and the American Stock Exchange. Lower Manhattan is home to major commodity exchanges (p 60), which trade in such products as gold, silver, oil, cotton, cocoa and coffee.

Closely related to New York finance are such large service industries as accounting, insurance and law. Four of the so-called "Big Six" accounting firms, over 700 insurance companies and 5,000 law firms, including many of the nation's top 25, are located in New York.

Transportation and Communication. – New York is the only US city accessible through three major airports (JOHN F. KENNEDY, LAGUARDIA and Newark), which annually serve 75 million passengers (52 million domestic and 23 million international). Travelers also arrive via a rail network that brings in 337,000 people daily, mostly commuters. Within the city, New Yorkers are served by the world's longest (708.6mi) rapid transit system, 12,000 taxicabs and 200 bus routes.

New York also reaches out to the world through communications. The city hosts three major television networks (ABC, NBC and CBS); telecasting, including cable, employs 23,000 people. Printing and publishing account for some 88,000 jobs in the city, which is home to two leading national newsmagazines (*Time* and *Newsweek*), 15 daily newspapers, the two major wire services (Associated Press and United Press International), and many prestigious book and magazine publishing companies, including McGraw-Hill, MacMillan and Bantam. Film production in New York, which increased 70 percent in the last decade, employs more than 10,000 New Yorkers.

New York is a world leader in advertising and public relations. The city's 1,400 ad agencies employ some 32,000 people. Madison Avenue is still the hub, but several agencies are moving into GREENWICH VILLAGE. Public relations employs 4,500 people. With its more than 90 two- and four-year colleges and universities, the city is renowned as an outstanding center for higher learning and scientific research.

Computer Technology. – New York City has more computer power than any other city in the nation. Its personal computers, microcomputers and mainframes are especially vital to the publishing, finance and medical industries. As a result, such service industries as electronic information, computer software, computer professional services and data processing have been growing at double-digit rates in the 1990s. New York City now has 1,600 data-processing firms employing nearly 33,000 people. Many are located in Manhattan, but the New York Stock Exchange, among others, has shifted its huge data-processing load to the city's large, new Metrotech Center in Brooklyn. Exemplifying the new growth is the city's computer software industry, which expanded by 400 percent in the 1980s and now accounts for some 6,000 high-pay jobs. Every large software firm has a major presence in New York.

Manufacturing. – Manufacturing's share of the economy has long been declining. Still, New York's highly diverse manufacturing base includes 24 industrial parks and 15,000 companies, many relying on a reservoir of specialized labor skills. From the city's 19C clothing workshops has emerged today's **garment industry**, embracing sophisticated midtown high-fashion designers and tiny factories in CHINATOWN. Pressed by foreign competition, New York is still the world leader, with nearly 100,000 people at work in the various trades. One fourth are on Seventh Avenue, where designers and showrooms are centered and hand trucks clatter through the streets. Some high-end manufacturing remains in this traditional Garment Center, but most has been moved to Chinatown, Sunset Park in Brooklyn and Flushing in Queens.

About 22 percent of the nation's **diamond and jewelry industry** is in Manhattan. The traditional centers are on West 47th Street ("Diamond and Jewelry Way" p 34), between Fifth Avenue and Avenue of the Americas, and on Canal Street. Diamond and jewelry trades employ 26,000 New Yorkers, many with unique skills.

The city's important emerging industries, such as semiconductors, health-care equipment and computer equipment, also bank on high-skill workers.

Tourism. – Some 25 million people who visit New York annually are drawn by the city's glamour, fine dining and shopping, and an array of tourist meccas and cultural attractions. A remarkable range of retail shops draw world-wide customers. Such names as TIFFANY & CO and Saks Fifth Avenue evoke images of smart shopping, and middle-class Macy's has long claimed the title of "the world's largest store."

In 1990, 783 organizations convened in New York, generating $1.1 billion in economic activity. The Broadway theater had an estimated $2.1 billion impact on the city's economy in 1992. The city's over 240 theaters range from Off-Off Broadway avant-garde houses to such large and famous showplaces as the RADIO CITY MUSIC HALL, CARNEGIE HALL and the LINCOLN CENTER.

Fine arts in New York is both an attraction to visitors and an industry in itself. Working artists are transforming entire Manhattan neighborhoods, including SOHO, NOHO, TRIBECA and parts of CHELSEA. The city boasts more than 400 art galleries and its 150 museums include such world-class art attractions as the METROPOLITAN MUSEUM OF ART, the MUSEUM OF MODERN ART and the GUGGENHEIM MUSEUM, as well as special-interest museums in such fields as photography, crafts, television and radio, and Jewish, African, American Indian and Latino culture. Overall the city estimates the annual impact of the visual and performing arts (fine arts, stage, dance and concerts) on the New York economy at $6.5 billion.

ARCHITECTURE AND CITY PLANNING

A stunning showcase for contemporary architecture, New York is first and foremost a city of skyscrapers. Yet beyond the skyline's perennially changing profile of steel and glass lies an architectural landscape remarkably rich in history and variety, including frame farmhouses and marble mansions, gilded theaters, soaring cathedrals and some of the finest brownstones and early 20C civic monuments in the US.

18C. – Colonial architecture flourished during the British occupation of New York. Prior to that, however, Dutch architectural elements distinguished the simple dwellings built in the area. The most important building from New York's Dutch colonial era is the Peter Claeson Wyckoff House (c.1652) in Brooklyn *(5902 Clarendon Rd)*, the oldest surviving structure both in the city and the state. Its sloping roof, flared eaves and columned porch are typical of the early Dutch frame farmhouses, also recalled by the DYCKMAN HOUSE (c.1785), the only Dutch structure extant in Manhattan (both are now museums).

With the arrival of the British came the **Georgian style**, influential in this country from about 1720 to 1780 during the reigns of kings George II and III. The symmetrical massing, heavy corner quoins (stone or wood blocks), pedimented porticos, and Palladian windows of such buildings as ST PAUL'S CHAPEL (1763), on lower Broadway, characterize this style; the MORRIS-JUMEL and VAN CORTLANDT mansions provide additional examples of typical Georgian residences.

Popular immediately after the Revolution, the gracefully proportioned **Federal style** drew on prototypes from ancient Rome to evoke pride in the new Republic; identifying characteristics include slender columns, refined Classical detailing and elegant fanlights. The 1828 Roman Catholic Orphan's Asylum (1828) at no. 32 Prince Street is among the most significant Federal buildings in the city. Located in the Hudson River Valley, BOSCOBEL represents another example of the style.

19C. – The Federal style persisted well into the 19C, shifting around 1815 to the heavier, more robust forms of the **Greek Revival**. Inspired by recently excavated monuments in ancient Greece, this style was superbly suited to grand civic buildings like the FEDERAL HALL NATIONAL MEMORIAL (1833), whose Doric portico was modeled on that of the Parthenon; the SNUG HARBOR CULTURAL CENTER on Staten Island also boasts some of the finest Greek Revival structures in the city.

The Victorian Era. – The period from the 1840s to the 1880s is noted for its eclectic, highly picturesque styles. The brownstone facades, elaborate tracery and pointed-arch windows of TRINITY CHURCH and GRACE CHURCH evoke the darkly romantic mood of the **Gothic Revival**. ST PATRICK'S CATHEDRAL represents another noted example of the style. Also rooted in the architecture of medieval Europe, the **Romanesque Revival** style featured rough cut stone, round arched windows, and heavy massing, displayed by such monumental structures as the AMERICAN MUSEUM OF NATURAL HISTORY, on Central Park West. The style also distinguishes numerous churches, apartment buildings and row houses.

The **Italianate style** was favored in the 1850s and 1860s. Its characteristically heavy cornices, pediments—with elaborate brackets—and tall arched windows appeared on countless cast-iron commercial buildings and brownstones. Designed by A. J. Davis in 1854, the Litchfield Villa in PROSPECT PARK is a prime example of the Italianate villa.

By the 1870s, the elegant **Second Empire** was the ultimate in fashion, as New Yorkers became obsessed with all things Parisian. This grandiose style, with its signature double-pitched mansard roof, is best represented by the loft and department store buildings dominating Ladies Mile *(Fifth Ave, between 23rd and 14th Sts)* and the SoHo Cast-Iron historic district, in particular the "King" and "Queen" on GREENE STREET.

The fanciful **Queen Anne** style appeared in the late 19C, distinguishing apartment buildings and row houses with elaborately decorated dormers, towers, patterned roof shingles and bay windows; the picturesque houses in the HENDERSON PLACE HISTORIC DISTRICT are typical of the style.

The Brownstones. – The quintessential symbol of the New York neighborhood, the brownstone is the legacy of various speculative booms of the 19C, when row after rhythmic row—punctuated by repeating patterns of stoops, cornices and plate-glass windows—appeared along the city's long residential blocks. Originally, the 4- or 5-story buildings housed a single family in grand style; now, most are divided into apartments, although a recent renovation movement has restored some to their original layout. Designed in the various popular styles of the day, many of the fine brownstones are located in BROOKLYN HEIGHTS and other areas of the borough. Brownstones abound in Manhattan particularly on the Upper East and West Sides, in GREENWICH VILLAGE, Murray Hill, GRAMERCY PARK and HARLEM.

Note: builders first used brown sandstone—a cheap substitute for limestone and marble—in the 1820s and 1830s. The term "brownstone" now refers to any row house, be it faced with stone or brick.

20C. – The classically inspired **Beaux-Arts** movement, based on the academic principles of the French Ecole des Beaux-Arts, ushered in the 20C with an explicit rejection of the eccentricities and excessive ornament of Victorian architecture. Among its leading lights were McKim, Mead and White, and Richard Morris Hunt (the first American graduate of the Ecole), whose designs derived from English, French and Italian Renaissance prototypes. The formal symmetry, classical columns and sumptuous interiors were the perfect expression for the East Side mansions of wealthy clients and such monumental public buildings as GRAND CENTRAL TERMINAL (1913), the NEW YORK PUBLIC LIBRARY (1911) and the UNITED STATES CUSTOMS HOUSE (1907) at Bowling Green, considered among the most masterful Beaux-Arts designs in the US.

The Skyscrapers. – By the early 20C, new structural technology led to a building type that would forever change the New York skyline: the skyscraper. Earlier, builders had been limited by the weight of load-bearing masonry, but the use of lighter steel framing and caisson foundations enabled them to attain greater heights. Even so, no tall building would have been financially feasible without another innovation—the passenger elevator—which, for the first time, made higher floors as rentable as lower stories. Among the significant early steel-framed skyscrapers that still soar in lower Manhattan are the 12-story Bayard-Condict Building (1899) on Bleecker Street (New York's only structure by Louis Sullivan); the 22-story Renaissance-style FLATIRON BUILDING (1901); and the Gothic Revival WOOLWORTH BUILDING, the world's tallest edifice (800ft) when completed in 1913.

While such buildings were a boon to developers, their ever increasing bulk also generated sizable controversy. Changes in design followed a 1916 zoning law, which regulated the height and volume of buildings in relation to the width of the street. It limited the maximum floor area to 12 times a site's area, resulting in setbacks and the base-and-shaft configuration of such stylized **Art Deco** masterpieces as the CHRYSLER BUILDING (1929) and the EMPIRE STATE BUILDING (1930). Another landmark skyscraper of this period is the 70-story GE BUILDING, notable as the first office building to use the slab form (with gentle setbacks).

Post-World War II. – Rising straight up with no setbacks, base or shaft, the slab found its first pure form in the sleek 1948 SECRETARIAT BUILDING at the United Nations, also the first New York skyscraper to employ another new technology: the glass curtain wall (hung from a supporting metal frame). Another pivotal building was LEVER HOUSE, first to use the slab to comply with the 1916 zoning rule (which stipulated that if a building occupied only twenty-five percent of its lot, no setbacks were necessary). The simple form and austere surfaces of Lever House inspired a new wave of office buildings in the **International Style**—free of all ornament and historical references—which reached its apogee in the bronze-and-glass SEAGRAM BUILDING (1956) designed by Ludwig Mies van der Rohe (his only New York City structure) and Philip Johnson.

While the 1960s became the era of the "glass box," dominating the FINANCIAL DISTRICT and the AVENUE OF THE AMERICAS in midtown, numerous towers in reinforced concrete also appeared, including I.M. Pei's Silver Towers Complex (1966), located in GREENWICH VILLAGE, one the city's first exposed concrete apartment houses. The walk-through atrium is a feature of many skyscrapers built since the 1970s—including CITICORP, TRUMP TOWER and the WORLD TRADE CENTER towers, which took advantage of a zoning bonus that allows up to twenty percent more space in exchange for a ground-level plaza. The twin World Trade Towers are also notable for an innovative metal mesh, instead of a curtain wall, used for support.

Recent Trends. – In the 1980s, a spurt of building activity concentrated on the East Side in midtown added no fewer than two dozen high-rise towers to the skyline. Notable are the granite-sheathed 5-sided IBM BUILDING by Edward Larrabee Barnes and the SONY PLAZA (former AT&T Building) by Philip Johnson and John Burgee. This tower—one of the most debated of recent decades—is the quintessential expression of post-Modern architecture, noted for its broken geometry and applied stylized ornament with overt Classical references; the pediment atop the building has been likened to the top of a Chippendale highboy.

Another recent trend is the multi-block "skyscraper city," in which several buildings are coordinated in a park-like setting. Recent versions of this scheme (initiated in ROCKEFELLER CENTER) include Cesar Pelli's BATTERY PARK CITY complex on the Hudson River, which incorporates residential and office buildings, landscaped promenades and docks for private yachts.

City Development. – For all its density, crowding and variety, New York retains a surprising sense of order, imposed by the neat grid of streets and avenues that creates a logical system of blocks. For almost two centuries after Nieuw Amsterdam was founded in 1621, however, the city developed haphazardly and roads were simply laid out as needed along old cart paths. (Many of the winding streets in lower Manhattan have their origins in these early byways).

During the 18C, the most extensive development was at the southern tip of Manhattan and along the shipping docks on the East River, which boasted superior anchorage because its high salt content made the water slow to freeze. After the Revolution, expansion continued steadily northward. As speculators competed to parcel off confiscated Loyalist land in a frenzy of development, the need for an organized plan was increasingly apparent. The result was the 1811 Randel Plan, which patterned Manhattan into a grid divided by 12 avenues, each 100ft wide, and 155 cross streets, each 60ft wide, designed specifically to facilitate "the buying, selling and improving of real estate." The standard city block was—and still is—200ft wide, and could hold two rows of lots each a 100ft deep.

Expanding with the addition of four outer boroughs after 1898, New York has continued to develop at a rapid pace. Today, the Department of City Planning is the major policy maker, setting zoning and overall land-use regulations. The New York City Landmarks Preservation Commission safeguards some 19,000 landmark buildings in the city; according to one of the strongest local landmark laws in the US, these cannot be torn down or altered in any way without a permit.

The city has also created many special districts, such as UNION SQUARE and Hunters Point, where specific design controls reinforce an area's particular character. An ongoing project is the redevelopment of 42nd Street *(p 52)* and the reopening of its legitimate theaters known more recently for showing B-movies.

THE ARTS

Prior to the 1930s, numerous American artists traveled abroad to study and observe the latest developments in experimental art. As war fermented and the depression lingered in Europe, many foreign artists began to arrive in the United States. This infusion of talent and ideas helped a great deal to shape an art that was uniquely American. The decade after World War II saw the birth of a truly American avant-garde art and the emergence of New York as cultural mecca and world leader in the production and promotion of modern art.

Hudson River School. – The painters of the first distinctly American school of painting (1825-1875) took their main inspiration from the dramatic scenery of the Hudson River Valley north of New York City. Artists Thomas Cole, Asher B. Durand, Albert Bierstadt and Frederic E. Church embraced a romantic vision of nature and art and imbued epic portrayals of America's grandiose landscapes with moral and transcendental meaning. These painters were among the many artists that swelled the ranks of the new art academies established in the city during the period, including the NATIONAL ACADEMY OF DESIGN (1825) and the ART STUDENTS LEAGUE (1875).

Emergence of Modern Art. – Founded in 1908, the artistic group "The Eight" sought to rebel against the conservatism of the New York academic establishment. Dubbed the **Ash Can school** in derisive reference to its bald urban realism, "The Eight" (particularly its most prominent members Robert Henri, George Luks and John Sloan) produced vivid, sympathetic portrayals of the rough edges of urban life, which inspired a rich tradition of 20C American realism (George Bellows and Edward Hopper) and found parallels in Jacob Riis' and Lewis W. Hine's documentary photographs of the growing immigrant population.

Photographer Alfred Stieglitz exhibited avant-garde European art in his Little Galleries of the Photo Secession from 1905 to 1917. Also known as "291," the gallery served as a laboratory and launching pad for New York's first modernist painters Arthur Dove, John Marin and Stieglitz's consort, Georgia O'Keeffe.

The main watershed event in the history of modern art in America was New York's 1913 **Armory Show**, or International Exhibition of Modern Art, which displayed over 1,300 objects—including works by European post-Impressionists, Fauves and Cubists—and introduced the most recent European art to a largely unprepared and bewildered American public. Marcel Duchamp's Cubist-inspired *Nude Descending a Staircase* provoked particular controversy. Despite the hostile public response, the exhibit attracted important collectors and can be credited with encouraging the tradition of patronage, which culminated in the founding of the MUSEUM OF MODERN ART in 1929, the WHITNEY MUSEUM OF AMERICAN ART in 1931 and the Guggenheim Foundation *(p 117)* in 1937.

After World War I, aspects of abstraction were explored by Stuart Davis, Patrick Henry Bruce and Charles Sheeler. The Depression brought an insular mood and public programs that fostered the social realism of Reginald Marsh and mural painting of Thomas Hart Benton.

Post-World War II Art. – During World War II, many of Europe's leading artists fled the war-torn continent for New York. The arrival of Frenchmen Léger and Masson, Spaniard Miró, and Germans Albers and Ernst brought an unprecedented opportunity for direct contact with Surrealist and abstract art. A period of fertile artistic activity ensued, culminating in the first radical American artistic movement, **Abstract Expressionism** (1946-late 1950s). Also known as the New York school, the Abstract Expressionists were divided among Action or Gesture painters (Jackson Pollock, Willem de Kooning, Franz Kline, Robert Motherwell and Clyfford Still), who emphasized the use of thick, sweeping brush strokes or dripped poured skeins of paint in the spontaneous intuitive act of painting; and Color Field painters (Mark Rothko, Barnett Newman), who employed equally large but color saturated canvases to envelop the spectator in meditative calm.

As the Abstract Expressionists received international recognition, post-war American affluence prompted collecting and gallery activity. New York gradually came to the fore, replacing Paris as the epicenter of the art world.

The late 1950s saw new artistic developments inspired by Abstract Expressionists: the brilliantly colored canvases of Stain Painting (Helen Frankenthaler), the simplified color fields of Hard Edge Painting (Al Held, Kenneth Noland) and the dramatic, shaped canvases of Frank Stella. In the 1960s, younger generation artists Roy Lichtenstein, Robert Rauschenberg, Andy Warhol and Claes Oldenburg debunked the high art notions of Abstract Expressionism and irreverently employed comic strip subjects and billboard painting techniques in the production of **Pop Art**.

Also emerging in reaction to Abstract Expressionism, 1960s **Minimalist** sculptors (Donald Judd, Carl Andre) used non-referential, geometric industrial forms to produce works of immediate and bold impact. The 1970s witnessed **Conceptual Art**, whose adherents—environmental sculptors and performance artists—proposed ideas rather than the collectible object as the essence of art, and the revival of Realism (Philip Pearlstein, Chuck Close, Alex Katz and George Segal).

The Current Art Scene. – The richly pluralistic artistic scene of the 1980s and 1990s embraces both post-Modernist movements—Neo-Expressionism (Julian Schnabel, David Salle), Graffiti Art (Keith Haring, Jean-Michel Basquiat) and Neo-Conceptualism (Barbara Kruger, Jenny Holzer)—and commitments to more long-standing traditions of representation and painterly abstraction. The principal stages for the viewing of the vast heterogeneity of current American art, as well as contemporary European trends, are New York's many museums (including the Whitney, which devotes a large Biennial Exhibit to recent American art); the "alternative spaces" for experimental and installation art, located mainly in TRIBECA; and the numerous commercial galleries, which line 57TH STREET and upper Madison Avenue (from 70th to 90th Streets) and proliferate in central SOHO and more recently on SoHo's eastern border.

LITERATURE

In the rich literary life of contemporary America, New York is no doubt the most vital force. Attracted by its intellectual climate and receptive public, publishing and printing have been leading industries in New York since the 19C.

18-19C: The Classics. – A distinguished literary tradition goes back to Washington Irving *(p 168)*, a native New Yorker, author of *A History of New York* (written in 1809 under the pen name of Diedrich Knickerbocker), an irreverent account of the city's first Dutch families. During the 19C, a galaxy of outstanding figures in American literature was associated with New York, either because they lived here for some time *(see Greenwich Village p 77 and Brooklyn Heights p 152)* or because they chose New York as the setting for their work. These include the poet and short-story writer Edgar Allan Poe *(p 149)*; the author of *Moby Dick*, New York-born Herman Melville *(Bartleby, A Story of Wall Street)*; the poet and New York journalist Walt Whitman *(Mannahatta* and *Crossing Brooklyn Ferry)*; the New York-born novelists Edith Wharton *(The Age of Innocence)* and Henry James *(Washington Square)*; Stephen Crane, the author of *The Red Badge of Courage (New York City Sketches)*; and Mark Twain, a correspondent for newspapers from the American West in his early days in New York.

All Around Town. – In the first decades of the 20C, artistic and literary life in New York centered around Greenwich Village, so much so that it was described, during that period, as "the home of American arts and letters." The names of the poet Edna St Vincent Millay, the playwright Eugene O'Neill and the novelist Theodore Dreiser *(p 81)* are remembered for their close associations with Greenwich Village.

Uptown, the Harlem Renaissance, which followed World War I and ended with the onset of the Great Depression in 1929, brought forth a flowering of black culture; Harlem composers, musicians, painters and writers drew world attention. Notable among the Harlem writers of the era were the poets, Countee Cullen, Langston Hughes and James Weldon Johnson; and the novelists, Claude McKay and Zora Hurston. They paved the way for a new generation of black writers, including novelists Richard Wright (*Black Boy* and *Native Son)* and Ralph Ellison *(The Invisible Man)* and playwright-novelist-essayist, James Baldwin *(The Fire Next Time)*.

While Harlem and Greenwich Village were flourishing, midtown was also enriching the city's literary tradition: a group of wits and writers made the ALGONQUIN HOTEL their headquarters. Among these poker-playing "knights" of what became known as the "Round Table" were the raconteur and drama critic, Alexander Woollcott; the columnist and diarist, Franklin P. Adams ("F.P.A."); and three figures closely associated with *The New Yorker* (founded in 1925): its long-time editor, Harold Ross, and two of its wittiest writers, Dorothy Parker and Robert Benchley. In the 1920s, *The New Yorker* established a literary standard, which continues to this day; contributors over the years have included essayists E.B. White and Edmund Wilson; novelists J.D. Salinger, Saul Bellow, John O'Hara and John Updike; film critic Pauline Kael; humorists Calvin Trillen and James Thurber; and musicologist Whitney Balliet.

The "Jazz Age" of the 1920s, which was also the age of the flapper, bathtub gin, the New York speakeasy and the "Lost Generation," saw the emergence of its prophet in F. Scott Fitzgerald *(The Great Gatsby)* and in his New York contemporary, John Dos Passos, whose critique of America was summed up in his best-known novels, *USA* and *Manhattan Transfer*. Broadway had its chronicler in the short-story writer Damon Runyon, who succeeded the author of *Bagdad-on-the-Subway*, O. Henry.

Contemporary Literature. – After World War II, Brooklyn-born Norman Mailer became an instant literary sensation with his first novel, *The Naked and the Dead* (1948). The period also inaugurated the careers of the era's pre-eminent New York playwright, Arthur Miller *(The Death of a Salesman)* and the ebullient North Carolina writer Thomas Wolfe *(Look Homeward, Angel; You Can't Go Home Again)*. Perhaps today's most renowned and authentically New York literary figure is E.L. Doctorow, whose novels capture the essence of the city; notable are the tragic *Ragtime* (1978) and the violent *Billy Bathgate* (1989). Among the best known literary figures of recent years is Tom Wolfe, whose best-seller *Bonfire of the Vanities (1987)* became an instant success.

The city is also the source of a distinct contribution to the national culture, New York Jewish humor, exemplified by the New York television comedy, "Your Show of Shows," which featured two young comedians, Sid Caesar and Imogene Coca, and was scripted by a crew of writers including Neil Simon (who became New York's most successful comedy playwright) and humorists Mel Brooks, Carl Reiner and Woody Allen.

"The Center of the Universe". – New York has always acted as a magnet, drawing unto itself the best the country had to offer. Long before the term "brain drain" was coined, the migration of the brightest young talents from farms, small towns and other remote areas to the big city was already an established phenomenon.

New York has stimulated the imagination of writers, foreign and American alike, because of the fascination exercised by this most exciting of all cities, "the center of the universe," as one of its mayors called it, essentially American but shaped by immigrants from a hundred lands. Among numerous writers from abroad who produced great works on the city are: Russian poet Vladimir Mayakovsky *(Brooklyn Bridge)*, Spanish poet Federico Garcia-Lorca *(Poet in New York)*, French novelist Paul Morand *(New York)*, English photographer and decorator Cecil Beaton *(Cecil Beaton's New York)* and Russian poet Andrei Voznesensky *(Airport in New York)*.

New York is the center of much of the nation's foremost literary criticism. In 1963, during a newspaper strike, editors Robert B. Silver and Barbara Epstein began *The New York Review of Books*, which now publishes 21 issues a year of influential literary reviews and social commentary and is available worldwide. Its contributors have included such New York literary figures as Susan Sontag, Dwight MacDonald, Gore Vidal, Paul Goodman and Norman Mailer. Another important source of criticism is *The New York Times Sunday Book Review*.

20C OUTDOOR SCULPTURE IN MANHATTAN

New York's plazas and open spaces have long been used as showcases of the city's monumental sculpture. A selection of 20C outdoor sculpture is listed below. Works by renowned artists are also displayed in the sculpture gardens of several museums, in particular the METROPOLITAN MUSEUM OF ART, the MUSEUM OF MODERN ART, the WHITNEY MUSEUM OF AMERICAN ART, the BROOKLYN MUSEUM and the ISAMU NOGUCHI GARDEN MUSEUM.

Title (Date)	Sculptor	Location

Downtown

Stabile (1971)	Alexander Calder	In front of 6 World Trade Center *(p 60)*
Bronze Sculpture (1971)	Fritz Koenig	World Trade Center Plaza *(p 59)*
The Red Cube (1967)	Isamu Noguchi	Plaza in front of Marine Midland Bank *(p 61)*
Group of Four Trees (1972)	Jean Dubuffet	Plaza in front of Chase Manhattan Bank *(p 64)*
Untitled (1973)	Yu Yu Yang	Plaza in front of Wall Street Plaza Building *(p 65)*
Korean War Memorial (1991)	Mac Adams	Battery Park
American Merchant Mariner Memorial (1991)	Marisol	Battery Park
Shadows and Flags (1977)	Louise Nevelson	Louise Nevelson Plaza, intersection of Maiden Lane, William and Liberty Sts *(p 64)*
The Family (1979)	Chaim Gross	Bleeker and W. 11th Sts (northwest corner)
Gay Liberation (1980)	George Segal	Christopher Park, at Christopher St and Sheridan Square *(p 81)*
Alamo (1967)	Bernard (Tony) Rosenthal	Astor Place, Lafayette and W. 8th Sts *(p 83)*

Midtown

Eye of Fashion (1976)	Robert M. Cronbach	Fashion Institute of Technology Plaza, at W. 27th St and Seventh Ave
Untitled (1973)	Forrest Myers	599 Broadway (north wall)
The Lover's Bench (1982)	Lea Virot	W. 33rd St and Seventh Ave (across from Pennsylvania Station)
The Garment Worker (1984)	Judith Weller	Plaza at 555 Seventh Avenue (W. 39th St)
Contrappunto (1963)	Beverly Pepper	777 Third Avenue (48th and 49th Sts)
Prometheus (1934)	Paul Manship	Lower Plaza, Rockefeller Center *(p 38)*
Atlas (1937)	Lee Lawrie	In front of International Building, Rockefeller Center *(p 38)*
News (1940)	Isamu Noguchi	Associated Press Bldg, Rockefeller Center
Lapstrake (1987)	Jésus Bautista Moroles	Plaza in front of 31 W. 52nd St *(p 40)*
Peace Form One (1980)	Daniel Larue Johnson	Ralph J. Bunch Park, United Nations
Single Form (1964)	Barbara Hepworth	Pool in front of Secretariat Building, UN *(p 51)*
No. 9 sign (1974)	Ivan Chermayeff	9 West 57th Street *(p 41)*

Uptown

Reclining Figure (1965)	Henry Moore	Plaza Pool, Lincoln Center
Le Guichet (1963)	Alexander Calder	In front of Library for the Performing Arts, Lincoln Center
Romeo and Juliet (1977)	Milton Hebald	Central Park, near entrance to Delacorte Theater at W. 81st St
Night Presence IV (1972)	Louise Nevelson	Center island at Park Avenue and 92nd St
Three-Way Piece: Points (1967)	Henry Moore	On overpass at W.117th St and Amsterdam Ave, Columbia University *(p 99)*
Bellerophon Taming Pegasus (1967)	Jacques Lipchitz	Over entrance of Law Building (W.116th St), Columbia University *(p 99)*

FURTHER READING

Above New York by Robert Cameron *(Cameron & Co, San Francisco)*.

Bricks and Brownstones by Charles Lockwood *(Abbeville Press, New York, 1972)*.

Guide to New York City Landmarks by the New York City Landmarks Preservation Commission *(The Preservation Press, 1992)*.

Inside New York by Joe Friedman *(Harper Collins, 1992)*.

New York, A Pictorial History by Marshall B. Davidson *(Charles Scribners Sons, New York, 1981)*.

New York, Then and Now by Edward B. Watson and Edmund V. Gillon, Jr *(Dover Publications, Inc, New York, 1976)*.

The AIA Guide to New York by Norval White and Elliot Willensky *(MacMillan Company, New York, 1988)*.

The City Observed: New York by Paul Goldberger *(Vintage Books, New York, 1979)*.

The Epic of New York City by Edward Robb Ellis *(Old Town Books, New York, 1966)*.

For works of fiction, see **Literature** *on p 27.*

Sights

Lower Manhattan, Brooklyn Bridge , Bud Freund/First Light

Manhattan

Area: 22 square miles
Population: 1,487,500

Celebrated for its spectacular skyline, Manhattan constitutes the heart of New York City's vibrant cultural and commercial activity. This tongue-shaped island, flanked on the west by the expansive Hudson River and on the east by the Harlem and East rivers, measures 13.4mi in length and 2.3mi at its widest point, making it the smallest of the city's five boroughs. Manhattan, whose name derives from an Algonquin word meaning "island of the hills," was acquired from the Algonquin Indians by Dutch governor Peter Minuit in 1626, in exchange for trinkets valued, during that period, at a mere $24. The Dutch settlement of Nieuw Amsterdam developed on the island's southern tip, giving rise to the irregular street pattern that has prevailed to this day in the Financial District. After British occupation the town expanded northward, following a neat grid of numbered streets and avenues *(p 25)* that eventually predominated throughout most of the island.

Today, the area south of 14th Street is known as "downtown"; it is bordered on the north by "midtown," which in turn gives way to "uptown" beyond 59th Street at the southern rim of Central Park. Fifth Avenue, one of Manhattan's grand north-south thoroughfares, marks the boundary between the east and west sides.

The following **22 walks** will help the visitor explore the rich variety of Manhattan's sights: busy avenues bordered by luxurious shops; historic and ethnic enclaves; bustling commercial districts; canyons of concrete and glass; airy landscaped plazas; and a multitude of soaring skyscrapers, grand civic structures and elegant mansions. The section on **Museums** *(p 110)* provides detailed information on over 35 of the city's reputed cultural institutions.

★★★ 1 FIFTH AVENUE (Midtown)

Time: 1/2 day. Distance: 1.8mi. Map pp 32-33.

New York's most prestigious thoroughfare, Fifth Avenue is studded with striking landmark skyscrapers, elegant churches, exclusive shops and grand public buildings. The elaborate window displays and the elegance of well-heeled New Yorkers contribute to make this one of the most fascinating walks in the city.

It is preferable to follow this itinerary on a weekday morning as some of the buildings are closed on Saturdays and Sundays.

HISTORICAL NOTES

Millionaires' Row. – Residences were first erected on the lower stretch of Fifth Avenue in 1824, and by 1850 this area had become more fashionable than Broadway. Following the Civil War, a housing boom increased the number of town houses by 350. Each home cost at least $20,000—a small fortune at the time.

By 1880, the avenue was a busy and noisy thoroughfare, teeming with carriages and horse-drawn omnibuses. Scattered among the stately mansions were elegant private clubs and more modest brownstones. The first fashionable stores were established in the mid-19C around 34th Street and continued to move northward on the avenue until the middle of this century.

From the very beginning, Fifth Avenue attracted the fabulously rich New York society. A.T. Stewart, a partner in several department stores, erected a splendid marble mansion at Fifth and 34th Street. The opposite corner was dominated by the huge brownstone of William Astor. Jay Gould, the American railroad tycoon, built a residence on the corner of 47th Street, while the Vanderbilt dynasty established itself around 50th Street.

The Talk of the Town. – In the spring of 1883, New York's high society was in a dither. William K. Vanderbilt, grandson of "The Commodore" *(p 46)*, was planning a ball in his Renaissance palace on 51st Street. The richest young belles of New York, including Miss Astor, daughter of William and Caroline Astor, rehearsed tirelessly to perfect graceful curtsies and complicated steps. However, when the invitations were sent out, Miss Astor was not included. Her mother, a descendant of an old Dutch family, had snubbed the nouveau riche Mrs Vanderbilt by not including her in her circle of friends.

Nevertheless, the story has a happy ending. Mrs Astor sacrificed her pride and invited Mrs Vanderbilt to her home. In turn, the precious invitation was sent, and Miss Astor could cavort in her period gown, dancing the minuet and the gavotte to music by Rameau.

The Marriage Mart. – Later, other balls caused nearly as much excitement. In 1892, Mrs Astor and Ward McAllister, social arbiter of New York society, launched the term "the Four Hundred" by sending exactly 400 invitations to a ball. Mrs Astor claimed that, unfortunately, her ballroom could accommodate only that number in proper style!

Fashionable balls at the Waldorf-Astoria were often graced by young European aristocrats whose titles were more brilliant than their fortunes. The results were sometimes spectacular: in one year, 1895, Consuelo Vanderbilt married the Duke of Marlborough, Pauline Whitney the grandson of the Marquess of Anglesey, and Anna Gould the day's leading dandy, Boni de Castellane.

WALKING TOUR

Begin at the corner of Fifth Ave and W. 34th St. ● *N, R train to 34th St.*

★★★ **Empire State Building.** – *350 Fifth Ave.* Rising to a height of 1,454ft with a grace, elegance and strength that have made it one of the finest and most breathtaking skyscrapers ever built, the Empire State Building has remained, since its completion in 1931, the most distinctive feature of the Manhattan skyline.

Named for New York, the "Empire State," the skyscraper was the world's tallest for four decades. Although it has been surpassed by the Sears Roebuck building in Chicago and the twin towers of the WORLD TRADE CENTER, the Empire State remains the world's quintessential sky-

Empire State Building

scraper. The view from the top is so impressive that it deserves two visits: by day, for an overview of the entire region, and then again in the evening, to enjoy the spectacle of the city's lights.

A Prestigious Site. – The edifice occupies the site of two mansions belonging to William Astor and his wife, the former Caroline Schermerhorn, in the late 19C. Known as "the beautiful Mrs Astor," Caroline presided over New York society and her house became the center of the city's social life. In the 1890s, her nephew, William Waldorf Astor, erected the **Waldorf Hotel** next to his aunt's house. This was seen as an act of vengeance because young Astor's wife had been unable to wrest the leadership of New York society from Caroline. Within a year, Mrs Astor had decided to move north to Fifth Avenue and 65th Street, and by 1897 her son, John Jacob Astor, had built the **Astoria Hotel** next to the Waldorf. They were operated together, despite the family tiff, to the benefit of both branches until 1929, when the structures were demolished to make way for the Empire State Building. The "new" WALDORF-ASTORIA HOTEL was erected uptown, on Park Avenue, in 1931.

The Construction. – Commissioned by a syndicate headed by Alfred E. Smith, governor of New York between the years of 1918 and 1928, the building was completed in May 1931, less than two years after the first excavations began in October 1929. Work progressed at a hectic pace; at times, the building rose more than a floor each day. Since there are only two stories of foundations, 60,000 tons of steel beams—enough to lay a double-track railroad from New York to Baltimore—were added to support the tower. Although there were initial doubts as to the stability of the building, it has proved to be extremely sound. Specialists intended to use the last floor as a mooring platform for dirigibles, but the project was abandoned after one trial in 1932, which nearly resulted in a catastrophe. Tragedy struck the building in July 1945, when a bomber crashed into the 79th floor killing 14 people including the crew.

Visible for miles, the 203ft television antenna installed in 1985 is 22 stories high. A beacon light at the top of the antenna serves as a warning signal for aircraft. The top 30 stories of the building are illuminated from dusk to midnight, often in colors that reflect the day or the season, e.g., green for St Patrick's Day; red, white and blue for

A Few Facts. – The Empire State cost almost $40,000,000 to build. Fifteen thousand people work there, and 35,000 visit it daily. A battery of 150 men and women wields vacuum cleaners during off hours, and 5 acres of windows are washed once a month. Seventy-three elevators serve the 102 floors. The express elevator will take you to the 80th floor in less than a minute. It takes half an hour to walk down the 1,860 steps.

national holidays such as Independence Day; and red and green at Christmas time. Lights are turned off on foggy nights during the spring and fall migratory bird seasons, lest the birds be confused by the diffused light and crash into the building.

Observatory. – *Enter the ticket office from Fifth Ave. Open daily 9:30am–11:30pm. $3.75. &. ☎736-3100 ext. 55. Consult the visibility notice before buying your tickets.* Magnificent **views★★★** of the metropolitan area can be enjoyed from the open-air platform on the 86th floor observatory. On clear days, the view extends for 80mi in all directions. Another elevator takes visitors to the glass-enclosed circular observatory on the 102nd floor.

Continue north on Fifth Ave.

The section of Fifth Avenue between 34th and 40th Streets is bordered by several large department stores, including the city's oldest, Lord and Taylor, known for fine clothing and its gaily decorated window displays during the Christmas season. B. Altman and Co, at 34th Street, had been the oldest, but is now closed. The Altman building, a conservative, 8-story Renaissance Revival edifice, is expected to become the city's new Central Research Library of Science, Industry and Business.

★★ New York Public Library. – *476 Fifth Ave, between W. 40th and 42nd Sts.* Founded in 1895 to combine the Astor Library, Lenox Library and Tilden Trust under one roof, the New York Public Library is the second largest research library in the United States, after the Library of Congress, in Washington DC. A Beaux-Arts masterpiece by Carrère and Hastings, the imposing marble temple (1911) is midtown Manhattan's most striking public edifice. Two famous marble lions (Edward C. Potter), often called Patience and Fortitude, guard the main entrance. On opening day, in 1911, President Taft declared "this day crowns a work of national importance."

Historical Notes. – The land now occupied by the Library building and Bryant Park *(p 34)* was the site of the first American World's Fair, which took place in 1853 in the **Crystal Palace.** The building was an imitation of the London Crystal Palace, completed two years earlier. The domed iron and glass pavilion sheltered a large assortment of works of art and industrial products. A fire destroyed it in 1858, leaving the open space that would become Bryant Park. To the east was the **Croton Distribution Reservoir** (1845), a fort-like building topped by a walkway, which surrounded a 4-acre reservoir supplied by water from Croton Lake in Westchester County. It remained in service until 1899 and was replaced

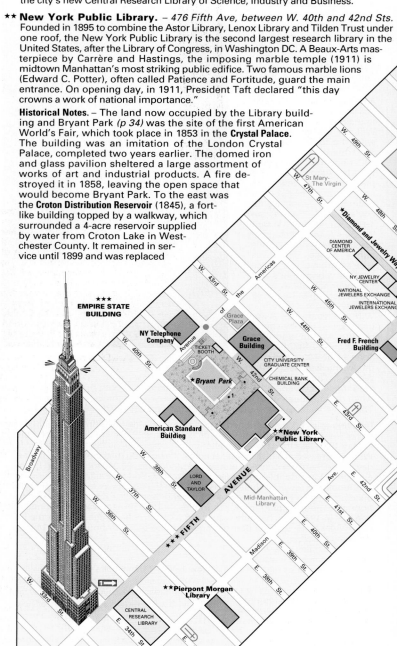

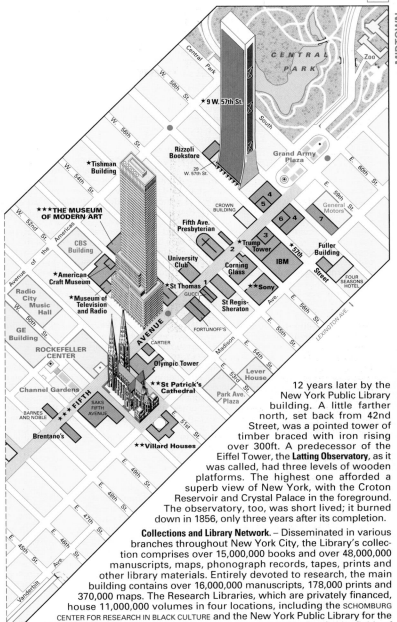

12 years later by the New York Public Library building. A little farther north, set back from 42nd Street, was a pointed tower of timber braced with iron rising over 300ft. A predecessor of the Eiffel Tower, the **Latting Observatory**, as it was called, had three levels of wooden platforms. The highest one afforded a superb view of New York, with the Croton Reservoir and Crystal Palace in the foreground. The observatory, too, was short lived; it burned down in 1856, only three years after its completion.

Collections and Library Network. – Disseminated in various branches throughout New York City, the Library's collection comprises over 15,000,000 books and over 48,000,000 manuscripts, maps, phonograph records, tapes, prints and other library materials. Entirely devoted to research, the main building contains over 16,000,000 manuscripts, 178,000 prints and 370,000 maps. The Research Libraries, which are privately financed, house 11,000,000 volumes in four locations, including the SCHOMBURG CENTER FOR RESEARCH IN BLACK CULTURE and the New York Public Library for the Performing Arts *(40 Lincoln Plaza)*, which features collections in the fields of theater, music and dance.

A network of 82 branch libraries serves Manhattan, the Bronx and Staten Island. The largest of these branches are located in the midtown area: the Mid-Manhattan Library *(455 Fifth Ave)*, the Library for the Performing Arts *(above)*, the Donnell Library Center *(20 W. 53rd St)* and the well-known Andrew Heiskell Library for the Blind and Physically Handicapped *(40 W. 20th St)*, containing thousands of braille and recorded materials.

Visit. – *Open Tue–Wed 11am–7:30pm, Thu–Sat 10am–6pm. Closed holidays. Guided tours (1hr) 11am & 2pm.* ☞ ☎ *869-8089*. Step into the grand, white marble **Astor Hall**, adorned with lavish decorations. Behind it, the **Gottesman Hall**, a handsome Beaux-Arts room enhanced by graceful marble arches and a carved oak ceiling, presents major temporary exhibits. In the south corridor, the richly paneled **DeWitt Wallace Periodical Room** contains a series of 13 murals by 20C artist Richard Haas. *Take the elevator at the far north end of the corridor to the right, up to the third floor.*
Rotating exhibits adorn the walls on the third floor. An exhibit room *(no. 318)* displays fascinating items from the Berg Collection of English and American literature, including portraits by noted American artists and printmakers. Selections from the library's special collections are presented in the **Salomon Room**, a 19C picture gallery. Among the rarities displayed on occasion are a draft of the Declaration of Independence in Jefferson's own hand and an edition of Galileo's works, which can be read only with a magnifying glass. The paintings on permanent display include

a group of five portraits of George Washington on the west wall. The large central hall, **McGraw Rotunda**, is decorated with wood paneling and murals depicting the story of the Recorded Word. Facing the Salomon Room is the **Public Catalog Room**, which consists of 800 retrospective volumes with 10,000,000 entries. Beyond is the enormous main reading room; it is 51ft high and covers a half-acre. In recent years, additional space for library stacks has been created beneath Bryant Park.

Continue west on W. 42nd St to Bryant Park.

★ **Bryant Park.** – *On Ave of the Americas, between W. 40th and 42nd Sts.* Located behind the Library, this formal garden is midtown's only large green space. Built on the site once occupied by the Crystal Palace and Croton Reservoir *(p 32)*, the park was named for **William Cullen Bryant** (1794-1878) in 1884 but remained vacant until 1934, when it was laid out by Lusby Simpson. Despite endeavors to keep the park a pleasant public space, it soon became a gathering spot for the unemployed and homeless, and in the 1960s was taken over by drug peddlers. After undergoing an extensive restoration effort, the park reopened to the public in late 1991.

Today, tourists and New Yorkers alike flock to Bryant Park to relax and enjoy concerts of live music and, on occasion, art exhibits. In summer, the park becomes an oasis of coolness in sweltering Manhattan, and is dotted with flower vendors, book-stalls and snack kiosks. At the Music and Dance Ticket Booth *(p 185)* on the 42nd Street side of the park, half-price tickets to music and dance events *(not theater)* are sold the day of performance.

Among the sculptures dotting the landscaped alleys, note the 1911 **memorial [1]** to the park's namesake, William Cullen Bryant, a bronze statue sheltered by a marble canopy. Bryant, author of the poem "Thanatopsis," was the editor and part owner of the *New York Evening Post,* an influential paper during the Civil War. He also gained renown as a political crusader and helped support the city's various cultural institutions.

Other works include a bronze bust of Goethe (1832) by Karl Fischer and life-size statues of William Earl Dodge (1895, J.Q.A. Ward) and José de Andrada e Silva, father of Brazil's independence (1954, José Lima).

Surrounding the park are several edifices of interest. At 40 West 40th Street is the **American Standard Building**, originally known as the American Radiator Building, designed by Raymond Hood in 1924. Inspired by the Gothic tradition, the black brick building is adorned with gold terra-cotta trim.

To the west rises the streamlined form of the **New York Telephone Company Building** *(1095 Ave of the Americas)*, faced with alternating columns of white marble and dark tinted glass. Dominating the north side of the park, at 1114 Avenue of the Americas, is the **Grace Building** (1974), the hyperbolic lines of its base merging without break into a 50-story tower of travertine and tinted glass. It was erected by the architec-tural firm of Skidmore, Owings & Merrill, who constructed a similar building that same year at 9 West 57th Street *(p 41)*.

The City University Graduate Center *(33 W. 42nd St)* is one of 20 individual educa-tional units within the City University of New York (CUNY). The Mall, a pedestrian arcade running from 42nd to 43rd Street between Fifth Avenue and Avenue of the Americas hosts art exhibits and occasional free concerts.

Return to Fifth Ave and continue north.

At the corner of 43rd Street is a branch of Chemical Bank (1954; Skidmore, Owings & Merrill). One of the first banks constructed in glass, it represented a radical depar-ture from the usual thick-walled buildings of masonry. The lobby is decorated with Macassar ebony furniture and Italian marble floors. Among the abstract sculpture, note the spectacular composition (1953, Harry Bertoia) of metallic strips hanging from the ceiling. The door of the main vault is visible through one of the windows.

On the corner of 45th Street, look up to admire the attractive multi-colored faience decoration embellishing the upper stories of the **Fred F. French Building** *(551 Fifth Ave)*. Constructed of masonry and solid in appearance, the ornate building (1927) rises 38 floors in a series of massed setbacks, in typical 1920s fashion.

Turn left into W. 47th St.

★ **Diamond and Jewelry Way.** – This 750ft block along 47th Street, between Fifth and Sixth Avenues, is home to some 80 percent of the diamond wholesale trade in America. A bewildering variety of languages—Spanish, Yiddish, Armenian, Russian and Arabic—serves to discuss carat, cut, color and clarity. The street is lined with shops, notably the International Jewelers Exchange, the National Jewelers Ex-change, the Diamond Center of America and the New York Jewelry Center, all displaying a superb array of precious stones. Much of the trade is carried on in booths located on the upper floors and in the rear of the buildings. A sophisticated security system protects the dealers from unwelcome intruders.

The merchants usually carry their precious bounty in suitcases, unobtrusive pack-ages or in their coat pockets. The exchanges take place either right on the sidewalk or in one of two private membership diamond-dealer clubs; major transactions may be sealed simply by a handshake. Offenders transgressing this honor code are reportedly blacklisted throughout the diamond world.

Return to Fifth Ave and continue north.

Between 48th and 49th Streets, the Barnes and Noble Bookstore offers bestsellers at discount prices. Across the avenue is **Brentano's Bookstore**, the former Charles Scribner's Sons shop. Designed by Ernest Flagg, who also conceived the Singer Building in SOHO, the edifice (1913) has retained its handsome turn-of-the-century cast-iron facade and genteel interior.

Across 49th Street is Saks Fifth Avenue, an exclusive department store offering designer collections for men and women.

★★★ **Rockefeller Center.** – *See description p 37.*

★★ **St Patrick's Cathedral.** – *On Fifth Ave, between E. 50th and 51st Sts. Open daily 7am–8:30pm. Guided tours available.* &. Designed by renowned architect **James Renwick** (1818-1895), New York City's major Roman Catholic Cathedral was one of the first examples of Gothic Revival ecclesiastical architecture in the US. When construction of the cathedral began in 1853, churchgoers complained that it was too far out in the country. However, the city continued its growth northward, and by the time the church was consecrated in 1879, St Patrick's dominated the city's most fashionable residential district. Today, the slender, balanced proportions seem rather dwarfed by the loftier ROCKEFELLER CENTER high-rises and the Olympic Tower *(to the north, across 51st St)*, in whose glass wall the church is mirrored.

The elegant granite and marble structure, with its 330ft spires (1888), is reminiscent of the much larger cathedral of Cologne, in Germany. Missing, however, are the extensive stone carvings (owing partially to the use of granite, a hard stone) and the flying buttresses, which are hallmarks of Gothic architecture.

Inside, the cathedral features a typical cruciform plan. Three portals with intricately sculpted bronze doors open into the spacious nave, illuminated by stained-glass windows of the Gothic type, most of which were manufactured in Chartres and Nantes, France. A series of slender, marble pillars supports the cross-ribbed vaults, which rise 110ft above the nave. Note also the elegantly designed baldachin over the high altar (Renwick), and the monumental organ. Located behind the apse, the lovely Lady Chapel was added by Charles T. Mathews in 1906.

The cathedral is dedicated to the patron saint of the Irish, who constitute a large segment of New York's population. The festivities of St Patrick's Day demonstrate their veneration for the apostle of Ireland. Each Easter Sunday, Fifth Avenue near St Patrick's is closed to traffic and New Yorkers stroll in their spring finery, an event memorialized in Irving Berlin's song *Easter Parade*.

Head east on E. 50th St to Madison Ave.

Facing Madison Avenue, the apse of St Patrick's is flanked by two small town houses: the rectory *(no. 460)* and the residence of the archbishop *(no. 452)*.

★★ **Villard Houses (New York Palace).** – *451-457 Madison Ave.* This graceful ensemble features a group of six mansions built in 1885 by McKim, Mead and White for Henry Villard, founder of the Northern Pacific Railroad. The Renaissance-style brown houses appear to be one mansion built in a U-shape around a central courtyard. Inspired by the Palazzo della Cancelleria in Rome, the architects successfully incorporated such elements as the window framing and the arcades into a 19C North American residential style. Following World War II, several companies used the mansions as office space until the Archdiocese of New York sold them to the Helmsley chain in 1976, on the condition that they be preserved as the hotel's public rooms.

Enter the pedestrian courtyard—formerly a carriage yard—through the wrought-iron gates fronting Madison Avenue, and step inside the central mansion. The interior, appointed in an ornate, rococo style, features several public rooms, which have been luxuriously restored. The **Gold Room** *(tea served daily; reservations suggested ☎303-6032)*, with its barrel-vaulted ceiling, musician's gallery and lunette paintings by John LaFarge, exudes an aura of 1930s high society. Beyond the Gold Room, continue through the great hallway adorned with Venetian mosaics to the sweeping staircase to admire the stained-glass windows by Louis Comfort Tiffany and the gilt-and-marble zodiac clock by Augustus Saint-Gaudens. The latter also designed the red marble fireplace dominating the second floor lobby.

Return to Fifth Ave on E. 51st St and continue north.

At no. 645 rises the 51-story **Olympic Tower**. This elegant brown-tinted glass building (1976; Skidmore, Owings & Merrill) houses shops, offices and luxury apartments on its upper stories. Located on the ground floor, H. Stern Jewellers enjoys a worldwide reputation for colored gemstones, stemming primarily from Brazil. Olympic Place, an indoor arcade, is a delightful public space, replete with a reflecting waterfall, palm trees and plants *(entrance on Fifth Ave)*.

The Renaissance-style palazzo on the southeast corner of 52nd Street houses the French jewelry firm Cartier *(651 Fifth Ave)*, which acquired the building in 1917. The edifice is one of the avenue's few remaining early 20C mansions originally built for the city's moneyed class.

★ **Tishman Building.** – *666 Fifth Ave.* Built in 1957, the 39-story edifice with its facade of embossed aluminum panels represents a worthy attempt at originality. The interior is equally imaginative, with its unusual ceiling composed of thin wavy hanging strips, and a cascade fountain on one wall. Designed by Isamu Noguchi, the space exudes an air of serenity often found in Japanese gardens. On the top floor, a restaurant and lounge, "Top of the Sixes," offers a magnificent view of Manhattan.

★ **St Thomas Church.** – *At corner of W. 53rd St. Open daily 8am–6pm. Guided tour (30min) Sun 12:30pm.* &. Topped by a single tower, St Thomas Episcopal Church was completed in 1913 by Cram, Goodhue and Ferguson, in a flamboyant Gothic Revival style. It replaces a building destroyed by fire in 1905. A wealth of statues and delicate tracery adorns the facade on Fifth Avenue. In the center of the main portal, St Thomas, flanked by six of the apostles, welcomes the worshippers. The remaining apostles are arrayed overhead in the tympanum. Below the sculptures, bas-reliefs depict the legend of St Thomas. Step to the left of the main portal to admire the narrow "Brides' Entrance," ornately decorated with symbolically joined hands. On entering the nave, the eye is drawn to the lovely **reredos★** of Dunville stone, which rises to a height of 80ft above the altar. Spotlighted, it forms a lighter contrast to the darker vault. Numerous recesses shelter statues of Christ, the Virgin Mary, the

Apostles and other saints, carved by Lee Lawrie. Also of interest are the stained-glass windows in deep reds and blues, the pulpit and the sculptured organ case. *Organ recitals (1hr 30min) Oct–mid-May Sun 5:15pm.*

Opposite St Thomas Church, on the east side of Fifth Avenue, is Fortunoff's, a 4-story jewelry and silverware emporium, distinguished by a sleek stainless steel and glass facade. Adjoining Fortunoff's, the Italian fashion and shoe boutique, Gucci, displays its wares, recognizable by the red and green stripe. Between 54th and 55th Streets, adjacent to a second Gucci shop, is the luxurious beauty and fashion salon of Elizabeth Arden **[1]**. Set on the northwest corner of 54th Street, the imposing **University Club** was designed by McKim, Mead and White (1899), in the Italian Renaissance style. Adorning the building's 3-tiered granite exterior are the shields of major American universities, all carved by Daniel Chester French.

At the corner of 55th Street is the elegant **St Regis-Sheraton Hotel** designed in 1904 in an ornate, Beaux-Arts style. It was commissioned by John Jacob Astor as the first luxury hotel in the city. Note the Maxfield Parrish mural in the King Cole Bar *(p 51)*.

Fifth Avenue Presbyterian Church. *–At corner of W. 55th St. Open daily Jun 28–Sept 5 Mon–Wed 8am–9pm, Thu–Fri 8am–5pm, Sat 8am–1pm, Sun 8am–3pm. Rest of the year daily 8am–6pm.* &. Erected in 1875 in the Gothic Revival style, this edifice is one of the last churches built in brownstone in the city. The sanctuary, with a seating capacity of 1,800, is notable for its magnificent organ casing and an intricately carved ash-wood pulpit.

The southwest corner of 56th Street is occupied by the small Renaissance palace of the jeweler Harry Winston **[2]**, who specializes in diamonds and precious stones. Standing opposite, the **Corning Glass Building** houses the New York City headquarters of one of the world's leading producers of fine glass, including Steuben crystal. Built in 1959, the 28-story building bears the characteristics of skyscrapers from that era: tinted-glass exterior, neat, trim lines, and an outdoor plaza with reflecting pool. The Steuben shop on the ground floor presents displays of new or historical designs and examples of crystal ware often chosen as gifts for heads of state.

★ **Trump Tower.** – *725 Fifth Ave.* Rising 58 stories above street level is the exuberant, bronze-mirror silhouette of Trump Tower, a luxurious mixed-use structure containing commercial space, condominium apartments and retail stores. Designed in 1983 by Der Scutt, this glass-sheathed tower, with its myriad of tiny setbacks often topped by trees and shrubs, is typical of the lively, innovative flair of the skyscraper style of the 1980s. The 6-story **atrium**★, a lavish pink marble shopping emporium featuring an 80ft-high waterfall cascading down one side, offers an array of fine boutiques and specialty shops, such as Asprey and Charles Jourdan.

At the corner of 57TH STREET, stop to gaze at the exquisite window displays at **Tiffany & Co [3]**, the internationally renowned jewelry store. Visitors can also admire the 128-carat Tiffany Diamond, displayed along the far left wall from the Fifth Avenue entrance. Across the avenue is the Crown Building (1921), its chateau-like upper section richly embellished in 23-carat gold leaf. Designed by Warren and Wetmore in the French Renaissance style, the building is named for the gilded crown at its pinnacle. Ferragamo, known for fine shoes and leather accessories, occupies a street-level shop.

On either side of the avenue between 57th and 58th Streets is Bergdorf Goodman's legendary emporium **[4]**, a bastion of haute couture. Adjacent to the store, the jewelry boutique of Van Cleef and Arpels **[5]** features a sparkling array of treasures, including the diamond tiara of the Empress Josephine.

A startling touch of Hollywood enlivens the northeast corner of West 57th Street and Fifth Avenue. The Warner Bros Studio Store **[6]**, named for the movieland film studio, occupies the basement and four floors of the Daichi Building, one of the city's choicest retail sites. The whimsical storefront is banded by 8ft-long friezes of Looney Tune cartoon action.

Towering over the east side of GRAND ARMY PLAZA is the General Motors Building, a 50-story tower (1968) articulated by white marble piers. Step inside the renowned FAO Schwarz toy store **[7]**, located within the building, to view the 28ft animated clock tower.

For a description of Fifth Avenue north of 59th Street see Upper East Side (p 91).

MUSEUMS

★★★ **The Museum of Modern Art (MOMA).** – *See description p 140.*

★★ **Pierpont Morgan Library.** – *See description p 145.*

★ **Museum of Television and Radio.** – *See description p 144.*

★ **American Craft Museum.** – *See description p 110.*

We welcome your assistance in the never-ending task of updating the texts and maps in this guide. Send us your comments and suggestions:

Michelin Travel Publications
Michelin Tire Corporation
PO Box 19001
Greenville, SC 29602-9001

Time: 1/2 day (including guided tours). Distance: 1mi. Map below.

Located in the heart of midtown Manhattan, between Fifth and Seventh Avenues and 47th and 52nd Streets, Rockefeller Center comprises an imposing group of harmoniously designed skyscrapers, dating primarily from the pre-World War II era. Vital, dignified and steeped in an air of festivity year-round, this jewel of an urban complex draws thousands of office workers and tourists daily.

Historical Notes. – In the early 19C, the site now occupied by Rockefeller Center was part of public lands administered by the city, collectively known as "Common Lands" or "The Fields," an area that extended from today's CITY HALL up to approximately 53rd Street. Dr David Hosack, a professor of botany, acquired 15 acres from the city for $5,000 to establish a public botanical garden. In 1811, he sold the land to the State of New York, which turned it over to COLUMBIA UNIVERSITY. The university then rented parcels to farmers for $100 a year.

The first buildings on the site appeared about 1850, when New York's present gridiron pattern of streets and avenues was laid out. The area soon developed into a fashionable residential district, where splendid mansions stood side by side with more modest brownstones. A few of these residences have survived to this day on 53rd Street. In the 1900s, the neighborhood began to decline. The area had become noisy especially after the construction of the Sixth Avenue "El" (the elevated railway) in 1878, and the millionaires and middle class moved away to FIFTH AVENUE, leaving their fine homes to poorer tenants. Later, during the Prohibition era, this once elegant district became notorious as the "speakeasy belt." Following the repeal of Prohibition, many speakeasies on 52nd Street were converted into jazz clubs, hosting such artists as Count Basie, Harry James and Coleman Hawkins.

The Rockefellers. – In 1870, the American oil magnate John Davison Rockefeller (1839-1937) created the Standard Oil Company of Ohio, and soon began dominating the US oil industry. When John Sr retired in 1911 as a multimillionaire, his son, **John D. Rockefeller Jr** (1874-1960), took over management of the company. During his tenure, he was known as one of the nation's greatest philanthropists. His most important contributions in New York City helped erect the UNITED NATIONS HEADQUARTERS, the CLOISTERS and RIVERSIDE CHURCH.

"John D.," as he was called, leased the land now occupied by the Rockefeller Center from Columbia University in 1928. With associates from the Metropolitan Opera, Rockefeller planned to erect a colossal new opera house on the site. The initial lease ran 24 years and was renewable until 2015, when the land and the building would revert to the university; however, the crash of 1929 brought this project to an abrupt halt. Left during the Depression days with a long-term lease on this parcel of land and a sizable rent to pay, John D. decided to build a commercial center, a "city within a city." In 1933, when the RCA Building (present GE Building) was opened, John D. celebrated by moving the Rockefeller family office from 26 Broadway to 30 Rockefeller Plaza.

An Urban Triumph. – Over a period of ten years, 228 buildings were destroyed and 12 edifices erected on an area of approximately 3 blocks (12 acres). Expected to trigger a boom and bring renewal to the area, the Center quickly fulfilled its goal. The project's core (12 buildings), including the RCA Building, was completed in 1940. Seven additional buildings were added between 1947 and 1973. The ensemble was designed by a team of seven architects, which included Wallace K. Harrison who was also responsible for the design of the UNITED NATIONS HEADQUARTERS and LINCOLN CENTER. The primary intent of the architects was to provide midtown Manhattan with an urban center that would foster a sense of community, openness, beauty and convenience. The result is a wonderful combination of buildings, open spaces, restaurants, shops and boutiques.

During the building of Rockefeller Center a practice was initiated, which New Yorkers now take for granted. It is said that Rockefeller himself stopped by to observe the progress that had been made one day, and was asked to move on. The occasion gave rise to the use of the peephole, now a part of every construction site. Today, 19 buildings cover about 22 acres and house a working population of 65,000. Add to that the number of tourists who visit the Center each day and the result is a workday population of more than 275,000 persons. The buildings are connected by a maze of underground passages, the **concourse**, lined with attractive shops and restaurants; the concourse also provides access to the subway system.

WALKING TOUR

Begin in front of St Patrick's Cathedral on Fifth Ave. ● *any train to 42nd St, or F, E train to 53rd St.*

Rising across the street from St Patrick's Cathedral, the 41-story **International Building** (1935) houses consulates, international airlines, travel agencies and a passport office on the mezzanine level. Standing in front of the building is a monumental bronze statue of Atlas (1937, Lee Lawrie) supporting the world.

Enter the vast lobby, with its piers and walls of marble from the Greek island of Tinos. The ceiling is covered with very thin gold leaf. If all this gold were removed from the ceiling, it would weigh about a pound and, melted down, could be held in the palm of your hand.

Continue to the Channel Gardens.

★★ Channel Gardens and Rockefeller Center

A relaxing spot, the Channel Gardens separate the Maison Française (1933) on the left, and the British Empire Building (1932) on the right, two low-lying, 7-story structures topped by roof gardens. The Channel Gardens contain a series of six pools surrounded by flower beds, which are changed regularly in season, beginning with

The Rockefeller Group

Rockefeller Center

Easter lilies on Good Friday. The benches along the flower beds will be especially appreciated if you have been window-shopping. The promenade leads down a gentle slope to the lower plaza—the centerpiece of Rockefeller Center—a sunken open area rimmed by the flags of the United Nations member countries. At the top of the steps leading to the lower plaza is a plaque citing John D.'s credo.

On the north side of the plaza, note the colorful limestone screen adorning the International Building's south facade. Designed in 1935 by Lee Lawrie, it represents man's progress in the fields of art, science, trade and industry. The west side of the lower plaza is dominated by the Center's best-known sculpture, the bronze statue of **Prometheus [1]** (1934, Paul Manship) stealing the sacred fire for humankind. The statue, covered in gold leaf, is flanked by two smaller figures (also by Manship) symbolizing a man and a woman receiving the fire.

An outdoor cafe in summer, the plaza serves as a **skating rink** in winter. Every December, a huge Christmas tree towers from 65ft to 90ft above this setting. Visitors come to admire the spectacular lighting displays and to observe the ice skaters in the rink below.

Rockefeller Plaza, a private street running from north to south between 48th and 51st Streets, was constructed to provide access to the GE Building. The street is closed one day each year so that it does not become public property, in accordance with local laws.

★★ **GE (General Electric) Building.** – *30 Rockefeller Plaza*. Soaring 850ft above street level, the 70-story GE Building (former RCA Building; renamed in 1990) is the loftiest of the Center's towers and is also the most harmonious architecturally. Slight setbacks in the massing of its slab-like form soften the severity of its lines. General Electric and National Broadcasting Company (NBC) are headquartered in the building, making it a major communications center.

A glass and limestone Art Deco panel (1933) by Lee Lawrie enlivens the main entrance at 30 Rockefeller Plaza. Step into the lobby decorated with immense ceiling and wall murals by the Spanish artist, José Maria Sert, depicting America's development and man's progress through time. These murals are actually the second series executed for the building. The first set, designed by Mexican muralist Diego Rivera, were considered too radical for this capitalistic enterprise and were subsequently destroyed.

On the 65th floor is the **Rainbow Room**, the legendary ballroom and restaurant, which reopened its doors in 1987 after a 2-year restoration effort. Spectacular views of the Rockefeller Center area and the Manhattan skyline can be enjoyed from all sides.

★ **NBC Studios.** – *Visit by guided tour (1hr) only, Apr–Aug Mon–Fri 9:30am–5pm, Sat 9:15am–7pm, Sun 9:30am–4:45pm, holidays 9:30am–7pm. Rest of the year Mon–Sat 9:30am–4:30pm, holidays 9:30am–7pm. Closed Jan 1, Labor Day, Thanksgiving Day, Dec 25. $8. Children under 6 not admitted. Tour leaves every 15min. Tickets are sold on a first-come-first-served basis. ☏664-4000. Disabled persons requiring assistance ☏664-7174. For audience ticket information and schedules ☏664-3055.* Several floors of the GE Building are devoted to the National Broadcasting Company television studios. After providing a brief overview of the company's "golden days" in radio, the tour takes visitors through the studio sets of the Today Show and Saturday Night Live. High-tech equipment, including NBC's "Van Go" mobile units, which monitor all major sporting events, can also be viewed. The tour ends in a simulated mini-studio where visitors appear on camera and learn a meteorologist's tricks for explaining the weather on television.

★★ **Radio City Music Hall [A].** – *1260 Ave of the Americas.* A treasured New York landmark, Radio City Music Hall is one of the city's most grandiose Art Deco creations and a spectacular entertainment venue. The Music Hall opened its doors to the public in 1932, under the direction of Samuel "Roxy" Rothafel, to present variety shows. At the time, it was the largest indoor theater in the world. In order to become more profitable, the Music Hall began operating as a movie house and soon hosted great movie premieres. When the movie business became unprofitable, plans were made to tear the building down. A great public outcry and hundreds of signed petitions from all over the country put an end to the plan, and the building was completely renovated in 1979.

Today, it is best known for musical spectaculars presented live on its Great Stage and for concerts by top performing artists.

The Rockettes. – *Major shows are the "Easter Extravaganza" (two weeks around Easter) and "The Christmas Spectacular" (mid-Nov–Jan 5). Concerts and special events are presented throughout the year. For show schedule ☏247-4777; for ticket information contact Ticketmaster ☏307-7171.* The Rockettes, founded in St. Louis, Missouri in 1925, have been a star attraction at the Music Hall since opening night, December 27, 1932. Known originally as the Missouri Rockets, then as the Roxyettes when they were resident performers at New York's Roxy Theater (named for Mr Rothafel), the troupe was renamed the Rockettes in 1934, the name by which they have gained international renown as the world's finest precision dance team.

★★★ **The Interior.** – *Visit by guided tour (1hr) only, Mon–Sat 10am–4:45pm, Sun 11am–4:45pm. $8. Tickets are sold on a first-come-first-served basis. ☏632-4041.* The luxurious Art Deco interior of Radio City Music Hall allows visitors to marvel at the same architectural splendor that awed the public a half-century ago.

On entering the Grand Foyer, designed by Donald Deskey, the eyes rise from the plush carpet, featuring a geometric pattern representing six musical instruments, up to the sweeping Grand Staircase and three mezzanine levels. Ezra Winter's enormous 60ft by 40ft mural, *Fountain of Youth,* adorns the wall behind the staircase. Magnificent chandeliers, considered among the largest in the world, emit a suffused light overhead. Each weighs 2 tons—a ton of crystal and a ton of steel—and can be lowered for cleaning merely by pushing a button. Note also the immense gold wall mirrors extending up to the sparkling ceiling, covered in gold leaf.

In the auditorium, the curved wall and ceiling design leads the eye toward the immense **proscenium arch** (60ft high), the most striking feature of the 5,882-seat theater. The stage itself, a masterpiece of technical expertise, is equipped with complex machinery: three elevators, a three-section turntable, and an orchestra elevator. The musicians in the orchestra and the two electric organs (with pipes up to 32ft high), complete with their organists, can be whisked away behind the walls or below the floor when necessary, without interrupting their playing.

On the lower level, the smoking and powder rooms also form a striking Art Deco ensemble.

Take W. 49th St to Ave of the Americas.

★ **Avenue of the Americas** *(47th to 54th Sts)*

An imposing series of tall office towers with spacious plazas lines the west side of the Avenue of the Americas; aligned like dominoes, these skyscrapers create a breathtaking canyon. Built in the 1950s and 1960s, the row of buildings became part of the Rockefeller Center but never quite managed to match its elegant style and refined beauty. Peek into the towers' spacious lobbies at your leisure to admire the decor and to view various art works and temporary exhibits.

Across 47th Street rises the **Celanese Building** (1973), a 45-story edifice similar in conception to the McGraw-Hill Building and 1251 Avenue of the Americas *(p 40)*; the striking trio was designed by Harrison, Abramovitz & Harris.

MIDTOWN

McGraw-Hill Building. – *No. 1221.* Housing the celebrated publisher, this 51-story building constructed of flame finished granite and solar bronze glass is surrounded by plazas. The lower plaza in front of the building features a sleek 50ft steel sun triangle, designed by meteorologist Athelstan Spilhaus in 1973. Each side of the triangle points to the four seasonal positions of the sun at solar noon in New York during the solstices and equinoxes. This plaza leads to the lower concourse and the McGraw-Hill Bookstore.

Bordering the western edge of the building, the McGraw-Hill Park features a moon-shaped walk-through waterfall, a tree-shaded mall with an ornamental pool, hanging plants, tables and chairs, and refreshment facilities *(park open May–Oct; concerts Jul–Aug Wed 12:30–1:30pm).*

Across the street behind 1251 Avenue of the Americas, another peaceful mini-park, replete with flowers, trees, food stands and a cascading waterfall, provides a welcome respite from the busy streets and sidewalks.

1251 Avenue of the Americas. – With its 53 stories, this is the second tallest skyscraper in Rockefeller Center after the GE Building, which it faces across the Avenue of the Americas. Rising 750ft from a landscaped plaza, the edifice (1971), former headquarters for Exxon Corporation, is marked by alternating limestone piers, bronze-tinted windows and steel beams.

Time & Life Building. – *No. 1271.* Across from Radio City rises the smooth, glistening exterior of the building where *Time, Life, Money, People, Sports Illustrated* and *Fortune* are published. Erected in 1959, the building was the first modern skyscraper constructed on the west side of the Avenue of the Americas.

Admire the pure vertical lines of the 48-story building, 587ft in height, featuring limestone, aluminum and glass. On two sides of the building is the Americas Plaza, paved with a two-toned terrazzo pattern. The undulating design contrasts pleasantly with the rectangular pools and their fountains.

★ **Equitable Center.** – *On Seventh Ave, between W. 51st and 52nd Sts.* The Equitable Center, a block-long complex named for the insurance company, features as its centerpiece Equitable Tower (1985), an elegant 54-story granite, limestone and glass structure designed by Edward Larrabee Barnes. In the Tower lobby *(entrance on Seventh Ave)* is Thomas Hart Benton's expressive ten-part mural *America Today,* depicting life across the nation on the eve of the Great Depression. An atrium, dominated by the bold images of Roy Lichtenstein's 65ft-high *Mural with Blue Brushstroke,* adjoins Equitable Tower on the west; the atrium houses the Equitable Gallery, a 3,000sq ft space dedicated to presenting works from all fields of the visual arts *(open Mon–Fri 11am–6pm; Sat noon–5pm;* & ☎554-4818).

To the east stands the **PaineWebber Building** (1961), presenting changing exhibits on the lobby level *(open Mon–Fri 8am–6pm;* & ☎713-2885).

★ **CBS Building.** – *51 W. 52nd St.* Known as the Black Rock, this abstract structure is the only high-rise building (38 stories) designed by the renowned architect, Eero Saarinen (1910-1961). Completed in 1965, the tower presents a framework of reinforced concrete, covered with dark granite, and triangular columns, exuding the sense of a grid. The building's sunken plaza and its indiscernible entranceways contribute to its aloofness and detachment from the busy thoroughfare.

Behind the CBS Building rises the E.F. Hutton Building *(31 W. 52nd St)*, a post-Modern pile sitting atop large piers of red granite, designed by Roche, Dinkeloo and Assocs. in 1987. In the benched courtyard separating the two buildings, note the large sculpture (1987, Jesús Bautista Moroles) reminiscent of ancient ruins.

Return to Ave of the Americas and turn left on W. 52nd St.

The tapered silhouette of the **Sheraton Center** (originally known as the Americana Hotel), one of the largest hotels in the world, is particularly elegant seen from the south, where the line is slightly broken. Built almost entirely of glass over a stone framework, it was erected in 1962 and contains 1,828 rooms on 50 floors.

Return to Ave of the Americas.

Adorning the plaza fronting the Crédit Lyonnais Building *(between W. 52nd and W. 53rd Sts)* are three huge (14ft to 23ft) bronze sculptures **[2]** by Jim Dine, representing the Venus de Milo statue; the ensemble (1989) is entitled *Looking Toward the Avenue.*

Covered with steel and blue glass panels, the 46-story **New York Hilton and Towers** hotel was completed in 1963. It includes a 4-story base housing service and reception facilities, and a slab-like tower given over to the 2,034 guest rooms and suites, each designed to have a view of the New York skyline.

On the main floor, next to the lobby, is the Promenade Cafe with its tall glass walls looking out onto the Avenue of the Americas.

Across 54th Street is the 50-story, brown-tinted Burlington House, which extends the row of tower buildings on the west side of the Avenue of the Americas.

"At night . . . the streets become rhythmical perspectives of glowing dotted lines, reflections hung upon them in the streets as the wisteria hangs its violet racemes on its trellis. The buildings are a shimmering verticality, a gossamer veil, a festive scene-drop hanging there against the black sky to dazzle, entertain, amaze.

Frank Lloyd Wright, *The Disappearing City,* 1932

Time: 2 hours. Distance: .8mi. Map pp 32-33, unless otherwise indicated.

One of New York's upscale thoroughfares, 57th Street spans the breadth of upper midtown Manhattan encompassing some of its most exclusive shops, galleries and office towers.

Once home to the Vanderbilts, Whitneys, Roosevelts and other members of the city's wealthy political elite, 57th Street was a premier residential address in the years following the Civil War. Commercial development after World War I transformed the area into a vibrant shopping district featuring tony department stores and specialty shops. Carnegie Hall's 1891 debut heralded the area's evolution as a center for classical music and the arts.

Today, East 57th Street is home to a wide range of art, home furnishings and decorator shops. The **Manhattan Art and Antiques Center** *(1050 Second Ave)* offers attractive displays of porcelain, jewelry, furniture and objets d'art in an urban bazaar setting. Venerable stores such as Tiffany & Co and Bergdorf Goodman vie for the sophisticated shoppers attention along with exclusive designer boutiques and the chic French department store, Galeries Lafayette. West of Park Avenue, 57th Street is known as a bastion of 20C art, housing one of the world's largest concentrations of art and antique dealers.

WALKING TOUR

Begin at corner of E. 57th St and Lexington Ave and walk west. ● *4, 5, 6 train to 59th St.*

Distinguished by the post-Modern *tempietto* fronting its plaza, 135 East 57th Street (1987; Kohn, Pederson and Fox) with its curved facade presents an original corner treatment for a Manhattan building. Located next door, at no. 125, **Place des Antiquaires** is a sophisticated showcase for antiques, paintings and decorative accessories from around the world. Erected in 1975, the Galleria *(no. 117)*, marked by a sharply angled facade, contains an inviting interior shopping mall. The building is flanked by a pleasant public arcade to the east.

Standing between Park and Madison Avenues, the Four Seasons Hotel, an I.M. Pei creation, rises to 46 stories through a series of setbacks. Its light stone facade is pierced by an enormous blind oculus.

Fuller Building. – *41 E. 57th St.* Once headquarters of the Fuller Construction Company, the elaborate 1929 Art Deco edifice showcases an assortment of contemporary art and antiques in over 20 galleries. The elegant black granite building, topped by a limestone tower, encloses a richly ornamented lobby: bronze elevator doors chronicle the building's construction while the mosaic floor displays other Fuller commissions, notably the FLATIRON BUILDING.

Turn left into Madison Ave to E. 56th St.

★★ **Sony Plaza (former AT&T Headquarters).** – *550 Madison Ave.* Presenting a radical departure from the metal and glass, box-like forms erected in the 1960s and 1970s, this 1984 stone building was designed by Philip Johnson and John Burgee in association with Henry Simmons. Distinguished by an unusual roof reminiscent of Colonial furniture design (a triangle split at the peak by a semi-circular hollow), the 40-story edifice has been dubbed the first post-Modern skyscraper. To conserve energy, only a third of its pink granite exterior is covered with windows. The building is elevated from the ground by massive, 110ft-high columns that enclose a pleasant outdoor pedestrian plaza, lit by oversize portholes and lanterns.

Enter the IBM Building through the E. 56th St entrance.

IBM Building. – *590 Madison Ave.* Clad in polished black granite, the 43-story highrise (1983, Edward Larrabee Barnes) features an imposing cut corner overhang above its entrance, defying the visitor to enter the monolith. Strips of windows set flush with the smooth stone exterior wrap around the building creating a pattern of horizontal bands. At the 56th Street entrance, a stylized, rough-hewn fountain containing horizontal flowing waters reflects the daily tides of pedestrian and automotive traffic. The cryptic striations at the fountain's edges are coded references to surrounding street addresses.

Return to E. 57th St and continue west.

The stretch of 57th Street between Madison and Fifth Avenues contains an array of signature boutiques, including Chanel, Hermès and Burberry's, whose attractive storefronts present the latest in fashion design.

Before reaching FIFTH AVENUE, note on the south side the Galeries Lafayette, housed in the TRUMP TOWER, and TIFFANY & CO **[3]**. Bergdorf Goodman's **[4]** exclusive department store flanks Fifth Avenue.

Cross Fifth Ave.

The intersection of Fifth Avenue and 57th Street is marked by several luxury shops, including VAN CLEEF & ARPELS **[5]**. The northwest corner is occupied by the WARNER BROS STUDIO STORE **[6]**, with its lively Looney Tune cartoon friezes.

The striking and controversial **9 West 57th Street**★ (1974; Skidmore, Owings & Merrill), a twin to the GRACE BUILDING on East 42nd Street, rises on the north side of West 57th. Articulated by tinted glass curtain walls and travertine edges, the 50-story high-rise slopes down to plazas on 57th and 58th Streets. The slightly distorted images of other buildings reflected in the sloping, curved exterior walls produce unusual visual effects. The award-winning sculptured red no. 9 sign on 57th Street is the work of graphic designer Ivan Chermayeff. The neighboring building, 29 West 57th

Street, is adorned with a colorful sculpted relief of the French Cross of the *Légion d'Honneur* on its tower. Located next door, the **Rizzoli Bookstore** *(no. 31)*, distinguished by a rounded archway, contains wood-paneled shelves lined with fine books.

Continue west between Avenue of the Americas and Seventh Ave.

The trendy Planet Hollywood restaurant *(no. 140)* sports a neon exterior featuring the handprints of celebrities from movies and television. The **Russian Tea Room** *(no. 150, map p 89)*, with its rustic facade of frosted glass windows and green and red trim, contains a richly appointed interior evoking the opulence of czarist Russia. Begun by Russian émigrés as a gathering spot for expatriate ballet corps members, this New York celebrity haunt serves over a ton of caviar a year and contains an extensive display of *samovars* (Russian tea services).

★ **Carnegie Hall.** – *Map p 89. 156 W. 57th St. Visit by guided tour (1hr) only, Mon, Tue, Thu 11:30am, 2 & 3pm. Closed Aug. $6. Special "Tea and Tour" (at the Russian Tea Room) available: $27. ♿. For performance schedule and ticket information ☎247-7800. Pre-concert buffet dinners with reservations ☎903-9689.* At the corner of Seventh Avenue, majestic Carnegie Hall is regarded as one of the world's most prestigious concert venues. Faced with orange-colored bricks, the building (1891) was designed by William B. Tuthill in the Italian Renaissance style.

Originally known as "Music Hall," it was renamed for steel magnate and philanthropist **Andrew Carnegie** (1835-1919), under whose auspices it was built. Carnegie Hall opened in 1891 with Tchaikovsky's American conducting debut. After narrowly escaping demolition in the 1960s, it was renovated in 1986. Today, this landmark concert hall seats 2,804 and is reputed to have the foremost acoustics of any performance space. Over the last century, Carnegie Hall has hosted luminaries from Gustav Mahler to the Beatles, Winston Churchill and Dr Martin Luther King. Two major additions, the Tuthill office tower on 56th Street and the Hardenbergh tower on 57th Street were added in 1895 and 1897 respectively. A 60-story tower added to the east by Cesar Pelli & Assocs. in 1990 completes the Carnegie Hall complex.

The small **Rose Museum at Carnegie Hall** *(access at no. 154; take elevator to second floor; open daily 11am–4:30pm; closed Aug)* features photos, programs and clippings detailing the history of the hall. Benny Goodman's clarinet and the batons of conductors Toscanini and von Karajan are also on display.

At the corner with Seventh Avenue, pause to look north to the ornate **Alwyn Court Apartments** *(182 W. 58th St, map p 89)*, built in 1909 by Harde & Short. This flamboyant building is faced entirely with terra-cotta panels decorated with Renaissance motifs.

Between Seventh and Eighth Avenues, on the northern side, stands the **Art Students League** *(no. 215, map p 89)*, founded in 1875 by former students of the NATIONAL ACADEMY OF DESIGN, who wanted to create an independent school that would admit women. Designed by Hardenbergh in 1892, the building resembles a 16C hunting lodge built by King François I of France. Located at no. 221, the London-based Hard Rock Cafe features a vintage Cadillac crashing into its facade. The Hard Rock is noted for its guitar-shaped bar and extensive displays of rock'n'roll memorabilia.

Cross-references to sights described in this guide are indicated by SMALL CAPITALS. ***Consult the index (p 187) for the appropriate page number.***

★★ 4 PARK AVENUE (Midtown)

Time: 2 hours. Distance: 1mi. Map p 44.

A majestic boulevard lined with broad sidewalks and divided by a series of islands embellished with flower parterres, shrubbery and sculpture, Park Avenue is considered one of the most desirable residential and commercial addresses in New York. The midtown section of the avenue, today taken over by corporate America, is the thoroughfare's busiest. Colorful in summer, it is also attractive at Christmas when the trees are decorated with multi-colored lights.

A Masterpiece of Urban Design. – Park Avenue has not always been such an attractive street. From the 1830s to the 1890s, the open railroad tracks ran straight down the thoroughfare, called Fourth Avenue, while bridges carried the cross-town traffic. The smoke and noise made the area almost unbearable.

In 1903, the New York Central Railroad Company commenced work on GRAND CENTRAL TERMINAL and sank the offensive tracks below street level. New engineering techniques made it possible to erect buildings on stilts, thereby isolating them from railroad vibrations. This innovation allowed the company to develop the real estate above both the tracks and the fan-shaped train yards, as far north as 50th Street. The newly named Park Avenue was quickly lined with uniform rows of apartment buildings, and the entire scheme was hailed as one of the great pieces of urban design of the early 20C.

During the post-war wave of construction, the original apartment houses were replaced by high-rise offices of varying styles, home mainly to banks. Today, the former residential elegance of Park Avenue's midtown section has vanished, giving way to a sometimes incongruous corridor of glass and metal towers.

WALKING TOUR

Begin at Park Ave and E. 46th St. ● *4, 5, 6 train to Grand Central Terminal.*

★ **Helmsley Building.** – *No. 230.* Erected in 1929 to house the headquarters of the New York Central Railroad Company, this distinctive building crowned by a pyramidal roof and cupola straddles Park Avenue. Designed by Warren & Wetmore, also responsible for Grand Central Terminal's imposing exterior, the structure sits atop two levels of railroad tracks. Once the dominant centerpiece of the area, the elegant tower is today dwarfed by the MET LIFE BUILDING (formerly the Pan Am Building), rising behind it *(illustration below)*. The edifice is pierced by two tunnels reserved for motor traffic and two street-level arcades for pedestrians.

Step inside the opulent lobby to admire the travertine walls and bronze detailing. At the time of construction, the sumptuous decor offered a dramatic contrast to the neighboring, sober office buildings and reflected the grandiose aspirations of the railway company. Acquired by the Helmsley chain in 1977, the edifice was covered with a new coat of gold leaf and is now illuminated at night.

Rising 53 stories from a small pedestrian plaza is **no. 270** *(between 47th and 48th Sts)*, a slender tower of contrasting black and white steel, erected in 1960 for Union Carbide Company by Skidmore, Owings & Merrill. Today, it houses the world headquarters of Chemical Bank. As is the case for many buildings in the vicinity of Grand Central, the main lobby and elevators are located on the second floor because the elevator shafts cannot be accommodated below ground.

No. 277, a silver gray tower built in 1962 by Emery Roth & Sons rises 50 stories on the east side of the street, balancing no. 270 through its similar height and axial alignment. A 3-story atrium protruding toward the street encloses a greenhouse, called **Chemcourt** (1982), dotted with exotic plants and mini-waterfalls. On the corner of East 48th Street, note the amusing bronze sculpture (1983) by J. Seward Johnson Jr, representing a business man hailing a taxi.

★ **Waldorf-Astoria Hotel.** – *No. 301, between 49th and 50th Sts.* This world-famous hotel designed by Schultze and Weaver in 1931, is the successor to the former Waldorf-Astoria, which occupied the present site of the EMPIRE STATE BUILDING. The massive structure, occupying an entire city block, is

Park Avenue with Helmsley and Met Life buildings

Ken Straiton/First Light

distinguished by its twin, chrome-capped towers rising 42 stories from an 18-story granite base, and a series of setbacks in limestone and brick, which contribute to the edifice's demure Art Deco look.

The elegant interior presents an eclectic mix of Art Deco ornamentation and Second Empire furnishings. Of particular interest is the main lobby, with its marble floor embellished by an intricate mosaic known as the *Wheel of Life*. The east lobby is noteworthy for the bronze clock, crafted in London in 1893.

A staff of 1,500 serve the more than 1,410 guest rooms, including luxury apartments and suites occupied by a succession of celebrities. Several suites are reserved for presidents or heads of state. A protocol service has been organized to decide delicate questions of precedence and etiquette. Thus certain dignitaries who stay at the Waldorf are entitled to see their national flags flying in front of the hotel. The private apartments have been occupied by every US president since President Hoover, and other notables such as General MacArthur, the Duke of Windsor and Henry Kissinger.

★ **St Bartholomew's Church.** – *At the corner of E. 50th St. Open daily 8am–6pm (Sun 4pm).* &. Considered one of architect Bertram G. Goodhue's most successful constructions, this Episcopal church illustrates the tenets of the Romanesque style, accentuated with Byzantine features. The edifice is marked by a multi-colored dome, salmon-colored brick and gray limestone walls. Set in a charming, terraced garden, the church and its adjoining community center offer a contrast to the surrounding modern skyscrapers.

In recent years, St Bartholomew's has been the focus of a bitter preservation dispute ultimately settled by the Supreme Court, which ruled against the church's proposal to demolish the community center.

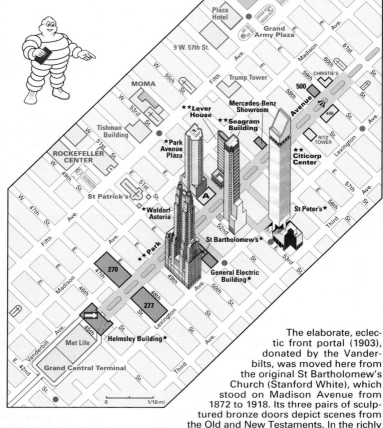

The elaborate, eclectic front portal (1903), donated by the Vanderbilts, was moved here from the original St Bartholomew's Church (Stanford White), which stood on Madison Avenue from 1872 to 1918. Its three pairs of sculptured bronze doors depict scenes from the Old and New Testaments. In the richly decorated, marble interior, note the mosaic of the Transfiguration located in the apse, above alabaster windows. In the baptistery stands the statue of a kneeling angel, the work of 19C English sculptor James Redfern. The church's Aeolian organ is the largest in the city.

Turn right on E. 51st St and continue to Lexington Ave.

★ **General Electric Building.** – *570 Lexington Ave.* Located immediately behind St Bartholomew's is this marvelous Art Deco creation, its reddish-orange spire topped by a spiky crown. The 51-story octagonal brick tower rising from a square base was designed to be viewed in conjunction with St Bartholomew's. It was constructed for RCA Victor Company, who deeded it to General Electric when the former moved to ROCKEFELLER CENTER in 1931. Decorative features include rays, flashes and lightning bolts, which are particularly appropriate to the building's principal tenant.

Return to Park Ave.

★★ **Seagram Building.** – *No. 375. Visit by guided tour (30min) Tue 3pm. Check with guard in lobby.* The headquarters of Joseph E. Seagram & Sons, Inc was designed in 1958 by **Mies van der Rohe** and **Philip Johnson**. Harmoniously proportioned, the 38-story tower is set back half an acre on a granite plaza with twin fountains. The subtle color scheme of the exterior bronze panels and the bronze colored windows, the refinement of the interior lobby with its travertine walls and the continuation of the granite plaza floor, give an air of classic distinction to this building. The only edifice in the city designed by Mies, the Seagram Building represents one of the finest International Style skyscrapers in New York.

Step inside the lobby to admire the huge Picasso painting adorning the entrance of the famed restaurant, The Four Seasons. The piece was executed in 1919 as a stage curtain for the ballet by Léonide Massine, "The Three-Cornered Hat" (Le Tricorne).

Facing the Seagram Building, the 1918 Italian Renaissance style "palazzo" housing the exclusive Racquet and Tennis Club **[A]** *(no. 370)* was designed by McKim, Mead and White. The edifice is one of the few survivors of a bygone era when this section of Park Avenue was lined with masonry buildings.

★ **Park Avenue Plaza.** – *E. 52nd to 53rd Sts, between Park and Madison Aves. Enter on 53rd St.* The massive bulk of this unusual 15-sided green mirror glass structure rises behind the Racquet and Tennis Club. Designed by Skidmore, Owings & Merrill and opened in 1981, this office building contains a 30ft, double-level pedestrian shopping arcade enhanced by a fountain resembling a wall of water. A monumental work, *Deauville* (1970), by Frank Stella hangs above the main desk on the upper level. Temporary exhibits are displayed in the lobby *(open Mon–Fri 9am–9pm; for exhibit schedule contact Chartwell Booksellers ☎ 308-0688).*

★★ Lever House. – *No. 390.* Designed by Skidmore, Owings & Merrill, and influenced by the architectural concepts of Le Corbusier, this building was considered avant-garde when it opened in 1952. The 21-story vertical slab of blue-green glass and stainless steel rising from a 2-story horizontal base presented an exciting contrast to the concrete and stone apartment buildings that lined the avenue in the 1950s. The Lever House inaugurated an era of glass-box structures throughout the city and firmly established the International Style for commercial constructions.

Changing art exhibits can be viewed in the main lobby *(open Mon–Fri 10am–5pm; Sun 1–5pm;* ♿ ☎*960-4685).*

From Park Ave, turn right on E. 53rd St and continue to Lexington Ave.

★★ Citicorp Center. – *153 E. 53rd St, at the corner with Lexington Ave.* Citicorp, parent company of Citibank, is headquartered in this spectacular aluminum and glass-sheathed tower (1978) whose top slopes at a 45° angle. This 900ft tower is Manhattan's fourth tallest building and one of its most conspicuous landmarks. The success of the complex designed by Hugh Stubbins & Assocs. has led to a surge of high-rise construction in the area between Lexington and Third Avenues. The tower stands on four colossal pillars, each 9 stories or 115ft high and 22ft square, set at the center of each side, rather than at the corners of the building. Beneath these cantilevered corners, which extend 72ft from the central columns, nestle St Peter's Church and a separate 7-story structure housing the **Market**, an attractive complex of shops and restaurants set around a landscaped atrium. Beneath the vast skylight, through which the main tower can be glimpsed, cafe tables have been placed among trees and shrubs. Popular and full of vitality, the atrium is often the scene of exhibits, concerts and other activities.

★ St Peter's Church. – *Access on 54th St. Open daily 9am–10pm. Guided tour (30min) available.* ♿. This Lutheran church sold its land to Citicorp on the understanding that a new church would be integrated within the complex. The result is a comparatively tiny structure whose roof lines repeat the angle of the tower above. The interior *(viewed from street level gallery)* is dramatic and simple, with stark white walls and floors. Roof and side wall skylights bring natural light into the structure, yet excellent soundproofing makes it an oasis of silence in this noisy corner of Manhattan. The altar, lectern, platform, steps and pews are constructed of red oak. Upon exiting the gallery, visit the adjoining **Erol Beker Chapel of the Good Shepherd★** designed by Louise Nevelson as a "place of purity" in Manhattan.

Return to Park Ave on 54th St.

Continuing north along Park Avenue, note the **Mercedes-Benz Showroom** *(no. 430)*. Designed in 1953 by Frank Lloyd Wright for Max Hoffman, a distributor of Mercedes automobiles, it is a symphony of ramp and reflection.

At the corner of 57TH STREET is the Ritz Tower *(no. 465)*, crowned by stepped obelisks, a typical Park Avenue apartment building. It was erected in 1925 by Emery Roth and Carrère & Hastings as part of the Hearst apartment hotel chain. Between 58th and 59th Streets, the black, glass and aluminum facade of 499 Park Avenue (1981) reflects the neighboring buildings. Designed by I.M. Pei, it houses the Banque Nationale de Paris. At this point, on either side of the street, the **view★★** south toward the Helmsley and Met Life buildings is resplendent.

500 Park Avenue. – *At the corner with 59th St.* Designed by Skidmore, Owings & Merrill, this elegant, 11-story structure (1960), formerly the Olivetti Building, seems dwarfed by the 1984 building (500 Park Tower) rising behind it. The geometric rigor of its lines, with glass panels resting on supporting pillars, is impressive.

On the northwest corner of 59th Street is Christie's, the fine-art auction house founded in 1766. Beyond 60th Street, Park Avenue becomes residential and one of the most fashionable addresses in the city.

For a description of Park Avenue north of 59th Street see Upper East Side (p 91).

EAST 42nd STREET

Time: 2 hours. Distance: .5mi. Map p 48.

Slicing across Manhattan from the East River to the Hudson, 42nd Street is New York's major crosstown artery. Its eastern section, between the UNITED NATIONS and FIFTH AVENUE, features a magnificent assortment of distinguished buildings reflecting changing architectural styles since 1900.

From Shanties to Skyscrapers. – In an attempt to encourage people to move uptown and away from the crowded tenements of lower Manhattan *(p 74)*, the city of New York opened 42nd Street to settlement in 1836. However, owing to the noise and pollution from steam trains, only factories and breweries would operate in the area, thereby stunting any residential development. By 1860, the district abounded in shanties, where newly arrived immigrants eked out an existence.

The construction of Grand Central Terminal in the early 20C created a catalyst for much needed change. The unsightly railroad tracks were covered up, and, following the station's completion in 1913, a boom in real estate opened up the area to office towers, apartment buildings and hotels. To the north, the WALDORF-ASTORIA HOTEL (1931) attracted a wealthy clientele to its high society events. Erected to the south and east, the Chanin, Chrysler and Daily News buildings inaugurated an era of architectural innovation. When six blocks of slaughterhouses were razed to make room for the UNITED NATIONS HEADQUARTERS in 1946, this area of New York became a recognized district in the city.

WALKING TOUR

Begin at Grand Central Terminal, at the corner of Park Ave. ● 4, 5, 6 train to Grand Central Terminal.

★★ **Grand Central Terminal.** – Often referred to as the "gateway to the nation," this world-famous railroad terminal represents a masterpiece of urban planning. Designed by the engineering firm of Reed and Stem and architects Warren and Wetmore, the grand Beaux-Arts edifice has remained a symbol of the city since its inception in 1913. Grand Central Terminal is one of the two major railroad stations servicing New York City.

From Depot to Terminal. – In the early 19C, the first steam trains in New York chugged down Fourth Avenue (now Park Avenue) to a depot on 23rd Street, where the coaches were hooked up to a team of horses, which pulled them to the end of the line near CITY HALL. By 1854, an ordinance was passed banning steam locomotives south of 42nd Street to reduce air and noise pollution. **Commodore Cornelius Vanderbilt** (1794-1877), who had acquired and consolidated all of the city's railroad companies by 1869, decided to build an enormous iron and glass terminal at the present site of Grand Central.

In 1902, a new state order banned steam locomotives from the city altogether, leaving the New York Central Railroad Company with the choice of relocating outside city limits or electrifying the line. Under the direction of chief engineer William J. Wilgus, the company chose to cover the tracks and bring trains in on two levels. Today, there is virtually no evidence that a vast underground railroad terminal exists at all. Some 500 trains carrying 200,000 commuters in addition to long distance travelers, arrive and depart daily via a subterranean tunnel that extends beneath Park Avenue from East 42nd to 59th Streets. The area surrounding Grand Central has developed into a prosperous commercial district.

The Building. – *Enter the terminal.* The cavernous **main concourse★**, measuring 375ft long by 120ft wide, soars to a height of 125ft (12 stories). The hall is pierced by a row of small windows and crowned by a vaulted ceiling decorated with the constellations of the winter zodiac. (One of the city's least-known oddities is that the zodiac was created backwards in 1913; terminal representatives say it will probably never be corrected.) The original ceiling, once illuminated by 2,500 stars, was covered over with painted panels in 1941, owing to water damage *(restoration is underway)*. Melon-shaped chandeliers highlight the elegant interior, lined with massive, square columns. Continuous streams of people flood past the central brass and onyx clock, a traditional New York City rendezvous point. Shops and service concessions line the two levels of ramps that lead to the tracks. The terminal is connected to many of the neighboring buildings underground.

Step outside to admire the sumptuous facade designed by Warren and Wetmore. Facing south down Park Avenue, it features three massive arched windows separated by an order of double columns. Surmounting the windows, note the immense 13ft clock and sculpture *Transportation* (1914) by Jules-Félix Coutan, which incorporates the figure of Mercury (Commerce) flanked by Hercules (Physical Energy) and Minerva (Intellectual Energy). Below the sculpture stands a bronze statue (1869) of Commodore Vanderbilt.

Towering 59 stories over Grand Central, the **Met Life Building★** (1963), formerly the Pan Am Building, was conceived by a group of architects that included **Walter Gropius** of the Bauhaus school. Its non-conforming design and the fact that it blocked the formerly unobstructed view down Park Avenue raised a storm of protest, which still rumbles occasionally today. Containing 2,400,000sq ft of office space at the time of completion, the edifice was exceeded in size only by the Pentagon.

Cross E. 42nd St to the south side.

Dominating the southwestern corner of Park Avenue and 42nd Street, the sober tower of granite, designed by Ulrich Franzen and Assocs., houses the **Philip Morris World Headquarters**. Completed in 1983, the 26-story building is distinguished by its glass facade articulated by vertical strips of granite.

Located on the ground floor, the midtown branch of the WHITNEY MUSEUM OF AMERICAN ART *(open Mon–Fri 11am–6pm; closed holidays; ⮜ ☎878-2550)* offers a welcome respite from the crowded sidewalks and traffic-clogged streets. Large 20C American sculptures are displayed in the 42ft-high enclosed sculpture court *(open Mon–Fri 11am–6pm; weekends 7:30am–9:30pm; closed holidays; ⮜ ☎878-2550)*, and an adjacent gallery serves for temporary exhibits covering the range of American art.

Continue east on E. 42nd St.

The **Bowery Savings Bank Building** *(no. 110)*, a monumental structure erected in 1923 by York and Sawyers, is well known for its richly ornamented banking hall, clad in marble and mosaic.

Grand Hyatt Hotel. – *No. 125.* Opened in 1980, this immense structure of silver mirror glass, rising to 30 stories, presents a striking contrast to its neighbors, Grand Central Terminal and the Chrysler Building, which are both reflected in it. Designed by Gruzen and Partners with Der Scutt, the H-shaped structure is actually the former Commodore Hotel, dating from 1920, a masonry building now sheathed in glass.

★ **Chanin Building.** – *No. 122.* A prime example of the Art Deco style, this 56-story building (1929) designed by architect and developer Irwin Chanin with Sloan & Robertson, features a series of setbacks, topped by a buttressed crown, rising from a massive base. Adorning the first four floors, an exquisite terra-cotta frieze of floral bas-reliefs reflects the typical curvilinear Art Deco elements. Step inside the intricately detailed **lobby** to view the door frames, convector grilles and mailboxes.

MIDTOWN

★★★ **Chrysler Building.** – *405 Lexington Ave.* Rising to 1,048ft (77 stories), this famous New York landmark is surmounted by a distinctive spire of radiant stainless steel arches that glimmers in sunlight and glows in the nighttime illuminations. Designed by William Van Alen and completed in 1930, it was briefly the tallest building in the world (the EMPIRE STATE BUILDING was opened in 1931). It was also one of the first buildings to feature exposed metal as an essential part of its design. The pinnacle resembles a radiator cap from a 1930 Chrysler car. Abundant automotive decorations adorning the various setbacks under the spire include silver hood ornaments, stylized racing cars and the huge radiator cap gargoyles at the fourth level, modeled after a 1929 Chrysler.

The **lobby★**, a superb example of Art Deco, is faced with red African marble. The elevator cabs feature ornate doors and richly paneled interiors. Note also the elaborate ceiling mural by Edward Trumbull. Chrysler no longer has offices in the building. Con Edison, the New York power corporation, presents a permanent display on conservation on the ground floor *(entrance on Lexington Ave; open Mon–Fri 7am–6pm; closed holidays).*

Chrysler Building - detail

Tom Sobolik/First Light

★ **Mobil Building.** – *No. 150.* Erected in 1955, this massive 45-story structure (Harrison & Abramovitz) occupies an entire city block between Lexington and Third Avenues. The largest metal-clad office building in the world at the time of construction, it represented an unsuccessful attempt by the steel industry to demonstrate that glass and aluminum were not the trends of the future. The stainless steel skin, backed by a masonry wall, measures about 1/3 of an inch in thickness. The large embossed panels were designed to be self-cleaning—the wind scours the splayed pattern and prevents dirt build-up.

★ **Daily News Building.** – *No. 220.* The original building (1930) was designed by Howells and Hood for the *Daily News*, a tabloid that once had the largest circulation of any metropolitan newspaper in the US but has been plagued by labor disputes in recent years. One of the city's first skyscrapers to abandon the Gothic style popular at the time, the News Building features white brick piers alternating with patterned red and black brick spandrels, giving the tower a vertical striped look and an illusion of height greater than its actual 37 stories. A flat roof, a remarkable innovation for 1930, crowns the slab-like edifice. The more recent annex (1958, Harrison & Abramovitz), stretching to Second Avenue, repeats the striped pattern.

Above the main entrance note the embellishments typical of the stylized decorative designs of the 1930s. The lobby is famed for its huge revolving **globe** (12ft in diameter) and the clock that gives readings in 17 time zones. The floor is laid out as a giant compass indicating most of the principal cities of the world and their distance, by air, from New York City.

Ford Foundation Building. – *320 E. 43rd St.* This 12-story glass and granite building (1967), designed by Roche, Dinkeloo and Assocs., provides an elegant home for the Ford Foundation, a private, non-profit institution established in 1936 by Henry and Edsel Ford. Foundation funds support research, training and other activities in the fields of social welfare, human rights, education, culture and international affairs. To date, the Ford Foundation has assisted more than 9,000 organizations all over the US and in many foreign countries.

The edifice reversed the trend of the 1960s to build in the center of a plaza and instead encompasses an open green space within the building. Rising to 10 stories and enclosed by a skylight, the interior **plaza**, covering 1/3 acre, contains a lush forest of trees, shrubs and flowering plants interspersed with pools and benches. Offices at the sides and top of the building overlook the greenhouse garden *(entrance on 42nd St; open to the public Mon–Fri 9am–5pm; closed holidays).*

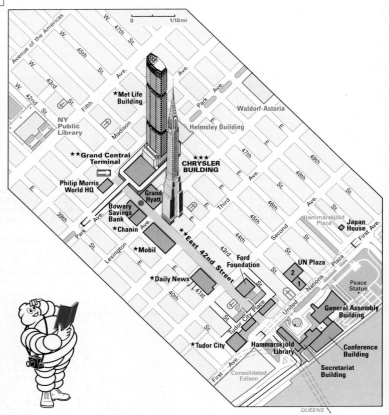

★ **Tudor City.** – *Tudor City Place.* Erected in the mid-1920s on a bluff overlooking the UNITED NATIONS HEADQUARTERS, this group of buildings was designed in the Tudor Gothic style, with such details as quatrefoils, pointed arches, pinnacles and crenellated rooflines. About 1925, the developer Fred F. French began acquiring dilapidated houses on this site with a view to creating a large housing project that would be accessible to the middle class. The complex was developed as a self-contained community with 3,000 apartments, a hotel, shops and parks.

The 12 brick buildings (6 apartment buildings, 5 apartment hotels, 1 hotel) enjoy a relative calm and isolation rare in New York. Facing two private parks to the west, the buildings are almost windowless on their east side because in the 1920s, the current United Nations plaza was an industrial area of breweries, slaughterhouses, glue factories and a gas works.

Tudor City Place, which crosses 42nd by a bridge *(access by steps from 42nd or 43rd Sts)*, affords a superb **view★** of 42nd Street to the west and of the United Nations to the east.

★★★
6 **UNITED NATIONS HEADQUARTERS**

Time: 2 hours. ●4, 5, 6 train to Grand Central Terminal. Map above and p 50.

Situated on 18 acres of land on the banks of the East River, between 42nd and 48th Streets, the United Nations complex comprises four buildings and various gardens that enjoy extraterritorial status. Composed of 181 member states, this international organization pledges to "preserve international peace and security, promote self-determination and equal rights, and encourage economic and social well-being."

Historical Notes. – The United Nations was created on June 16, 1945, when representatives of 51 nations, meeting in San Francisco, signed the original UN charter, hoping to provide a framework in which nations could work together in the cause of international security and peace. The UN succeeded to the role performed by the League of Nations, created under President Woodrow Wilson following World War I. The Charter's ambitious goals include: international cooperation to solve economic, social, cultural or humanitarian problems; peaceful solutions to international disputes; and an end to threats or use of force against any nation. Over the years the UN has undertaken several military efforts to repel aggression, beginning with an intervention in 1950 to turn back North Korea's incursion into South Korea and extending through the Gulf War in 1991, in which Iraqi forces were ousted from Kuwait. Many of the most heated conflicts were outgrowths of the Cold War between the US and the former Soviet Union.

One of the most striking developments in the UN's evolution has been the increasing influence of the so-called Third World, which has resulted from the end of colonial empires and the rapid growth in the number of independent states. Since 1988, 25 nations have been added to the list of member states.

The Buildings. – In December 1946, John D. Rockefeller, Jr *(p 37)* offered the United Nations a gift of $8.5 million to acquire the present site on the East River. At the time, this area known as Turtle Bay consisted mainly of slums, slaughterhouses and breweries. The construction program, costing over $67 million, was financed in large part by the US government, which made available an interest-free loan of $64 million that was entirely reimbursed by annual payments. The balance was paid from the regular United Nations budget. The UN buildings were designed by a group of international architects, including Le Corbusier (France), Oscar Niemeyer (Brazil) and Sven Markelius (Sweden), under the direction of the American architect, Wallace K. Harrison.

The Secretariat Building opened in 1950, and two years later the first meetings of the Security Council and the General Assembly was held at the permanent site. The Dag Hammarskjöld Memorial Library (Harrison, Abramovitz & Harris) was completed in 1962.

United Nations

United Nations Headquarters

The Organs of the UN. – The United Nations, governed by a charter of 111 articles, is composed of six principal organs and a number of subsidiary organs. Working closely with the UN are 16 specialized international agencies such as the United Nations Educational, Scientific and Cultural Organization (UNESCO) in Paris; the Food and Agriculture Organization (FAO) in Rome; and the International Monetary Fund (IMF) in Washington, DC, which helps to stabilize exchange rates. The UN and these specialized agencies make up what is known as "the United Nations family."

The Secretary-General, at present Dr Boutros Boutros-Ghali of Egypt, is the organization's chief administrative officer. He performs such functions as are necessary to carry out decisions or recommendations adopted by the General Assembly and the Councils.

VISIT

Open daily 9:15am–4:45pm. Closed Jan 1, Thanksgiving Day, Dec 25; weekends Jan–Feb. Guided tours (1hr) leave every 20min from Tour Desk in main lobby of the General Assembly Building. Children under 5 not admitted on tours. $6.50. ✗ ⅙ ☎963-7713. Tours in foreign languages by reservation on day of tour ☎963-7539.

The corner of 45th Street and First Avenue offers a fine view of the four buildings and the flags of the 181 member states lining the United Nations plaza. These flags are arranged north to south in English alphabetical order, from Afghanistan to Zimbabwe. Delegations seated in the General Assembly follow the same order.

Diagonally across from the Secretariat and General Assembly buildings, at the northwest corner of 44th Street and First Avenue, rise the spires of **United Nations Plaza** (1976), two commercial office buildings. Designed by Roche, Dinkeloo and Assocs., the irregularly shaped towers sheathed entirely in green reflecting glass present an appropriate counterpart to the straight shaft of the Secretariat Building.

Around the corner is Ralph J. Bunche Park, a small resting place honoring the first black UN official from the United States. The park is a frequent rallying point for demonstrations on issues before the UN.

The esplanade in front of the visitors entrance affords a pleasant view of the spacious gardens, dotted with various works of outdoor sculpture. The bronze equestrian statue, *Peace* (1954, Antun Augustincic), was a gift from Yugoslavia. A stairway located nearby leads to a lower terrace and the riverside promenade, which provides good views of the UN complex, the river and buildings lining the bank. Beneath the lawn to the north of the building, three underground levels are occupied by printing facilities.

The Buildings

General Assembly Building. – Forming the heart of the United Nations, this long, low-lying structure topped by an elegantly curved roof contains the vaulted Assembly Hall.

Visitors enter through one of the seven doors—donated by Canada—that pierce the huge exterior wall of concrete and glass. To the left of the entrance is the information desk, and to the right, the Meditation Room, dedicated to those who have died in the name of peace. The room is highlighted by a dramatic, 15ft by 20ft stained-glass window by Marc Chagall. Unveiled in 1964 as a memorial to Dag Hammarskjöld, the window was contributed by members of the UN staff and the artist. Various objects enhance the lobby, including a model of Sputnik I, a Foucault pendulum, a statue of Poseidon and a chunk of moon rock.

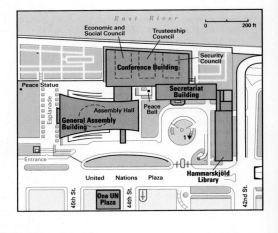

Assembly Hall. – Lighted from above, the oval Assembly Hall measures 165ft by 115ft and is 75ft high. The speaker's rostrum is surmounted by a dais on which sits the President of the General Assembly flanked by the Secretary-General and an Under Secretary-General for Political Affairs. Above the dais, the emblem of the United Nations hangs between the illuminated boards that indicate members' votes. On either side are glass-enclosed booths for radio and television, and for the interpreters who work in the six official UN languages (Arabic, Chinese, English, French, Russian, Spanish). The side walls are decorated with murals designed by the French artist, Fernand Léger.

The General Assembly regularly meets in an annual 3-month session, which starts on the third Tuesday in September. Special sessions may be called at the request of the Security Council or by a majority of the member states. The Assembly may discuss any matters within the scope of the Charter, except those under consideration by the Security Council. It also receives and discusses annual reports from the other organs and votes on the UN budget. Decisions on important questions are made by a two-thirds majority of members present and voting; a simple majority suffices for other matters. Member states are required to obey only those decisions of the Assembly concerning the UN budget. The Assembly may pass resolutions, initiate studies and make recommendations for the maintenance of peace and security and the promotion of international cooperation. It also elects its own president and vice-presidents, admits new members on the recommendation of the Security Council and chooses the non-permanent members of the Security Council.

Conference Building. – Thus named because of its council and committee meeting rooms, this low, rectangular building links the Secretariat and the General Assembly buildings. The Security Council, the Economic and Social Council, and the Trusteeship Council meet here.

The five stories of the Conference Building house—from the basement up—technical installations (air conditioning, printing presses, television and recording studios, photographic dark rooms), Conference Rooms, Council Chambers, Delegates' Lounges, and the Delegates' Dining Room.

A number of works of art, gifts of member nations, adorn the premises. They include a Persian carpet; a mosaic from Morocco; a Belgian tapestry; two Brazilian murals depicting Peace and War; a painting by Rouault, *Christ Crucified*; an ivory carving from China illustrating the Chengtu-Kunming Railway; and a scale model of a Thai royal barge. In the garden, in front of the Conference Building and the Secretariat, is a Japanese peace bell, made of copper coins and metal donated by the people of 60 countries.

Security Council. – Donated by Norway, this chamber is decorated with gold and blue wall hangings, and a mural by Norwegian artist Per Krohg symbolizing Peace and Liberty, Equality and Fraternity. The public gallery seats 200 people.

The primary responsibility for the maintenance of international peace and security lies with the Security Council. Amendments, which were adopted by the General Assembly and came into force in 1965, have increased the number of members of the Security Council from 11 to 15; 10 are elected for 2-year terms, and the other 5 (China, France, United Kingdom, Russian Federation, United States) are permanent. Votes on procedural matters require an affirmative vote of 9 members, and for important questions, these 9 must include the 5 permanent members. This rule of unanimity for the "great powers" is better known as the veto, but an abstention by a permanent member does not in practice prevent a decision from being adopted. The members of the Security Council preside in rotation; the president changes every month.

Trusteeship Council. – The furnishings in this room were donated by Denmark. Precious woods sheathe the walls and provide the backdrop for a large teak statue of a woman releasing a bluebird, which symbolizes Hope and Independence. The Trusteeship Council, created with the goal of aiding non-autonomous colonies attain independence, supervises the Trust Territories administered by member states. Out of 11 original Trust Territories, only one remains that has not become independent: Belau (part of the Carolines in the Pacific Islands), which is administered by the US.

Economic and Social Council. – This functional room was decorated with funds contributed by Sweden. The plain walls and exposed heating apparatus symbolize the council's never ending tasks. The 54-member council coordinates the efforts and resources of various UN and affiliated organizations towards the alleviation of economic and social problems. Subjects under consideration include the environment, population, women's rights, health, transportation, human rights, crime prevention and freedom of information. All the decisions of the Council are subject to the approval of the General Assembly.

Secretariat Building. – *Not open to the public.* Constructed entirely of white Vermont marble and glass and aluminum panels, this slab-like building is architecturally striking for its pure, clean lines. The simple grid-like pattern of the exterior rises 39 floors without a break. In front of the building lies a circular marble pool donated by American school children, with black and white stones collected by the children of the Greek island of Rhodes. Highlighting the pool, *Single Form* **[1]**, an abstract sculpture (1964) by Barbara Hepworth of Great Britain, commemorates Dag Hammarskjöld.

The 7,400 international civil servants and other employees who work here are drawn from many of the member nations, and include interpreters and translators, experts in international law and economics, press officers, printers, librarians, statisticians, United Nations security officers and other supporting staff. Young people in uniform or their native dress serve as tour guides for approximately half a million visitors who come each year.

Hammarskjöld Library. – *Not open to the public.* Located on the southwest corner of the complex, the library, a gift of the Ford Foundation *(p 47)*, is dedicated to the memory of the second Secretary-General, **Dag Hammarskjöld**, killed in 1961 in a plane crash during a peace-keeping mission to the Congo.

Its marble walls enclose 380,000 volumes for the use of UN delegates, Secretariat staff members and scholars. In addition, there are newspapers, reading rooms, a collection of 80,000 maps, a microfilm laboratory, tape recording services and an auditorium.

BROADWAY – TIMES SQUARE ★★ 7

Time: 2 hours. ● *any train to 42nd St. Map p 52.*

Running the entire length of Manhattan, Broadway, "the longest street in the world," has given its name to the city's famous entertainment district, which extends approximately from 40th to 53rd Streets, between Broadway and Seventh Avenue. Times Square, referred to as the "Crossroads of the World," marks the center of this concentration of world-renowned theaters, cinemas, night spots and bars. Best seen at night, Broadway lights up when a colorful crowd throngs beneath its huge illuminated billboards.

New York Convention & Visitors Bureau

Times Square after dark

Times Square Yesterday... – At the end of the 19C, the Times Square district, then named Longacre Square for a similar area in London, was a center for livery stables and harness makers. The American Horse Exchange remained at 50th Street and Broadway—the present site of the Winter Garden Theater—until 1910. The square was renamed in 1904 when the *New York Times* moved its headquarters here *(p 53)*.

On the southeast corner of Broadway and 42nd Street, stood the ornate Knickerbocker Hotel *(142 W. 42nd St)*. The Knickerbocker housed the fashionable King Cole Bar, with a renowned Maxfield Parrish mural. When the hotel was converted to offices, the Parrish mural was rescued and now graces the King Cole Bar at the ST REGIS-SHERATON HOTEL. The Hotel Astor (1904), one of the grandest in New York, stood on the west side of the square between 44th and 45th Streets and was replaced in 1968 by an office building.

In the first decade of the 20C, Times Square abounded with vaudeville houses. The mecca for vaudeville performers was the prestigious Palace Theater *(1564 Broadway)*, now a legitimate theater. As vaudeville waned, live entertainment persisted during the "big band" era of the 1930s and 1940s. Opened in 1919, the legendary Roseland Dance City *(239 W. 52nd St)* quickly became a haven for devotees of ballroom dancing, attracting Fred Astaire and Ginger Rogers "wannabes."

... And Today. – Noisy and congested, lined with movie houses, restaurants, discount and record shops, interspersed with bars, "adult" bookstores and other tawdry establishments, Times Square reveals little of its former grandeur. Efforts to revitalize the square have been on-going since the mid-1970s rehabilitation of West 42nd and 43rd Streets between Eighth and Tenth Avenues. The construction of **Manhattan Plaza** (1977), a complex of shops, restaurants and two residential towers, and the reconversion of tenements between Tenth and Dyer Avenues into **Theater Row**, a series of Off-Off Broadway theaters, have upgraded the westerly fringe of Times Square. During the last decade, the completion of the Marriott Marquis Hotel *(p 54)* and the new construction at a number of sites at the north end of Times Square seemed to herald the area's long-awaited rebirth. An ambitious plan involving construction of four large office towers (designed by Philip Johnson and John Burgee) on all four corners of the square has been suspended owing to insufficient funding and a disagreement on what image the square should project. However, architects and planners are at work on a revised plan that will use the existing structures to create new entertainment and retail spaces.

Legitimate Theaters. – *For ticket information see p 185.* One of the area's first theaters was opened by Oscar Hammerstein in 1899 at the corner of 42nd Street and Seventh Avenue. This far-sighted gentleman was the grandfather of Oscar Hammerstein II, composer of such popular musicals as *Oklahoma* and *South Pacific.* Many of the early theaters in the Broadway area specialized in vaudeville or burlesque. The 1920s and 1930s saw the emergence of the Theater Guild and the Actor's Studio, which helped promote classic dramas as well as the works of local playwrights. Political and satirical plays popular in the 1960s were often performed in locales situated off Broadway, giving rise to a new category of theaters, which present a varied repertoire.

The 38 theaters remaining in the theater district are concentrated between 40th and 57th Streets and Avenue of the Americas and Eighth Avenue *(see listing p 53)*, an area which has been designated a special theater district to protect its exceptional character. Today, most of these establishments present musicals, some of which run many years to sold-out houses. In the theatrical year ending in May 1992, over 7 million people spent $292 million on Broadway theater productions, creating a major contribution to the city's economy. Off and Off-Off Broadway theater developed as a response to the soaring cost of mounting Broadway productions after World War II. The movement encourages experimentation with new talent (authors, directors and performers) and the revival of classic plays.

Movie Theaters. – In the 1920s, the rise of the film industry was reflected in the number of movie palaces that began to appear in the area. The **Paramount Building** (1926), located between 43rd and 44th Streets, was erected to house a movie theater and offices. The theater has been taken over by a bank, but the building, its symmetrical silhouette culminating in a clock tower crowned with a glass ball, remains as a monument to the movie era.

Today, scores of movie theaters are concentrated in the Broadway area, including some "grinds" open around the clock, showing second-run films. Along

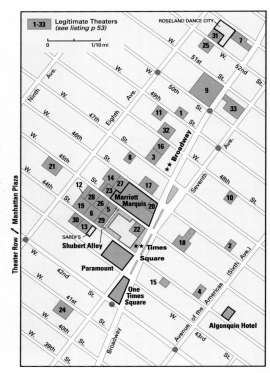

42nd Street, between Seventh and Eighth Avenues, stands a series of converted legitimate theaters, virtually a solid row of marquees. The once-magnificent New Amsterdam, built in 1903 by Florence Ziegfield, welcomed such stars as Maurice Chevalier and the Italian actress, Eleonora Duse, and offered "Midnight Folies" on its roof during the summer.

Farther north on Seventh Avenue, or Broadway, larger movie houses were originally built to accommodate two to three thousand spectators at a sitting. On their screens passed such famous figures as Shirley Temple, Deanna Durbin, Gary Cooper, Irene Dunne, Clark Gable, Doris Day, James Dean and Marilyn Monroe. Most of these giant prewar houses have since been demolished or transformed into multi-screen cinemas.

Legitimate Broadway theaters:

- *Actors Studio (432 W. 44th St, ☎757-0870)*
1 *Ambassador Theater (215 W. 49th St, ☎239-6200)*
2 *American Place Theater (111 W. 46th St, ☎840-2960)*
3 *Barrymore Theater (243 W. 47th St, ☎239-6200)*
4 *Belasco Theater (111 W. 44th St, ☎239-6200)*
5 *Booth Theater (222 W. 45th St, ☎239-6200)*
6 *Broadhurst Theater (235 W. 44th St, ☎239-6200)*
7 *Broadway Theater (1681 Broadway, ☎239-6200)*
8 *Brooks Atkinson Theater (256 W. 47th St, ☎719-4099)*
9 *Circle in the Square (1633 Broadway, ☎307-2704)*
10 *Cort Theater (138 W. 48th St, ☎239-6200)*
- *Douglas Fairbanks Theater (432 W. 42nd St, ☎239-4321)*
11 *Eugene O'Neill Theater (230 W. 49th St, ☎239-6200)*
9 *Gershwin Theater (222 W. 51st St, ☎586-6510)*
12 *Golden Theater (252 W. 45th St, ☎239-6200)*
13 *Helen Hayes Theater (240 W. 44th St, ☎944-9450)*
14 *Imperial Theater (249 W. 45th St, ☎239-6200)*
15 *Lambs Theater (130 W. 44th St, ☎997-1780)*
16 *Longacre Theater (220 W. 48th St, ☎239-6200)*
17 *Lunt-Fontanne Theater (205 W. 46th St, ☎575-9200)*
18 *Lyceum Theater (149 W. 45th St, ☎239-6200)*
19 *Majestic Theater (245 W. 44th St, ☎239-6200)*
20 *Marquis Theater (1535 Broadway, ☎382-0100)*
21 *Martin Beck Theater (302 W. 45th St, ☎239-6200)*
22 *Minskoff Theater (1515 Broadway, ☎869-0550)*
23 *Music Box Theater (239 W. 45th St, ☎239-6200)*
24 *Nederlander Theater (208 W. 41st St, ☎921-8000)*
25 *Neil Simon Theater (250 W. 52nd St, ☎757-8646)*
- *New Dramatists (424 W. 44th St, ☎757-6960)*
26 *Plymouth Theater (236 W. 45th St, ☎239-6200)*
27 *Richard Rodgers Theater (226 W. 46th St, ☎221-1211)*
28 *Royale Theater (242 W. 45th St, ☎239-6200)*
29 *Shubert Theater (225 W. 44th St, ☎239-6200)*
30 *St. James' Theater (246 W. 44th St, ☎239-6200)*
31 *Virginia Theater (245 W. 52nd St, ☎239-6200)*
32 *Walter Kerr Theater (219 W. 48th St, ☎239-6200)*
- *Westside Theater (407 W. 43rd St, ☎315-2244)*
33 *Winter Garden Theater (1634 Broadway, ☎239-6200)*

SIGHTS

We advise you to visit these sights after dark, so as to best appreciate the illuminations.

★★ **Times Square.** – Located at the intersection of Broadway and Seventh Avenue, Times Square is best known for its **nighttime illuminations**★★★, which generate great excitement: it is here that the quick pulse of the city can best be felt, as the milling theater crowds merge with the thousands strolling under the flashing neon signs. Although the first electric advertising sign in the city was erected on Madison Square in 1892, the sign industry soon moved to Times Square, attracted by its combination of huge crowds and large vistas. In 1916, a city zoning bill formally encouraged large electric signs in Times Square and the "Great White Way" was born. Corporate advertisers still outdo themselves to create eye-catching displays. Among the best remembered is the smoke-ring sign between 43rd and 44th Streets. Sponsored by Camel and later Winston cigarettes, it employed a steam box to produce about 1,000 rings a day through the lips of a gigantic smoker. It began puffing in 1941 and succumbed in 1977.

Times Square is also often the setting for huge gatherings such as political demonstrations or the annual vigil to celebrate the twelfth stroke of midnight on New Year's Eve. The December 31 celebrations began in 1908 to mark the anniversary of the occupancy of the square's new building by *The New York Times*. The former Times Tower, now known as **One Times Square**, dominates the southern end of the square; it was erected for Adolph S. Ochs, owner of the *Times*. Rising to 25 stories, the building seemed prodigiously tall at the time of construction. Demolished except for its steel framework in 1964, the edifice was remodeled into a marble-clad structure and is now best known for the lighted ball—now replaced by a big apple—which falls to mark the arrival of the New Year. On the facade, a giant computer-generated display (20ft by 40ft) features a mix of art and advertisements. The Motogram, a 5ft-high ribbon of lights, circles the building, flashing news and weather reports. Ironically, the news ribbon is sponsored by *New York Newsday*, a major competitor of the *Times*, which has long since consolidated its operations at 229 West 43rd Street, just west of Times Square.

The futuristic profile of the **Marriott Marquis Hotel** *(1535 Broadway)*, a 50-story glass and concrete structure (1985) that is the second largest hotel in Manhattan, towers above the western side of Times Square. The Marriott Marquis hosts conventions and seminars year-round. Designed by John C. Portman and Assocs., the 1,874-room hotel has as its centerpiece a 37-story landscaped **atrium**, which ranks among the world's tallest. Note, on the Broadway facade, the 4-story electronic billboard.

Shubert Alley. – Parallel to Broadway, behind the former Hotel Astor site, this alley forms the heart of the theater district. This short private street, reserved for pedestrians, was laid down in 1913, between 44th and 45th Streets. The Shubert Brothers built the Booth and Shubert Theaters, and were required to leave this passage as a fire exit. At intermission or after the show, many theatergoers drop into Sardi's restaurant, well known for the caricatures of celebrated theatrical personalities lining the walls, and their more or less famous successors who gather in the bar or the restaurant.

The Algonquin Hotel. – *59 W. 44th St, between Fifth and Sixth Aves.* A landmark of the theatrical and literary world, this hotel was the site of Alexander Woollcott's famous "Round Table" in the 1920s. This celebrated clique of writers counted Robert Benchley, Dorothy Parker and Robert Sherwood among its regulars. Some of the old aura of the period and virtually the entire original decoration have survived to this day. The Algonquin is now noted for its bar and after-theater suppers.

The "Broadway" theater rules cover all productions in the area between Fifth and Ninth Avenues, from 34th through 57th Streets, and between Fifth Avenue and the Hudson River, from 55th to 72nd Streets.

Off-Broadway theaters are outside this territory and operate with fewer than 500 seats. Union rules are more flexible here.

As the Off-Broadway theaters flourished (and became more expensive), the more experimental Off-Off Broadway movement took up the avant-garde mantle. These theaters are limited to 100 seats; they are found in churches, vacant factory lofts, and storefronts in many parts of the city.

Time: 1 day. ● 1, 9 train to South Ferry. Map below.

At the entrance to New York harbor stands the Statue of Liberty, her upraised torch lighting the world with the promise of freedom and justice for all. A dignified, stirring reminder of the ideals upon which the nation is founded, "Miss Liberty" has been welcoming travelers arriving by sea for more than a century.

Nearby in the harbor is Ellis Island, the immigration station and entry point for millions during the peak years of immigration.

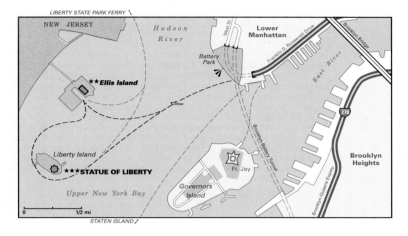

★★★ STATUE OF LIBERTY

The Birth of an Idea. – The idea to present the American people with a memorial commemorating the friendship of France and the United States (which dated back to the American Revolution) was first conceived at a dinner party hosted by law professor Édouard-René de Laboulaye in 1865. Six years later, a committee formed under the chairmanship of Laboulaye selected Alsatian sculptor **Frédéric-Auguste Bartholdi**, who then traveled to America for the purpose of studying and promoting the project.

The Inspiration. – Bartholdi had attended the opening ceremonies of the Suez Canal in 1869, in hopes of securing a commission for a huge statue-lighthouse at the entrance to the new canal. Unsuccessful in obtaining the commission, he now turned his energy to creating a similar monument in the United States.

Entering New York harbor, he was overwhelmed and inspired by the grandeur of the scene before him, and its significance as the main gateway to the New World. Then and there he knew that the envisaged monument would be a figure of Liberty, and that one of the tiny harbor islands in this breathtaking setting would be an ideal site for the statue.

A Franco-American Union was established, with Laboulaye as president, to raise funds and coordinate all matters regarding the statue. The project was to be a joint effort reflecting the shared commitment of both nations: the French would underwrite the statue itself, and the Americans, the pedestal. A private subscription of $250,000 was planned.

The Difficulties: technical.... – Bartholdi began to work on the sculpture in 1874. He first made a clay figure 4ft high, and then three successively larger working models in plaster, which were corrected and refined before the final dimensions were achieved. Turning his attention to the framework that would support the statue, the sculptor first selected Violet le Duc as the engineer for his project. Following le Duc's death in 1879, Bartholdi called upon the skill and knowledge of the inventive French engineer, **Gustave Eiffel**, who was later to build the Eiffel Tower. Employing construction techniques similar to the ones used for the skyscrapers of the 1880s, Eiffel created an intricate iron and steel skeletal frame to which the 300 copper plates (each 3/32in thick) forming the skin of Liberty were applied.

... and financial. – With the technical problems solved, the financial difficulties assumed an increasing urgency. The cost of construction had almost doubled—from $250,000 to $450,000—since work on the statue had begun. To reach their goal, the French launched a massive fund drive, and by 1884 the statue was complete. At a special ceremony held July 4, 1884, the statue was presented to the ambassador of the United States as a gift from the people of France. Following the festivities, Liberty was dismantled and packed in 220 crates, in preparation for the ocean voyage to her permanent home across the Atlantic.

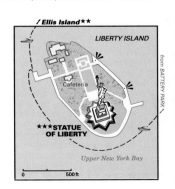

In the meantime, in the US, little progress had been made in rasing funds for the pedestal. At the American centennial exhibit in Philadelphia in 1876, the statue's forearm and torch were displayed to the delight of numerous visitors who took great pleasure in being photographed on its balcony; but purse strings were slow to open. Benefit balls, theatrical and sporting events, even a poetry contest were held to support the pedestal campaign. Inspired by the spirit of liberty and affected by the persecutions then taking place in Russia, **Emma Lazarus** wrote her poem *The New Colossus* (1883). Included were the memorable lines:

> *Give me your tired, your poor,*
> *Your huddled masses yearning to breathe free,*
> *The wretched refuse of your teeming shore.*
> *Send these, the homeless, tempest-tost to me,*
> *I lift my lamp beside the golden door!*

In 1884, in another effort to raise money, Liberty's arm, complete with torch, was exhibited in the center of MADISON SQUARE. By 1885, with the statue awaiting shipment to the US and contributions still not forthcoming, the committee once again acted. An urgent appeal to patriotism was issued stating: "If the money is not now forthcoming the statue must return to its donors, to the everlasting disgrace of the American people." As a result, numerous donations were received. The success of the project was due largely to the fund raising campaign of **Joseph Pulitzer**, the publisher of the New York *World*. In front page editorials, Pulitzer criticized the rich for not providing the mere "pittance" required and encouraged all Americans to contribute to the project as the masses of French people had. In addition, he promised to publish in his newspaper the names of every donor, no matter how small the amount of the gift. With this, the drive rapidly assumed a new impetus, and contributions began to pour in daily.

The Dedication. – In May 1885, the French ship *Isère,* carrying its precious cargo, set sail from Rouen and approximately one month later dropped anchor in New York harbor. Bartholdi traveled once more to New York to confer with the engineers and the architect chosen to design the pedestal, **Richard Morris Hunt**, one of the leading American architects of the day. Hunt's final design for the pedestal blended in character and scale to form an integrated unit with the statue.

Declared an official holiday in New York City, the festivities took place on October 28, 1886. Presiding over the unveiling of the statue on Bedloe's Island (renamed Liberty Island in 1956) was **President Grover Cleveland** who had arrived by boat, accompanied by a 300-ship escort. National and international dignitaries huddled together at the foot of the statue while speech after speech was heard. The excitement that had been mounting throughout the day eventually reached a climax as the statue was unveiled. As fog horns bellowed, the roar of a 21-gun salute sounded from nearby batteries. Liberty's crown was illuminated simultaneously, symbolizing prophetically the beacon of hope she would be to the millions who would soon begin to flock to these shores.

A Magnificent Restoration. – Through the wear and tear of the years, the statue suffered degradation. The idea of restoring the statue to its former splendor originated in France, in 1981. After three years of extensive research and experiments designed to test the statue's soundness, an elaborate restoration effort was begun with the financial assistance of the Statue of Liberty-Ellis Island Foundation, Inc— headed by chairman emeritus Lee Iacocca of Chrysler Corporation. The 5-year project, costing millions of dollars, involved a thorough cleaning of the statue's copper skin and the replacement of various parts that had been damaged beyond repair: the torch, the flame and the 1,700 iron bars supporting the structure. Additional improvements included the installation of new elevators and staircases and the creation of a museum chronicling the statue's history *(p 57)*.

Visit

Open Jul–Aug daily 9am–6pm. Rest of the year daily 9:30am–5pm. Closed Dec 25. Audio tours available. Expect long lines at entrance to the Statue and at ferry piers. ✕ ⧖ ☏363-3200. Ferry departs from Battery Park South Ferry and from Liberty State Park, Jersey City daily (except Dec 25) every half hour. First sailing 9:30am, last sailing 3:30pm. Ticket office (open 8:30am–3:30pm) located at Castle Clinton National Monument, Battery Park, and at Liberty State Park. Fare includes round-trip and visits to both sights. $6. ✕ ⧖. For sailing schedule ☏269-5755 or 201/435-9499 in New Jersey. Expect long lines during the summer.

> From the ferry slip, walk up the landscaped mall past the visitor center and the cafeteria to the Statue. From there visitors may proceed directly to the pedestal or to the Statue of Liberty Exhibit.

The brief crossing *(15min)* affords magnificent **views★★★** of the lower Manhattan skyline gradually receding into the background, and of the majestic and massive Statue of Liberty standing at the eastern end of the island, above the star-shaped walls of Fort Wood (1808-1811). Declared a National Monument and administered by the National Park Service, the statue receives about 3 million visitors a year.

Weighing 225 tons, the statue is 151ft high and the head is 10ft by 17ft. The right arm, holding the torch, measures 42ft in length with a diameter of 12ft, and the index finger is 8ft long. Liberty represents a crowned woman trampling beneath her feet the broken shackles of tyranny; the seven points in her crown signify liberty radiating to the seven continents and the seven seas. In her left hand she holds a tablet representing the Declaration of Independence and bearing the date of its proclamation, July 4, 1776. Her right hand raises the torch, symbolizing a beacon of hope, 305ft above sea level. The torch and the crown are lighted in the evening. Miss Liberty's grandeur is best appreciated from the base of the statue.

Pedestal. – *Observation deck at the top of the pedestal. Access by elevator.* An elevator from the main entrance accesses this four-sided balcony, which provides spectacular **views★★★** of the New York harbor, lower Manhattan and the FINANCIAL DISTRICT, the VERRAZANO-NARROWS BRIDGE and New Jersey.

Climb to the Crown. – The 364-step climb (22 stories) from the ground to the crown begins just inside the main entrance. A narrow, circular metal staircase *(visitors prone to claustrophobia are advised to proceed with caution)* winds its way up through the statue's interior, culminating in a narrow platform from which a **view** of the New York harbor is visible through the openings in the crown.

Statue of Liberty Exhibit. – *2nd level in the pedestal.* The badly corroded torch (replaced in 1986) is featured in this exhibit, which recounts the history of the statue from Laboulaye's conception to the present. Bartholdi's working models of the statue illustrate the evolution of his ideas, and a cutaway model provides an excellent view of the complex inner structure. The repoussé technique used in forming the copper exterior is explained in a continuous videotape, and a substantial collection of postcards and souvenirs depict the statue's role as a symbol of liberty both in America and abroad.

Before returning to the ferry pier, stroll along the waterfront **promenade**. Glancing across the harbor, note the contrast between Manhattan's striking high-rises and the older, lower-scale buildings found in Brooklyn.

★★ ELLIS ISLAND

Situated in New York Harbor, approximately halfway between lower Manhattan and the Statue of Liberty, Ellis Island stands as living testimony to the millions of immigrants who passed through its gates to enter the "land of golden opportunity." A multi-million dollar restoration project transformed this 27.5-acre parcel of land into a national monument that pays tribute to the ancestors of nearly 40 percent of Americans by commemorating their hope and determination.

America's Great Immigrant Gateway. – Inaugurated in 1892 on the site of an abandoned fort, Ellis Island was America's first and most comprehensive immigration facility and quickly became the main port of entry for newcomers to America. During the peak immigration years from 1880 to 1924, nearly 5,000 new arrivals were processed daily, the majority in less than half a day. After World War I, restrictive laws and quotas diminished Ellis Island's importance as a reception site and, by 1954, the island had slipped into decay and was officially closed. Most immigrants quickly booked passage beyond New York City joining friends or family already in America; unfortunately, two percent of them were denied admission and shipped back to their country of origin. During its 30 years of operation, Ellis Island received over 12 million immigrants, attesting to one of the greatest mass migrations in history, which helped shape the face of 20C America.

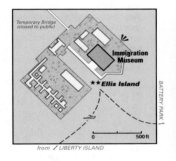

from / LIBERTY ISLAND

In 1984, with funding and supervision by the Statue of Liberty-Ellis Island Foundation, Inc *(p 56)*, the main structure in the 33-building complex underwent one of the most elaborate restorations of any public building in the US and re-opened its doors in September 1990, as the Ellis Island Immigration Museum. So far, only the main building has been restored. Plans to destroy 12 buildings in order to make way for a conference facility were met with public outcry, and the project was put on hold.

Visit

Open Jul–Aug daily 9am–6pm. Rest of the year daily 9:30am–5pm. Closed Dec 25. Audio tours available. Expect long lines at ferry pier. ☂ ⚘ ☏363-3200. For ferry information see Statue of Liberty p 56.
We recommend getting free tickets to the "Island of Hope/Island of Tears" film (below) as soon as you enter the main building, since the shows fill up quickly.

Immigration Museum. – A glass-and-metal canopy leads from the ferry slip to the elegant brick and limestone Beaux-Arts main building. Completed in 1900 by Boring and Tilton, it replaced an earlier structure that had burned down in 1897. Crowned by four copper-domed towers and pierced by three arched entrance portals, the former processing center has been restored to reflect its appearance in the early 1920s. It houses the Ellis Island Immigration Museum, presenting a series of permanent and temporary installations on three floors.

First Floor. – Visitors enter into the baggage room, where immigrants were separated—sometimes forever—from their precious belongings. The old railroad office, to the north, houses the "Peopling of America" exhibit, which uses statistical displays to chronicle the history of immigration and ethnicity in the US, from the late 19C to present day. Highlights include a 6ft globe that traces worldwide migration patterns since the 18C, and the "Word Tree," which explains the origin of many American words. A poignant short film ("Island of Hope/Island of Tears") portraying the human face of migration is screened in the two small theaters located in the eastern wing *(30min, shown every half hour)*. The western wing displays temporary exhibits.

57

National Park Service

Ellis Island Immigration Museum

Second Floor. – The sweeping 2-story Registry Room/Great Hall was the site of the initial inspection of immigrants, who awaited their fate while queuing behind metal pens. The hall that once accommodated thousands has been left empty, save for a few scattered benches, to serve as a grand, quiet memorial. The pride of the 17,300sq ft hall is its impressive vaulted Guastavino ceiling: only 12 of the 28,000 tiles had to be replaced during restoration.

In the western wing, a 14-room exhibit ("Through America's Gate") re-creates the step-by-step inspection process that often culminated in the dividing of families at the "Staircase of Separation." The displays in the eastern wing chronicle the immigrants' hopes and hardships through photographs, memorabilia and recorded commentaries. Life-size portraits enliven the hallways in the two wings.

Third Floor. – The highlight of this floor, "Treasures from Home," presents objects donated by immigrants and their families, from a teddy bear to an elaborate wedding gown. In "Silent Voices," large photographs taken before the restoration evoke the eerie feeling of an abandoned place, while furnishings recall the daily routine of processing, registering and caring for immigrants. Another exhibit, tracing 300 years of the island's history, displays four detailed models showing the evolving floor plans of the island between 1897 and 1940.

Along the north wall of the mezzanine, a narrow dorm room has been furnished to reflect the cramped living conditions experienced by some of the detainees.

Grounds. – Facing Manhattan, a newly rebuilt "American Immigrant Wall of Honor" serves as a memorial to the nation's immigrant heritage. The 652.5ft, double-sided, semi-circular wall contains the names of over 420,000 individuals and families whose descendants have honored them by donating to the Ellis Island restoration project *(for more information on how to add a name, contact the Statue of Liberty-Ellis Island Foundation ☎883-1986).* The terrace offers breathtaking **views★★** of the Manhattan skyline.

Sights described in this guide are rated:

★★★	*Highly recommended*
★★	*Recommended*
★	*Interesting*

FINANCIAL DISTRICT – LOWER MANHATTAN

Time: 1 day. Map p 62.

The site of the city's earliest Dutch settlement, the Financial District today is defined by gigantic skyscrapers towering over a maze of narrow streets, thereby creating some of the city's most spectacular canyons. Feverishly busy during the week, the area is almost deserted on weekends. Through the years, Wall Street, hub of the district's activity, has come to symbolize the nation's financial power.
It is best to visit this area during weekday mornings.

HISTORICAL NOTES

17-18C. – The general area now called the Financial District was the birthplace of New York in 1625. Trade flourished under the Dutch West India Company and the town of Nieuw Amsterdam quickly developed as the center of Dutch hegemony in the colonies. Occupying a limited area, the small town was defended to the south by a fort and to the north by a wall of thick wooden planks constructed in 1653 between the Hudson and East rivers. Erected to protect the town from marauding Indians, the wall (the origin of the name of Wall Street) was instead regularly dismantled by residents, who would take the planks to shore up their houses or to heat their homes.

About 1,000 persons occupied the 120 wood and brick houses topped with characteristic Dutch gables and tile roofs. A windmill and a canal, "the Ditch," dug in the middle of Broad Street, attested to the town's Dutch heritage. The inhabitants, however, were of varied origins; in 1642, when the first Stadt Huys (City Hall) was built at 71 Pearl Street, no less than 18 languages were spoken in Nieuw Amsterdam. Governing the town was first a commercial agent of the Dutch West India Company, and later a succession of governors, including Peter Stuyvesant *(p 74)*.

When the British took over Nieuw Amsterdam in 1664, "the Ditch" was filled in and the wall torn down. During the 18C, colonial Georgian houses, such as Fraunces Tavern *(p 65)*, began to replace the narrow Dutch dwellings.

Wall Street: the Birth of a Financial Center. – Completely dismantled by the British in 1699, the wooden wall *(above)* was replaced by a new street where, on the corner of Broad Street, the City Hall was built (today the Federal Hall National Memorial, *p 63)*. Wall Street became an administrative and residential street, lined with rows of fine houses ornamented with Georgian pilasters and porticos. After the Revolution, the east end of the street harbored a series of coffee houses and taverns. The famous **Tontine Coffee House**, built in 1792 at the corner of Water Street, served as the first home of the New York Stock Exchange *(p 63)*.

As the area specialized in shipping and warehousing, accounting and banking developed. Following an 1835 fire that destroyed 700 houses in the area, storehouses, shops and banks moved into the reconstructed buildings. Speculation flourished, especially after 1860. On September 24, 1869, the financier **Jay Gould** (1836-1892), who had tried to corner the gold market with his associate James Fisk, sold out and brought about the financial panic known as "Black Friday." **Cornelius Vanderbilt** (1794-1877), nicknamed "The Commodore" owing to his interests in the shipping industry, began to extend his activities to the railroads in 1862. First the owner of small lines (the Harlem, the Hudson, and New York Central), he launched the famous New York-Buffalo line in 1873. At the same time, banker **J. Pierpont Morgan** (1837-1913) financed the great new industries: steel, oil and railroads. Generous but a ruthless businessman, the founder of the famous PIERPONT MORGAN LIBRARY was succeeded by his son, John Pierpont Morgan, Jr, who was the target of an assassination attempt in 1920: on September 16 a bomb exploded in a cart near the bank *(p 63)*, missing Morgan, Jr, but killing 38 innocent people caught in the noonday rush.

The business activities and interests of the Vanderbilts, Goulds, Morgans and other financiers, contributed to the leading position gained by New York in the 1920s. Wall Street gradually replaced London as the financial capital of the world and has maintained this role despite the crash of 1929.

★★ WORLD TRADE CENTER

Occupying a 16-acre site, the seven buildings of the World Trade Center are grouped around a central plaza, creating a vast, open space in this densely developed section of Manhattan.

Two years after the concept of a trade center was proposed, in 1960, legislation was passed, authorizing the Port Authority to realize the project. Architects Minoru Yamasaki & Assocs. and Emery Roth and Sons designed the complex, which was completed in 1970. Today, over 50,000 people work in the various buildings, and an additional 50,000 visitors come to the center daily.

The stated mission of the trade center is the advancement and expansion of international trade. Referred to as a "United Nations of Commerce," it has become the central market of world trade, and all international business services are concentrated here—exporters, importers, American and overseas manufacturers, freight forwarders, Custom House brokers, international banks, federal, state and overseas trade development agencies, trade associations and transportation lines.

In addition to the various buildings, the complex includes a concourse with a PATH (Port Authority Trans-Hudson) railroad terminal, access to the New York subways and 8 acres of shops and services.

★★★ **Twin Towers [A, B].** – The two 110-story towers, the second tallest buildings in the nation after the Sears Roebuck Building in Chicago, rise to 1,350ft, adding a distinctive landmark to the Manhattan skyline. The towers dominate the sweeping 5-acre central **plaza**, which links the various buildings of the center and interconnects with other pedestrian systems in the area. A huge bronze sculptured sphere **[1]** by the German, Fritz Koenig, marks the center of the fountain-pool.

The engineers responsible for laying foundations in the wet landfill terrain, without disrupting existing communication lines and surrounding structures, developed the "slurry wall" foundation system by erecting an underground concrete wall around the site. With the wall in place, excavation work began within this "bathtub" area, without danger of subsidence due to water pumping. The excavated material was used to create 23 acres of landfill for Battery Park City *(p 60)*.

The conventional skyscraper is generally built with a maze of interior columns. In these towers, however, the architects used a new structural design in which the exterior walls bear most of the load, thereby providing a maximum of open, column-free floor space. These outer walls consist of closely spaced vertical columns of steel, tied together by horizontal spandrel beams, which girdle the towers at every floor. The columns are covered with a thin skin of aluminum and separated by tinted floor to ceiling windows recessed ten inches.

The introduction of the "skylobby" system minimizes the floor space occupied by elevator shaftways. Each building is divided into three zones: 1st-43rd floor, 44th-77th, 78th-110th. The 44th and 78th are the skylobbies, which are connected to the ground floor lobby by express elevators traveling 1,600ft per minute. A battery of local elevators then serves all floors within each zone.

The glass-enclosed **observation deck** of Two WTC *(107th floor; open Jun–Sept daily 9:30am–11:30pm; rest of the year daily 9:30am–9:30pm; $4; ✗ ㅎ ☎435-7397)* offers spectacular **views★★★** of the entire metropolitan area from a downtown vantage point. Weather permitting, it is also possible to take an escalator up to the 110th floor to the rooftop promenade for a stroll at a quarter of a mile in the sky. On the 107th floor of One WTC, the views can be enjoyed from the Windows of the World restaurant.

The 9-story **Plaza Buildings [D, E]** flank the main entrance of the complex, on Church Street. Four WTC serves as headquarters of four exchanges (New York Cotton Exchange; New York Coffee, Sugar and Cocoa Exchange; Commodity Exchange, Inc and New York Mercantile Exchange) and their Commodities trading floor. *Trading activities may be observed from the visitors gallery (open Mon–Fri 9:30am–3pm; closed holidays; ㅎ ☎938-2000).*

Five WTC contains the offices of a variety of international trade and financial firms. Designed by Skidmore, Owings & Merrill in 1981, the 22-story **Vista International Hotel [C]** has the distinction of being the first major hotel in almost 150 years to be built in the downtown area.

Seven WTC, a 47-story office tower (1987) clad in insulated glass and polished red granite is the most recent addition to the World Trade Center complex. Bounded by Vesey, Washington, Barclay and West Broadway Streets, the building has a trapezoidal shape reflecting the irregular site on which it stands. An open plaza and a covered walkway link the upper lobby level of Seven WTC to the main plaza of the WTC. Note on the open plaza, a bright orange sculpture by Alexander Calder.

Bordering the northwest corner of the site, the 8-story **US Custom House [F]** consolidates all intricate customs functions relating to the movement of goods in and out of the port, in one convenient location.

★ BATTERY PARK CITY

From the World Trade Center, take the north bridge from the US Custom House.

This vast commercial-residential complex adjoining the World Trade Center rises on 92 acres of landfill edging the Hudson River. An extension of lower Manhattan, Battery Park City has a working population of almost 25,000 and will provide housing for 25,000 residents when completed *(scheduled completion: early 2000s).*

Development. – In the late 1960s, Governor Nelson Rockefeller came up with the concept of erecting a residential complex in lower Manhattan that would provide space away from Manhattan's hustle and bustle in a modernistic setting. The landfill and infrastructure were completed in the mid-1970s, but residents protested the fact that the project was so isolated from the rest of the island. In 1979, during the administration of Mayor Ed Koch and Governor Hugh Carey, a new plan to develop the area as an integrated extension of the island—following the same street grid—was adopted, and construction resumed.

The Complex. – The **World Financial Center**, designed by Cesar Pelli & Assocs., forms the commercial heart of Battery Park City. Its four glass and granite-sheathed office towers extending from Vesey to Albany Streets encompass 7,000,000sq ft of office space, and are home to some of the nation's most prestigious brokerage and financial services firms—American Express, Dow Jones, Merrill Lynch. Marked by setbacks and notches, and topped with geometrically shaped copper roofs, the buildings of the World Financial Center present a graceful blend of traditional and contemporary design elements and provide an elegant counterpoint to the World Trade Center towers. Highlighting the WFC is the **Winter Garden★** (1987), a barrel-vaulted glass and steel structure reminiscent of London's 19C Crystal Palace. This attractive space offers performing arts programs and events, and houses shops and a variety of restaurants. Sixteen 45ft palm trees dot the large plaza, which culminates in the grand central staircase. Weary shoppers can rest on the benches and admire the fascinating play of light on the glass.

On the fringe of the WFC rise the buildings of Gateway Plaza (1982), the first of Battery Park City's residential developments, which will eventually stretch north to Chambers Street and down to the Battery. Just to the south lies the Rector Place area, a 10-building ensemble containing 2,200 residential units.

The enormous complex also includes landscaped parks, public plazas and outdoor sculpture. Especially pleasant is the 1.2mi riverside **esplanade** *(access from Liberty St)* with its cast-iron benches and lampposts, lush trees and flowering shrubs. A stroll along the boardwalk affords spectacular **views★★** of the harbor.

WALKING TOUR   *1/2 day. Distance: 2mi.*

Begin at Liberty Plaza. ● 1, 9 or A, C, E trains to World Trade Center.

Liberty Plaza. – *At Liberty St between Church and Broadway Sts.* This small, pleasant square is surrounded by prestigious buildings. **One Liberty Plaza**, a 54-story building (1974; Skidmore, Owings & Merrill) of thick, horizontal steel beams and tinted gray windows, borders the northeast side. The slender, dark glass tower dominating the east side of the plaza houses the **Marine Midland Bank** (1967). Rising 55 stories without a single setback, the edifice is characteristic of the buildings erected in the 1960s. Crafted by Isamu Noguchi in 1967, a reddish-orange **cube [2]** enlivens the plaza fronting the bank. Resting solely on one corner, the sharply angled, brightly colored sculpture provides a foil for the stark yet elegant bank building. The US Realty Building (1907) towers to the south of the park.

Continue south on Broadway.

Located immediately behind the US Realty Building, the Trinity Building **[G]** is connected to the former by a pedestrian walkway on the top floor. The two limestone structures were designed in an elaborate Gothic style in order to harmonize with neighboring Trinity Church.

Rising across the street, the **Equitable Building** *(no. 120)*, an immense Beaux-Arts edifice (1915), comprises twin towers connected by a recessed central section. Protests over the fact that the building encompassed 1,200,000sq ft of office space on an area of less than one acre gave rise to the first zoning resolution *(p 25)*, passed in 1916, which limited the amount of floor space allowed on a particular plot of land.

★★ **Trinity Church.** – *Open Mon–Fri 7am–6pm, weekends 8am–4pm. Guided tour (45min) daily 2pm.* &. Located on Broadway at the head of Wall Street, this lovely Gothic Revival church, now dwarfed by the surrounding high-rises, was the tallest building in New York at the time of construction. It is lined on three sides by a grassy cemetery, where several famous New Yorkers are buried.

The First Anglican Parish of New York. – An Episcopal church, Trinity was founded by a charter granted by King William III in 1697. Among the influential local citizens aiding in its construction was **William Kidd**, the famous captain-turned-pirate

who lived at nearby Hanover Square *(p 65)*, and who was hanged for piracy in London in 1701. The first church building (1698), resembling a country chapel with a spire and narrow, spear-shaped windows, burned in the great fire of 1776 and was replaced by another, the roof of which collapsed in 1839. The present edifice, designed by Richard Upjohn, was completed in 1846. The Chapel of All Saints was added in 1913, and the Bishop Manning Memorial Wing in 1966.

The Building. – The rose sandstone exterior is distinguished by the square bell tower and its 280ft spire, which soared above the nearby houses when it was built. The tower contains ten bells, including three of the original eight bells dating from 1797. Handsome bronze doors (designed by Richard Morris Hunt), inspired by those of the Baptistery in Florence, Italy, lead to the interior. Note the highly colored stained-glass windows by Upjohn above the white marble altar (1877), and the elaborate wooden vault and screen of the Chapel of All Saints at the right of the choir.

Jonathan Wallen

View of Trinity Church from Wall Street

To the left of the chancel is **Trinity Museum** *(Mon–Fri 9–11:45am, 1–3:45pm, Sat 10am–3:45pm, Sun 1–3:45pm)*, which presents exhibits portraying the history of Trinity Church and its interrelationship with the city of New York from colonial days to the present.

The Cemetery. – The parcel of land occupied by the churchyard is worth several million dollars, at the going rate in the area. Dotted with old and worn tombstones, the cemetery offers a pleasant, shady green space among the Financial District skyscrapers. The oldest stone marks the grave of Richard Churcher, who died in 1681 *(right of the church)*. Notice also the graves of the publisher, William Bradford, Jr *(right of the church)*; Robert Fulton, the inventor of the steamboat *(left of the church, near Rector St)*; two Secretaries of the Treasury, Alexander Hamilton *(left of the church, near Rector St)*, and Albert Gallatin *(right of the church, near Trinity Pl)*; and Francis Lewis *(right of the church, near entrance)*, a New York signer of the Declaration of Independence.

Turn left on Wall St.

The nation's center of high finance, **Wall Street**★★ winds its narrow way in the shadows of the surrounding skyscrapers.

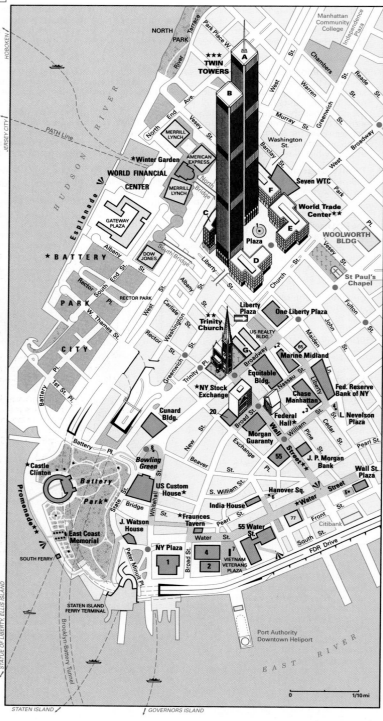

A few facts about New York City:

- some 25,000,000 visitors annually
- 6,400 miles of streets
- 504.3 miles of sidewalks
- some 15,500,000 hotel rooms occupied annually
- some 12,000 licensed taxis
- some 3,200,000 daily subway riders
- 708.6 miles of subway tracks
- 3,500 churches and synagogues in all five boroughs

★ **New York Stock Exchange.** – *8-18 Broad St.* Facing Broad Street, this 17-story building (1903) presents a majestic facade of Corinthian columns crowned by an elaborate pediment with sculpted figures symbolizing Commerce. Marking the entrance, a tree recalls the buttonwood tree at Wall and William Streets where 24 brokers met to found the forerunner of the New York Stock Exchange in 1792. The traders dealt in stocks and bonds issued by the government and a few private companies; a handshake or tap on the shoulder sealed a bargain.

The stock exchange gained popularity among the "little people" in the early 20C, at a time when fraud and debauchery were running rampant among city officials (the Tammany political machine still wielded great power in the city). By the late 1920s, guided by an invincible feeling of prosperity, over one million Americans were members of the stock exchange, many taking enormous gambles. On Thursday, October 24, 1929, thereafter known as Black Thursday, the New York Stock Exchange experienced a financial panic that ushered in the Great Depression of the 1930s. In a matter of weeks, over 9 million savings accounts were depleted and the national income was cut in half.

Today, some 1,366 Exchange members trade the shares of more than 2,000 domestic and foreign companies listed on the Stock Exchange. These companies include virtually every leading industrial, financial and service corporation in the United States. They have available for trade on the stock exchange some 120.7 billion shares worth $4 trillion. On an average day, about 276 million shares are traded, valued at more than $9 billion. One American in five is a shareholder.

On the ground floor is the actual exchange where trading takes place Mondays through Fridays 9:30am to 4pm.

Visitors Center. – *Entrance 20 Broad St. Open Mon–Fri 9:15am–4pm. Closed holidays. Tickets (free) are distributed outside the building for same day visit. It is advisable to obtain tickets early. Taped information in foreign languages available.* ⟨ ☎656-5167*. The public may visit exhibits that trace the history of the New York Stock Exchange, present the workings of the Stock Market and explain the financial organization of companies listed. The **Visitors Gallery★** *(3rd floor)* overlooks the hectic pace of activity on the trading floor below; a taped explanation on the Exchange may be heard in English, French, German, Japanese, Italian and Spanish. The staff is available to answer questions.

★ **Federal Hall National Memorial.** – *26 Wall St.* This imposing Westchester marble edifice, reminiscent of a Doric temple, marks one of the city's most historic locations. The site was first occupied by New York's City Hall, which was remodeled in 1789 to serve as Federal Hall, the country's first Capitol.

Construction of the first City Hall began in 1699 on land donated by Abraham de Peyster *(p 65)*, and in 1702, the city government moved in. The pillory where minor offenders were exposed to public derision, and the stake to which they were bound for flogging stood in front of the edifice. The first City Hall also served as a courthouse and a debtor's prison. The Stamp Act Congress met in the same place 30 years later to oppose British colonial policy.

Reconstructed in 1789 under the supervision of **Pierre Charles L'Enfant** (1754-1825), the Frenchman who designed the master plan of Washington DC, the building became Federal Hall, the first capitol of the United States under the Constitution. George Washington took the oath of office as the first president on the balcony of Federal Hall on April 30, 1789. The Federal Government was transferred to Philadelphia the following year, and the building was used for state and city offices, then torn down and sold for salvage in 1812 for $425.

The present building (Town & Davis) dates from 1842 and served as the US Custom House until 1862, when it became the US Subtreasury. Later the site of a number of government offices, it was designated as an historic site in 1939 and a national memorial in 1955. Today, it attracts businessmen and tourists to its wide steps overlooked by a towering bronze **statue** of Washington, designed in 1883 by John Q.A. Ward.

The **interior** *(open Mon–Fri 9am–5pm; concerts Wed noon; ⟨)* is dominated by a splendid central rotunda. Sixteen marble Corinthian columns support the large dome and balconies, embellished with ornate bronze railings. Mementos of George Washington are displayed alongside an exhibit on the Constitution. In the section devoted to the history of the building and New York, several dioramas depict the three buildings that have stood on this site. The balcony galleries feature changing exhibits year-round.

Morgan Guaranty Trust Company. – *23 Wall St, at the corner of Broad St.* Erected in 1913, this austere, white marble building was the setting of a terrorist attack on J. Pierpont Morgan, Jr *(p 59)*. The narrow Beaux-Arts structure with salmon-colored trimmings, adjoining the building on the Wall Street side, also belongs to the Morgan Company.

Continue to William St, turn left then left again on Pine St.

Chase Manhattan Bank. – *On Pine St, between Nassau and William Sts.* Born of the merger between the Chase National Bank and the Bank of the Manhattan Company, this institution became, in 1961, the first bank to occupy a prestigious modern building in lower Manhattan. The stately glass and aluminum structure, designed by Skidmore, Owings & Merrill, rises 813ft from a paved plaza enlivened by various sculptural elements.

Historical Notes. – In 1798, a yellow fever epidemic, attributed to polluted water, broke out in the city. The following year, **Aaron Burr** (1756-1836) founded the Manhattan Company to provide and distribute drinking water to the city. The company laid down a network of hollow pine log pipes, which still come to light occasionally during excavations. Burr then decided to expand the company's activities to the realm of banking and finance. On September 1, 1799, the Manhattan Company opened its first office of discount and deposit. The extension of its activities was a serious blow to **Alexander Hamilton** (1755-1804), who had political and financial interests in two other banks functioning in New York at the time. The two men's financial differences reinforced by their long-standing political rivalry finally led Burr to challenge Hamilton to their historic duel (July 11, 1804), in which Hamilton was fatally wounded.

The Chase Bank was founded in 1877 by John Thompson and his son, who named it in honor of **Salmon P. Chase** (1808-1873), US senator and governor of Ohio. Chase also served as Lincoln's secretary of the Treasury and chief justice of the US Supreme Court. He drafted a bill enacted by Congress as the National Currency Act of 1863, establishing a national currency and the present Federal banking system. The portrait of Chase appears on the largest bill in circulation ($10,000).

The Building. – The 2.5-acre tract of land originally purchased by the Chase Manhattan Bank was large, but unfortunately bisected by a street. Under an agreement with the city, the bank was able to acquire the part of the street connecting the two parcels and to build on it. Almost five years were required for the completion of the building, a steel frame structure covered with a glass curtain wall. One of the largest office buildings constructed since the 1960s, the edifice soars to 813ft and contains 65 stories (including 5 below street level). Located in the fifth basement, the bank vault is reputed to be the world's largest: longer than a football field, it weighs 985 tons and has 6 doors, each 20in thick (four of them weigh 45 tons a piece and the other two 30 tons).

Note, on the esplanade fronting the bank, Jean Dubuffet's striking sculpture [3] *Group of Four Trees* (1972). The undulating figures present a vivid contrast to the sober Chase tower. To the left, the Plaza Banking Office curves around the sunken Japanese water garden, designed by Isamu Noguchi (*p 160*) in 1964.

Continue on Pine St to Nassau St; turn right and continue to Liberty St.

Located west of Nassau Street, at no. 65 Liberty Street, the imposing, marble Beaux-Arts structure (the ex-Chamber of Commerce, 1900) now houses the International Commercial Bank of China.

Federal Reserve Bank of New York. – *33 Liberty St. Visit by guided tour (45min) only, Mon–Fri 10:30 & 11:30am, 1:30 & 2:30pm. Closed holidays. Reservations required at least four weeks in advance. Contact Public Information Dept, Federal Reserve Bank of New York, 33 Liberty St, New York, NY 10045 ☎720-6130.* &. Facing the Chase Manhattan Bank, this imposing 14-story masonry edifice occupying an entire block was completed in 1924. The design for this structure, distinguished by massive rusticated walls, was inspired by several 15C Italian Renaissance palaces, which were built to house the wealthiest banking and merchant families in Florence. Inside the building, at a depth of 80ft below the street level, is the Federal Reserve's gold vault. Approximately half the length of a football field, this chamber contains the gold reserves of 80 foreign nations, thought to be the largest accumulation of gold in the world—about 325 million troy ounces, with a market value (1993) of over $107 billion.

The guided tours allow the public to view the gold vault and an exhibit on cash processing, including many examples of old currency and coins.

Continue east on Liberty St to William St.

In the small park at the triangle formed by William and Pine Streets and Maiden Lane, note the seven huge, black welded steel sculptures [4] crafted in 1977 by **Louise Nevelson**, for whom the space is named.

Turn right on William St to return to Wall St.

55 Wall Street. – This massive, Greek Revival temple is distinguished by its double colonnade of Ionic and Corinthian columns. Until 1992, the building was occupied by Citibank, which is now located at 120 Wall Street. Created in 1812, Citibank succeeded the first financial establishment founded in New York by Alexander Hamilton ten years earlier. Designed in 1841 by Isaiah Rogers, as the Second Merchants Exchange, the building was enlarged and renovated by McKim, Mead and White in 1907.

Especially impressive is the ornate interior, restored to its original neoclassical appearance. The Great Hall, embellished with arches and colonnades, and clad in marble and travertine, culminates in a 72ft coffered and domed ceiling.

J.P. Morgan Bank Headquarters. – *60 Wall St.* Designed by Roche, Dinkeloo and Assocs. in 1988, this massive, 47-story tower is one of the tallest skyscrapers in the Financial District. Protruding from the granite and reflective glass facade are representations of classical pilasters, replete with base, shaft and capital. The motif recurs on the top ten stories. The white marble lobby, enlivened with trellis work and a multitude of mirrors, provides an inviting public space, dotted with ficus trees, flowers, tables and chairs.

Continue east to Water St.

Before reaching Water Street, turn around and admire the **vista★** down the celebrated "canyon," which ends with the dwarfed, dark silhouette of Trinity Church.

Turn left on Water St.

Water Street★ reflects the astonishing pace of development that has occurred in lower Manhattan since the late 1960s, owing principally to the creation of new office space. Here progressive planning has re-established the human and recreational elements in the architectural landscape. Laid out on landfill, Water Street is lined with office buildings in a variety of shapes, colors and construction materials, greatly altering the skyline of this seafront area.

At the corner of Water and Pine Streets rises the elegant glass and aluminum **Wall Street Plaza**, designed by I.M. Pei in 1973. Highlighting the building's plaza is Yu Yu Yang's tantalizing two-part sculpture **[5]**, consisting of a pierced slab and a disk. Just beside, a plaque commemorates the *Queen Elizabeth I*, the largest and fastest ocean liner ever built, whose last proprietor, Morley Cho, also owned Wall Street Plaza.

Double back and return towards Wall St.

Continuing west along Water Street, pass the small, welcoming plaza of 77 Water Street, known as Bennett Park, where pools, fountains, sculpture and benches provide a pleasant recreational ensemble.

Continue west on Water St.

To the right is **Hanover Square**, a quiet little plaza dotted with trees, benches and a bronze **statue [6]** of Abraham de Peyster (1896), a prosperous Dutch merchant and mayor of the city. William Bradford established his first printing press in 1693 in one of the shops originally lining the square. **India House**, a handsome Italianate brownstone erected in 1853, borders the south side of the plaza.

Continue west to **55 Water Street**, a 2-building complex flanking a raised plaza *(access by escalator from Water St)*, which affords an expansive **view★** across the East River to BROOKLYN HEIGHTS.

At Vietnam Veterans Plaza, a street level plaza, pause to view the 1985 **Vietnam Veterans Memorial [7]**, a 70ft by 14ft granite and glass block wall dedicated to the nation's men and women who served in the conflict. The memorial is inscribed with passages from letters, diary entries and poems written by American soldiers.

The buildings of **New York Plaza** (nos. 1, 2 and 4) form a varied ensemble, linked by plazas and a ground-level concourse lined with shops and restaurants. Note in particular the 22-story red brick building of 4 New York Plaza, punctuated by narrow slit windows.

At the corner with Broad St, turn right and continue north to Pearl St.

★ **Fraunces Tavern.** – *54 Pearl St. Open Mon–Fri 10am–4:45pm, Sat noon–4pm. Closed Jan 1, Thanksgiving Day, Dec 25. $2.50. Guided tours (30min) available. ☎425-1778.* This handsome yellow brick house, with its slate roof, portico and balcony, represents a fine example of Georgian Revival architecture. The original house was built in 1719 as the home of Etienne de Lancey, the ancestor of a prominent New York family, which gave its name to Delancey Street, in the Lower East Side. The house became a tavern in 1763 when Samuel Fraunces acquired the building. Governor De Witt Clinton gave a dinner here, celebrating the British evacuation of New York in 1783, and in December of the same year, the tavern was the scene of Washington's farewell to his officers. The present building is a 1907 restoration. Fraunces Tavern has been preserved by the Sons of the Revolution. A restaurant occupies the main floor. A wooden stairway leads to the museum on the upper two floors, where permanent and changing exhibits trace the early history of New York City and the Revolutionary War. In addition, American decorative arts are displayed in period settings.

Continue west on Pearl St. Turn right on Whitehall St and continue to the Former US Custom House.

★ **Former US Custom House.** – *1 Bowling Green.* Erected in 1907 by Cass Gilbert, this magnificent Beaux-Arts building stands on the site occupied originally by a fort and later by the Government House, which served as residence for the state governors until its demolition in 1815. The current imposing edifice presents a monumental gray granite facade adorned with white Tennessee marble sculptures. The lower series, by Daniel Chester French (renowned for his statue of Lincoln in the Lincoln Memorial in Washington DC), depicts Asia, America, Europe and Africa. The statues above represent some of the most famous trading cities and nations of the world: notice, to the left of the central shield, a woman depicting Lisbon, by Augustus Saint-Gaudens, and the doge with death's head evoking Venice.

The building was vacated in 1973, when the customs offices moved to the new US Custom House at 6 World Trade Center *(p 60)*. Formerly located on AUDUBON TERRACE, the National Museum of the American Indian is in the process of moving a large part of its collection to this site *(to open in spring 1994; for visiting hours ☎283-2420)*. The new name of the museum will be the George Gustav Heye Center of the National Museum of the American Indian. The remainder of the collection will be housed in a new museum on the Mall, in Washington DC, to be completed by the year 2000.

Cunard Building. – *25 Broadway, on Bowling Green.* Now converted into a post office, this grand structure, which once housed a steamship ticket office, is noteworthy for its **lobby**. Designed in 1921 by Benjamin W. Morris, the lobby features a 68ft rotunda and a series of large murals.

Bowling Green. – Named for the lawn where gentlemen could bowl for the modest annual fee of one peppercorn, this egg-shaped park is surrounded by a 1771 wrought-iron fence. The prosperous residences that lined the small park in the 19C have since made way for office buildings. A 3.5-ton bronze statue **[8]** of a charging bull (1988), symbolizing a rising stock market, guards the northern entrance to the green.

From Bowling Green, continue southwest to Battery Park.

DOWNTOWN

★ BATTERY PARK

On the southwestern tip of Manhattan, the maze of stone and steel monoliths dominating the Financial District suddenly gives way to a vast expanse of greenery, known as Battery Park. Here, strolling along the waterfront promenade, visitors may enjoy one of the most spectacular panoramas on the eastern seaboard.

Historical Notes. – During the 17C and 18C, the shore followed the lines of State Street, between Bowling Green and Pearl Street. In order to protect the harbor during the War of 1812, the British erected the West Battery (Castle Clinton) some 300ft offshore, and the East Battery (Castle Williams) on Governor's Island *(below)*. In 1870, the land was filled in between the West Battery and Manhattan proper, creating a pleasant park subsequently named Battery Park.

Today, the area encompasses 21 acres extending from Bowling Green to the junction of the Hudson and the East rivers. The view of New York Bay, enlivened by the movement of boats of all sizes entering and leaving the harbor, attracts large numbers of tourists year-round. The park, dotted with commemorative monuments, is also the departure point for ferries to the STATUE OF LIBERTY and ELLIS ISLAND.

The Brooklyn-Battery Tunnel (about 2mi) linking Manhattan to Brooklyn passes under Battery Park.

★ Castle Clinton National Monument. – *Open daily 8:30am–5pm. Closed Dec 25. Guided tours (30min) available.* ♿ ☎344-7220. *Information center, bookstore & ticket booth for Statue of Liberty & Ellis Island ferry on the grounds.* Built on a small artificial island between 1808 and 1811, the structure known as West Battery was part of a series of forts erected to protect the New York harbor. However, it was never used for its original purpose and, in 1824, the fort (renamed Castle Garden) was ceded to the city and remodeled into a concert hall. That same year a gala evening honoring French General Lafayette was held here. On another grand occasion in 1850, Castle Garden served as the setting for a famous concert promoted by P.T. Barnum—the American debut of the "Swedish Nightingale," Jenny Lind. It was here also, that Samuel Morse first demonstrated his revolutionary invention, the telegraph.

In 1855, the former fort and opera house was transformed into an immigrant landing depot. Over 7 million immigrants were processed here before construction of the Ellis Island station, in 1890. Six years later, the NEW YORK AQUARIUM (now in Coney Island) moved in and occupied the building until 1941. Designated as a national monument in 1950, the structure was restored to its original appearance and reopened to the public in 1975. Today Castle Clinton, named for De Witt Clinton, governor of New York State in the early 19C, consists of 8ft thick walls, pierced with gun-ports for cannons; the entrance is framed by pilasters. The large interior courtyard contains a ticket office for various ferries and boat tours to the Statue of Liberty and Ellis Island.

Stroll south along the promenade.

★★ Promenade. – From Castle Clinton to the Staten Island Ferry Terminal *(below)* where the famous Staten Island ferries *(p 164)* dock, the walk meanders pleasantly along the shore of New York Bay. South of the fort stands a statue of Giovanni da Verrazano *(p 157)*. Near the South Ferry stands the **East Coast Memorial** (1961), dedicated to those who died in the Atlantic during World War II. The powerful statue of a landing eagle with outspread wings, is flanked on both sides by four granite columns inscribed with the names of the deceased.

The promenade offers magnificent **views★★★** of the bay. Among points of interest, visitors can spot from west to east: **Jersey City**, with its tall Colgate clock; Ellis Island, the former processing center for immigration; Liberty Island, formerly known as Bedloe's Island, home to the colossal Statue of Liberty; and Brooklyn, with its docks at the foot of BROOKLYN HEIGHTS. Also visible from this vantage point is **Governors Island**, known in Dutch times as Nutten's Island, because of the many nut trees which grew there. The island affords spectacular views of Manhattan and Brooklyn, and is the site of two pre-1800 structures: the Governor's House and Fort Jay. Another fort, Castle Williams, was erected on the island at the beginning of the 19C, at the same time as Castle Clinton. Since then the island has remained a government reservation and is home to the US Coast Guard *(visit by guided tour only; 2hrs 30min; $12; for schedule & reservations contact Big Onion Walking Tours ☎439-1090)*. Further in the background are Bayonne, New Jersey, with its oil refineries and its naval port; the hills of Staten Island; the Narrows and the cobweb of cables of the VERRAZANO-NARROWS BRIDGE, half hidden by Governors Island.

Continue toward the Staten Island Ferry Terminal.

Badly damaged by fire in 1991, the Ferry Terminal is currently defunct, but plans are underway to restore the building. The preliminary design by Venturi, Scott Brown and Anderson & Schwartz calls for the construction of the world's largest clock—a 120ft-diameter timepiece that will overlook the harbor. A makeshift terminal at Whitehall Street is in use until reconstruction begins *(scheduled completion: 1997)*.

Turn left on State St and continue to the corner of State and Water Sts.

At 7 State Street, note the handsome, Federal-style Shrine of St Elizabeth Seton, one of the few remaining grand mansions erected in the late 18C on the waterfront. The part of the building on the right, the former **James Watson House**, dates from 1792; the graceful Ionic colonnade was added in 1806. Elizabeth Ann Seton (1774-1821), America's first saint, was canonized in 1975.

Cross-references to sights described in this guide are indicated by SMALL CAPITALS. *Consult the index (p 187) for the appropriate page number.*

SOUTH STREET SEAPORT

Time: 2 hours. ● 2, 3 train to Fulton St. Map below. Admission is free to historic district, its shops, restaurants, piers & Fulton Market. Free concerts, festivals, maritime events & holiday celebrations throughout the year. $6 general admission covers gallery, historic ships, the museum's special programs (films) & guided tours (50min). Purchase tickets at visitor center. ✗ ♿ ☎669-9424.

Fronting the East River, south of Brooklyn Bridge, the South Street Seaport Historic District comprises an 11-block district, which was the heart of the port of New York and the center of its world-wide shipping activities during the early 19C. The South Street port declined after the Civil War, as shipping moved to the deepwater piers on the Hudson River. Its once-busy counting houses, shops and warehouses, at first converted to a variety of uses, were gradually abandoned and left to decay.

In the 1960s, efforts to preserve the port's historic buildings, piers, streets and vessels led to the establishment of the South Street Seaport Historic District and the South Street Seaport Museum. In the 1980s a large-scale development project was launched to revitalize the district. Extensive restoration and new construction have transformed the area bounded by John, South, Water and Beekman Streets into a complex of pedestrian malls, restaurants, shops and boutiques animated with a vitality reminiscent of the district's days as a major seaport.

VISIT

Museum Block. – The block bounded by Fulton, Water, Beekman and Front Streets contains a group of fourteen 18C and 19C buildings, many of which have been converted into exhibit galleries. The **visitor center** *(open Jun–Sept daily 10am–6pm; rest of the year 5pm; closed Jan 1, Thanksgiving Day, Dec 25; ☎669-9424),* located at 12 Fulton Street, features a permanent exhibit on the history of the seaport. On Water Street, note the three similar edifices—**nos. 207, 211, 215**—housing the Bowne & Co Stationers, a re-creation of a 19C printing and stationery shop, the Chandlery, and The Gallery, which displays changing exhibits related to the history of the South Street district and

the waterfront. The **New "Bogardus" Building** *(17-19 Fulton St)* is a steel and glass low-rise structure (1983) inspired by the cast-iron buildings of James Bogardus *(p 76).*

Schermerhorn Row. – Distinguished by a uniform brick facade and sloping roofs, this handsome group of 19C buildings exemplifies the Federal style. Constructed for the ship chandler and developer, Peter Schermerhorn, between 1811 and 1813, the row was occupied by a string of counting houses and warehouses during South Street's heyday. Today these buildings house a number of specialty shops as do the Greek Revival structures located across the street in Cannon's Walk Block.

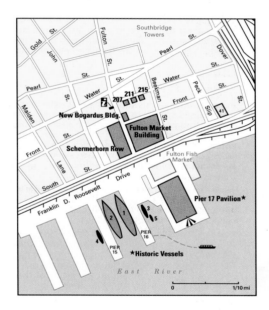

The Fulton Market Building. – This brick and granite market (1983), designed by Benjamin Thompson & Assocs., is the fourth market to be built on this site since 1822. A hub of activity both day and night, the market shelters an assortment of food stalls and restaurants, serving international cuisine as well as ice cream, hot dogs and other favorites. The marketplace is a good spot to people-watch and enjoy the festive atmosphere of the Seaport.

The South Street side of the building incorporates stalls of the **Fulton Fish Market**, which has been operating at this waterfront site for more than a century and a half. A visit to the market in pre-dawn hours is recommended to catch a glimpse of the bustling activity *(midnight–8am).*

★ **Pier 17 Pavilion.** – Rising from a pier that extends 400ft into the East River, the Pavilion (Benjamin Thompson & Assocs.), a 3-story glass and steel structure, encompasses more than 100 shops, restaurants and cafes. The spacious public promenade decks overlook the river on three sides, creating the marvelous illusion of being on board a ship. The **vistas★★** are magnificent: north to the Brooklyn Bridge, east to Brooklyn Heights and the Brooklyn waterfront, and south to New York harbor.

★ **Historic Vessels.** – *Pier 16. Same hours as the visitor center (above).* Moored at piers 15 and 16 along South Street is the fleet of historic ships: the **Peking [1]**, a square-rigged, four-masted barque (1911); the **Wavertree [2]**, a square-rigger (1885) built for the jute trade between India and Europe; the *Ambrose* **[3]**, the first lightship to serve as a guide to vessels approaching the entrance to Ambrose Channel in the New York harbor; the *Lettie G. Howard* **[4]**, one of the last extant Gloucester fishing schooners (1893); and the *W.O. Decker* **[5]**, a 1935 wooden tugboat.

Harbor Cruises. – *Pier 16. May–Sept 3-4 cruises daily. First cruise 11am. Round-trip 2hrs. $15. For schedule: Seaport Line Harbor Cruises* ☎*233-4800.* The Seaport Line Company offers cruises of New York harbor aboard a replica side-wheeler (the *Andrew Fletcher*), or by sail, aboard an 1885 schooner (the *Pioneer*).

During the summer, there are frequent open-air concerts on the piers. Before leaving the Seaport, notice at no. 41 Peck Slip the *trompe l'œil* painting *The Brooklyn Bridge,* one of several outdoor murals in the city by 20C artist Richard Haas.

★★ 11 CIVIC CENTER – BROOKLYN BRIDGE

Time: 3 hours. Map p 69.

Located at the foot of Brooklyn Bridge, north of the FINANCIAL DISTRICT and west of CHINATOWN, the Civic Center area encompasses Foley Square and City Hall Park. Once covered by swamps and marshland that formed part of the Common Lands *(p 37)*, the district developed as one of New York's principal gathering places during the 18C; residents would often assemble for protest or celebration here. The northern section of the Common Lands contained a large body of water called the Fresh Water or Collect Pond, on which John Fitch tried out a prototype of the steamboat in 1796. Located west of the pond was a burial ground for free and enslaved blacks, who according to law had to be buried outside the city limits.

After completion of City Hall in 1811, several federal, state and municipal buildings were erected in the immediate vicinity. Although the city continued its northward expansion, the area around City Hall remained the heart of governmental activities. Today, it is a bustling area during the work week, alive with crowds of office workers rushing to and from work. In 1993, during the course of archaeological excavations, part of the ancient African burial ground was uncovered and declared a historic landmark by the Preservation Commission.

★ CIVIC CENTER *2hrs. Distance: .8mi.*

Begin at Foley Square. ● *N, R train to City Hall.*

Foley Square. – This square stands on the former site of the Collect Pond. The area was drained in 1808 to make room for a recreational center. Owing to inadequate drainage and poor foundations, several houses began to sink, and the structures were quickly abandoned. In the early part of the century, government buildings sprung up around the square, which was named in 1926 for Thomas F. Foley (1852-1925), a city alderman, sheriff and saloon-keeper. Today, the square is surrounded by monumental structures that unfortunately present a quite disjointed architectural ensemble.

Jacob K. Javits Federal Office Building and US Court of International Trade. – *26 Federal Plaza.* The Federal Office Building, a 1967 high-rise resembling a checkerboard of granite and glass, is attached by a bridge to a smaller glass building (the Court), which is suspended from concrete beams.

New York State Supreme Court. – *60 Centre St.* Formerly housing the New York County Courthouse, this granite-faced, hexagonal Classical Revival edifice (1927) is distinguished by its monumental Corinthian colonnade. The imposing interior radiates from an elaborate central rotunda. Note the rich polychrome marble floor with copper medallions representing the signs of the zodiac, and the murals (1930s) adorning the dome, by Attilio Pusterla.

United States Courthouse. – *40 Centre St.* Completed in 1936 by Cass Gilbert, designer of the Woolworth Building *(p 70)*, the courthouse presents a curious blend of architectural elements. A square, 32-story tower capped by a pyramidal top bursts through the roof of a Classical Revival temple. Step inside the main hallway, flanked by marble columns, to admire the ceiling murals.

South of the building lies the attractive St Andrew's Plaza, particularly pleasant in summer, with its tables, umbrellas and food stalls.

Walk south along Centre St.

★ **Municipal Building.** – *1 Centre St.* Located at the foot of Chambers Street, this 40-story edifice was erected in 1914 by McKim, Mead and White. Rising from a limestone base distinguished by a neoclassical colonnade, the tower culminates in a gilded finial—the heroic statue, *Civic Fame.* Designed by Adolph A. Weinman in 1914, the 25ft statue is the tallest in Manhattan. Weinman was also commissioned to create the carvings adorning the monumental central arch.

A pedestrian walkway leads to Police Plaza and the New York City Police Headquarters, an orange and brown brick structure completed in 1973. Highlighting the plaza is Bernard (Tony) Rosenthal's imposing 75-ton rusted steel sculpture, *Five in One* **[1]**, composed of five disks that have come to represent the city's five boroughs.

Surrogate's Court. – *31 Chambers St.* This richly ornamented Beaux-Arts structure, completed by John Thomas in 1907, houses the Hall of Records—the city archives. The profusion of sculptural detail includes statues of mythical figures and famous New Yorkers embellishing the granite facades. The central hall features marble walls and floors and a mosaic ceiling.

** **City Hall.** – Surrounded by a pleasant, tree-shaded park, this handsome edifice contains the office of the Mayor and the City Council Chamber.

The "New" City Hall. – The present building is New York's third city hall. The Dutch established their "Stadt Huys" in 1653 in a former tavern on Pearl Street (their city council consisted of two burgomasters, a public attorney and five magistrates). During the 18C, the British City Hall stood at the corner of Wall and Broad Streets (the present site of FEDERAL HALL NATIONAL MEMORIAL).

Today's city hall, built between 1802 and 1811 at a cost of about $500,000, is the work of architects **Joseph F. Mangin** and **John McComb, Jr**, who won a competition for the design and a prize of $350. Solemnly inaugurated on May 5, 1812, the building has been the scene of several memorable events. In 1824, Revolutionary War hero Lafayette was officially entertained here during his triumphal return to America. The first parades on Broadway for visiting dignitaries began at that time.

In the middle of the night of April 9, 1865, the city learned of General Lee's surrender at Appomattox, and the following day the city was draped with flags. The gaiety was brief, for less than a week later Abraham Lincoln's assassination plunged the nation into sadness. Lincoln's body lay in state at City Hall while 120,000 grief-stricken New Yorkers filed past. Then, on April 25, the hearse, pulled by 16 black horses, proceeded slowly up Broadway to the Hudson River Railroad where the coffin was placed in a special train for Springfield, Illinois, Lincoln's home.

The 1860s witnessed less solemn and dignified proceedings at City Hall and nearby Tammany Hall (formerly located at the corner of Park Row and Frankfort Street). The Tammany political machine founded by Aaron Burr at the beginning of the 19C, flourished under the leadership of **"Boss" William M. Tweed** (1823-1878). Once in control of local government, Tweed and his infamous Tweed Ring are said to have filched the city out of approximately $30,000,000. The pendulum swung against him during the 1870s. Discontented city officials, aided by the incisive cartoons Thomas Nast drew for *Harper's Weekly*, brought about his downfall and imprisonment.

The City Hall building was restored in 1956 at a cost of about $2,000,000. It remains the focus of welcoming ceremonies for visiting dignitaries and the finishing point of ticker tape parades during which the honoree is deluged with tons of paper shreds.

The original impromptu ticker-tape parades used paper from the thousands of stock-transaction machines in the offices of Wall Street brokers. With the advent of electronic systems, paper must be imported to carry on the "blizzard-of-paper" tradition.

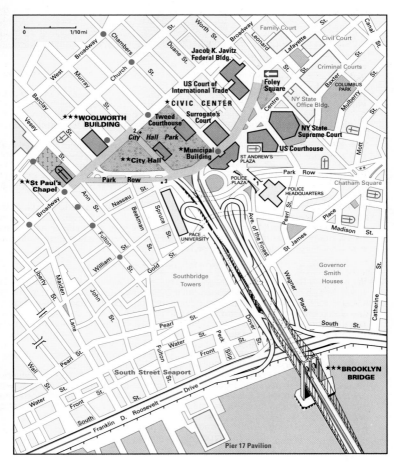

The Building. – *Open Mon–Fri 9am–5pm. Closed holidays.* ঌ. Distinguished by a well-proportioned French neoclassical facade and a superb Georgian interior, City Hall ranks among the city's most elegant buildings. It was originally constructed of marble on its downtown side and brownstone on the uptown face. According to tradition, the City Fathers, in an economy drive, decided that since hardly anyone lived north of Chambers Street, no one would notice! City Hall was entirely refaced with Alabama limestone in 1956.

In the central rotunda, note the bronze statue (1853-1860) of Washington by William James Hubbard, a replica of the original marble by Jean-Antoine Houdon. A pair of graceful, cantilevered stairs lead to the second floor. The gallery is ringed with slender Corinthian columns, supporting the coffered dome, and a delicate wrought-iron railing. Located at the top of the stairs, the **Governor's Room** *(open Mon–Fri 10am–noon, 1–4pm)* consists of a suite of three rooms once used by the governor on official visits. Today it houses a small museum of furniture (note the 18C mahogany writing desk used by George Washington) and paintings (note John Trumbull's portraits of Washington, John Jay and Alexander Hamilton). To the right is a public hearing room, and to the left the City Council Chamber, which features a statue of Thomas Jefferson by David D'Angers and a portrait of Lafayette by Samuel F.B. Morse, inventor of the telegraph.

John Carucci

City Hall

The Park. – Before the Revolutionary War, this area encompassed a common planted with apple trees. Liberty poles were erected here by the Sons of Liberty, and in July 1776, the Declaration of Independence was read in the presence of Washington, his troops and other patriots. Afterward the crowd rushed down to BOWLING GREEN to attack the statue of the British monarch, George III.

A statue (1890) by MacMonnies, erected on the Broadway side of City Hall Park, commemorates **Nathan Hale [2]**, one of the heroes of the Revolutionary War, whose famous last words were: "I only regret that I have but one life to lose for my country." A statue (1890) of Horace Greeley by John Q.A. Ward and a plaque to Joseph Pulitzer are reminders that this was once the center of newspaper publishing in New York *(p 71)*.

Behind City Hall, the old New York County Courthouse, generally known as the **Tweed Courthouse**, stands as a monument to "Boss" Tweed *(p 69)* who allegedly pocketed some $10 million of the building's $14 million construction cost! The edifice contains one of the city's finest 19C interiors. Of particular interest are the cast-iron staircases and the Gothic-style courtroom.

Pass in front of City Hall and turn left into Broadway.

★★★ **Woolworth Building.** – *233 Broadway.* This 1913 skyscraper, Cass Gilbert's masterpiece, was the tallest in the world until the CHRYSLER BUILDING's completion in 1930. Created for F.W. Woolworth (the founder of the ubiquitous five-and-ten-cent store), the Gothic-style building cost more than $13.5 million for which Woolworth paid cash. Soaring without setbacks to a height of 792ft, the tower is ornamented with gargoyles, pinnacles, flying buttresses and finials. During recent renovation efforts, much of the terra-cotta facade has been replaced with cast stone.

At the highlight of the opening ceremony, President Woodrow Wilson pressed a button in Washington that lit up 80,000 light bulbs on the building.

An ornate entrance leads to the spectacular **lobby**★★ *(open Mon–Fri 7am–6pm; closed holidays).* Rising to three stories, it features a barrel vault covered with Byzantine-style mosaics and second floor balconies decorated with frescoes. A marble stairway, bronze furnishings, plaster grotesques and ornate gilt decoration complete the Gothic theme. Note the six whimsical caricatures, among them Woolworth (counting his nickels and dimes) and Gilbert (clutching a model of the building), under the supporting crossbeams on the Barclay Street side.

Continue south on Broadway.

DOWNTOWN

★★ **St Paul's Chapel.** – *On Broadway, between Fulton and Vesey Sts. Open Mon–Fri 9am–3pm, Sun 7am–3pm. Closed holidays.* Belonging to Trinity Parish *(p 61)*, this small chapel constructed of native Manhattan schist is the oldest church in Manhattan and one of the city's finest Georgian buildings. Completed in 1766, it resembles the Church of St Martin in the Fields in Trafalgar Square, London, possibly because its architect, Thomas McBean, studied under James Gibbs who was responsible for St Martin's. The lovely spire, which contrasts so well with the twin towers of the WORLD TRADE CENTER behind it, and the portico on Broadway were added in 1794. Pierced by a Palladian window, the portico contains a memorial to Major General Montgomery who was killed at Quebec City in 1775 *(see Michelin Green Guide to Quebec)*. Montgomery's grave lies under the church.
The graveyard flanking the chapel provides a delightful green oasis dotted with 18C tombstones.

Interior. – The chapel has a surprisingly elegant Georgian interior. Painted in pastel colors and lit by Waterford crystal chandeliers, it was remodeled in the 1790s. The flamboyant altar is attributed to Pierre Charles L'Enfant, who later laid out Washington DC. Above the cream and gold pulpit, the feathers of the Prince of Wales can be seen reminding visitors that this was the "Established" church prior to the Revolution. Despite this fact, Washington worshipped here regularly after his inauguration *(p 63)*. His pew can be seen in the north aisle, and that of Governor Clinton in the south aisle (the arms of the State of New York hang on the wall beside it). *Classical music programs Mon & Thu noon–1pm. $2.*

Turn east into Park Row.

Park Row. – The stretch of road bordering the edge of City Hall Park, between St Paul's Chapel and the Municipal Building, was a fashionable promenade in the 19C. It became known as Newspaper Row at the end of the century because so many newspapers—including *The Times, Tribune, Herald, World* and *Sun*—had their offices there. The intersection with Nassau Street was called Printing-House Square. Park Row is no longer the center of journalism in the city, and today only 4 general-interest, English-language newspapers remain from a former total of 19.
Near the bronze statue (1872) of Benjamin Franklin **[3]**, holding a copy of his *Pennsylvania Gazette*, stands Pace University (Civic Center Campus). The main building, adorned with a copper-relief sculpture, surrounds a garden and pool *(visible from Spruce St).*

★★★ BROOKLYN BRIDGE

The pedestrian walkway can be reached by crossing Park Row from City Hall Park, or from the "Brooklyn Bridge–City Hall" subway station. The Brooklyn side is accessible from the "High St–Brooklyn Bridge" subway station. Allow 1/2hr to cross the bridge on foot. If walking from Manhattan to Brooklyn, continue on to nearby Brooklyn Heights (p 152).

The first bridge to link Manhattan and Brooklyn, this famed bridge was one of the great engineering triumphs of the 19C and the world's longest suspension bridge for 20 years. Its graceful silhouette set against the New York skyline has inspired many artists, writers and poets. *See illustration p 29.*
The stroll across the bridge is one of the most dramatic walks in New York. The **view★★** of the city and harbor through the filigree of cables is magnificent, especially as the sun sets.

Construction. – In 1869, German-born **John Augustus Roebling**, a pioneer bridge builder responsible for the Niagara Falls and Cincinnati, Ohio, suspension bridges, was commissioned to design a bridge linking Manhattan and Brooklyn. Shortly after approval of the plans, Roebling's foot was crushed while he was taking measurements for the piers. Despite an amputation, gangrene set in and he died three weeks later. His son, Washington Roebling, carried on his work, adopting new methods in pneumatic foundations, which he had studied in Europe.
To construct the foundations, workers used caissons immersed in water and then filled with compressed air to prevent water infiltration. In order to adapt to the air pressure, the workmen underwent periods of gradual compression before going down to work, and decompression afterward. Despite these precautions, a few had burst eardrums or developed the "bends," which cause convulsions and can bring on partial or total paralysis. Washington Roebling himself was stricken with the bends. Confined to his sickbed he, nevertheless, continued to direct the operation from his window overlooking the bridge. Finished in 1883, the bridge cost $25 million. With its intricate web of suspension cables and its majestic, pointed arches, the bridge represents an aesthetic and technical masterpiece.
The bridge has a total length of 3,455ft with a maximum clearance above water of 133ft. The central suspended span between the two stone towers is 1,595ft long. The span is made of steel—the first time this metal was used for such a mammoth undertaking—and it is supported by four huge cables (15 3/4in thick) interconnected by a vast network of wires.

History and Legend. – The bridge immediately became the busy thoroughfare its planners had foreseen. On opening day, 150,000 people walked across the bridge. However, less than a week after its inauguration by President Arthur, tragedy struck. A woman fell on the stairway and her screams set off a panic killing 12 persons and injuring many more.
Fifteen years after inauguration of the bridge, the city of Brooklyn was incorporated into New York. The bridge played a significant role in the development and growth of Brooklyn, the city's most populous borough.

Monumental and awe-inspiring, the Brooklyn Bridge has fascinated, obsessed and haunted New Yorkers. Immortalized in the works of Walt Whitman, it has also been painted on numerous occasions. Colorful, cubist renditions of the bridge, created in the 1920s by Joseph Stella, are among the best known depictions of the monument. Some people have felt compelled to jump from the bridge, not all of them in despair. New Yorker Steve Brodie who purportedly jumped off Brooklyn Bridge in 1886 without harm, later gained fame as an actor on Broadway.

Since the end of the 19C, the bridge has provided an opportunity for confidence men to fleece strangers to the city by extorting exorbitant "tolls" (the original toll, now abolished, was one cent for pedestrians), or by "selling" it to the gullible.

In 1972, the cables and piers were re-painted in their original colors—beige and light brown. The walkway was rebuilt in 1981-1983 and the cables undergo regular maintenance.

★★
12 CHINATOWN – LITTLE ITALY

Time: 2 hours. ● *B, D, Q train to Grand St. Map p 73.*

Situated on the western edge of the LOWER EAST SIDE, Chinatown and Little Italy form the other two neighborhoods in New York City's traditionally immigrant East Side district. Sprawling Chinatown is a veritable city within a city. The narrow streets lined with colorful shops and restaurants teem with people, particularly on weekends. Little Italy, concentrated on Mulberry Street, draws crowds to its neighborhood stores, plentiful restaurants and pastry shops, and annual feasts.

★★ CHINATOWN

Trains and Tongs. – The first Chinese to settle in New York came via the western states, where they had worked in the California gold fields or on the transcontinental railroad. The majority were men who had no intention of staying, unlike other immigrants. They just wished to make their fortunes and return to a comfortable life in China. By the 1880s, the community numbered about 10,000. The Chinese Exclusion Acts passed in 1882 stopped further immigration, and growth was effectively halted. By the turn of the century, Chinese immigrants began to form **tongs** or associations designed to ease their adaptation to American culture. Organized gambling and prostitution eventually sprang up in Chinatown, and the tongs fell into conflict with each other. During the resulting tong wars, accounts were often settled with hatchets and revolvers, giving rise to the term "hatchet men."

Chinatown

Present-day Chinatown. – Following the 1943 repeal of the Chinese Exclusion Acts, New York experienced a new influx of immigrants from Taiwan and Hong Kong, as well as mainland China. Once bounded by Baxter, Canal, the Bowery and Worth Streets, Chinatown is rapidly encroaching on Little Italy and the formerly Jewish Lower East Side, both of which now contain a multitude of Chinese factories and laundries. The present-day Asian community of New York has been estimated at 512,000, of which roughly three-fourths are Chinese. The majority of Manhattan's 110,000 Asians live in Chinatown.

Chinatown comes to life with a bang for the Chinese New Year *(the first full moon after January 19)*, when dragons dance down the streets accompanied by banner-carrying attendants while evil spirits are driven away by displays of fireworks.

Visit. – Canal, **Mott**, Bayard and **Pell** Streets form the heart of Chinatown. Strung with colorful banners and sporting signs in Chinese calligraphy, Catherine and East Broadway Streets are especially lively. Columbus Park, located on the former site of a large slum area, provides much-needed green space in this congested part of the city.

DOWNTOWN

A stroll through the heart of Chinatown leads past stalls and shop windows piled high with exotic displays of herbs and condiments, snow peas, bean curd, dried fungi, duck eggs, real birds' nests for soup and bundles of Chinese mushrooms resembling strange marine plants. Other shops offer jade and ivory carvings, brocade dresses, silks, fans, "Chinese" lanterns and tea sets. Elements of Chinese architecture adorn the otherwise undistinguished tenement buildings, and several telephone booths are crowned with mini-pagoda roofs. Note the gaily ornamented pagoda-roofed structures at 41 Mott Street and 241 Canal Street.

At the corner of the Bowery and Division Street, adjacent to Confucius Plaza, stands a bronze **statue [1]** of the Chinese philosopher (551-479 BC). Just across the intersection, traffic flows past the 1962 Kim Lau Memorial *(on Chatham Square)*, which honors those Chinese-Americans killed in US conflicts. The Chinese culture is kept alive here by a number of Chinese film theaters, by Buddhist temples (Grace Gratitute, Buddhist and Easter Buddhist) and by the local cultural center on Mott Street. The red brick **Edward Mooney House** *(18 Bowery)* is reputed to be the earliest surviving row house in Manhattan. Dating from the Revolutionary era (1785-1789), it reflects both Georgian and Federal styles.

A visit to Chinatown is of course not complete without a meal in a Chinese restaurant. The cuisine of China is as varied as the country is large and many different regional specialties are available, including Cantonese, Hunan, Mandarin and Szechuan.

★ LITTLE ITALY

Roughly bounded by Canal, Lafayette, Houston Streets and the Bowery, this district was populated by Italian immigrants who arrived at ELLIS ISLAND between the 1880s and 1920s. Hailing primarily from southern Italy and Sicily, the immigrants were

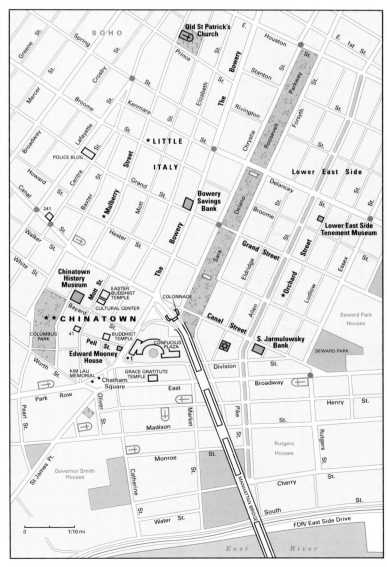

fleeing their country's rampant poverty and epidemics. Although many Italians have left the neighborhood, they return for family gatherings, marriages, funerals, festivals and saints' days. The friendly atmosphere of neighborhood grocery stores displaying their wares of pastas, salamis, olives and cheeses, and the inviting smells drifting from the cafes have turned this area into a popular tourist attraction.

Visit. – The hub of Little Italy centers on **Mulberry Street★**, sometimes called the Via San Gennaro, in particular the section north of Canal Street. The area abounds in cafes serving espresso and cappuccino, pizzerias, restaurants and clam bars. During the feast of San Gennaro *(September)*, the patron saint of Naples, the street is a vast alfresco restaurant.

At the corner of Prince and Mulberry Streets stands **Old Saint Patrick's Church** (1815, Joseph F. Mangin), New York's Roman Catholic Cathedral until 1879, when it was replaced by the larger Gothic Revival structure on Fifth Avenue *(p 35)*. Marking the corner of Grand and Centre Streets, the Police Building, a massive Renaissance palazzo (1909), served as the city's police headquarters until 1973. Neglected for over a decade, it was restored in the late 1980s and converted into cooperative apartments.

MUSEUM

Chinatown History Museum. – *See description p 114.*

13 LOWER EAST SIDE

Time: 2 hours. ● *4, 5, 6 or N, R trains to Canal St. Map p 73.*

Encompassing the area below Houston Street bounded by the Bowery and the East River, the Lower East Side is best known historically as a melting pot for newly arrived immigrants. Once primarily home to Jewish and Ukrainian families, the neighborhood has undergone continual change as successive waves of immigrants have staked their claim. Lining the narrow streets, an eclectic ensemble of tenement buildings, bustling open-air markets and grand houses of worship combine to create one of America's landmark ethnic neighborhoods.

HISTORICAL NOTES

The Governor's Farm. – The last Dutch governor of Nieuw Amsterdam from 1647 to 1664, **Peter Stuyvesant** (1592-1672) established a farm (*bouwerie* in Dutch) on the land he wrested from the Indians between Broadway and the East River and the present 5th and 17th Streets. In order to facilitate transport to his farm, Stuyvesant laid out a broad, straight road, known today as the Bowery. His own home was located near a small chapel, rebuilt in 1799 by one of his descendants—the present-day ST MARK'S-IN-THE-BOWERY CHURCH.

Neighborhood of Beginnings and Dreams. – The first mass migration to the Lower East Side occurred in the mid-1800s with the arrival of Irish immigrants seeking relief from famine. From the late 19C until World War I, millions of southern and eastern Europeans arrived via ELLIS ISLAND, America's great immigrant gateway. After being processed at Ellis Island, these new arrivals were diverted to the Lower East Side by "street birds" who directed them to neighborhoods already populated by other recently arrived immigrants. The tide of immigration was halted in the 1920s with the passage of restrictive legislation.

The neighborhood still contains many of the cramped tenement buildings that were constructed specifically to house immigrants. Entire families were often crowded into one room apartments under oppressive living conditions. Reformers such as Jacob Riis chronicled the plight of the immigrant through photographs, while service groups were established to ease the assimilation process.

Although many second-generation immigrants moved away as they prospered, the Lower East Side today remains a neighborhood of ethnic contrasts where visitors are likely to hear Chinese, Spanish and Yiddish as well as English. Strolling along the narrow streets, it is easy to conjure up the sights and smells encountered by its turn-of-the-century residents. Open markets selling exotic fare and buildings with multilingual signs bear witness to the successive waves of immigrants who have made the Lower East Side their home.

VISIT

It is best to visit the area on Sundays, when most stores are open and the neighborhood becomes a lively and colorful bazaar. We recommend walking south on the Bowery, then turning on Grand and Orchard Sts, and completing the walk along Canal St.

The Bowery. – Once a notorious entertainment center where vaudeville became fashionable and risqué revues flourished, the Bowery was nicknamed "the poor man's Broadway." After World War I, the area degenerated into an undesirable neighborhood frequented by vagrants and alcoholics. Although the street is still home to shelters and soup kitchens, it is also known for its stores specializing in electrical goods—especially lighting fixtures—and wholesale restaurant equipment. Designed in 1895 by McKim, Mead and White, the Beaux-Arts **Bowery Savings Bank** *(no. 130, near Grand St)* is distinguished by imposing Corinthian columns and opulent detailing, making it one of the most striking buildings on the Lower East Side. The interior features an ornate coffered vault marked in the center by a large, opaque skylight.

Grand Street. – In past years, this thoroughfare was known for its shops selling wedding gowns and linens. Today fresh fish stalls, bustling open-air vegetable markets and small restaurants support the growing Chinese and Asian communities who have spilled into this area north of CHINATOWN.

★ **Orchard Street.** – Once jammed with pushcarts and street vendors, this bustling artery and its surrounding streets are closed to traffic on Sundays, becoming a veritable mecca for those seeking bargains on clothing and accessories. Over 300 tiny stores display their wares on stalls in the street. Enthusiastic merchants and street hawkers vie for the customer's attention with colorful invitations to inspect their merchandise. At no. 97 stands the Lower East Side Tenement Museum *(p 119)*.

Canal Street. – This busy east/west thoroughfare separating SOHO from CHINATOWN is noted for its jewelry and diamond merchants. Once the tallest structure on the Lower East Side, the now vacant **S. Jarmulowsky Bank** *(nos. 54-58, at Orchard St)* was established in 1873 to cater to newly arrived Jewish immigrants.

A short detour on Eldridge Street leads to the **Eldridge Street Synagogue** *(nos. 12-16)*, the first great house of worship built by eastern European Jews in America. Currently undergoing restoration and transformation into a Jewish heritage center, this 1887 Herter Brothers commission displays a striking rose window set against an ornate Moorish facade. Inside, hand-stenciled walls rise to a 70ft vaulted ceiling *(open Mon–Fri 9am–5pm, Sun 10am–4pm; closed Jewish holidays; suggested contribution $5; guided tours available)*.

At the base of the Manhattan Bridge linking Manhattan with Brooklyn stands the sorely neglected Manhattan Bridge colonnade (1915, Carrère and Hastings). Designed as part of the "City Beautiful" movement, the gateway features an arch flanked by curved colonnades. Heavy traffic at its base coupled with vandalism and graffiti have taken their toll on this once-noble civic commission.

MUSEUM

Lower East Side Tenement Museum. – *See description p 119.*

SOHO

★★ 14

Time: 3 hours. ● *1, 9 train to Prince St, or N, R train to Spring St. Map p 80.*

The heart of Manhattan's fashionable downtown art scene, SoHo (an acronym for south of Houston—pronounced Howston—Street) is New York at its most trendy and colorful. This once largely industrial area is now an international center for artists and collectors, and the place where the hottest fashions in clothing, collectibles and home furnishings are likely to appear first. Declared an historic district in 1973, the 26 blocks bounded by Canal, West Broadway, West Houston and Crosby Streets, also boast the largest concentration of 19C cast-iron buildings in the US.

From Farmland to Fashion. – While SoHo's lively facade makes it hard to imagine a quieter past, the area was actually remarkably rural from the early Dutch colonial period well into the 1800s. The site of the first free black community on Manhattan, this area was settled in 1644 by former slaves of the Dutch West India Company who were granted the land for farms. Serious development did not begin until the early 19C, when the city drained and filled the area's badly polluted waterways.

By 1809, Broadway was paved and a number of prominent citizens, including James Fenimore Cooper, had moved in, bringing considerable cachet to the new residential district. In the late 1850s, large stores, including Tiffany & Co, E.V. Haughwout, Arnold Constable and Lord & Taylor began lining Broadway, soon joined by grand hotels like the St Nicholas, which occupied most of a city block. Theaters, casinos and the numerous brothels found on Crosby, Mercer and Greene Streets offered still more diversion. As the area grew more commercial in character, respectable middle-class families began to move uptown and the district evolved into a thriving industrial dry-goods center during the second half of the 19C. SoHo's remarkable cast-iron and stone commercial buildings date from this period.

By the 1950s, the district became known as "Hell's Hundred Acres" and was threatened with decimation by a proposed Lower Manhattan Expressway. After fierce local opposition, the scheme was abandoned and, during the 1960s, SoHo came to life as an artistic community. Painters began moving into the old warehouses, or lofts, attracted by low rents and huge, open spaces that could accommodate enormous canvases. Although the area was zoned for manufacturing, a 1971 provision allowed artists to legally convert the lofts into living/working quarters. Uptown galleries arrived and, as the area became desirable, real-estate values skyrocketed. While affluent professionals moved in, many artists were priced out, drawn to cheaper warehouse space in Brooklyn, Queens and New Jersey. However, scores of aspiring and struggling artists still work and live here.

Today, SoHo caters primarily to the well-heeled with its smart restaurants, trendy coffee bars and pricey boutiques. Yet here, where "shabby chic" is the epitome of style, light manufacturing still exists and dumpsters and loading docks are as common a sight as black leather jackets, especially in the more industrial area south of Broome Street. And while the district is home to many of the city's most expensive galleries, several early outposts for experimental film and video, dance and drama still hold their own. Indeed, SoHo is a thoroughly incongruous area, but that is precisely its attraction.

DOWNTOWN

Construction in Cast Iron. – Although cast iron has a long history of use for tools and household utensils, it was not exploited as a building material until the late 1700s, when the English developed a novel iron framing technique used in spinning and textile mills that would be the prototype for commercial buildings in the US some 50 years later. Among the material's two greatest American proponents were Daniel Badger and **James Bogardus**, who both established foundries in New York in the 1840s.

Limited primarily to the fronts, beams, and interior columns of a building, cast iron had many virtues. Sold through catalogues, the prefabricated parts were relatively easy to produce and assemble. Moreover, the columns, which eliminated the need for interior loadbearing walls and allowed much more open space, were ideal for warehouses. Formed in molds, the material introduced an inexpensive way to reproduce the elaborate stone balustrades, cornices and columns that distinguished the architectural styles of the day. At far less the cost of carved granite or marble, a style-conscious merchant could turn a suitably grandiose facade to the street with a Second Empire design like the elaborate confections of architect **I.F. Duckworth** or the elegant compositions of **Richard Morris Hunt**.

Used for both full and partial facades, cast iron remained extremely popular until the 1890s, when it was eclipsed by a new taste for styles better interpreted in brick or stone. At the same time, the development of steel framing and elevators made possible taller buildings, more difficult to face with cast-iron units.

Note: Finished with paint, cast iron can look remarkably like stone, another widely used building material in SoHo. Apart from tell-tale signs of rust, the only sure way to identify the metal is to use a magnet.

VISIT

The best way to experience SoHo is to wander at will, taking time to window shop, to browse in galleries and boutiques, and to engage in one of the most popular downtown rituals of all: people watching.
Most galleries and museums are closed on Monday and many shut down for part or all of the summer.

★ **Broadway.** – Overflowing with traffic, pedestrians and sidewalk vendors, this lively thoroughfare is a street of contrasts, where hardware stores and bargain outlets stand side by side with tony emporiums selling everything from antiques to Armani. Modern signs obscure some of the proud old storefronts, but there are still many outstanding architectural landmarks.

The impressive brick-and-stone building at no. 575, dating to 1882, has been renovated as the setting for the **Guggenheim Museum SoHo★**, the famed museum's *(p 117)* downtown branch, which offers changing exhibits on two floors of airy gallery space *(open Wed–Mon 11am–6pm, Thu, Fri & Sat 10pm; closed Thanksgiving Day, Dec 25; $5; guided tours available; & ☎423-3500).*

The 1903 **Singer Building** *(nos. 561-563)* designed by Ernest Flagg is a handsome example of the new skyscraper architecture that emerged in the early 20C. Twelve stories high, it features a fireproof facing of brick and terra-cotta, but wrought-iron tracery and expanses of glass keep the tall office building from appearing heavy. An earlier, 1883 brick-and-stone store at no. 560 now houses Dean and DeLuca, renowned purveyor of specialty foods.

The remarkable **E.V. Haughwout Building** *(nos. 488-492)*, on the northeast corner of Broome Street, boasts the oldest complete cast-iron facades in the city, produced by Daniel Badger's ironworks in 1857. Unfortunately today, it has fallen into neglect and is in a deteriorated state. With its rhythmic pattern of arched windows, balustrades and Corinthian columns—repeated 92 times—this "Venetian palace" proved a suitably pretentious setting for the cut-glass chandeliers, silver and clocks originally sold here. Inside is the country's first safety passenger elevator, installed by Otis Elevators.

On the southwest corner of Broome Street at no. 487 stands a handsome example of the tall brick-and-stone office buildings that appeared in SoHo in the 1890s; the graceful ornament is terra-cotta. Across Broadway, at 435 Broome Street, is an unusual building, designed in 1873 in a Victorian Gothic style, seldom used for commercial cast-iron architecture; the tracery arches, typical of the style, would have been extremely expensive to produce in stone. Further south on Broadway is the elegant facade of nos. 478-480 Broadway (1874, Richard Morris Hunt), distinguished by slender colonnettes, large plate-glass windows and an unusual concave cornice.

★ **Greene Street.** – One of the richest collections of cast-iron building facades in SoHo is found on this thoroughfare, where the original cobblestones and wide granite sidewalks accentuate the 19C atmosphere. The notable facade at 112-114 Prince Street on the southwest corner of Greene may look like cast iron, but it is actually a *trompe l'œil* design painted on brick by artist Richard Haas in 1975. The "King" of Greene Street is located at **no. 72**, a grandiose composition with massive projecting bays designed by Isaac F. Duckworth in 1872. Around the corner at 469-475 Broome stands the Gunther building; this impressive 1871 creation of Griffith Thomas features a curved corner bay and curved plate-glass windows. Located nearby is another architectural gem, 91-93 Grand Street. This building, dating to 1869, appears to be two stone row houses; closer inspection, however, reveals that the facade is actually cast iron, complete with imitation mortar joints. Called the "Queen" of Greene Street, the 6-story warehouse at **nos. 28-30** was built the same year as the "King" and is also the work of I.F. Duckworth; the enormous mansard roof, projecting central bay and ornate dormers are hallmarks of the Second Empire style.

Spring Street. – This vibrant shopping street is notable for its mix of clothing boutiques, fruit and vegetable markets, galleries and antique stores. The oldest building in the district is located at **no. 107**. Completed prior to 1808, the corner house has been faced with stucco, but its small scale is immediately apparent, recalling the pre-cast-iron days of SoHo, when the neighborhood was primarily residential. With its large expanses of glass and slender columns, the 1870 building at **no. 101** is among the most distinguished cast-iron structures on the street.

West Broadway. – This wide, busy avenue is lined with T-shirt shops and expensive clothing boutiques alike. It comes alive on weekends, as it is also home to some of SoHo's oldest and best known galleries, including Mary Boone *(no. 467)*, Leo Castelli and Sonnabend *(no. 420)* and OK Harris *(no. 383)*. At 141 Wooster Street is the New York Earth Room, where 280,000lbs of dirt, exactly two inches deep, have been on display since 1980 *(open Tue–Sat 10am–6pm)*. This installation is the work of environmental artist Walter de Maria.

Ken Straiton/First Light

Art galleries on Spring Street

MUSEUMS

Alternative Museum. *– See description p 110.*
★ **The Guggenheim Museum SoHo.** *– See description p 76.*
★ **Museum for African Art.** *– See description p 139.*
The New Museum of Contemporary Art. *– See description p 145.*

GREENWICH VILLAGE ★★ 15

Time: 3 hours. Distance: 2mi. Map p 80.

Greenwich Village occupies approximately the area bounded by Spring Street to the south and 14th Street to the north, between Greenwich Street and Broadway. The heart of this heterogeneous district is Washington Square and the area just to the west of it. Here Federal and Greek Revival town houses line narrow streets that play havoc with Manhattan's grid system. Restaurants and coffee houses abound, interspersed with craft shops, boutiques, theaters and galleries.
During the day, a serene small-town atmosphere pervades, enlivened on Sunday afternoons by strollers who gather to hear street musicians or have their portrait painted. The night, however, reveals a countenance reminiscent of Montmartre and Saint-Germain-des-Prés in Paris: a cosmopolitan tourist crowd rubs shoulders with artists, intellectuals and students. People flock to theaters and movie houses, and folk, rock and jazz musicians perform in dimly lit nightclubs and cafes.

HISTORICAL NOTES

A Country Village. – In 1609, when Henry Hudson sailed up the river, which was later named for him, the countryside that was to become Greenwich Village was covered with woods and streams abounding with fish, and sheltered an Algonquin Indian settlement called Sapokanikan. Later, British colonists settled here and, in 1696, a village sprung up, named after the English town Greenwich (actually, the name "Greenwich Village" is redundant, since "wich" means village or town). Between rows of wooden houses ran Greenwich Street, then the main street of the village overlooking the Hudson River.
During the 18C, wealthy landowners such as the De Lanceys, Van Cortlandts, Sir Peter Warren and Abraham Mortier built estates in the area, and it became a settled and well-known part of the city, with good taverns and even a road that led directly out of town. Thomas Paine, the famous revolutionary figure and pamphleteer, lived in Greenwich Village for a time. After the Revolutionary War, six parallel streets south of the area that became Washington Square Park were named for Revolutionary generals. The "Streets of the Six Generals," from west to east, are (Major General Alexander) MacDougal, (Brigadier General John) Sullivan, (Brigadier General William) Thompson, (Brigadier General David) Wooster, (Major General Nathanael) Greene and (Brigadier General Hugh) Mercer.

The early 19C saw recurrent outbreaks of smallpox and yellow fever ravaging the downtown area, and residents, thus, sought the healthy country air of Greenwich Village. The present Bank Street, in the northern part of the Village, was named for the Wall Street banks that took temporary refuge here, in 1822, during the city's most virulent yellow fever epidemic.

In the 1830s, prominent families brought cachet to the area by constructing elegant town houses here, but they moved further north when industry developed near the waterfront. Irish and Chinese immigrants, as well as free blacks, came to live in the Village, and Italian immigrants settled in the area south of Washington Square Park, creating LITTLE ITALY. Lower rents attracted artists and writers following the example of **Edgar Allan Poe**, who took up residence at 85 West 3rd Street in 1845, where he wrote *Gordon Pym* and *The Fall of the House of Usher*.

Village Bohemia. – During the early 1900s, Greenwich Village became New York's Bohemia. Intellectuals, social reformers and radicals descended in droves to join the writers and artists, and it seemed as though the entire avant-garde of the US was concentrated in these few streets. *The Masses,* a publication founded in 1910, was the mouthpiece of radicals who attacked the complacency of American society and its Victorian morality. The favorite haunt of the Village rebels was the **Liberal Club**, frequented by such social critics as **Upton Sinclair**. At its headquarters, at 133 MacDougal Street, the club organized cubist art exhibits, lectures and debates, and all-night dances called "Pagan Routs." There were soon so many "Pagans" that the festivities had to be moved to other quarters. Polly Holliday's restaurant, located below the Liberal Club, became the favorite meeting place of anarchists.

Ferment also swept the arts. A new group of painters known as **The Eight**—or the Ash Can school—challenged established academic concepts, and was instrumental in organizing the 1913 Armory Show *(p 26)*. Literary salons helped to create an intellectual climate in the Village, which stimulated such writers as Walt Whitman, Mark Twain and Henry James. Theodore Dreiser, Richard Wright, O. Henry and Stephen Crane also lived here for a certain time. Not surprisingly, the Village attracted the theater. In 1915, the **Washington Square Players** ensemble, later to become the Theater Guild, was founded at the Liberal Club. In the following year, the **Provincetown Players** made their New York debut on the ground floor of a bottling plant, after a summer season in Provincetown on Cape Cod. Among the members of the company was the poetess and playwright, Edna St. Vincent Millay. It was here that Eugene O'Neill first gained recognition. The jazz age of the 1920s touched off a wave of eccentricity with **F. Scott Fitzgerald**, a predominant figure of the Lost Generation.

The Village has historically been the stomping ground for the city's large gay population. Although the Village still claims an active gay community, other sections of the city, including the Upper West Side and Chelsea, are also home to a growing population of gays and lesbians.

Today, Greenwich Village, although still a hive of non-conformism and originality, is not as radical, Bohemian and avant-garde as it once was. High rents have driven away struggling and would-be artists to cheaper areas (such as the EAST VILLAGE and TRIBECA). Nonetheless, scattered among the small houses in the narrow streets, high-rise buildings accommodate New Yorkers who prefer the vitality of the Village to the conventionality of suburbia or residential uptown and are attracted by a community, which welcomes talent, offers serious and light entertainment, caters to the bibliophile and to the gourmet, and cherishes diversity of lifestyle. These residents, as well as their neighbors, are deeply committed to preserving the character of their unique neighborhood.

New Yorkers and visitors alike have always flocked to the Village for its innumerable cafes. Enjoy an espresso or cappuccino at one of the following establishments:

- *Café Borgia (185 Bleecker St)*
- *Caffé dell'Artista (46 Greenwich Ave)*
- *Caffé Lucca (228 Bleecker St)*
- *Caffé Manatus (340 Bleecker St)*
- *Caffé Raffaella (134 Seventh Ave South)*
- *Caffé Reggio (119 MacDougal St)*
- *Caffé Sha Sha (510 Hudson St)*
- *Caffé Vivaldi (32 Jones St)*
- *Le Figaro Café (168 Bleecker St)*
- *Pane e Cioccolato (10 Waverly Place)*

WALKING TOUR

This walk links the most typical parts of the Village. We advise you to follow it twice, once during the day and once at night. Begin at Washington Square. ● A, C, E or 6 trains to Spring St, or N, R train to Prince St.

★★ Washington Square. – Forming the heart of present-day Greenwich Village, this large square is the main gathering place for Villagers and visitors alike. It stands at the beginning of Fifth Avenue, its monumental arch a fitting entry to this famous thoroughfare.

Originally a marshland and favorite hunting ground of the early colonists, the site of the present square became a potter's field in the 18C (skeletons of about 1,000 early New Yorkers were found during the renovation of the square in the 1960s). It was also popular as a dueling ground and the site of public hangings. Following its transformation into a park in 1826, it served as a military parade ground and later spurred the growth of a fashionable residential enclave of elegant red brick town houses.

Washington Square

D & J Heaton/First Light

Henry James's novel *Washington Square*, later adapted for stage and screen as *The Heiress*, depicts the life of the local aristocracy. Mark Twain, O. Henry, Walt Whitman and the painter, Edward Hopper, also frequented Washington Square and evoked it in their works.

After the founding of New York University, Washington Square became the unofficial university campus, and a large number of the surrounding buildings now belong to the university *(p 82)*.

Today, the park is a veritable people watcher's paradise: throngs of visitors stop to listen to impromptu performers and soapbox orators, admire skateboard and frisbee enthusiasts, or gaze at the eclectic mix of people dressed in all sorts of wild and wonderful outfits. Radiating from the central fountain, the park offers entertainment for young (children's park) and old (large chess tables). Even dogs can frolic in their own little play area.

Twice a year for three weeks, the square and surrounding streets are the scene of the **Washington Square Outdoor Art Exhibit** *(p 178)*. More than 500 emerging artists display their work, many for the first time.

★ **Washington Arch [1].** – Designed by Stanford White in 1892, this white marble triumphal arch replaced a temporary wooden one commemorating the centenary of President Washington's inauguration *(p 63)*. The arch, 30ft across and 77ft high, is best viewed from Fifth Avenue. Gracing this side are two sculptures of Washington—as a soldier by Herman MacNeil and as a civilian by A. Sterling Calder, father of the renowned 20C sculptor, Alexander Calder. On the south side, note the frieze with the American eagle, the "W's" for Washington at the center and the trumpet-blowing statues of fame.

Located to the east of the arch, the 1888 bronze **statue of Garibaldi [2]** forms a rallying point for the inhabitants of nearby LITTLE ITALY. A hero of the Italian struggle for independence, Garibaldi stayed in New York in 1850.

Walk to north side of the square.

★ **Washington Square North.** – Often referred to as "the Row," this is the most attractive side of the square. Two blocks of Greek Revival town houses *(nos. 1-13 and 21-26)* remain from the 1830s, suggesting what the entire square once looked like. The residences have housed such renowned individuals as Richard Morris Hunt, Henry James, Edward Hopper and John Dos Passos, who wrote *Manhattan Transfer* while living at no. 3. Doric or Ionic columns grace the entrances topped by flat lintels, and elaborate cast-iron railings separate the red brick houses from the sidewalk. Some of the residences *(nos. 7-13)* only retain their original facades as the interiors have been gutted and converted into an apartment complex *(entrance on Fifth Ave)*.

Continue up Fifth Ave to Washington Mews.

Washington Mews. – Behind Washington Square North, this secluded alley once contained stables and servants' quarters for the town houses on Washington Square North. The charm and intimacy of this street with its whitewashed and brick facades, climbing shrubs and cobblestone pavement has long attracted artists, writers and actors.

Continue north on Fifth Ave and turn left on W. 8th St.

West 8th Street. – This lively artery caters to a motley crew of regulars and tourists alike, who can be observed poking around the bookshops, shoe stores and vintage clothing boutiques. Also lined with antique stores, arts and crafts galleries and jewelry stores, West 8th Street has become the main shopping street of the Village. A variety of eating places and watering holes add to the colorful atmosphere.

Turn left on MacDougal St to MacDougal Alley.

★ **MacDougal Alley.** – Yet another picturesque lane, similar to Washington Mews, this alley was inhabited by sculptor Gertrude Vanderbilt Whitney (1875-1942) who opened a gallery in a converted stable that was the precursor of the WHITNEY MUSEUM OF AMERICAN ART. Lit by gas street lamps, the row houses have been converted into private studios.

Return to W. 8th St, turn left, continue to Ave of the Americas and glance north to the corner of W. 10th St.

Renowned as one of the Village's more eccentric landmarks, **Jefferson Market Library** *(425 Ave of the Americas)*, a castle-like red brick structure (1877, Frederick Clarke Withers and Calvert Vaux), was modeled after King Ludwig II's Neuschwanstein castle in Bavaria, Germany. Designed in an ornate Victorian Gothic style, the building is adorned with pinnacles, gables, turrets, arches and traceried windows, and dominated by a whimsical clock tower. Originally used as a courthouse, the building was threatened with destruction in the 1960s. At the urging of the local populace, the building was considered for adaptive re-use and today houses a branch of the New York Public Library system.

Continue south on Ave of the Americas, turn right on Waverly Place and right again on Gay St.

Lined with quaint, Federal-style brick houses, the charming Gay Street bears no trace of its past as a black ghetto.

Continue to the end of Gay St and turn left on Christopher St.

Historically the center of the city's gay population, **Christopher Street** is lined with an array of eccentric shops. Occupying the intersection with Waverly Place is the imposing, triangular **Northern Dispensary**, New York's oldest medical clinic, established in 1831 to dispense free medical care to the poor and now being refurbished as a residence for homeless people with AIDS. A little farther down the street, at the

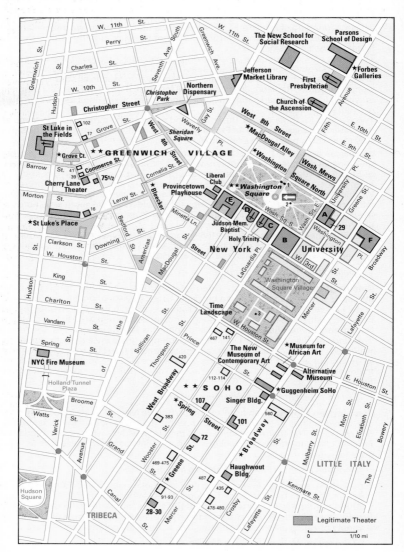

intersection with West 4th, **Christopher Park**, a small square, became the focus of controversy in 1990 owing to the installation of a sculpture by George Segal, representing two gay couples. On the north side of the park stands the Stonewall bar *(no. 51)*, scene of the historic 1969 riot between police and gays that sparked the Gay Liberation movement.

Turn left on W. 4th St.

A lively artery, **West 4th Street** is jammed with a succession of restaurants, coffee houses and craft shops. Take a minute to admire the splendid assortment of shrubs and flowers of the viewing garden at **Sheridan Square**, a welcome spot of greenery on this commercial street.

Turn right on Cornelia St, left on Bleecker St and right on Leroy St. Cross Seventh Ave and continue on Leroy St to St Luke's Place.

West of Seventh Avenue, the Village presents a series of charming, tree-lined streets, quaint houses and a few choice restaurants. Exuding a quiet, residential atmosphere, this area contrasts vividly with the more vibrant section centering around 8th and Bleecker Streets. Lining the winding streets, 2 1/2-story Federal houses, topped by slate roofs and brick chimneys, and enlivened with elaborate wrought-iron gates and railings, recall the area's 19C elegance.

★ **St Luke's Place.** – Located across from a public swimming pool and park, this attractive row of brick and brownstone residences from the 1860s is shaded by gingko trees and fragrant wisteria. It was here, at no. 16, that Theodore Dreiser wrote *An American Tragedy*. South of this area, near Charlton and Vandam Streets, an elegant estate known as Richmond Hill served as a headquarters for General Washington, and later as a residence for both John Adams and Aaron Burr.

Turn right on Hudson St and again on Morton St.

Lined with fine trees, the curving Morton Street features stately homes, some adorned with elaborate doorways, especially no. 59. *Turn left on Bedford St.* Erected in 1873, **75 1/2 Bedford Street** is reputed to be the narrowest house in the city (9.5ft wide, 30ft long, 3 stories high). Edna St. Vincent Millay lived here from 1923 to 1924.

Turn left on Commerce St.

A charming, rambling, residential alley, **Commerce Street** well represents the "village" feel of West Greenwich. Housed in an old barn at no. 38, the **Cherry Lane Theater**, a venue for Off-Broadway productions since the 1920s, has hosted the American premieres of plays by Beckett, Ionesco and Edward Albee. Around the corner at nos. 39 and 41, rise two handsome brick houses (1832), called "The Twin Sisters"; legend has it that they were built by a sea captain for his two daughters who could not live together under the same roof.

Turn left on Barrow St, continue to Hudson St and turn right.

On the west side of Hudson Street stands the **Church of St Luke in the Fields**, an austere, brick structure erected in 1822 and reconstructed following a fire in 1981. A little farther north, Hudson Street is lined with cafes, boutiques and bookshops.

Turn into Grove St across from St Luke's.

Grove Street, like Bedford, is a peaceful byway that seems miles away from feverish Manhattan. At nos. 10-12, peak through the gate of **Grove Court★**, an attractive fan-shaped cul-de-sac surrounded by brick-fronted Federal houses of the 1850s. A 3-story wood-frame house *(no. 17)*, unusual for New York, marks the northern corner of Grove and Bedford Streets. Before turning right on Bleecker, take a look at the "twin peaks" of 102 Bedford Street, an eccentric 1925 renovation of a traditional Village house.

Continue to Bleecker St, turn right and continue to Ave of the Americas.

★ **Bleecker Street.** – This is one of the most active commercial thoroughfares in the Village, along with West 8th and Hudson Streets. Part of an old Italian neighborhood, Bleecker is famed for the displays of fruits and vegetables, the specialized grocery stores and pastry shops, and the coffee houses for espresso lovers.
The 4-block stretch of Bleecker between Avenue of the Americas and LaGuardia Place is an old 1960s stomping ground. Today the stretch still abounds with small cabarets, coffee houses, music clubs and bars.

Continue on Bleecker St and turn left on MacDougal St.

Erected for Aaron Burr *(p 63)*, a block of Federal style residences *(nos. 127-131)* dominate the west side of the street. At no. 133 is the **Provincetown Playhouse** *(p 78)*, one of the oldest Off-Broadway theaters.

Jazz up an evening in the Village:
- *Blue Note Jazz Club (131 W. 3rd St, ☎475-8592)*
- *Bottom Line Cabaret (15 W. 4th St, ☎228-6300)*
- *Sweet Basil (88 Seventh Ave South, ☎242-1785)*
- *Village Gate/Top of the Gate (160 Bleecker St, ☎475-5120)*
- *Village Vanguard (178 Seventh Ave South, ☎255-4037)*
- *Cornelia Street Cafe (29 Cornelia St, ☎989-9318)*
- *Bradley's (70 University Place at W. 11th St, ☎228-6440)*

NEW YORK UNIVERSITY

The largest private university in the United States, NYU was founded by **Albert Gallatin**, secretary of the Treasury under Jefferson, in 1831. Today, NYU has 13 colleges, a staff of 14,500 and over 49,000 students. The principal campuses are: Washington Square (Sciences, Arts and Letters, Business, Law, Education), the Medical Center on First Avenue (Medicine and Dentistry), the School of Continuing Education on Trinity Place in the Wall Street area, the Real Estate Institute on West 42nd Street and the NYU INSTITUTE OF FINE ARTS on Fifth Avenue.

Main Building [A]. – *100 Washington Square East.* Built in 1895, this neoclassical structure replaced the original building erected in 1836. An impressive row of four paired Doric columns adorns the facade fronting Washington Square. The ground floor houses the **Grey Art Gallery** *(entrance on 33 Washington Place; open Tue, Thu & Fri 11am–6:30pm, Wed 11am–8:30pm, Sat 11am–5pm; closed holidays; suggested contribution $3.50; guided tours available; & ☎998-6780),* which features changing exhibits encompassing various aspects of the visual arts, including painting, sculpture, photography, decorative arts and video.

Elmer Holmes Bobst Library [B]. – *70 Washington Square South. Not open to the general public.* This imposing red sandstone cube on the southeast corner of the square was designed by Philip Johnson and Richard Foster in 1972. Rising to 150ft, its 12 stories house over 2 million books.

The **Loeb Student Center [C]** (1959, Harrison & Abramovitz) stands on the site of a boarding house known as the House of Genius, which had been home to Herman Melville, Stephen Crane and Eugene O'Neill. It features an aluminum-panel sculpture (1960, Reuben Nakian) on its facade, representing birds in flight. Adjacent to it, the triangular-shaped Roman Catholic **Holy Trinity Chapel** is distinguished by modern, stained-glass windows.

Judson Memorial Baptist Church. – *55 Washington Square South.* Creating a marked contrast to Holy Trinity Chapel, this distinctive structure of mottled yellow brick and white terra-cotta presents an eclectic mix of Greco-Romanesque and Renaissance motifs. Built in 1893, it is considered one of architect Stanford White's finest designs in the city. Inside, note the superb stained-glass windows by John LaFarge. The separate, 10-story campanile now houses a student dormitory.

Hagop Kevorkian Center for Near Eastern Studies. [D] – *At corner of Washington Square South and Sullivan St.* Dominating a small corner lot, this stark, granite building was designed by Philip Johnson and Richard Foster in 1972. It contains a surprising and delightful **entrance hall★** *(on Sullivan St)*, a reconstruction of a Syrian courtyard complete with tiled floor, fountain, moldings and door panels. The various pieces came from a merchant's house (1797) in Damascus.

The 1951 red brick, Georgian Revival **Vanderbilt Hall [E]**, which houses NYU's School of Law, features a pleasant courtyard at its entrance on Washington Square South.

Tisch School of the Arts [F]. – *721 Broadway.* The recycled NYU loft building is where such well-known movie directors as Spike Lee, Martin Scorsese and Oliver Stone learned their trade.

Sylvette [3]. – *In Silver Towers Plaza located on Bleecker St, between LaGuardia Place and Mercer St.* Located in the center of the Silver Towers complex (designed for NYU by I.M. Pei in 1966) stands this 36ft-high bust of Sylvette David, a young woman Picasso met in the 1950s. The original Picasso sheet-metal sculpture was enlarged in concrete and stone by Carl Nesjar and Sigurd Frager in 1968.

ADDITIONAL SIGHTS

Time Landscape. – *At corner of LaGuardia Place and West Houston St.* Designed by environmental sculptor Alan Sonfist, this patch of greenery represents the vegetation found on the island of Manhattan prior to the arrival of Europeans. Planted in 1978, the garden includes oak, sassafras, maple trees, wild grasses and flowers.

29 Washington Place East. – *At the northwest corner of Washington Place East and Greene St.* In 1911, a Saturday afternoon fire in the workrooms of the Triangle Shirtwaist Company on the top three floors of this 10-story industrial building killed 145 people, most of them women and young girls. Many plunged into Washington Place. The outcry led to the passage of the first factory safety laws. A modest plaque commemorates the disaster and the International Ladies Garment Workers Union marks the event every March 25 with an on-site memorial service.

Church of the Ascension. – *36-38 Fifth Ave, at the corner with W. 10th St. Open daily noon–2pm, 5–7pm.* Built of local brownstone, this Gothic Revival Episcopal church (1841) was designed by Richard Upjohn during the Village's first wave of development, which included the construction of prominent institutional buildings. Of particular interest in the soaring interior, remodeled by Stanford White in 1888, is John LaFarge's superb **mural** of the Ascension over the altar, the stained-glass windows and the box pews.

Located one block north, at the corner with West 11th Street, the **First Presbyterian Church** (1845, Joseph C. Wells), topped by a square, pinnacled tower, exemplifies a more elaborate Gothic Revival style.

The New School for Social Research. – *Main building at 66 W. 12th St.* The New School for Social Research, founded in 1919 by historians Charles Beard and James Harvey Robinson, and philosophers John Dewey and Thorstein Veblen, was originally conceived as a small informal center for adults, where a broad range of economic and political issues could be discussed. Over the years, the New School has evolved into a diversified institution of higher learning and today, with its six divisions and total enrollment of more than 30,000 students, it is one of the nation's most innovative universities. In 1970, it joined with **Parsons School of Design** *(66 Fifth Ave between 12th and 13th Sts)* in order to broaden its curriculum. The Parsons School, founded in 1896 by William Merritt Chase, has garnered a world-wide reputation in the fields of fine arts, photography, illustration, design marketing, and the design of interiors, fashions and products. Some 1,800 undergraduate students attend the school. In 1989, the Mannes College of Music, founded in 1916 by violinist David Mannes, joined the New School, adding a distinguished classical music conservatory to its array of academic programs.

MUSEUM

★ **Forbes Magazine Galleries.** – *See description p 114.*

ASTOR PLACE – EAST VILLAGE

Time: 2 hours. ● *4, 5, 6 train to Astor Place. Map p 84.*

This somewhat seedy but lively district, bounded by Houston and 14th Streets east of Broadway, is an active center for dance, theater (Off-Off Broadway), and visual and performance art. Trendy bars and restaurants abound in the **NoHo** (NOrth of HOuston) and Astor Place neighborhoods; east, toward Second Avenue and Avenue A, second-hand shops, ethnic boutiques, bakeries, restaurants and coffee houses are an adventure to explore, especially in the evening.

From Posh to Punk. – In the 17C, the area was part of a 600-acre farm tract owned by Governor Peter Stuyvesant *(p 74).* Briefly in the early 1800s, the now-commercial district west of Second Avenue boasted fashionable town houses; the working-class neighborhoods farther east were home to Polish, Ukrainian and German immigrants until the early 20C. In the 1950s, low rents and an air of romantic seediness attracted such beat-generation writers as Jack Kerouac and William S. Burroughs. In the 1960s and 1970s came the "hippies," then the "punkers" and eventually every other imaginable layer of New York's counterculture. The glory days were the 1980s, when rock bands like the B-52's and Talking Heads made their name at the CBGB Club *(315 Bowery)*—still a center of the underground music movement—, transvestites danced on the bars of popular nightspots like the Pyramid *(101 Avenue A)*, and store-front galleries and performance spaces appeared, and often disappeared, overnight. In 1985, the Palladium *(126 E. 14th St)*, housed in the 1920s Academy of Music converted by Arata Isozaki and decorated by artists Francesco Clemente and Keith Haring, opened as one of the city's most popular discotheques. A magnet for the homeless, the run-down Tompkins Square Park *(east of Avenue A)*, once the center of a German neighborhood known as Kleindeutschland, was the scene of riots during the financial panic of 1873, and again in 1991, when the police uprooted a colony of homeless people from the park, which led to a temporary closing. While the district has become somewhat gentrified, the area is still home to urban housing projects, mainly in Alphabetville, and retains much of its avant-garde flavor.

ASTOR PLACE

The restored 1904 Astor Place subway kiosk is the pride of this busy street connecting Third Avenue to Broadway. Below ground, the station has also been restored to its former glory; note in particular the bas-relief beavers celebrating John Jacob Astor's primacy in the 19C beaver trade. Located opposite the kiosk is Bernard (Tony) Rosenthal's sculpture *Alamo*, popularly known as the "black cube."

Cooper Union for the Advancement of Science and Art. – Located between Third and Fourth Avenue, the Cooper Union comprises three colleges emphasizing architecture, engineering and art. This free institution was founded in 1859 by Peter Cooper (1791-1883), a self-made industrialist who wanted to benefit working-class students with the formal education he himself never had. Art shows, dance performances, literary evenings and lectures—open to the public—occur regularly in the main **Cooper Union Foundation Building**★, the oldest extant steel frame structure in the US. Noted figures who have delivered speeches here include Gloria Steinem, Jimmy Carter, Susan B. Anthony and Abraham Lincoln, who gave his famous "right makes might" anti-slavery speech here in 1860.

Lafayette Street. – In the early 1800s, this area was the site of Vauxhall Gardens, a popular pleasure ground of outdoor cafes and bars. It was developed as a fashionable residential neighborhood in 1825 by John Jacob Astor, then the richest man in America. **Colonnade Row**, the four marble-columned houses at nos. 428-434, features the remnants of nine magnificent Greek Revival houses erected in 1833. Originally called La Grange Terrace, after Lafayette's country estate near Paris, this was a coveted address for such society members as Cornelius Vanderbilt and Warren Delano (grandfather of Franklin Roosevelt).

The monumental brick and stone building across the street was originally the Astor Library, funded by John Jacob Astor and opened in 1854. Offering about 100,000 volumes without charge—a revolutionary idea at the time—it eventually formed the nucleus of the NEW YORK PUBLIC LIBRARY. In 1967, the late impresario Joseph Papp converted the then-abandoned building into the Public Theater *(no. 425)*. Home of the New York Shakespeare Festival, the Public also screens films and hosts new plays in its six theaters; *Hair* (1967) and *A Chorus Line* (1975) were both launched here.

EAST VILLAGE

The main artery of this lively and colorful district is **Second Avenue**, the spine of the Jewish intellectual community during the first half of the 20C. The Entermedia Theater *(189 Second Ave)*, originally the Yiddish Art Theater, is located here, along with an astounding variety of inexpensive ethnic eateries offering Caribbean, Ukrainian, Russian, Chinese, Yemenite, Italian, Japanese, Tibetan, Mexican and Israeli food. Indian restaurants line both sides of East 6th Street between Second and First Avenues, known as "Curry Lane" or "Little India." McSorley's Ale House on East 7th Street *(no. 15)* has been a popular neighborhood bar since 1854.

St Mark's Place between Second and Third Avenues is packed with shops and stalls where you can buy everything from vintage hats and comic books to leather goods.

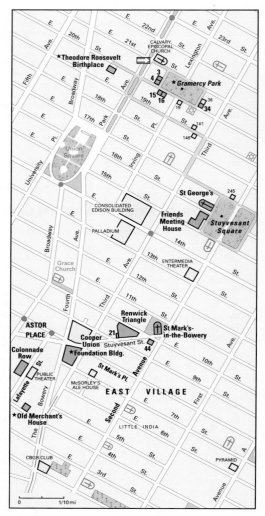

St Mark's-in-the-Bowery Church. – *E. 10th St and Second Ave. Open Mon–Fri 9am–5pm, Sun 10:30am–2pm. Closed holidays. To visit enter through the churchyard gates and go to the rear door.* This Georgian-style Episcopal Church, crowned by a Greek Revival steeple (added in 1828), was built in 1799 on the site of Peter Stuyvesant's 1660 family chapel and is the second oldest church in Manhattan after ST PAUL'S CHAPEL. Damaged by fire in 1978, the church was restored and rededicated in 1983. Seven generations of Stuyvesants are buried under the building. The church hosts literary readings and a resident theater company *(weekly Sept–Jun; for schedule ☎674-6377)*.

Nearby in the St Mark's Historic District are the **Nicholas William Stuyvesant House** *(44 Stuyvesant St)*, built in 1795, and the 1804 **Stuyvesant-Fish House** *(no. 21)*, among the finest and very few surviving Federal-period town houses in the city. Also on Stuyvesant Street, the **Renwick Triangle** *(23-25 Stuyvesant St and 114-128 E. 10th St)*, an ensemble of 5-story row houses (1861) attributed to James Renwick, once shared a large garden with the Stuyvesant-Fish house.

17 GRAMERCY PARK – STUYVESANT SQUARE

Time: 1 1/2 hours. Distance: .8mi. Map above.

Located north of the EAST VILLAGE and east of CHELSEA, within easy walking distance of midtown, these two squares come as pleasant surprises in an otherwise undistinguished area of the city. Surrounded by mid-19C buildings reflecting a variety of Revival styles, the squares are remnants of a once-elegant district that became engulfed by commercial structures at the turn of the century. Today, the area's old-fashioned residential charm is again in vogue, attracting mainly young professionals in search of moderate rents.

DOWNTOWN

WALKING TOUR

Begin walk at Park Ave and E. 21st St. ● *N, R train to 23rd St.*

Dominating the northeast corner of Park Avenue, the red sandstone Calvary Episcopal Church (1846) was designed in the Gothic Revival style by James Renwick, architect of ST PATRICK'S CATHEDRAL.

Continue east on E. 21st St.

★ **Gramercy Park.** – This attractive square and its immediate surroundings form an elegant and tranquil residential enclave in a largely commercial area of the city. The patch of greenery was laid out in 1831 by Samuel B. Ruggles who drained an old marsh—Gramercy is a corruption of the Dutch for "little crooked swamp"—and patterned the area after London's residential squares. Ruggles sold over 60 lots surrounding the square on the understanding that each owner would have access to the park at the center. He also laid out Irving Place, named for his friend Washington Irving *(p 168)*, and Lexington Avenue, as extensions of the park. The first grand homes appeared in the 1840s, and the area quickly attracted prosperous residents. Following several decades of high life, the district's prestige began to wane and apartment houses were erected. By the early 20C, artists and intellectuals moved into the town houses, many of which were converted into cooperatives and duplexes.

Today, surrounded by an 8ft-high cast-iron fence, Gramercy Park remains private—the only such square in New York. Access (by key) is restricted to owners and tenants. A statue (1916, Edmont Quinn) of actor Edwin Booth *(below)*, dressed in his favorite role of Hamlet, stands at its center.

Walk around the park.

Gramercy Park West, the most attractive side of the square, presents a harmonious front of red brick town houses. **Nos. 3** and **4**, designed by Alexander Jackson Davis, boast elaborate cast-iron porches, reminiscent of New Orleans architecture. No. 4, the former home of James Harper, mayor of New York in 1844 and one of the founders of Harper & Bros publishers, is flanked by a pair of iron lanterns, called "Mayor's lamps": the mayor could request to have such lamps installed in front of his house to facilitate locating him in case of night-time emergencies.

The south side features two distinguished clubs. The present site of the National Arts Club, at **no. 15**, was the home of Samuel Tilden, an opponent of Tammany Hall *(p 69)*, governor of New York State from 1874 to 1876, and unsuccessful Democratic nominee for the presidency in 1876. Designed in 1884 by Calvert Vaux in a Victorian Gothic style, the building is embellished with sculptural detailing ranging from flowers and birds to famous authors and thinkers. Fearing for his life after having destroyed the Tweed Ring, Tilden had an underground passageway built to 19th Street as a possible escape route. Located next door at **no. 16**, the Players Club was founded in 1888 by Edwin Booth, the brother of John Wilkes Booth, President Lincoln's assassin. Booth commissioned Stanford White, of McKim, Mead and White, to renovate the facade. Note the ornate, wrought-iron street lamps and the elaborate ironwork of the 2-story porch.

No. 19 was the domain of Mrs Stuyvesant Fish, grande dame of New York society (succeeding Mrs William Astor, *p 30*), whose innovations included reducing the time for a formal dinner from several hours to 50 minutes.

At the east end of the square stand two apartment buildings. Dating from 1883, the red brick **no. 34** is marked by an octagonal turret corner. Adjacent to it, the white terra-cotta building at no. 36 (1910) represents the Gothic Revival style; two concrete knights in armor flank the entrance way.

Follow E. 20th St and cross Park Ave.

★ **Theodore Roosevelt Birthplace National Historic Site.** – *28 E. 20th St. Open Wed–Sun 9am–5pm. Closed holidays. $2. Guided tours (45min) available. ☎260-1616.* This reconstructed Victorian brownstone stands on the site of the home of Theodore Roosevelt (1858-1919), who lived here until he was 14 years of age. Harvard graduate, rancher in the Dakota Territory, colonel in the Rough Riders, hunter-naturalist and author of some 30 books, "Teddy" Roosevelt—who gave his name to Teddy Bears—was a colorful personality and a dynamic force in US politics for 40 years. McKinley's vice president in 1901, he succeeded to the Oval Office on the assassination of the president. Elected in his own right in 1904, he declined to run for re-election in 1908 and failed in an attempt for the presidency in 1912. He received the Nobel Peace Prize for his mediating efforts between Russia and Japan. The 32nd US president, Franklin Delano Roosevelt, was a distant cousin of Teddy and married the latter's niece, Eleanor Roosevelt, in 1905.

The Building. – Erected in 1848, the original 3-story brownstone was torn down in 1916 and replaced by a 2-story commercial building. Three years later, prominent New York citizens acquired that structure and the adjacent building (which once belonged to Teddy's uncle, Robert) and rebuilt the house as a memorial. Opened to the public in 1923, the museum features five period rooms adorned with family heirlooms and the original color schemes, selected by interior designer Leon Marcotte in 1865. The room located to the right of the entrance contains exhibits tracing Roosevelt's career through letters, mementos, cartoons and other memorabilia. On the second floor are the parlor, library and dining room. The master bedroom and nursery occupy the third floor. The "lion's room," which showcases Roosevelt's hunting trophies and his large writing desk, can also be found on this floor. The house was donated to the Park Service in 1963 and has been designated a National Historic Site.

Return to Park Ave, continue south one block and turn left on E. 19th St.

At the intersection with Irving Place, look south to see the Consolidated Edison Company Building (1915). Designed by Henry Hardenbergh who also drew plans for the DAKOTA and the PLAZA HOTEL, the tower is crowned by a landmark clock.

Lined with graceful trees, the stretch of East 19th Street between Irving Place and Third Avenue is known as the "block beautiful." Renovated in the 1920s by Frederick J. Sterner, the houses present a curious yet harmonious blend of stuccoed facades. Note in particular no. 141 with its jockey hitching posts. The artist George Bellows (1882-1925) lived at no. 146 from 1910 until his death.

Turn right on Third Ave and left on E. 17th St.

Stuyvesant Square. – A gift to the city from the Stuyvesant family in 1836, the square formed part of an elegant residential quarter in the 19C. Today, unfortunately, the fenced-in park is bisected by Second Avenue, thereby losing much of its original charm. Hospitals surround the east side, and the towers of Stuyvesant Town, a middle-income housing project built by the Metropolitan Life Insurance Company, are visible beyond. On the north side, at no. 245, the Sidney Webster House (1883) is reputedly the only surviving residential structure in New York designed by Richard Morris Hunt.

The west side of the square attests to the area's former elegance. Located on Rutherford Place, the austere, red brick **Friends Meeting House** and Seminary (1860) and the neighboring **St George's Episcopal Church** (1856) lend the square the appearance of a "village green." St George's, a Romanesque brownstone edifice constructed in 1856 by Blesch and Eidlitz, was known as "Morgan's Church" when the elder J.P. Morgan *(p 145)* was a parishioner here. Its massive, round arches represent an early Romanesque Revival style. Destroyed by fire in 1865, the church was rebuilt to the original specifications *(for visiting hours ☎475-0830)*. Crafted by Gertrude Vanderbilt Whitney, a 1936 bronze statue of Governor Stuyvesant *(p 74)*, easily recognizable by his peg leg, stands in the square, facing St George's Church.

Films that have immortalized New York throughout the years:

A Tree Grows in Brooklyn (1945)	*Elia Kazan*
On the Waterfront (1954)	*Elia Kazan*
West Side Story (1961)	*R. Wise and J. Robbins*
Breakfast at Tiffany's (1961)	*Blake Edwards*
America, America (1963)	*Elia Kazan*
Funny Girl (1968)	*Williams Wyler*
Midnight Cowboy (1968)	*James Schlesinger*
Hello Dolly! (1969)	*Gene Kelly*
Next Stop, Greenwich Village (1976)	*Paul Mazursky*
Taxi Driver (1976)	*Martin Scorsese*
Hair (1979)	*Milos Forman*
Manhattan (1979)	*Woody Allen*
Arthur (1981)	*Steve Gordon*
Ragtime (1981)	*Milos Forman*
Splash (1984)	*Ron Howard*
The Cotton Club (1984)	*Francis F. Coppola*
Ghostbusters (1984)	*Ivan Reitman*
Desperately Seeking Susan (1985)	*Susan Seidelman*
After Hours (1985)	*Martin Scorsese*
Hannah and her Sisters (1986)	*Woody Allen*
Moonstruck (1987)	*Norman Jewison*
Bright Lights, Big City (1988)	*James Bridges*
Slaves of New York (1989)	*James Ivory*
When Harry Met Sally (1989)	*Rob Reiner*
Crimes and Misdemeanors (1989)	*Woody Allen*
New York Stories (1989)	*F. F. Coppola, W. Allen, M. Scorsese*
Green Card (1990)	*Peter Weir*
Bonfire of the Vanities (1990)	*Brian de Palma*
GoodFellas (1990)	*Martin Scorsese*

CENTRAL PARK

Time: 1/2 day. Map p 89.

A sweeping, rectangular greensward located in the geographical center of Manhattan, Central Park provides a haven of greenery, light and air to the more than 15 million people who flock to the park each year. Covering 843 acres and measuring 2.5mi long by .5mi wide, the man-made park extends from 59th to 110th Streets, and Fifth Avenue to Central Park West. Framed by the silhouettes of surrounding buildings, the park offers a quiet oasis in the heart of bustling Manhattan, with many opportunities for recreation.

HISTORICAL NOTES

An Idea Takes Shape. – Foreseeing the need for recreational open spaces in the fast-growing city, the editor and poet, **William Cullen Bryant** *(p 34)*, launched the idea of Central Park in 1850 through a press campaign in his newspaper, *The New York Evening Post*. With the aid of two well-known authors, Washington Irving and George Bancroft, and other public-minded New Yorkers, Bryant urged the city government to acquire a "waste land, ugly and repulsive," located well beyond 42nd Street, which marked the northern border of the city at that time. It was in fact a swamp inhabited by squatters, who raised pigs and goats. After acquiring the land, the city held a competition for the design of the park. The $2,000 prize was awarded to landscape architects **Frederick Law Olmsted** (1822-1903) and **Calvert Vaux** (1824-1895). Clearing began in 1857 with a labor force of 3,000 mostly unemployed Irish workers and 400 horses.

In spite of fierce resistance by the squatters who bombarded the workers with stones, the project got underway and proceeded at a steady pace. The workers moved an estimated billion cubic feet of earth, and after 19 years of extensive drainage, planting, road and bridge building, and ingenious landscaping, the park emerged essentially as we now know it.

Using nature as their main source of inspiration, Olmsted and Vaux skillfully blended natural and man-made elements to create a park inspired by the "picturesque" or romantic style that was highly favored in the mid-19C. Sparse vegetation in parts of the park where the thin layer of top soil barely covers outcropping rocks, accentuates the rugged character of the topography. In the northern part, hills and dales, rocky crags, trees, bushes and shrubs produce a landscape of great scenic beauty. Wide open spaces and meadows where sheep grazed until 1934 lend other sections a pastoral charm, unimpaired by asphalt-covered roads. Over 185 acres were set aside by the designers for lakes and ponds. A formal atmosphere prevails at the Mall and in the Conservatory Garden.

Central Park with Upper West Side skyline

A Popular Park. – From its beginnings, Central Park enjoyed great popularity among New Yorkers. Soon after its completion, it became the testing ground for the finest equipages. On sunny afternoons, carriages lined up at the park entrance were avidly eyed by the populace. Victorias, broughams, phaetons and barouches carried society ladies in elegant attire who pitilessly judged the rigs of their rivals. Trotters too were in great favor, and they whipped through the park to the speedways of Harlem. In 1875, it became fashionable for gentlemen to drive their own four-in-hands. A year later, Leonard Jerome, the maternal grandfather of Sir Winston Churchill, founded the select Coaching Club together with the financier and sportsman, August Belmont. Bicycle riding, which became popular in the 1890s, was denounced as unbecoming for young ladies because of undue freedom of dress and movement. However, the trend was too strong to resist, and before long the curved paths of Central Park were teeming with cycling women.

In the early 1930s, Central Park served as a camping ground for victims of the Depression. The emptied reservoir sheltered "Hooverville," a cluster of shanties. Following several decades of peace and prosperity, the city entered the "flower child" era of the 1960s, and the park became a gathering place for the counter-culture, and a haunt of hustlers and drug dealers. Owing mainly to a shortage of city funds, the park gradually fell into a state of neglect. In the early 1980s, a private organization, the Central Park Conservancy, was created to launch a large-scale renovation effort. Working in tandem with the city of New York, the Conservancy has raised almost $100 million to renovate the park to its former splendor.

Practical Information

The park is open every day from a half hour before sunrise to midnight. The best-known areas are south of the Reservoir, but there are now important attractions to the north. However, it is recommended to limit your strolls to the southern areas. The park is most lively on weekends.

The park's **Visitor Information Center** is located in the Dairy (open Tue–Thu 11am–5pm, Fri 1–5pm, weekends 11am–5pm; closed holidays except Memorial Day & Labor Day; ☎794-6564), a restored Victorian Gothic structure located at 65th Street, between the zoo and the Carousel. Maps, a seasonal calendar of events and other materials may be obtained here as well as at the Belvedere Castle (same hours). For recorded information on events currently being held in the park ☎360-3456. To speak to a representative about park activities, call the Park's 24hr hotline ☎800/834-3832.

Central Park encompasses a zoo, skating rinks, tennis courts, various athletic fields and other recreational facilities. Guided walks and talks (90min) on the history, geology, wildlife and botany of the park are conducted regularly by Urban Park Rangers. For schedule and topics, consult the seasonal calendar of events or call ☎427-4040.

In summer the Parks Administration offers opera, symphony concerts and a variety of light entertainment. One of the great attractions, the annual "Shakespeare in the Park" festival, is held at the Delacorte Theater (Calendar of Events, *p 178*). In addition, one can boat on two lakes, swim in the large Lasker Pool near E. 106th Street, ride horseback on the 4.4mi of bridle paths, cycle on the several miles of bicycle paths, jog on the 1.5mi running track around the Reservoir, join lively roller skaters near the Mall or play quieter games at the Chess and Checker House. Bicycles can be rented at the Loeb Boathouse (Apr–Nov; $6/hr or $24/day; ☎861-4137). Horse rentals at Claremont Stables, 175 W. 89th St (daily from sunrise to 1hr before sunset; $33/hr; English riding experience required; for reservations ☎724-5100). Trolleys depart from the Central Park information kiosk at Fifth Ave and 60th St and stop at the Conservatory Garden, Glen Span Arch, Strawberry Fields and Bethesda Terrace (late-Apr–mid-Oct Mon–Fri 10:30am, 1 & 3pm; round-trip 90min; $14; commentary; advance ticket purchase ☎397-3809; recorded information ☎360-2727; ⚭). Park drives are closed to vehicular traffic during certain hours to permit safe cycling, jogging and walking.

Eating facilities include the Tavern on the Green (*p 90*); a cafeteria at the zoo, with outdoor tables; and a restaurant at the Loeb Boathouse (East Dr and 74th St), affording pleasant views over the lake.

Of particular interest for children are the zoo, a marionette theater, fishing and other recreational facilities. Natural history exhibits and children's programs are offered at the Central Park Learning Center (*see* Belvedere Castle *p 90*). Storytelling takes place in summer on fine Saturday mornings (11am), in front of the statue of Hans Christian Andersen, located near the statue of Alice in Wonderland, which tops a giant toadstool.

Horse-drawn carriages, a New York tradition, can be hired for a ride in Central Park, at the southeast corner near the Plaza Hotel (daily year-round unless temperatures are below 18°F or above 89°F 10am–4pm, 7pm–midnight; 1-4 passengers $34 for 20min, $10 every additional 15min; Chateau Stables ☎246-0520).

VISIT

Begin at Artist's Gate on Central Park South. ● any train to Columbus Circle/59th St or N, R train to 57th St.

Enter through the "Artist's Gate" across from Avenue of the Americas on Central Park South. A bronze equestrian statue (1919) of Simón Bolívar overlooks this entrance. Turn right, taking the path leading down to the crescent-shaped **pond**, surrounded by luxuriant vegetation. Continue around the pond to your right, past the bird sanctuary atop a rocky outcrop, and head northwest to the Wollman Memorial Rink, which is used for ice skating in the winter, and rollerblading and rollerskating in summer.

Turn eastward toward the zoo.

★ **Central Park Zoo/Wildlife Conservation Center.** – *Open Apr–Oct Mon–Fri 10am–5pm, weekends 10:30am–5:30pm. Rest of the year daily 10am–4:30pm. $2.50. 🍴⚭ ☎861-6030.* Occupying 5.5 acres, the zoo houses over 450 animals of 100 species in a newly renovated naturalistic habitat, which represents three distinct climatic regions: the tropical zone, the temperate regions and the polar circle.

On the Fifth Avenue side of the zoo stands a severe, massive building in gray stone and red brick. Built in the 1840s in the Gothic Revival style, the Arsenal of the State of New York now serves as the headquarters of the New York City Parks and Recreation Department.

Continue a short distance to the northwest to visit the Mall.

Conservatory Garden, Harlem Meer ↑

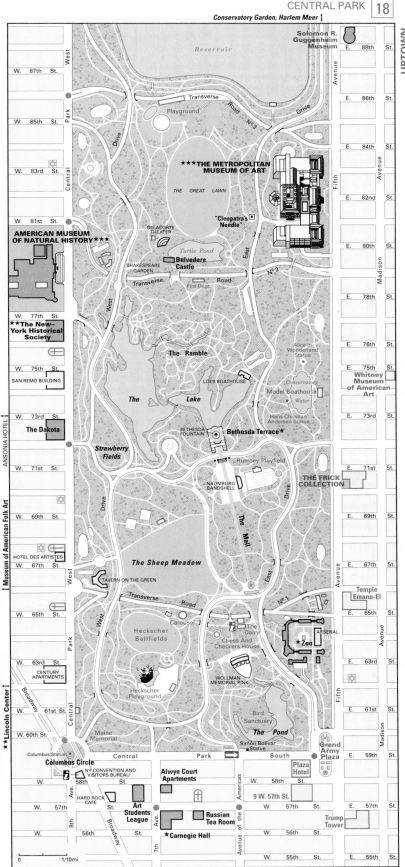

UPTOWN

Reservoir

Solomon R.
Guggenheim
Museum

W. 87th St.

West

E. 88th St.

Avenue

Transverse Road N° 3

Playground

E. 86th St.

Drive

Park

W. 85th St.

Drive

E. 84th St.

Central

W. 83rd St.

★★★THE METROPOLITAN
MUSEUM OF ART

Avenue

E. 82nd St.

THE GREAT LAWN

Fifth

W. 81st St.

"Cleopatra's
Needle"

AMERICAN MUSEUM
OF NATURAL HISTORY★★★

DELACORTE
THEATER

E. 80th St.

East

Turtle Pond

N° 2

SHAKESPEARE
GARDEN

Belvedere
Castle

E. 78th St.

W. 77th St.

Transverse Road

Fire Dept

★★The New-
York Historical
Society

E. 76th St.

Alice in
Wonderland
Statue

E. 75th St.

W. 75th St.

The Ramble

Whitney
Museum
of American
Art

SAN REMO BUILDING

LOEB BOATHOUSE

Conservatory

ANSONIA HOTEL

Model Boathouse

W. 73rd St.

The

Lake

Water

E. 73rd St.

The Dakota

Hans Christian
Andersen Statue

BETHESDA
FOUNTAIN

Bethesda Terrace ★

Strawberry
Fields

W. 71st St.

Rumsey Playfield

E. 71st St.

THE FRICK
COLLECTION

Museum of American Folk Art

NAUMBURG
BANDSHELL

Drive

W. 69th St.

E. 69th St.

The Mall

HOTEL DES ARTISTES

W. 67th St.

The Sheep Meadow

E. 67th St.

West

Temple
Emanu-El

Avenue

TAVERN ON THE GREEN

East

W. 65th St.

Transverse Road

E. 65th St.

Park

Carousel

Heckscher
Ballfields

The
Dairy

Avenue

W. 63rd St.

Chess And
Checkers House

ARSENAL

★ Zoo

E. 63rd St.

CENTURY
APARTMENTS

Broadway

Central

Heckscher
Playground

WOLLMAN
MEMORIAL RINK

Fifth

W. 61st St.

Madison

Lincoln Center ↑

Bird
Sanctuary

Maine
Memorial

The Pond

W. 60th St.

Simon Bolivar
Statue

Grand
Army
Plaza

E. 59th St.

Columbus Statue

Central

Park

South

Plaza
Hotel

Columbus Circle

NY CONVENTION AND
VISITORS BUREAU

Alwyn Court
Apartments

W. 58th St.

E. 58th St.

W. 58th St.

Ave.

Americas

9 W. 57th St.

HARD ROCK
CAFE

8th

Broadway

W. 57th St.

St.

Art
Students
League

Ave.

Russian
Tea Room

the

E. 57th St.

Trump
Tower

7th

W. 56th St.

of

W. 55th St.

★Carnegie Hall

Avenue

W. 55th St.

E. 55th St.

0   1/10mi

The Mall. – One of the few formal areas in the park, the Mall consists of a straight path lined with handsome elms and two rows of busts depicting famous writers. At the north end of the Mall is the small Naumburg Bandshell, once a popular concert site and now unused. Summer evening concerts are now performed at the Rumsey Playfield, east of the bandshell. (Occasional large public-benefit concerts and rallies take place on the Great Lawn, behind the Metropolitan Museum.) Lying to the west of the Mall, the **Sheep Meadow** attracts throngs of people to its rolling hills, which also offer superb views of the city skyline.

Located to the far west of the Sheep Meadow, near the West 66th Street entrance, stands the renowned restaurant, Tavern on the Green, housed in a former sheep's barn (1870).

From the Mall, take the steps down to Bethesda Terrace.

★ **Bethesda Terrace.** – Considered the centerpiece of the park, this lovely plaza resembles a Spanish courtyard with its arcaded bridge adorned with ornate friezes, sweeping stairs and central fountain. Crowning the fountain is a statue by Emma Stebbins, *Angel of the Waters* (1868).

The Lake. – Steps, banks and irregular shores make the lake seem almost transplanted from some far-off mountains. A graceful iron bridge located a short distance from Bethesda Fountain has been reproduced innumerable times in engravings and photographs. *Boats may be rented at the Loeb Boathouse located at the east end of the lake Mar–Oct daily 10am–6pm; $8 ($20 deposit); minimum age: 16; ☎517-3623.*

To the west lie the **Strawberry Fields** and the International Garden of Peace honoring the late Beatle, John Lennon. The 3-acre garden, containing 161 species of plants representing the 150 nations of the world, is steps away from New York's first luxury apartment house, the DAKOTA, where Lennon lived and was murdered.

Between the Lake and Fifth Avenue, Conservatory Pond is given over to young mariners. To the north of the lake, the **Ramble** is a heavily wooded hill with a number of hidden paths that seem to wind aimlessly and a meandering brook.

Continue up the Ramble to Belvedere Castle.

Belvedere Castle. – *Open mid-Feb–mid-Oct weekends & holidays Tue–Thu 11am–5pm, Fri 1–5pm. Rest of the year Tue–Thu 11am–4pm, Fri 1–4pm, Sat 11am–4pm. ☎772-0210.* Created by Vaux, this imitation medieval Scottish castle complete with merlons and crenels, serves as the Central Park Learning Center *(p 88)*. From its site atop Vista Rock, the Castle overlooks the entire northern part of the park, affording good views of the park and neighboring parts of the city. Just to the north are Turtle Pond, Delacorte Theater and the Shakespeare Garden, originally planned to include every species of flower, herb, tree and shrub mentioned in the works of the bard. Beyond lie the vast reaches of the Great Lawn, which contains several playing fields. It was built on the site of the Receiving Reservoir, dug in 1862 to supply the city water system.

From Belvedere Castle walk northeast toward the METROPOLITAN MUSEUM, whose massive silhouette appears through the trees. Just before reaching the museum, note **"Cleopatra's Needle,"** a 77ft pink granite Egyptian obelisk (16C BC) from Heliopolis, given to the City of New York in 1880 by the Khedive Ismael Pasha. The hieroglyphs, translated onto plaques, tell the story of Pharaoh Thotmes III (18th dynasty).

ADDITIONAL SIGHTS

The Conservatory Garden. – *Enter at E. 103rd St, opposite El Museo del Barrio.* Step into Central Park's only formal garden through the ornate wrought-iron Vanderbilt Gate, crafted in Paris for the VANDERBILT MANSION in 1894. Created in the 1930s, the garden gained enormous popularity, especially as a spot for weddings, and fell into disrepair during the 1970s. A 12-year restoration project gave it its present luster. Opposite the entrance is the Center Garden, a half-acre greensward flanked by two crab apple alleys and culminating in a wisteria pergola at the west end. The South Garden, known as "The Secret Garden" after Frances Hodgson Burnett's children classic, is graced by 175 varieties of perennials. The North Garden, a formal garden in the French style, features two dazzling floral displays each year.

Harlem Meer. – *E. 110th St at Fifth Ave.* Once a beautiful lake with coves and inlets, Harlem Meer (Dutch for "lake") was surrounded by a concrete rim in the 1940s and almost abandoned. In recent years, the 11-acre lake was dredged *(boats are available for rental).* As part of ongoing renovation efforts in the northern area of the park, a visitor and educational center, named Charles A. Dana Discovery Center, is being constructed near the lake *(for hours ☎794-6564).* The Lasker Pool and Skating Rink (1964) mark the lake's west end.

MUSEUM

★★★ **The Metropolitan Museum of Art.** – *See description p 120.*

There is no place like it [New York], no place with an atom of its glory, pride, and exultancy. It lays its hand upon a man's bowels; he grows drunk with ecstasy; he grows young and full of glory, he feels that he can never die.

Thomas Wolfe, *From Death to Morning*, 1935

UPTOWN

Time: 1/2 day. Map pp 92-93.

Known primarily as an enclave for the wealthy and fashionable, the area between CENTRAL PARK and the East River, stretching from 59th Street to 97th Street, actually represents a broad cross-section of New York neighborhoods. In the most desirable areas near the park, are located some of the city's great museums and an impressive concentration of galleries, along with elegant shops, restaurants, clubs and residences. East of Lexington Avenue, the atmosphere becomes more casual. Here, modern high-rises dominate, sharing space with a variety of delis, bars, pizza joints and parking garages.

Historical Notes. – Dotted with squatters' shanties and a few farms, the East Side remained largely rural until the 19C. One of the first sections to be developed was **Yorkville**, a hamlet just south of Harlem centering on present-day 86th Street, east of Lexington Avenue. Several prominent families of German descent, including the Schermerhorns, Astors and Rhinelanders, had built country estates here in the late 18C. Along with its **Carnegie Hill** neighbor to the west *(between 86th and 96th Sts, east of Fifth Ave)*, Yorkville soon became a suburb for middle-class Germans, many of whom worked in nearby piano factories and breweries.

New horsecar lines established on Madison, Third and Second Avenues in the 1860s spurred development south of 86th Street after the Civil War. By the 1880s, speculative builders had lined the streets with rows of brownstones. Churches, synagogues, armories and charitable institutions soon followed.

Attracted by large lots on and near Fifth Avenue, fashionable society also continued the migration uptown, gradually extending "Millionaire's Row" *(p 30)* northward with lavish mansions and club buildings. The boldest, Andrew Carnegie *(p 42)*, purchased land in the remote area of East 90th Street and Fifth Avenue in 1898. Other prominent financiers, including Otto Kahn, bought land from Carnegie north of 90th Street, while the haughty Mrs Astor *(p 30)*, the Goulds and Whitneys stopped farther down in the 60s and 70s.

In the 1920s, stylish apartment buildings replaced many of the town houses. Over the years, the posh East Side neighborhoods have continued to attract celebrities—Greta Garbo, Andy Warhol, Richard Nixon and Woody Allen among them—as well as old New York families and young Wall Streeters. Perhaps most changed is the Yorkville region, which has lost much of its old European flavor. Most of the area's German residents, along with Hungarians and Czechs who arrived in the mid-1900s, have been replaced by an influx of young urban professionals.

Note: the sights on the following avenues are described from south to north.

★★ FIFTH AVENUE

The section of Fifth Avenue bordering CENTRAL PARK has long been New York's most prestigious residential area. Luxury apartments abut with former mansions, most of which have now become museums, consulates, clubs or cultural institutions.

Surrounded by luxurious and distinguished hotels, **Grand Army Plaza★★**, a large and flowered square, marks the division between the Fifth Avenue *(p 30)* of luxury shopping and the residential section. Highlighting the plaza is the **Pulitzer Fountain** (1915) with its gracefully cascading waters. Just to the north, notice the statue of General Tecumseh Sherman on horseback (1903, Augustus Saint-Gaudens).

The **Plaza Hotel★** (1907), designed by **Henry J. Hardenbergh** in the French Renaissance style, is a New York institution of elegance and standing where coming-out parties and charity balls draw the cream of New York society. Nearly as celebrated as the Plaza, the Hotel Savoy stood across the square until 1966 when it was replaced by the General Motors Building *(p 36)*. Across 59th Street stands the Sherry-Netherland Hotel (1927), its graceful tower overlooking the park. The north corner of 60th Street is dominated by the Hotel Pierre (1930), the last of the grand hotels erected around the plaza.

At the corner with 62nd Street rises 810 Fifth Avenue, former home of such famous personalities as William Randolph Hearst, Richard Nixon and Nelson Rockefeller. On the south corner of 64th Street, note the Tuscan Renaissance mansion built in 1896 for the coal baron, Edward J. Berwind. On the same street, at 3 East 64th Street, is the **New India House**, headquarters of the Consulate of India and the Indian delegation to the United Nations. Built in 1903 by Warren and Wetmore (architects of GRAND CENTRAL TERMINAL) as a private residence for Mrs Astor's daughter, Carrie, its exterior features a lavish entranceway, tall second-story windows and a dormered mansard roof.

Located on the site of Mrs Astor's former mansion, **Temple Emanu-El★** *(1 E. 65th St)* was built in 1929 in the Byzantine Romanesque style. It is the leading Reform synagogue in New York and the largest in the US. The majestic nave, rising to 103ft, can welcome 2,500 worshippers. The ceiling, the marble columns in low relief and the great arch covered with mosaics are reminiscent of the basilicas of the Near East. The sanctuary harbors the tabernacle, or Holy Ark, which contains the Torah scrolls *(open Mon–Thu 10am–5pm; Fri 10am–4pm; Sat 12:30–5pm; Sun 10am–5pm; closed Jewish holidays)*.

Occupying the block between 70th and 71st Streets, Henry C. Frick's former mansion *(p 115)*, surrounded by terraced flower beds, now houses a world-class collection of Old Masters.

At the corner with 75th Street, an attractive wrought-iron fence protects **Harkness House** (1900), an Italian-style palace built for Edward S. Harkness, son of a partner of John D. Rockefeller *(p 37)*. Today Harkness House serves as headquarters of the Commonwealth Fund, a philanthropic foundation.

UPTOWN

The renowned **New York University Institute of Fine Arts** *(1 E. 78th St)*, a division of NEW YORK UNIVERSITY, is located in the James B. Duke House (1912), built for one of the founders of the American Tobacco Company. Architect Horace Trumbauer's Classical Revival design for the house was modeled after a Louis XV-style chateau in Bordeaux. Duke's wife donated the splendid mansion to NYU in 1957. The institute offers courses in art, architecture, conservation and museum training to graduate students.

The cultural and press services of the French Embassy are housed in the former Payne Whitney home *(no. 972)*, designed by McKim, Mead and White in 1906. The turreted mansion on the southeast corner of 79th Street, the former Stuyvesant Fish House, now serves as the home of the **Ukrainian Institute of America**.

On the northeast corner of 80th Street is one of the first and most luxurious apartment houses erected on Fifth Avenue—no. 998. Completed in 1914 by McKim, Mead and White, the Renaissance-style building attracted a wealthy clientele and inspired the creation of countless similar structures on Fifth, Madison and Park Avenues. Dominating the Central Park side of Fifth Avenue between 80th and 84th Streets is the imposing facade of the Metropolitan Museum of Art *(p 120)*.

The brick and stone mansion at the southeast corner of 86th Street, houses the headquarters of the **Yivo Institute for Jewish Research**, whose holdings encompass a comprehensive collection of Yiddish manuscripts and letters dating back to the 17C *(open Mon 9:30am–8:30pm; Tue–Thu 9:30am–5:30pm; ☎535-6700)*.

The section of Fifth Avenue between 70th and 103rd Streets is known as "Museum Mile" *(see p 94 for listing)*.

★ MADISON AVENUE

Lined with exclusive stores, galleries and haute couture boutiques, this is a street for moneyed shoppers, where the pedestrians often look as chic as the window displays. Most of the small designer boutiques are concentrated south of 79th Street, but the stretch north to 96th Street, with its neighborhood bookstores, shops and trendy bistros, also has great appeal.

Many of the fine brownstones that made the avenue a choice residential district in the late 19C remain, now remodeled with stylish storefronts at street level. Several early prestigious apartment buildings and apartment hotels, including 45 East 65th Street and the 1929 **Carlyle Hotel** *(35 E. 76th St)*, also enhance the street's genteel character. Note also the 1895 Gertrude Rhinelander Waldo house *(no. 867)*, modeled after a French Renaissance chateau for an eccentric dowager who never occupied the mansion.

The rich and famous not only come to Madison to shop, but some—including Tennessee Williams, Judy Garland, John Lennon and Arturo Toscanini—have even passed on to their next lives by way of the prestigious Frank E. Campbell Funeral Chapel, located at 81st Street. Also on Madison Avenue *(no. 945)* is the renowned Whitney Museum of American Art *(p 146)*.

★ PARK AVENUE

A meticulously landscaped mall and dignified apartment houses define this European-style boulevard, originally called Fourth Avenue. Although the two-way street is now a highly coveted address, the first occupants were not society members, but hospitals and educational institutions that took advantage of the inexpensive land adjacent to the

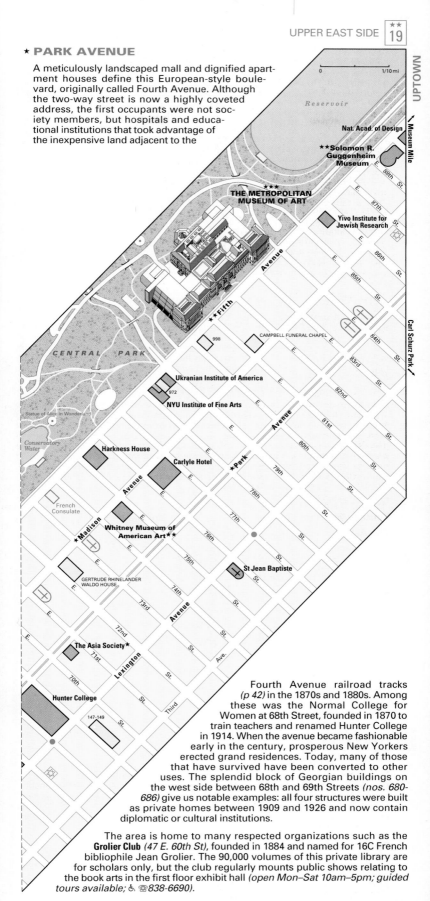

UPTOWN

Reservoir

Nat. Acad. of Design

★★Solomon R. Guggenheim Museum

Museum Mile

Carl Schurz Park

★★★ THE METROPOLITAN MUSEUM OF ART

Yivo Institute for Jewish Research

★★ Fifth Avenue

CAMPBELL FUNERAL CHAPEL

998

CENTRAL   PARK

Ukranian Institute of America

972

NYU Institute of Fine Arts

Statue of Alice in Wonderland

Conservatory Water

Harkness House

Carlyle Hotel

★ Park Avenue

French Consulate

★ Madison Avenue

Whitney Museum of American Art ★★

St Jean Baptiste

GERTRUDE RHINELANDER WALDO HOUSE

The Asia Society ★

Lexington Avenue

Hunter College

147-149

Third Ave.

Fourth Avenue railroad tracks *(p 42)* in the 1870s and 1880s. Among these was the Normal College for Women at 68th Street, founded in 1870 to train teachers and renamed Hunter College in 1914. When the avenue became fashionable early in the century, prosperous New Yorkers erected grand residences. Today, many of those that have survived have been converted to other uses. The splendid block of Georgian buildings on the west side between 68th and 69th Streets *(nos. 680-686)* give us notable examples: all four structures were built as private homes between 1909 and 1926 and now contain diplomatic or cultural institutions.

The area is home to many respected organizations such as the **Grolier Club** *(47 E. 60th St)*, founded in 1884 and named for 16C French bibliophile Jean Grolier. The 90,000 volumes of this private library are for scholars only, but the club regularly mounts public shows relating to the book arts in the first floor exhibit hall *(open Mon–Sat 10am–5pm; guided tours available; &. ☎838-6690).*

UPTOWN

Designed by Charles W. Clinton, the monumental fortress occupying the block between 66th and 67th Streets houses the **Seventh Regiment Armory** (1877), headquarters of the New York National Guard. Many of the original Victorian fixtures and furnishings still found in the vast entry and in the regimental and company rooms include works by such prominent designers as Louis Comfort Tiffany and Stanford White *(open by appointment only, Mon–Fri 8am–4pm;* ♿ ☏ *744-2968).*

LEXINGTON AVENUE

With its mix of apartment houses, brownstones, coffee shops and bookstores, this busy thoroughfare has a neighborhood feel and a pleasant scale unbroken by high-rise buildings. A famous landmark is the Art Deco-style **Bloomingdale's** department store at 59th Street. Here, high fashion not only applies to clothes, but to all of the merchandise, from designer bonbons to trendy shower curtains.

Located at no. 869, the **Church of St Vincent Ferrer** *(open daily 7am–7pm;* ♿*),* designed by Bertram Goodhue and completed in 1918 for the Dominican order, features a lovely rose window dominating the granite facade adorned with carvings by Lee Lawrie. Note also the 1880 Victorian Gothic priory just to the south.

East of Lexington, at 147-149 East 69th Street, stands a charming group of late 19C carriage houses that originally served fashionable town houses closer to the park. At East 76th Street and Lexington rises the imposing Roman Catholic **St Jean Baptiste Church** *(open Mon–Fri 7:30am–7pm; weekends 9am–8pm),* founded by French Canadians in 1913. The gold-leafed interior contains a handsome altar and a French-style organ.

ADDITIONAL SIGHTS

Islamic Cultural Center of New York. – *1711 Third Ave at 96th St. Open Sun–Fri 9am–5pm.* ♿ ☏ *722-5234. Women are requested to cover their heads with a scarf and wear long sleeves.* Completed in 1991 from designs by Skidmore, Owings & Merrill, this pink marble center for Muslim worship is the first major mosque built in New York City. The 2-story domed prayer hall, where light streams through a curtain wall of windows distinguished with Eastern motifs, is particularly stunning. Designed to serve the city's 400,000 Muslims, the mosque is flanked by a 12-story minaret, from which the faithful are called to prayer.

Carl Schurz Park. – *Located along East End Ave from 84th to 90th Sts.* This appealing sliver of green, completed in 1891 and remodeled in 1938, stretches along East End Avenue, capturing fine East River views from the promenade. It is named for a famous 19C German immigrant who served as US senator and as secretary of the Interior under President Hayes, and who lived nearby in Yorkville *(p 91).* At the northern end stands GRACIE MANSION, official residence of New York's mayor. Fronting the park across East End Avenue at 86th Street is the **Henderson Place Historic District**, comprising 24 turreted houses (1881) designed in the Queen Anne style.

MUSEUMS

★★ **Whitney Museum of American Art.** – *See description p 146.*

★ **The Asia Society.** – *See description p 113.*

Fifth Avenue between 70th and 103rd Streets is known as "Museum Mile":

★★★ **The Frick Collection.** – *See description p 115.*

★★★ **The Metropolitan Museum of Art.** – *See description p 120.*

★★ **Solomon R. Guggenheim Museum.** – *See description p 117.*

★★ **Museum of the City of New York.** – *See description p 140.*

★ **Cooper-Hewitt National Museum of Design.** – *See description p 114.*

★ **International Center for Photography.** – *See description p 118.*

★ **The Jewish Museum.** – *See description p 119.*

El Museo del Barrio. – *See description p 114.*

National Academy of Design. – *See description p 144.*

UPPER WEST SIDE

Time: 1 1/2 days. Maps p 89 and p 97.

This ethnically diverse area reaching northward from Columbus Circle between the Hudson River and CENTRAL PARK is home to many of the city's great cultural institutions, including Lincoln Center, Columbia University and the American Museum of Natural History. Relatively free of modern high-rise development, it also boasts numerous historic districts and some of the most harmonious blocks of row house architecture in Manhattan.

From Wasteland to Wealth. – In the late 19C, development reached the rural area of Bloomingdale, dotted with shantytowns and saloons and populated by stray goats, when New York's first luxury apartment house was erected on West 72nd Street and Central Park West in 1884. Even then, the building was considered to be so far out west in the middle of nowhere that it was dubbed the "Dakota" *(p 95).*

From the late 1880s onward, middle-class tenements and flats began to appear along Amsterdam and Columbus Avenues, with stylish row houses lining the cross streets. In the 1890s, the area also gained numerous studio buildings designed specifically for artists, along with another late 19C innovation: **apartment hotels.** These featured fancy suites with parlors, dining rooms, bedrooms and baths, but no kitchens; residents brought meals up from a main kitchen via a dumbwaiter, or ate downstairs in the main dining room.

The fine residences of the West Side were home to bankers, lawyers and other well-to-do professionals, and, after the 1930s, to prosperous Jewish families from the LOWER EAST SIDE. In the 1960s, low rents in the old tenement buildings attracted an element of bohemia, while urban renewal projects brought further diversity to the area. Recent gentrification of the older row houses has made the cross streets quite desirable, particularly among young professionals drawn to the area by the friendly neighborhoods.

The tree-lined residential blocks make a quiet contrast to the bustle of Broadway, the area's commercial spine, which features everything from discount shoe stores to the famous food shop, Zabar's *(at W. 80th St)*—along with some of the most popular restaurants in town.

Famous Buildings and Famous Residents. – *Map p 89.* Some of New York's best-known apartment buildings are found on the West Side and have long attracted a famous clientele. At 1 West 72nd Street stands the 1884 **Dakota**, whose ornate finials and Gothic gables made it a suitable setting for the film, *Rosemary's Baby* (1968, Roman Polanski). The work of Henry Hardenbergh, who also created the PLAZA HOTEL, it contains apartments with as many as 20 rooms. Past and present residents include Leonard Bernstein, Lauren Bacall and John Lennon, who was killed just outside the 72nd Street entrance in 1980.

Dominating the Central Park West skyline are the twin-towered 1931 Century Apartments *(no. 25)*, a superb Art Deco design by Irwin Chanin *(p 46)*, and the elegant San Remo *(nos. 145-146)*, home to Dustin Hoffman, Paul Simon and Diane Keaton. Featuring one of the first drive-in courtyards in the city, the ornate 1904 Ansonia Hotel *(2101-2119 Broadway)* was a fashionable apartment hotel that attracted residents such as Babe Ruth and Arturo Toscanini. Norman Rockwell, Rudolf Valentino and Noel Coward, in turn, all lived at the popular Hotel des Artistes *(1 W. 67th St)*, erected in 1907, designed with duplex studio spaces lit by huge 2-story windows.

COLUMBUS CIRCLE *Map p 89*

The focal point of this busy traffic circle is the 1894 statue of Christopher Columbus. Three bronze ships' prows represent his famous fleet: the *Niña*, the *Pinta* and the *Santa Maria*. At the entrance to Central Park is the Maine Memorial, dedicated to the 260 men who lost their lives when the battleship Maine was destroyed in Havana Harbor in 1898.

The building on the south side of Columbus Circle houses the New York Convention and Visitors Bureau *(open Mon–Fri 9am–6pm; weekends & holidays 10am–6pm; ☎397-8222)* and the City of New York Department of Cultural Affairs.

COLUMBUS AND AMSTERDAM AVENUES

Both of these thoroughfares have enjoyed a renaissance as lively districts for shops and night spots, in particular on the stretches below 86th Street. As young singles moved to the Upper West Side in the 1970s, Columbus Avenue, once lined with local hardware stores, laundries and markets, became almost overnight the site of dozens of specialty shops and sidewalk cafes. In the past few years, Amsterdam Avenue has followed suit and is now the setting for several popular bars, coffee houses and bistros.

★★ LINCOLN CENTER

On Broadway between W. 62nd and 67th Sts.

Devoted to drama, music and dance, Lincoln Center for the Performing Arts is a 16-acre complex comprising five major theater and concert buildings, a library, a bandshell and two outdoor plazas.

The idea for such a grand cultural center, where operas, ballets, plays and concerts could take place simultaneously, originated in 1955, and two years later the city bought the necessary land in what was then a rundown neighborhood (the setting for the film *West Side Story*). Despite considerable controversy—the new complex caused the demolition of 188 buildings, forcing some 1,600 residents to relocate—the project proceeded, with John D. Rockefeller III chairing the building committee. A board of architects headed by Wallace K. Harrison, who had helped design the UNITED NATIONS and ROCKEFELLER CENTER, went to work, analyzing some 60 theater designs in 20 countries.

Construction finally began in 1959 with Avery Fisher Hall, and continued over the next ten years, ending with the Juilliard School. Private contributions largely accounted for the total budget (about $350 million). In 1991, the Samuel B. and David Rose Building, a multi-purpose structure, was added to the complex, to the northwest of the Juilliard School. The sleek rectangular buildings of glass and Italian travertine marble can accommodate 13,666 spectators at a time.

Visit. – *Visit by guided tour (1hr) only, daily 10am–5pm. No tours Jan 1, Thanksgiving Day & Dec 25. Visit includes Metropolitan Opera House, the New York State Theater & Avery Fisher Hall. $7.75. 24hrs advance reservation advised. Tours leave from the concourse level under the Metropolitan Opera House. ♿ ☎875-5350.*

Lincoln Center Information Hotline ☎875-5400. For ticket information on performances *see p 185.* *Free performances are held outdoors in the summer.*

Metropolitan Opera House, Lincoln Center

Metropolitan Opera House. – *Backstage tours (90min) with reservation only, mid-Oct–mid-Jun Mon–Fri 3:45pm, Sat 10am. $7. ♿ ☎769-7020 Mon–Fri 10am–4pm.* Distinguished by a 10-story colonnade, this opera house, which opened in 1966 with Samuel Barber's *Anthony and Cleopatra*, forms the centerpiece of the main plaza. Designed by Wallace K. Harrison with seating for 3,788 persons, it replaced the celebrated "Met" at Broadway and 39th Street, closed in April 1966 and later demolished. The building hosts both the Metropolitan Opera and the American Ballet Theater, and contains seven rehearsal halls and storage space for 15 opera sets. In the lobby hang large murals by Chagall, the *Sources of Music* and *The Triumph of Music*. The double staircase carpeted in red is accentuated by crystal chandeliers, donated by Austria.

Avery Fisher Hall. – Originally called Philharmonic Hall, this concert hall, designed by Max Abramovitz and set to the right of the main plaza, was renamed in 1973 in recognition of a gift from Avery Fisher, the founder of Fisher Radio. The 2,742-seat auditorium is home to the New York Philharmonic, the country's oldest orchestra, which previously played at CARNEGIE HALL.

New York State Theater. – Designed by Philip Johnson, this theater is home to the New York City Opera and the New York City Ballet. The City Center of Music and Drama, which oversees the two companies, operates the theater, owned by the City of New York. Completed in 1964, it seats 2,792 spectators.

The Lincoln Center complex also includes the Guggenheim Bandshell (in Damrosch Park, behind the Opera House to the south), the site of free concerts. Behind the Opera House to the north is the New York Public Library at Lincoln Center *(open Mon noon–8pm, Wed–Sat noon–6pm. Closed holidays. ♿ ☎870-1630)*. This building (1965; Skidmore, Owings & Merrill) houses an extensive music library, a museum of the performing arts and a 200-seat auditorium. Two small stages are located in the Vivian Beaumont Theater and Mitzi E. Newhouse Theater, built according to plans by Eero Saarinen. These are home to the Lincoln Center Theater Company, which opened in 1980. A footbridge leads across West 66th Street to the Juilliard Building (1968; Pietro Belluschi, Catalano and Westerman). The building contains the Juilliard School (for musicians, actors and dancers) and Alice Tully Hall, used by the Chamber Music Society of Lincoln Center. The New York Film Festival is also held here every fall.

★★ CATHEDRAL OF ST JOHN THE DIVINE *Map p 97*

On Amsterdam Ave at W. 112th St. Open daily 7am–5pm (Sun 8:30pm). Guided tour (45min) Tue–Sat 11am, Sun 1pm. ♿.

The seat of the Episcopal Diocese of New York, this is reputedly the largest cathedral in the world built in the Gothic style. The massive stone edifice—begun in 1892 and still under construction—can welcome up to 8,000 worshippers at a time and is also the setting for frequent dance, music, film and drama performances, many of them free. The 13-acre area on Broadway between Cathedral Parkway and West 113th Street contains seven ancillary buildings, gardens, a park and a stone-cutting yard.

A Challenging Task. – Although the idea for a monumental cathedral in the city dates back to 1828, the building was not conceived until 1872, when Horatio Potter, then Bishop of New York, presented a proposal to the diocesan convention. After several delays, the Bishop's nephew and successor, Henry Potter, settled on this site in Morningside Heights *(western fringe of Manhattan between Cathedral Pkwy and 125th St)*, and construction began in 1892. From the start, excavation and structural problems plagued the builders. Twenty-five years into the project, the original 1888 Romanesque design by Heins and LaFarge was scrapped for a revised plan in the Gothic style by Ralph Adams Cram. The choir and sanctuary were completed in 1916 and construction of the nave began in 1925. Another century is needed to finish the towers, central spire, transepts and portal carvings and limestone interior facing, along with a planned chapter house, sacristy building and Greek amphitheater. A crew of apprentice stoneworkers, many of them neighborhood youths, is currently on the job, training under a master mason.

Visit. – Two square Gothic towers (to reach 266ft when completed) flank the symmetrical west facade, where the central Portal of Paradise features a double set of bronze doors bearing scenes from the Old *(left doors)* and New *(right doors)* Testaments. The doors, each weighing three tons, were produced in Paris by Ferdinand Barbedienne, who also cast the STATUE OF LIBERTY. Between the doors is the carved figure of St John the Divine surmounted by a tympanum adorned with a Christ in Glory.

The portals open into the narthex, or vestibule, where striking stained-glass windows from the studio of Ernest W. Lakeman represent the Creation *(on the left)* and scenes from the Old Testament *(on the right)*. Note also the Greek icons and 15C paintings of the Virgin and Child.

The majestic nave measures 248ft long and is as wide as 112th Street. Along the flanking side aisles are 14 bays honoring as many prominent institutions, in the fields of education, art, medicine and religion. The aisles are also the setting for a group of 17C tapestries depicting the Acts of the Apostles, woven in Mortlake, England, after cartoons painted by Raphael in 1513.

The 100ft-wide crossing, a holdover from the original Heins and LaFarge design, features a second set of 17C tapestries, woven on papal looms founded by Cardinal Barberini in Rome; these scenes are from the New Testament. The crossing offers an excellent view back to the great rose window in the narthex, which was made by the Connick studios in the 1920s and contains 10,000 pieces of glass.

A semi-circle of eight granite columns (each weighing 130 tons) encloses the sanctuary, containing the great choir and the high altar. Niches in the marble historical parapet fronting the altar hold statues of notable figures, including St Paul, Lincoln and Washington; a stone block representing the 20C still remains to be carved.

The apse aisle, or ambulatory, contains seven chapels and, on the south side, displays several paintings of the 16C Italian school, a glazed terra-cotta Annunciation (15C, Della Robbia school) and a 16C silk-embroidered cloth, representing the Adoration of the Magi.

The domed baptistery, located to the north of the choir, is decorated with eight niches holding figures associated with the early history of Nieuw Amsterdam, including Peter Stuyvesant *(p 74)*, depicted

with his wooden leg. In the gift shop, located in the north transept, you will find a model of the completed cathedral. Just outside is the stone yard, where apprentice masons are sometimes at work.

To the east of the south transept lies a small Biblical Garden, planted with flora mentioned in the Bible. The distinctive Peace Fountain [1], which celebrates the triumph of good over evil, is by Greg Wyatt, artist-in-residence at the cathedral. It dominates the Children's Sculpture Garden to the south, where animal sculptures by the city's youths have been cast in bronze.

★ **RIVERSIDE CHURCH** *Map above*
On Riverside Dr between W. 120th and 122nd Sts. If west portal is closed, use entrance on Claremont St. Open daily 7am–10pm, holidays 9am–4pm. Guided tour (1hr) Sun 12:30pm. ⅃.

With its soaring 400ft tower—containing the largest carillon in the world—this streamlined Gothic Revival building is a dominant West Side landmark. It is also an important community center offering a broad range of social services and cultural programs.

Founded before 1850 as a small Baptist congregation in the LOWER EAST SIDE, the church is associated with the American Baptist Churches and the United Church of Christ; interdenominational and interracial, it is perhaps best known for its liberal stance on social issues. John D. Rockefeller, Jr helped fund the present 1927 building of limestone, designed by Allen and Collens and Henry C. Pelton (the south wing was added in 1960).

The magnificent west portal faces Riverside Drive and recalls the sculptures at Chartres Cathedral, in France. Prophets from the Old Testament are carved into the columns on the left, with New Testament figures on the right. The tympanum above features a Christ in Glory and symbols of the Four Evangelists.

In the narthex you will see two striking **stained-glass windows** depicting the Life of Christ, made in the 16C for the Cathedral of Bruges, in Belgium. From the narthex, enter the nave, which is 100ft high and 215ft long, with space for 2,500 worshippers. The clerestory windows are modeled after those at Chartres, while the chancel screen is notable for 80 panels depicting figures whose lives embodied Christian ideals—among them Luther, Milton, Lincoln and Pasteur.

A passage from the narthex leads to a small, very lovely **Romanesque-style chapel**. You may visit the observation deck *(Sun 12:30–4pm; $1)* by taking an elevator to the 20th floor. Ascending the final 147 steps, you will pass by the chambers of the 74-bell carillon. A stunning 360° **panorama**★★ from the summit encompasses Riverside Park *(p 99)*, the Hudson River, New Jersey shore, CENTRAL PARK, STATUE OF LIBERTY and GEORGE WASHINGTON BRIDGE.

★ GENERAL GRANT NATIONAL MEMORIAL
On Riverside Dr at W. 122nd St. Open Wed–Sun 9am–5pm. Closed Wed after holidays. Guided tours (30min) available. ☎666-1640.

Popularly known as Grant's Tomb, this classically inspired monument is the final resting place of Ulysses Simpson Grant (1822-1885) and his wife, Julia Dent Grant (1826-1902). Grant was commander of the Union Army during the Civil War and president of the US from 1869 to 1877.

The white granite mausoleum, crowned by a stepped cone, was designed in 1890 by John H. Duncan and took six years to build. The tablet above the Doric portico bears the words "Let us have peace," part of Grant's written reply to the Republican Party in 1868, in which he accepted his nomination as presidential candidate. Gold-tinted clerestory windows create a soft glow in the marble interior, which recalls Napoleon's tomb at the Invalides in Paris. A dramatic coffered dome is suspended directly over the sunken crypt, where niches contain busts of Grant's comrades-in-arms: Sherman, Sheridan, Thomas, Ord and McPherson. Two small rooms display photographs illustrating Grant's life and achievements.

The free-form mosaic benches flanking the tomb outside were designed by Pedro Silva in the early 1970s and created as part of a community project to involve neighborhood youths with the monument.

★ COLUMBIA UNIVERSITY *Map p 97*
W. 114th to 120th Sts, between Amsterdam Ave and Broadway. Main entrance at W. 116th St.

The first college in New York and the fifth oldest in the nation, Columbia is one of the country's wealthiest and largest private Ivy League universities, with almost 20,000 students. The main, Morningside Heights campus occupies 36 acres.

From King's College to Columbia University. – Founded in 1754 by charter from George II, King's College was first located in lower Manhattan, where the original class of eight men met in the schoolhouse of TRINITY CHURCH. Among the early graduates of King's College were Alexander Hamilton, aide-de-camp to General Washington and later secretary of the Treasury, and John Jay, first chief justice of the US.

After the Revolution, the school reopened in 1784 under a new name—Columbia College. In 1897, it moved to the present site after 40 years at Madison Avenue and East 49th Street. It was during the 20C that the university earned its reputation for excellence, claiming among its noted administrators Dwight D. Eisenhower, who served as Columbia president from 1948 to 1953, when he left to become president of the US.

Today, the coeducational university has an endowment of $1.7 billion and boasts 71 academic departments and some 5,700 faculty. Of the 15 schools, it is particularly renowned for the Law, Architecture, Journalism and Medical Schools; Teachers College; and the School of International and Public Affairs. The two undergraduate divisions are Columbia College (co-ed since 1983) and Barnard College, an affiliated liberal arts school for women founded in 1889. The Barnard campus is located on the west side of Broadway between 116th and 120th Streets.

Visit. – Visitors may stroll around the campus at their leisure. Free guided tours (1hr) enabling visitors to see the interior of many of the buildings Mon–Fri. Reservations required. ♿ ☎854-2845.

Campus. – Located on the site of the former Bloomingdale Insane Asylum, Columbia's campus has a formal, axial arrangement typical of the turn-of-the-century Beaux-Arts movement. Charles McKim envisioned Low Memorial Library as the focus of his 1894 design, which encompasses the area north of 116th Street. Added in 1934, Butler Library faces Low Library across a majestic mall, while handsome limestone and brick classroom buildings define the quadrangles. The university began expanding outside the old campus in the early 20C, adding the 1926 Casa Italiana by McKim, Mead and White, and the more recent Law School Building and School of International and Public Affairs, all on Amsterdam Avenue.

★ **Low Memorial Library.** – The gift of Seth Low, president of Columbia from 1890 to 1901, this elegant neoclassical building (1894-1898) was the first major structure on the campus. Designer Charles McKim modeled the library on the Roman Pantheon. Since 1934, the building has served as an administrative center and exhibit hall. Step inside to view the magnificent marble rotunda, with its 130ft dome and 16 colossal columns.

Temple Hoyne Buell Hall. – The only building remaining from the former Bloomingdale Insane Asylum, this 1878 edifice is the oldest structure on campus and now serves as a center for the study of American architecture. Frequent exhibits are mounted in the first-floor galleries *(open to the public).*

★ **St Paul's Chapel.** – This elegant structure (1907), a Northern Italian Renaissance design by Howells & Stokes, features a beautiful vaulted interior, with salmon-colored Guastavino tiling and striking cast-iron chandeliers. The carved pulpit, choir stalls, and organ front recall those in the Church of Santa Croce in Florence, Italy. Owing to the chapel's excellent acoustics, many concerts are held here.

Schapiro Research Center. – Completed in 1992 for $62 million, this classically inspired building was designed by Hellmuth, Obata and Kassabaum and contains state-of-the-art laboratories for computer and telecommunications research. A glass-enclosed skyway connects it to the 1927 Pupin Physics Laboratories, where Columbia professor Harold C. Urey discovered heavy water in 1934. The Manhattan Project, which pioneered the development of atomic energy in the US, was founded in the Pupin lab.

Outdoor Sculpture. – A number of sculptures by European and American artists also distinguish the campus. Fronting Low Library is the regal *Alma Mater* [2]; designed by Daniel Chester French in 1903, the classical bronze figure, emblem of the university, survived a bombing during the 1968 student riots. Admire Rodin's famous bronze, *The Thinker*, cast from the 1880 model in 1930, in front of Philosophy Hall *(east of Low Library)*; and the *Great God Pan* (1899) by George Grey Barnard, originally intended for the DAKOTA *(west of Low Library)*. Modern works include *Bellerophon Taming Pegasus* [3] by Jacques Lipchitz (1967), mounted over the entrance to the Law School; *Tightrope Walker* (1979) by Kees Verkade and *Three Way Piece: Points* (1967) by Henry Moore, both on the Amsterdam Avenue overpass; and *Curl* (1968) by Clement Meadmore, fronting the Business School *(Uris Hall, behind Low Library).*

★ **RIVERSIDE PARK AND DRIVE** *Map p 97*

Designed as a single entity in 1875 by Frederick Law Olmsted (creator of CENTRAL PARK), Riverside Drive and Park take advantage of the beautiful views and sloping topography along the Hudson River. The traditional home of artists and musicians, the curving drive is complete with majestic elms, walkways and scenic overlooks, boasting fine 19C row houses, turn-of-the-century mansions and elegant early-20C apartment buildings. The park, in turn, extending from West 72nd to 155th Streets, contains some of the city's most important monuments *(recommended area: below 100th St).* These include Grant's Tomb *(p 98)*; the 1902 Soldiers' and Sailors' Monument at West 89th Street, dedicated to Civil War veterans; the Joan of Arc Statue at West 93rd Street; and the Firemen's Memorial at West 100th Street. The 91st Street garden, a beautiful English garden maintained by local residents, is also noteworthy. Together, the park and drive are a designated New York City Historic Landmark.

MUSEUMS

★★★ **American Museum of Natural History.** – *See description p 111.*

★★ **The New-York Historical Society.** – *See description p 144.*

HARLEM

Time: 1/2 day. Map p 2.

Embracing most of northern Manhattan, above 125th Street and St Nicholas Avenue on the West Side and above 110th Street on the East Side, Harlem is home to a sizable segment of New York's black and Hispanic communities. This multi-faceted "city within a city," with its broad boulevards, brownstones, tenements, bodegas and bargain stores, was world-famous in the 1920s as a center for black arts and culture. Although it is better known today for the poverty, drug problems and social unrest that have afflicted the area in the last half century, Harlem encompasses some outstanding architecture, several landmark historic districts and renowned churches and institutions.

Historical Notes. – Dutch farmers founded Nieuw Haarlem in 1658, establishing numerous farms and country estates in this largely rural area. Residential development began after 1837, when the New York and Harlem Railroad connected the neighborhood to downtown Manhattan. By the 1880s, working-class immigrants were pouring into new tenement buildings east of the train tracks running along Park Avenue (then known as Fourth Avenue). Western Harlem, by contrast, became a fashionable middle-class white suburb, with fine row houses and apartment buildings, an opera and a symphony.

At the turn of the century, however, the bottom fell out of the real estate market. As speculators went bust, a black realtor named Philip Payton bought up 5-year leases very inexpensively, turning them over to hundreds of black families whose houses in the West 30s section of midtown Manhattan were being condemned to make way for Pennsylvania Station and its tunnels. This was the first time decent housing was available to blacks in the city, and by 1914, more than 50,000 families had arrived in Harlem— while as many whites had left for northern suburbs.

Harlem experienced its heyday in the 1920s: as bootleg liquor flowed, popular night spots including the original Cotton Club on Lenox Avenue drew nightly crowds (some white-only) with jazz greats like Duke Ellington, Count Basie and Cab Calloway. The area also provided a serious cultural forum for emerging writers (Langston Hughes) and artists, and a haven for prosperous middle-class black families. This era, dubbed the Harlem Renaissance, came to an end with the Depression, however. While a wave of new-comers from the American South and the Caribbean solidi-

Duke Ellington (1899-1974)

fied the black community after World War II, few jobs were waiting. Artists gravitated to GREENWICH VILLAGE and by the 1960s, Harlem's celebrities were more likely to be civil rights activists like Malcolm X, who worked with the Black Muslims Temple of Islam at 116th Street and Lenox Avenue. In 1965 he was assassinated at the Audubon Ballroom on West 166th Street. More recently, Harlem has been the home of prominent public officials, including the city's first black mayor, David Dinkins.

Hard hit by inflation, rent control and vandalism, some Harlem landlords simply abandoned their buildings or torched them for insurance money, leaving behind a bleak landscape of rubble-strewn lots and public housing projects. Recovery is slow, but the city, acquiring thousands of buildings for non-payment of taxes, has initiated several rehabilitation programs in recent years, including the 1992 renovation of the 19C Astor Row houses at 8-62 West 130th Street. Other historic districts also recall Harlem's glory days, including Hamilton Heights *(p 101)*, AUDUBON TERRACE, Mount Morris Park and the elegant brick houses on West 139th Street known as **Strivers Row**. (The Strivers refer to the prominent middle-class blacks who moved in during the 1920s.)

Today, as in the past, Harlem has a distinct, two-part character. East of Fifth Avenue is Spanish Harlem, or "El Barrio," primarily a Puerto Rican enclave; to the west, north of St Nicholas Avenue and 125th Street, is central Harlem, where some 200,000 of the city's 1.7 million blacks live (the largest black population is concentrated in the Bedford-Stuyvesant area of Brooklyn). The main commercial arteries are lively, particularly Luis Muñoz Marin Street *(116th St)* and Martin Luther King Jr Boulevard *(125th St)*, where Senegalese vendors offer Kente cloth, wood carvings and jewelry. The **Apollo Theatre** *(253 W. 125th St)*, famous for its all-black revues of the 1930s, hosts varied shows, including Wednesday's Amateur Night, which still draws would-be stars to the stage.

VISIT

Although many parts of Harlem are safe, visitors can feel unwelcome at times, and it is advisable to limit your visit to daylight hours. Harlem Spirituals, Inc offers the following guided tours: visit of Harlem including soul food lunch (Thu 9am–1:30pm; $37); evening visit of Harlem including soul food & jazz (Mon, Thu, Fri, Sat 7pm–midnight; $65); Sunday Gospel & visit of Harlem (9am–12:30pm; $29) with brunch ($52); mid-week Gospel & visit of Harlem (Wed 9am–12:45pm; $32). Reservations required ☎757-0425. Tickets available at departure point for tours, 1697 Broadway, Suite 203. Once you are familiar with the area, you may want to return and explore on your own. Harlem is accessible by taxi, bus and subway (● any train to 125th St).

The Schomburg Center for Research in Black Culture. – *515 Malcolm X Blvd. Open Mon–Wed noon–8pm, Fri–Sat 10am–6pm. Hours during summer may vary.* ♿ ☎491-2200. This branch of the New York Public Library system contains the world's largest archive relating to black heritage. **Arthur Schomburg** (1874-1938), a black Puerto-Rican who was an influential cultural leader during the Harlem Renaissance of the 1920s, began the collection in an effort to discredit the contemporary belief that African-Americans had no history. Today, more than 5 million books, photographs, manuscripts, films, recordings and works of art are kept in the center, which is housed in a 1905 landmark library building designed by McKim, Mead & White (restored in 1990) and a modern 1980 annex. The center also presents exhibits, screenings and educational forums throughout the year.

The Abyssinian Baptist Church. – *132 W. 138th St. For visiting hours* ☎*862-7474.* This 1923 Gothic Revival church is home to New York's oldest black congregation, founded in 1808. It was built during the tenure of Adam Clayton Powell, Sr, and became prominent in the 1930s under the leadership of **Adam Clayton Powell, Jr** (1908-1972), the controversial pastor and civil-rights advocate who was elected to Congress in 1944. Under financial investigation, Powell was stripped of Congressional office in 1967, but reinstated two years later. Clippings and photos in the memorial room trace his career.

★ **Morris-Jumel Mansion.** – *W. 160th St and Edgecombe Ave. Open Tue–Sun 10am–4pm. $3. Closed holidays.* ☎*923-8008.* Occupying a hilltop site with a superb view of the Harlem valley, this handsome Georgian mansion is the only colonial home to survive in northern Manhattan. Colonel Morris built the house, originally known as Mount Morris, in 1765 but fled a decade later to England, where his Loyalist sentiments were better appreciated. During the Battle of Harlem Heights in 1776, the estate served as General Washington's headquarters, and in 1810, it passed to Stephen Jumel, a wealthy French wine merchant. Jumel's wife, Eliza Bowen, was never fully accepted in New York society, and the Jumels set sail for France in 1815, where they traveled more comfortably in Napoleonic circles. Jumel died in 1832, and a year later, his widow married Aaron Burr *(p 63)*, the third vice president of the US, in the front parlor of her mansion. After a year of marriage, the couple separated. Their divorce was granted on the day Burr died, in 1836.
While constructed of brick, the mansion features wood facades, corner quoins and a lovely 2-story Federal-period portico. The interior is particularly notable for the rear drawing room on the first floor—possibly the first octagonal room in the US. The front parlor contains a fashionable Empire-style settee and chairs, and a French chandelier that belonged to Madame Jumel. On the second floor, Madame Jumel's bedroom and dressing room feature Empire furniture that once belonged to the Bonaparte family; note especially the 19C mahogany slipper chairs.

The mansion is part of the **Jumel Terrace Historic District**, which also includes 20 simple 2-story row houses built in the 1880s on the original carriage drive, now known as Sylvan Terrace. The homes are among the few surviving wood frame structures that once proliferated in the area.

Hamilton Heights. – This elevated area, which encompasses the historic district east of Amsterdam Avenue between West 140th and West 145th Streets, was once part of a 35-acre estate owned by statesman **Alexander Hamilton** (1757-1804). The picturesque gabled row houses on Hamilton Terrace and Convent Avenue include some unusual Dutch and Flemish Revival residences dating from the 1880s, when the district was developed as a suburb for prosperous New Yorkers. Note the imposing brownstone St Luke's Episcopal Church *(285 Convent Ave)*, designed in the Romanesque Revival style in 1892.
On the heights between Edgecombe and St Nicholas Avenues lies **Sugar Hill**★. This affluent black neighborhood of elegant 4-story houses was home to such famous residents as Cab Calloway, Duke Ellington, Thurgood Marshall and Langston Hughes between the 1920s and 1950s. Just to the south is City College's campus, begun in 1897. Some 14,000 students, mainly black, Hispanic and Asian, are enrolled here.

Hamilton Grange National Memorial. – *287 Convent Ave. Closed for renovation. For information* ☎*283-5154.* Designed in 1801 by John McComb, Jr (architect of CITY HALL), this Federal-style clapboard residence was Alexander Hamilton's country estate and his principal residence when he was killed in a duel with Aaron Burr in 1804. In 1889, it was moved about 100yds to its current location and altered; the rear facade now faces the street. The building was later used as a rectory for St Luke's Church and is now owned by the National Park Service.

MUSEUMS

★ **Audubon Terrace.** – *See description p 113.*

★ **The Studio Museum in Harlem.** – *See description p 146.*

THE CLOISTERS

Time: 1/2 day. Map p 102.

Isolated on a hill in Fort Tryon Park, the Cloisters re-creates a fortified monastery, a part of the Old World transplanted to the New. Housed in four reconstructed medieval cloisters and part of a fifth, its collections, which include innumerable works of sculpture, stained glass, tapestries and other objects spanning over one thousand years, enjoy an unrivaled reputation among lovers of medieval art.

HISTORICAL NOTES

Rockefeller to the Rescue. – The core of the collection is made up of medieval sculptures and architectural remains assembled by the American sculptor, **George Grey Barnard** (1863-1938), during his frequent trips to Europe. When the collection was opened to the public in 1914, in a special brick building on Fort Washington Avenue, it already included large sections of the cloisters of Saint-Michel-de-Cuxa, Saint-Guilhem-le-Désert, Bonnefont-en-Comminges and Trie, all from regions in southern France.

In 1925, **John D. Rockefeller, Jr** *(p 37)* donated a large sum to the Metropolitan Museum to purchase the Barnard collection and to improve its presentation. At that time, the Rockefellers also donated over 40 sculptures from their collection.

In 1930, Rockefeller decided to give to the City of New York an estate he owned in the area, which is now Fort Tryon Park. He stipulated that the northern part be reserved for the new Cloisters, today home to this extraordinary institution.

Designed by **Charles Collens** of Boston, also responsible for RIVERSIDE CHURCH, the building was completed in 1938. Considerably enriched by gifts and acquisitions, the museum has remained administratively a part of the METROPOLITAN MUSEUM OF ART.

★★★ THE CLOISTERS

To reach the Cloisters take bus no. 4, "Fort Tryon Park–The Cloisters" on Madison Ave or the subway "190th St–Overlook Terrace" (A line), and walk. Parking available. Open Mar–Oct Tue–Sun 9:30am–5:15pm. Rest of the year Tue–Sun 9:30am–4:45pm. Closed holidays. $6 (same day admission to the Metropolitan Museum of Art, p 120). Guided tour (1hr) Tue–Fri 3pm, Sun noon. &. ☎923-3700. Recorded concerts of medieval music daily. Concerts Sat & Sun afternoons (Nov–Apr). Tickets available by mail or phone order only: The Cloisters, Fort Tryon Park, New York, NY 10040 ☎923-3700.

The central structure, containing a group of cloisters, chapels and halls, is arranged around a square tower inspired by that of Saint-Michel-de-Cuxa, in the Pyrenees Mountains in southern France. There is little unity of style since both Romanesque and Gothic elements are incorporated, as was often the case in European monas-

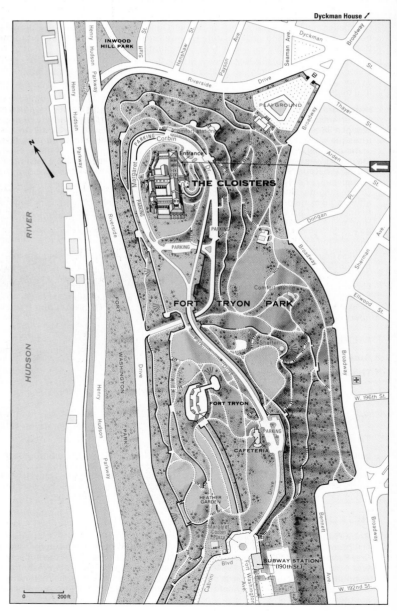

teries. The weathered stone and pleasing proportions, however, combine to create a harmonious ensemble, resembling an ancient monastery. A stroll along the rampart wall affords different views of the building, the park and the Hudson River. On the east side of the building, a postern serves as the entrance. As you exit the building, note the driveway paved with Belgian blocks—originally from New York streets—reminiscent of European cobblestones.

Main floor   *Map below*

Fuentidueña Chapel. – This "chapel" is largely devoted to Spanish Romanesque art. The apse comes from the church of San Martin at Fuentidueña in Old Castile, Spain, and dates from about 1160. Notice the capitals depicting Daniel in the Lion's Den *(right side)* and the Adoration of the Magi *(left side),* and pier figures of the Annunciation *(right side)* and St Martin, Bishop of Tours *(left side).* The two niches in the wall probably contained the cruets of water and wine used during Mass, and held the ewer for the priest's ceremonial handwashing.

The semi-dome bears a fresco of the Virgin and Child with the three Wise Men and the archangels Michael and Gabriel. It once graced the apse of the small Catalan church of San Juan de Tredos, in the Spanish Pyrenees.

In the nave of the chapel is an Italian Romanesque doorway from San Leonardo al Frigido in Tuscany, carved from Carrara marble about 1175. Just to its left, a Tuscan, cream-colored marble holy water font depicts Raynerius, patron saint of Pisa, who is believed to have performed miracles such as separating water from wine. The font was carved in 1160, the year of Raynerius' death. On the left wall of the nave hangs a well-preserved 12C crucifix from the Convent of Santa Clara, in Spain.

Romanesque Hall. – The entrance features a barrel vault characteristic of the Romanesque style. On the left side, the capitals are carved with graceful birds feeding upon acanthus plants. The capitals on the right bear imaginary animals surmounted by a delicate acanthus motif. The doorway is believed to come from Poitou in France.

The portal leading to the Saint-Guilhem Cloister *(below)* is from a church in Reugny, in the upper Loire Valley, and dates from the late 12C; it represents a transitional style between the Romanesque and Gothic styles. The Gothic portal (13C) leading to the Langon Chapel *(p 104),* was the entrance to a transept of the former abbey of Moutiers-Saint-Jean in Burgundy. The statues represent, on the left, Clovis, the first Christian French king, and on the right, his son Clothar, who protected the abbey after its foundation by his father at the end of the 5C.

On the right wall can be found the Torso of Christ (12C), a fragment of a Deposition group; the statue's head is one of the treasures of the Louvre in Paris.

Saint-Guilhem Cloister. – The covered walkway contains a magnificent series of columns and capitals from the Benedictine abbey of Saint-Guilhem-le-Désert, near Montpellier, France. The property was sold during the French Revolution, and some of the columns were being used to support grape vines, when George Grey Barnard acquired them in 1906. Admire the intricately carved capitals (12C-13C), adorned with plants and figures; a number of the capitals bear the mark of Roman inspiration. Several columns are also incised with geometric patterns of vegetation.

The fountain in the center of the cloister was once a Romanesque capital in the church of Saint-Sauveur in the Auvergne region of France. The grotesque corbels supporting the ribs and cornice of the gallery vaults hail from the Abbey of Sauve-Majeure, near Bordeaux.

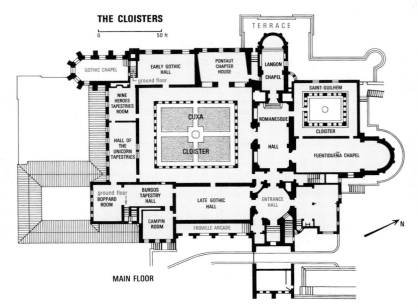

THE CLOISTERS

Langon Chapel. – The original parts of this chapel came from the choir of the Romanesque church of Notre-Dame du Bourg at Langon, near Bordeaux, used as a Jacobin Club during the French Revolution, and later transformed into a dance hall and movie theater. A 12C Italian marble ciborium (tabernacle) symbolically protects a poignant 12C Virgin Mary from Autun, Burgundy, carved in birch. Located near the door, another 12C representation of the Virgin and Child, from Auvergne, creates an interesting contrast.

Pontaut Chapter House. – Notre-Dame-de-Pontaut was first a Benedictine and later a Cistercian abbey in Gascony, France. Its chapter house, where the monks met every morning to discuss community affairs, exemplifies both the late Romanesque style and the transition to Gothic with rounded-arch windows and doors, and a rib-vaulted ceiling. On the other side of the open arches, lay brothers gathered in the cloister to follow the debates, while monks were seated along the wall. The capitals are particularly worth noting for the simple but forceful carving of ornamental geometric or plant forms.

The Metropolitan Museum of Art, Cloisters Collection

Chapter House from Notre-Dame-de-Pontaut

Cuxa Cloister. – Although this is the museum's largest cloister, it represents only half the size of the original structure. The various elements came from the Benedictine monastery of Saint-Michel-de-Cuxa, near Prades, in the French Pyrenees, an active center of art and learning in the 12C. Abandoned during the French Revolution, the monastery was sold in three parts, and during the 19C, its elements were widely scattered. In 1913, Barnard was able to bring together about half of the original Romanesque capitals, 12 columns, 25 bases and 7 arches. Rose-colored Languedoc marble was cut from original quarries to complete the restoration. Note the capitals carved with plants, grotesque personages and fantastic animals possibly inspired by motifs from the Near East; curiously, there are very few that bear any clear religious significance.

Early Gothic Hall. – This room features several fine examples of early stained glass, which played such an important role in Gothic design. There are also a number of interesting statues in this hall, including a 13C Virgin *(on the wall)* from the former choir screen of the Strasbourg Cathedral.

Nine Heroes Tapestries Room. – The doorway from the Cuxa Cloister is capped by ornamental ogee arches, exemplary of the Flamboyant Gothic style. Contained within this room is a large part of a set of **tapestries** (1385) that are among the oldest in existence, along with the Apocalypse tapestries at Angers, France. The theme of the Nine Heroes, very popular in the Middle Ages, includes three pagans (Hector, Alexander, Julius Caesar), three Hebrews (David, Joshua, Judas Maccabeus) and three Christians (Arthur, Charlemagne, Godfrey of Bouillon). Their feminine counterparts were the Nine Heroines.

The surviving tapestries on display depict five of the nine Heroes. David is recognizable by his golden harp, and Arthur by his banner with three crowns representing England, Scotland and Brittany. Joshua, Alexander and Caesar are also portrayed. A number of lesser personages escort the Heroes, giving an edifying view of the medieval social structure. The arms of Berry, with golden fleurs-de-lis on the tapestries depicting the Hebrew heroes, indicate that the set may have been woven for Jean, Duke of Berry, a patron of the arts and brother of the French king, Charles V. Before continuing into the next room, pause to admire the 16C Gothic stone doorway from Auvergne, carved with unicorns.

Hall of the Unicorn Tapestries. – The magnificently colored **Unicorn tapestries** are among the most exceptional of the golden age of tapestry, which flourished at the end of the 15C and the beginning of the 16C. To be admired is the fine craftsmanship and attention to detail with which the artist has depicted the people and animals, their expressions and poses. The set of seven tapestries originally hung in the Chateau of Verteuil in Charente (southwestern France), the home of the well-known La Rochefoucauld family. Six of the tapestries were acquired by John D. Rockefeller, Jr in 1922 (the seventh was added in 1938). A narwhal tusk, strongly resembling a unicorn's horn leans against a 15C limestone fireplace from Alençon, in Normandy.

Boppard Room. – This room is named for the German town of Boppard on the Rhine, where the six stained-glass panels were created for the Carmelite Church (late 15C). There is also a Spanish alabaster altarpiece (15C) and a brass eagle lectern (16C) from Belgium.

Burgos Tapestry Hall. – Among the large tapestries (1495) hung in this hall, one represents a Glorification of King Charles VIII of France, after his accession to the throne in 1483. The young king appears at least five times and can be identified by his crown. His sister, Anne de Beaujeu, the regent during his minority, and his fiancee, Margaret of Austria, are also represented. Other scenes in the complicated iconographic scheme include the story of Adam and Eve, Esther and Ahasuerus, the Emperor Augustus and the three Christian Heroes *(p 104)*.

Campin Room. – This room, with its painted Spanish ceiling, has been furnished with medieval domestic objects: table and benches, bronze chandelier and a 15C iron birdcage (the only one known to have survived from the Middle Ages).
Above the chest is the famous **Annunciation altarpiece** by 15C Flemish artist Robert Campin. The central panel represents the Annunciation. The side panels depict the donors, on the left, and on the right, St Joseph in his workshop: notice the mouse-trap on St Joseph's workbench and the painstakingly reproduced details of the town square in the background.

Late Gothic Hall. – This large gallery designed to resemble a monastery refectory is lighted by four 15C windows from the convent of the Dominicans at Sens, in Burgundy. There is a remarkable example of a Spanish 15C altarpiece, in painted wood, carved and gilded. You may also admire the pure lines of a kneeling Virgin (late 15C, Italy) and the Adoration of the Magi (late 15C, Swabia, Germany). In an effort to recreate the original positioning and perspective, the statue of St Michael (16C, Spanish) has been placed above the doorway.

Ground Floor *Map below*

Gothic Chapel. – Inspired by a chapel in the church of Saint-Nazaire at Carcassonne and by the church at Monsempron, both located in France, this structure provides a superb setting for an interesting collection of tomb effigies and slabs. Among the former note the effigy of Jean d'Alluye (13C) and four monumental Catalan sarcophagi of the Counts of Urgel (13C). The tombs come from the Premonstratensian monastery of Santa Maria de Bellpuig de las Avellanas, north of Lérida in Spain. The apsidal windows are now glazed with 14C Austrian stained glass, mostly from the pilgrimage church of St Leonhard in Lavanthal.

Bonnefont Cloister. – This cloister is bordered on two sides by twin columns. Their double capitals in gray-white marble, from the quarries of Saint-Béat, come from the cloister (13C-14C) of the former Cistercian abbey at Bonnefont-en-Comminges, in southern France.

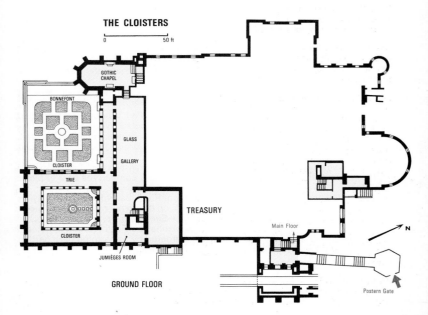

THE CLOISTERS

0   50 ft

GOTHIC CHAPEL

BONNEFONT

GLASS

CLOISTER

GALLERY

TRIE

TREASURY

Main Floor

CLOISTER

N

JUMIÈGES ROOM

GROUND FLOOR

Postern Gate

The other two sides of the cloister form terraces offering a view on Fort Tryon Park and the Hudson River. A medieval garden of herbs and flowers adds to the charm of this spot.

Trie Cloister. – Because of its small size, this cloister evokes in an especially pleasant manner the atmosphere of serenity and meditation associated with a monastery. Its capitals, dating from the late 15C, are decorated with coats of arms or religious scenes; note those on the south arcade, which illustrate the Life of Christ.
The central fountain is a composite of two 15C-16C limestone fountains discovered in France's Vosges region.

Glass Gallery. – This room is named for the roundels and panels of stained glass (15C-16C) representing scenes from the Old and New Testaments. A fine selection of 15C and 16C statues in wood, alabaster, stone and ivory is gathered here along with a Nativity altarpiece painted in the workshop of 15C Flemish artist Roger van der Weyden. At the far end of the gallery note the intricately carved wood panels that originally surrounded the courtyard staircase of a 16C house in Abbeville, in northern France.

Jumièges Room. – The group of 37 carved wooden panels is believed to have been part of choir stalls, probably from the royal abbey of Jumièges in Normandy (early 16C). The panels are decorated in late Gothic style with scenes from the life of the Virgin and Christ. The wall case contains the magnificent *Belles Heures* (Book of Hours) manuscript, which belonged to Jean, Duke of Berry who also commissioned the Nine Heroes Tapestries *(p 104)*.

Treasury. – The Cloisters' collection of smaller objects of exceptionally fine quality is displayed in the room adjacent to the Jumièges Room.
The most outstanding piece is a walrus-ivory cross from the 12C, the so-called Bury St Edmund's Cross, which has been traced to the monastery of Bury St Edmund's in Suffolk, England. Both the front and back surfaces of the cross are covered with figures, inscriptions and minuscule scenes from the Old and New Testaments, which have been skillfully carved with great attention to detail; note the expressiveness of the hands, and on the back of the cross, the individuality of the twelve figures set in frames: the facial expression of each figure is different and no two hold the scroll in the same manner.
Also of interest are the enamels (13C, Limoges) and reliquaries used for personal devotions, and a rosary bead of boxwood, with a tiny representation of the Passion inside (15C, Germany).
Superb wall hangings embroidered with silk and gold threads depict biblical scenes. Note the late 14C German hanging with scenes from the Life of Christ and the Old Testament.

★★ FORT TRYON PARK *Map p 102*

Covering 62 acres of wooded hills above the Hudson River, this peaceful, green space, landscaped by Frederick Law Olmsted, Jr, seems miles away from the bustle of the heart of the city. Although fairly small, the terrain is varied with hills, dales and cleverly arranged terraces overlooking the river. In the 19C, the area was covered with farms and pastures, replacing earlier Indian camps. John D. Rockefeller, Jr acquired the site in 1909 and donated it to the city in 1930.
A lookout built upon the site of **Fort Tryon** caps a hill 250ft above the river. The fort, named for the last English civil governor of New York, William Tryon, was an outpost of Fort Washington, which was the last to resist the British invasion of Manhattan during the American Revolution. It was here that American heroine Margaret Corbin replaced her husband killed in action and fought until severely wounded. With the fall of Fort Washington on November 16, 1776, the British occupied all of New York City, which remained in their hands for seven years. Until recently, fortunate strollers could find cannon balls and Revolutionary buttons and belt buckles.
The lookout point affords fine **views★** of the Hudson River and the George Washington Bridge to the west, and the East River to the east.
Between Fort Tryon and Margaret Corbin Plaza to the south, is the 3-acre Heather Garden planted with colorful and ornamental flower beds.

Set at the northwestern tip of Manhattan, **Inwood Hill Park** is separated from Fort Tryon Park by a ravine dotted with several apartment houses. Wooded and hilly, the terrain seems to have changed very little since the Algonquins inhabited the area, then known as Shora-Kapkok. During the Revolution, British and Hessian troops were quartered here.
Today, the park is quite empty on weekdays, and it is unwise to walk here alone. On Sundays, however, New Yorkers in search of greenery come to the park to picnic and relax.
Located to the northeast of the park along Harlem River, Baker Field is the playing field of COLUMBIA UNIVERSITY. To the east of the park, on the corner of West 204th Street and Broadway, stands **Dyckman House** *(open Thu–Sun 11am–4pm; ☎304-9422)*, the only extant 18C Dutch Colonial farmhouse in Manhattan. Restored and appointed with period Dutch and French furniture, and bordered by a charming herb garden and a smokehouse, it illustrates life in colonial America.

Additional Sights in Manhattan

Roosevelt Island. – *Map of Principal Sights p 3. Access by public transportation: tramway or subway (● Q or B trains from 63rd St). The tramway, located on Second Ave and 60th St, operates daily 6–2am (weekends 3am) every 15min (4:30–7pm every 7min). $1.40 one-way. ⑆ ☏832-4543. Access by car from the borough of Queens across the bridge at 36th Ave. Because automobile traffic is restricted on the island, all cars are required to park at the Motorgate Garage, just across the bridge on the island. From there, visitors can take the minibus to the center of the island.*

Roosevelt Island is located in the East River, 300yds off the shore of Manhattan. Formerly the site of various public health facilities, and therefore known as "Welfare Island," it is now the home of a residential "town-in-town" built by the New York State Urban Development Corporation in the 1970s. Politically a part of the borough of Manhattan, the island is 2.5mi long, 800ft wide at its broadest point and 147 acres in size. It is linked to Manhattan by bridge and by an aerial tramway that provides a 3min ride across the East River with views in each direction.

The buildings in the first phase of the Roosevelt Island Community—designed by the noted architectural firms Johanson & Bhavnani and Sert, Jackson and Assocs.— were based on a master plan by Philip Johnson and John Burgee, while Gruzen Sampton Steinglass conceived the Manhattan Park complex, containing 1,108 units. The community encompasses mixed-income housing, retail shops, schools, two city hospitals, parks and other recreational facilities. Several of the island's landmarks have been restored, including the **Chapel of the Good Shepherd**, erected in 1889; the **Blackwell Farm House** (late 18C), one of the oldest farm houses still standing in New York City; and the **Lighthouse**, built in 1782 under the supervision of James Renwick. Octagon Tower, the remains of the New York City Lunatic Asylum, the city's first mental health institution, is currently being restored. A waterfront promenade on both sides of the community affords good vantage points for viewing river traffic and the Manhattan skyline.

★ **Chelsea.** – *Time: 3hrs. Map of Principal Sights p 4. ● 1, 9 train to 23rd St.* Situated between busy 34th and 14th Streets and bordered by the bustling Garment District along Seventh Avenue, Chelsea is a multifaceted neighborhood known for its leafy historic district and bohemian air. Named for England's Old Soldier's home at Chelsea, this distinct enclave was staked out by Capt Thomas Clarke in 1750, and divided into plots by his grandson, Clement Clarke Moore (author of "A Visit from St Nicholas").

Attracted to the growing movie industry, which prospered here at the turn of the century, a vibrant artistic community continues to flourish along Chelsea's industrial west side where many 19C warehouses have been converted to galleries, theaters and performance venues, such as The Kitchen *(512 W. 19th St)* and the dance-oriented Joyce Theater *(175 Eighth Ave)*.

Visit. – The blocks between 23rd and 19th Streets encompass the heart of Chelsea's historic district. Located on 23rd Street *(between Seventh and Eighth Aves)* in the center of what once was New York's theater district, the eclectic **Hotel Chelsea** (1884, Hubert and Pirsson), festooned with wrought-iron balconies, has long been the hotel of choice for writers and artists from Dylan Thomas and Mark Twain to Jackson Pollock and Andy Warhol, whose cult classic *Chelsea Girls* was filmed here. The somewhat shabby lobby features works by various residents past and present. *Head south on Eighth Ave and turn right on W. 22nd St.*

Lining this quiet street, stylish Italianate brownstones (early 19C) are characterized by low stoops and sunken basements. At Ninth Avenue, take a peek south to the L&S Dairy and adjacent buildings *(nos. 183-187 1/2)*, examples of the few remaining 1-story wooden homes that once abounded in the neighborhood. *Continue to Tenth Ave and walk south.*

At the corner of 21st Street and Tenth Avenue stands the Guardian Angel Church, erected in 1930 in the Romanesque Revival style and distinguished by an elaborate portal. *Continue south on Tenth Ave and turn left on W. 20th St.* Well-preserved Greek Revival houses with elaborate iron balustrades are found along **Cushman Row** *(406-418 W. 20th St)*. Constructed in 1840 by dry goods merchant Don Alonzo Cushman, these graceful residences typify the quiet, genteel air of a bygone era.

Occupying an entire city block, the **General Theological Seminary** sports a non-descript, modern facade (1960) on its Ninth Avenue entrance *(no. 175)*. The remainder of the brick and brownstone buildings, grouped around a green quadrangle and enclosed by a tall iron gate, evoke a classical English university campus. Note especially the 1836 fieldstone West Building, the oldest Gothic Revival building in New York. Dominated by a prominent tower, **St Peter's Episcopal Church** *(346 W. 20th St)* features an eclectic mix of early 19C architectural styles, including Gothic and Greek Revival. Located next door at no. 336, the Off-Broadway Atlantic Theater, occupying the church's 1852 brick parish house, specializes in new American plays.

★ **Tribeca.** – *Time: 2hrs. Map of Principal Sights p 5. ● 1, 9 train to Franklin St.* Named for its location in the TRIangle BElow CAnal, this wedge-shaped area derives its acronym from a realtor who bestowed it in the 1980s in order to give this area an identity as trendy as that of SOHO. The heart of this emerging neighborhood, sandwiched between the FINANCIAL DISTRICT to the south and GREENWICH VILLAGE and SoHo to the north and east, lies north of Chambers Street. Lining Tribeca's unpretentious streets and occupying its asymmetrical nooks and crannies are a variety of 19C cast-iron buildings, galleries, shops and cafes. Several street segments have been designated as landmark districts by the city.

During the latter half of the 19C, much of the shipping and warehousing industry formerly located at the SOUTH STREET SEAPORT moved to deepwater piers on the Hudson River. As activity on the East River declined, the western flank of lower

Manhattan boomed. The heart of Tribeca, then known as the Lower West Side, developed as a wholesale produce and meat exchange, called Washington Market. Warehouses, designed to store fruits and vegetables, sprung up, and the grand, brick and granite **New York Mercantile Exchange**, built in 1884, housed the offices of food brokers for the nearby Market. Today, Washington Market refers to the area extending south along Greenwich to Chambers Streets (produce merchants have relocated to the Hunts Point section of the Bronx). This pleasant stretch now features a mixture of specialty food and retail outlets selling items from imported cheeses to dried fruits.

With the departure of the produce industry and small-scale manufacturing, many Tribeca lofts were taken over by artists. About 9,000 people now live in what had long been considered an exclusively commercial and industrial district.

Visit. – *Begin at the corner of White and Broadway Sts and walk west.* On the section of White Street between Broadway and Church Street, note the curved exterior of the Center Synagogue *(no. 49)* and the **Let There Be Neon Gallery** *(no. 38)*, featuring the creations of founder Rudi Stern and other American neon artists. Past Avenue of the Americas, White Street is lined with buildings reflecting Tribeca's cast-iron history, such as **nos. 8-10** and **no. 17**, crowned by a mansard roof. These ornamented edifices illustrate the mixing and matching of styles common to Tribeca. *Walk south on West Broadway to Franklin St and turn right. At Hudson St, continue south until Harrison St. Continue west on Harrison St to the corner of Greenwich St.*

A group of four restored 1828 Federal-style row houses, **Harrison Street Row** *(nos. 37-41)* is the sole remnant of the merchant homes once common to this area. *Continue south on Greenwich St to Washington Market Park.*

Surrounded by a charming, wrought-iron fence, the **Washington Market Park** *(Duane at Greenwich Sts)* constitutes a quiet oasis of neatly kept lawns and shrubbery embellished by a lacy gazebo.

Grace Church. – *Map p 84. 802 Broadway at E. 10th St. Open Mon–Fri 10am–5:45pm, Sat noon–4pm, Sun for services only. Guided tour available.* &. Founded by the TRINITY CHURCH parish in 1808, this Episcopal church was erected in 1846 by James Renwick Jr, who later designed ST PATRICK'S CATHEDRAL. Distinguished by an elegant spire, the church is a fine example of the Gothic Revival style. In 1863, P.T. Barnum arranged for the rector to marry two midgets from his circus: Charles S. Stratton, better known as Tom Thumb, and Lavinia Warren.

Located to the left of the church, the rectory (also by Renwick) is one of New York's earliest Gothic Revival residences.

The Little Church Around the Corner (Church of the Transfiguration). – *Map of Principal Sights p 4. 1 E. 29th St. Open daily 8am–6pm.* &. This charming Episcopal church with its peaceful garden seems dwarfed by the surrounding skyscrapers, especially the EMPIRE STATE BUILDING. Built of red brick in the mid-19C, the edifice reflects the 14C Gothic style and is sometimes referred to as an example of "English Cottage Gothic."

The church earned its nickname in 1870, when the pastor of a nearby church refused to hold funeral services for an actor; at that time, those associated with the theater were not looked upon favorably. The cleric did, however, suggest that the actor's friends try "the little church around the corner" where a monument still commemorates its pastor's charitable decision. It has remained a favorite parish for theater people, and also one where many weddings are held.

The interior is remarkable for its luminous stained-glass windows dedicated to great New York actors: note the window depicting Edwin Booth as Hamlet, designed by John LaFarge and the one in the vestibule *(leading to the south transept)*, which is studded with raw diamonds. It is dedicated to the memory of the Spanish actor, José Maria Muñoz. The Transfiguration, designed by Frederick Clark Withers, adorns the high altar reredos.

Church of St Mary the Virgin. – *Map p 32. 139 W. 46th St. Open Mon–Sat 11am–7pm, Sun 8am–6pm. Guided tours (30min) Sun.* Distinguished by a Gothic Revival facade, this Episcopal church was founded in 1868. The interior of the church was extensively decorated during the first part of the century. Note in the left side aisle the Madonna and Child, a 19C Majolica bas-relief from the Della Robbia workshop in Florence, Italy. The murals adorning the Lady Chapel represent the Annunciation and the Epiphany. In the baptistery admire the colossal pulpit and the wooden font cover embellished with 73 delicately carved figures. The Chapel of Our Lady of Mercy contains a black marble altar and a 15C plaque depicting the death of St Anthony. In the apse above the high altar, three large stained-glass lancet windows (early 20C) were crafted by Kempe of England.

★ **Jacob K. Javits Convention Center.** – *Map of Principal Sights p 3. 655 W. 34th St.* New York's Convention Center, a low-rise building stretching along the Hudson River from West 34th to 39th Streets, is named for Jacob K. Javits (1904-1986), the former US senator from New York. Designed by I.M. Pei and Partners in 1986, the center has 1,800,000sq ft of enclosed space, including two main exhibit halls, more than 100 meeting rooms, and restaurant and service areas; it can accommodate 85,000 persons daily.

Of special architectural interest is the enormous exposed-steel space frame that shapes the main exhibit hall. Some 76,000 tubes, containing tension rods, and 19,000 nodes were used in constructing the space frame, giving it the appearance of an assemblage of gigantic tinker-toy components. Extremely flexible from a structural point of view, the frame serves as beams, walls and roof of the hall and is supported by columns rising 90ft.

★★ **George Washington Bridge.** – *Round-trip toll per passenger car: $4.00 (toll booth on New Jersey side only).* This toll bridge, which links 179th Street in Manhattan to Fort Lee on the New Jersey side, was for a number of years the longest bridge in the world and is still the only 14-lane suspension bridge. Designed by **O.H. Amman** (an American engineer of Swiss origin, who also conceived the VERRAZANO-NARROWS BRIDGE) and architect Cass Gilbert, the bridge was opened on October 25, 1931 and cost about $59 million. In 1959, the growing volume of traffic required the construction of a lower level, opened in 1962. At the same time, an intricate system of interchanges was installed. In 1992, nearly 100 million vehicles used the bridge. A tremendous feat of engineering, the George Washington Bridge spans the Hudson River in one pure line 3,500ft long. The towers are 604ft high and the supporting cables have a diameter of 36in. The upper level, 250ft above the river, comprises eight lanes; the lower level is divided into six lanes.

The best view of the George Washington Bridge may be had from the sightseeing boats *(p 12)* that circle Manhattan, or from the Henry Hudson Parkway, along the river. To the north, note the Little Red Lighthouse on Jeffrey's Hook, a point of land on the Hudson near 178th Street.

Union Square. – *Map p 84. E. 14th to 17th Sts, between Park Ave South and University Pl.* Once the scene of political gatherings, a New York equivalent of London's Hyde Park where political radicals indulged in soap box oratory, Union Square is now no more than a busy crossroads between Broadway and Park Avenue South and 14th and 17th Streets.

In 1836, the garden at the center of the square was enclosed by iron grillwork and locked at night. At the time, the square marked the northern border of the city. By the mid-19C, it had become a fashionable address for New York's finest families, rivaling ASTOR PLACE. As the city spread northward in the late 19C, wealthy residences gave way to theaters, the Academy of Music (now converted into the Palladium, *p 83*), commercial establishments such as Tiffany's and Brentano's, and restaurants like Delmonico's. During the first decades of the 20C, Union Square witnessed mass demonstrations such as the one on August 22, 1927, when Sacco and Vanzetti were executed in Boston. A number of participants were wounded in the fray.

Today, the square is best known for its popular Greenmarket, held on Wednesdays and Saturdays *(8am–6pm)*, to which New Yorkers flock en masse to purchase fresh produce, flowers, bread, honey and eggs. The park contains three statues of interest: George Washington *(south)* and Abraham Lincoln *(north)*, both by Henry Kirke Brown, and Lafayette *(east)* by Bartholdi, better known as the sculptor of the STATUE OF LIBERTY. To the east rises the **Consolidated Edison Building** *(4 Irving Pl at 14th St)*, headquarters of the company that provides gas, electricity and steam for most of the city.

Madison Square. – *Map of Principal Sights p 4. E. 23rd to 26th Sts, between Madison and Fifth Aves.* Created in 1847 on a patch of swamp-infested land, Madison Square originated as a military parade ground. Following on the heels of its southern neighbor, Union Square, it became an elegant residential enclave during the second half of the 19C, when it was surrounded by fashionable hotels, fine restaurants and expensive shops. In 1884, in an effort to raise money for the Statue of Liberty's pedestal *(p 56)*, Liberty's arm, complete with torch, was exhibited in the center of the square, attracting thousands of visitors.

The square was long associated with sporting events. In 1845, it had been the site of the city's first baseball games. From 1853 to 1856, the Hippodrome, a type of circus, drew as many as 10,000 spectators at a time to the square. Then, at the end of the last century, the Madison Square Garden, an ornate sports arena with room for 8,000 spectators, was built on the northwest corner of the square. It was designed by Stanford White, architect and man about town, who was shot on the roof garden in 1906 by a jealous husband who resented White's attentions to his actress-wife, Evelyn Nesbitt. Destroyed in 1925 in order to make room for the New York Life Insurance Building *(below)*, the "Garden" was relocated to a site on West 49th Street, between Eighth and Ninth Avenues. In 1968, the latter was replaced by the current Madison Square Garden, which covers two city blocks between 31st and 33rd Streets and Seventh and Eighth Avenues, the former site of McKim, Mead and White's grandiose Pennsylvania Station. Although no longer at the height of its glory, this pleasant spot of greenery is still surrounded by several noteworthy buildings. At the northeast corner, between East 26th and 27th Streets, where the "Garden" once stood, stands the New York Life Insurance Building (1928), designed by Cass Gilbert in the Gothic style and embellished with impressive gargoyles.

Marking the corner of East 25th Street, the elegant white marble building (1899) fronted with Corinthian columns houses the Appellate Division of the Supreme Court of the State. The roof balustrade depicts symbolic figures and great teachers of law (including Moses, Justinian and Confucius). Formerly on the far right, the statue of Mohammed has been removed at the request of the city's Islamic community, since the Koran forbids the corporeal representation of the Prophet. The vestibule inside features a gilded ceiling, supported by yellow marble columns.

Farther south, between East 24th and 23rd Streets, the 700ft **Metropolitan Life Insurance Company Tower** (1909, Stanford White) resembles the campanile of St Mark's in Venice, Italy. Note the enormous clock with its four faces: the minute hands each weigh 1,000lbs and the hour hands 700lbs.

On the south side of the square stands one of New York's first skyscrapers, the **Flatiron Building**★. Built in 1902 by Chicago architect Daniel H. Burnham, the striking 22-story brick and limestone structure features an unusual, triangular shape, resembling an iron. Originally erected for the Fuller Construction Company (who also commissioned the FULLER BUILDING on East 57th Street), the Renaissance-style edifice, with its three-tiered palazzo format and articulated cornice, was soon dubbed the Flatiron Building and later adopted its nickname as its official title.

Museums in Manhattan

(in alphabetical order)

New York Convention & Visitors Bureau

The Metropolitan Museum of Art

ABIGAIL ADAMS SMITH MUSEUM

Time: 1 hour. 421 E. 61st St. ● 4, 5, 6, R or N trains to 59th St. Map p 3. Visit by guided tour (1hr) only, Jun–Jul Mon–Fri noon–4pm; Sept–May Mon–Fri noon–4pm, Sun 1–5pm. $3. ☏838-6878.

This 1799 Federal-style stone building, now located in a largely commercial area of midtown Manhattan, is among the few surviving 18C residences remaining in the city. The house was designed to be part of a 23-acre estate acquired by Colonel William Smith and his wife Abigail Adams Smith, daughter of President John Adams. The couple, however, soon encountered financial trouble and had to sell the property to a merchant, William T. Robinson, who in turn erected a manor house and various outbuildings, including this structure, a former coach house and stable. Fire destroyed the manor house in 1826 and the coach house/stable was converted the same year to an inn and tavern, the Mount Vernon Hotel. The Colonial Dames of America purchased the building in 1924 and restored it to its mid-19C appearance. Nine period rooms, appointed with 18C and 19C antiques, as well as a neatly manicured garden, are open to the public.

ALTERNATIVE MUSEUM

Time: 1 hour. 594 Broadway. ●6 train to Spring St or N, R train to Prince St. Map p 80. Open Tue–Sat 11am–6pm. Closed holidays & 2 weeks in Aug. $3. ♿ ☏966-4444.

This issue-oriented museum was founded in 1975 expressly to offer programs that represent equitable participation by both men and women from all economic, ethnic and social backgrounds. The three galleries, located in a SoHo loft building, are the scene of some eight or nine visual arts exhibits a year, along with periodic panel discussions, dance and media performances, and concerts of New Age music and jazz. Designed to "test the definitions and boundaries of art in contemporary society," the programs address such topical subjects as cultural disenfranchisement and ethnic and gender stereotypes. They are often organized by guest curators and feature emerging artists as well as established names, including Adrian Piper, Ida Applebroog, Andres Serrano and Lorna Simpson.

★ AMERICAN CRAFT MUSEUM

Time: 1 hour. 40 W. 53rd St. ● E, F train to 53rd St. Map p 33. Open Tue–Sun 10am–5pm (Tue 8pm). $4.50. ♿ ☏956-3535.

Housed in a mottled, pink granite office tower (1986; Roche, Dinkeloo & Assocs.) and flanked by stylized columns and 20ft smoked glass windows, this delightful museum displays contemporary craft with an eye towards both traditional craftsmanship and avant-garde materials. Created in 1956 by the American Craft Council, the museum presents rotating selections from permanent and traveling collections emphasizing the scope and spirit of 20C crafts. Inside, the gracefully arching, 4-story atrium features a Guggenheim-inspired spiral stairwell *(p 118)* leading to galleries that highlight thematic exhibits as well as recent acquisitions. Executed by international and American artists, the works range from fiber art, glass and ceramics to synthetic and mixed media creations.

★★★ AMERICAN MUSEUM OF NATURAL HISTORY

Time: 1 day. Central Park West, between 77th and 81st Sts. ● *B, C train to 81st St or 1, 9 train to 79th St. Map p 89.*

Ranking among the most venerated New York establishments, this institution is the largest of its kind in the world. Its outstanding collections, dealing with all facets of natural history, range from minerals and gems to dinosaurs, and from Indian totem poles to Tibetan gowns.

The Building. – Founded in 1869 by Albert S. Bickmore, the museum was first installed in the Arsenal, in CENTRAL PARK. Calvert Vaux *(p 87)* designed the present structure to be erected on a swampy area north of the Dakota *(p 95)*. Construction of the colossus, today composed of 23 interconnected buildings, began in 1874, when Gen Ulysses S. Grant, then president, laid the cornerstone. It was formally opened three years later by his successor, Rutherford B. Hayes. Finally completed in the 1930s, the complex is a curious mixture of styles, the result of a program directed by various architects at different periods.

On the Central Park side is the main entrance *(2nd floor)*, part of a majestic 800ft-long facade. The Ionic colonnade bears the statues of the explorers and naturalists, Boone, Audubon *(p 144)*, Lewis and Clark. Another entrance on West 77th Street leads to the first floor and the Naturemax Theater. As part of an ongoing $45 million renovation project, by Roche, Dinkeloo & Assocs., the museum is restoring the building to its original appearance and former grandeur, thereby revealing windows, arches and cast-iron columns that had been hidden for years. The museum has also erected an 8-story library, on West 77th Street, to hold its 450,000 volumes on natural history.

The Collections. – The museum's holdings include more than 30 million artifacts and specimens, only a small part of which are on view in 40 exhibit halls on four floors. The various displays include life-size **dioramas** of animals shown in their natural habitats: the ground and vegetation are faithfully reproduced, and the background scenes are effectively painted by artists using sketches made at the original sites. The lighting contributes to the realism of the scenes.

VISIT

Open daily 10am–5:45pm (Fri & Sat 8:45pm). Closed Thanksgiving Day & Dec 25. $5. Guided tours (1hr 15min) available every hour until 3:15pm. ✕ ♿. *For further information and to consult the day's special shows & lectures* ☎769-5100.

Owing to the museum's numerous collections, it is impossible to see every exhibit in a single day. The following description presents only the highlights on each floor. In order to plan an itinerary that suits your interests, we recommend stopping by the Information Desk to pick up the museum's detailed floor plan.

Begin in the Theodore Roosevelt Memorial Hall on the 2nd floor.

Second Floor. – The central rotunda is dominated by the tallest free-standing dinosaur model in the world, **Barosaurus**, a herbivore dating from the Jurassic period. Rising 5 stories (55ft), the skeleton is a resin-and-foam replica of the original fossilized bones, which are too fragile to be mounted in a display.

Just west of the rotunda is a spectacular hall dedicated to **African Mammals★**. Highlighted by an impressive herd of African elephants on the alert, the hall consists of realistic dioramas along the walls, presenting zebras, antelopes, gorillas, lions and gazelles in their natural surroundings. In the galleries on the third floor level of this hall, other dioramas depict different species of monkeys, rhinoceroses, leopards and hyenas. To the north of the Central Park West entrance is the **Hall of Oceanic Birds**. Winged creatures from New Guinea to New Zealand are represented in various dioramas, while albatrosses fly overhead, set off by a light blue sky.

The **Hall of African Peoples** traces the development of complex human culture on the African continent. The **Hall of Mexico and Central America** displays an outstanding pre-Columbian collection. Of special interest are the exhibits related to the Aztec and

Barosaurus, Theodore Roosevelt Memorial Hall

American Museum of Natural History

Mayan civilizations, the gold ornaments of the Americas dating from 2,500 years ago, and clay sculptures from central Veracruz. The **Hall of South American Peoples** exhibits Andean and Amazonic treasures, including the 2,300-year-old Paracas mantle, which are testimony to the religious beliefs and social organization of the ancient, existing and recently extinct cultures of this continent.

The **Hall of Asian Peoples★** features a comprehensive exhibit of life from prehistoric times to the late 19C when Western technology began to influence the traditions of the Orient. Daily life in Asian trading cities and villages from Arabia to Japan and Siberia to India, and colorful ceremonies and rituals are portrayed by life-size displays and dioramas. Over 60,000 artifacts comprise the Asian collection, making it the largest such assemblage in the Western hemisphere.

First Floor. – The 77th Street foyer is dominated by a seagoing Haida war canoe from the Queen Charlotte Islands, in British Columbia. Carved out of one piece of cedar, the craft can hold over 30 passengers. Devoted to Indians of the northwest coast, this floor's highlight is the **Pacific Northwest Hall★**, presenting superb totem poles, American Indian and Inuit tools and handicrafts.

To the left of the foyer is the **Hall of Mollusks and Our World**, covering the many uses of mollusks and their shells by past and present cultures around the globe. The **Hall of Human Biology and Evolution**, opened in 1993, is divided into three sections focusing on human anatomy, the path of human evolution and the origins of human creativity. In the section on **Meteorites, Minerals and Gems★★**, you may feast your eyes on the more than 6,000 rubies, emeralds and diamonds as well as the Star of India, the world's largest star sapphire (weight: 563 carats). The 34-ton meteorite, Ahnighito, and the Brazilian Princess Topaz are among the other highlights of the collection.

Also of interest are the North American Mammals and North American Forests halls. The 2-story Hall of Ocean Life and Biology of Fishes contains an immense (94ft long) model of a blue whale suspended in a dive position and a magnificent diorama on the Bahamian Coral Reef Group.

Opened to children, the **Discovery Room** features "discovery boxes" designed to encourage learning about the natural sciences. Films on several different subjects are shown in the Naturemax Theater, a 996-seat auditorium equipped with a gigantic movie screen 4 stories high and 66ft wide.

Third Floor. – The **Hall of Reptiles and Amphibians** features the world's largest living lizards, the 10ft Komodo dragon. The **Hall of Primates** displays animals from the same biological order as man, beginning with the tree shrew. To the west of the primates, displays on the lifestyles of the Eastern woodlands and Plains Indians include model houses, weapons, tools and utensils. In the Hall of North American Birds, a variety of birds from all corners of the country includes the wild turkey, which Benjamin Franklin wanted to designate America's national bird.

The **Hall of the Pacific Peoples★**, inspired by the work and ideas of Dr Margaret Mead (1901-1978), contains exhibits related to six cultural areas of the Pacific: Australia, Indonesia, the Philippines, Melanesia, Micronesia and Polynesia. A large display case toward the center of the hall holds sacred masks, carved figures and boldly decorated shields illustrating the rich and diverse art of the peoples of the Sepik River basin.

Fourth Floor. – *This floor is under renovation until 1995.* When reopened, the floor's six halls will encompass one of the world's most comprehensive displays of vertebrate fossils, organized according to physiological similarities rather than chronologically. An orientation center will allow visitors to experience the world of dinosaurs through interactive displays. Four of the halls will feature the museum's greatest attraction: dinosaur skeletons and fossil mammals. Other exhibits will focus on fossil fish and amphibians.

★★ Hayden Planetarium

Open Mon–Fri 12:30–4:45pm, Sat 10am–5:45pm, Sun noon–5:45pm. Closed Thanksgiving Day & Dec 25. $5 (includes Sky show). ⚥ ⚐. For further information and to consult the show schedule ☎769-5920.

Crowned by a huge dome, the Hayden Planetarium is located just west of the Museum of Natural History. Opened in 1935, it contains the astronomy department of the museum.

The Guggenheim Space Theater. – *1st floor.* The space theater offers an exciting series, presented in sight and sound on the 360-degree space-screen, covering such topics as the Earth, Moon, Solar System and rocketry. Suspended from the ceiling is an animated model of the solar system 48ft in diameter. Around the central sun move six of the planets, simultaneously rotating on their axes. They are the Earth, Mars and Jupiter with their moons; Saturn with its rings; Mercury and Venus. Owing to the enormous distances separating them from the sun, the three outer planets, Uranus, Neptune and Pluto are not represented. The model is lighted so that each planet and satellite shows "daytime" on the side facing the sun.

The Sky Theater. – *2nd floor.* Projected onto the hemispherical dome of the Sky Theater, rising 48ft and 75ft in diameter, forty-five minute shows, changed three times a year, offer exceptional insight into the various planets of the universe.

The spectators are seated around the Zeiss VI projector, which weighs 2.5 tons and is 12ft long. Placed at either end, large globes emit images of the fixed stars of the northern hemisphere and the southern hemisphere. The sun, moon and planets are projected from the cylinder, which supports the globes.

Devoted entirely to the sun, the exhibits in the Hall of the Sun explain the huge star's place in the universe and its effects on our planet.

Two additional galleries contain exhibits illustrating the history and progress of astronomy. Among the astronomical murals is the 35ft, scientifically accurate representation of the surface of the Moon. Other displays focus on rockets and artificial satellites. Specially conceived scales permit you to find out how much you would weigh on the various planets and stars.

★ THE ASIA SOCIETY

Time: 1 hour. 725 Park Ave. ● 6 train to 68th St. Map p 93. Open Tue–Sat 11am–6pm (Fri 8pm), Sun noon–5pm. Closed holidays. $2. & ☎288-6400.

This intimate museum was founded in 1956 under the guidance of John D. Rockefeller 3rd, with a view to promoting an increased understanding and appreciation of Asian cultures. In addition to providing an elegant setting for showcasing Southeast Asian and Indian art, the Asia Society offers lectures, films and performances in its 258-seat auditorium, designed as a forum for cross-cultural exchanges. The well-stocked bookstore contains an impressive collection of resource materials on Asian history and culture.

Designed by Edward Larrabee Barnes in red granite and sandstone, the distinguished headquarters building (1981) rises to eight stories. Upon entering the large foyer, note among the sculptures the 6C Chinese tympanum incised in low relief, showing the Buddha preaching *(on the left)*, and the elephant-headed Ganesha (8C), Hindu god of good fortune.

On the ground floor, a large gallery is reserved for special exhibits on specific themes in Asian art. The two galleries on the second floor host rotating exhibits from the outstanding Mr and Mrs John D. Rockefeller 3rd's collection of Asian art, donated to the society in 1978. Objects on view include lively animated Indian bronzes, Chinese and Japanese ceramics, exquisite screen paintings and hanging scrolls, wood carvings and manuscripts. Also of interest are the three-dimensional and low-relief stone sculptures from Southeast Asia.

★ AUDUBON TERRACE

Time: 3 hours. On Broadway between 155th and 156th Sts. ● 1 train to 157th St.

Grouped around a wide, barren plaza located to the northwest of HARLEM, stand some of the city's lesser known museums and cultural institutions. Naturalist John Audubon *(p 144)* once had a country house named Minniesland on the site. The present buildings were erected at the beginning of the 20C in the Classical Revival style by Charles Pratt Huntington, nephew of Archer M. Huntington *(p 144)* who conceived the Audubon Terrace project in 1908 and provided the financial backing.

National Museum of the American Indian. *– The museum is in the process of relocating part of its collection to the US Custom House (p 65). The museum will be renamed The George Gustav Heye Center of the National Museum of the American Indian. The remainder of the collection will be housed in a new museum on the Mall in Washington DC, to be completed by the year 2000.*

★★ **Hispanic Society of America.** *– Open Tue–Sat 10am–4:30pm, Sun 1–4pm. Closed holidays.* ☎926-2234. This small yet fascinating museum, which offers a panorama of Spanish civilization from pre-Roman times to the present century and houses a collection of high-quality Old Masters, comes as quite a surprise in this part of the city. Located opposite a bronze statue of El Cid, the 2-story edifice contains a lavish and well-appointed interior. Designed as an interior courtyard in the Renaissance style, the first floor gallery presents a large selection of traditional and ritual objects such as choir stalls, exquisite silverware, Paleolithic tools, Renaissance tombstones, tabernacles, silk brocades and altar frontals. Upon entering, the eye is drawn to two life-size portraits by 18C Spanish artist Goya, including one of the Duchess of Alba. To the right of the gallery, note the 15C Mudejar door surrounded by colorful tiles. The Sorolla room *(far right)* features an ensemble of paintings by Sorolla y Bastida entitled *Provinces of Spain*. A research library is also located on the first floor.

The second floor balustrade contains a rich collection of earthenware, ceramics, metalwork, porcelain, lusterware and jewelry displayed in glass cases. **Portraits** by renowned artists El Greco, Morales, Ribera, Velasquez and Goya line the walls.

★ **American Numismatic Society.** *– Open Tue–Sat 9am–4:30pm, Sun 1–4pm. Closed holidays.* ☎234-3130. Founded in 1858, this small museum houses one of the world's foremost collections of coins and medals, as well as a comprehensive research library and archives. Two galleries on the first floor display medals of historic or artistic interest and rotating exhibits on the history and the various uses of coins throughout the world. A major exhibit, "The World of Coins," traces the history of money as a medium of exchange from ancient to modern times.

American Academy of Arts and Letters. *– Open for special exhibits Mar, May–Jun & Nov Tue–Sun 1–4pm.* ☎368-5900. This is the nation's highest honor society for the arts, with a membership of 250 of America's foremost artists, architects, writers and composers. Recurrent art and manuscript exhibits are held three times a year *(call ahead for schedule)*. The Academy's collection of Childe Hassam paintings can be viewed year-round by appointment.

CHINATOWN HISTORY MUSEUM

Time: 1/2 hour. 70 Mulberry St, 2nd floor. ● *N, R or 6 trains to Canal St; B, D trains to Grand St. Map p 73. Open Sun–Fri noon–5pm. Closed holidays. $1.* ☎619-4785.

Created in 1980, this small museum presents the history and culture of Chinese people in New York and promotes awareness of Chinese communities throughout the Americas. The permanent exhibit traces the development of the city's Chinatown using the museum's vast collection of artifacts and oral histories. Rotating exhibits focus on special related themes such as the arts and culture.

★ COOPER-HEWITT (Nat. Museum of Design)

Time: 1 hour. 2 E. 91st St. ● *4, 5, 6 train to 86th or 96th Sts. Map p 3. Open Tue–Sat 10am–5pm (Tue 9pm), Sun noon–5pm. Closed holidays. $3. Guided tours available.* ♿ ☎860-6868.

Founded in 1897 by New York socialites **Sarah**, **Eleanor** and **Amy Hewitt**, this museum of the decorative arts is devoted to historical and contemporary design, with a focus on its uses in industrial and interior design, architecture, fashion and advertising. The extensive collection that resulted from the three sisters' eclectic tastes and unorthodox acquisition methods encompasses some 250,000 objects representing artists from around the world and spanning over 3,000 years.

The collection was first displayed at the COOPER UNION OF NEW YORK, the college of art, architecture and engineering founded by the sisters' grandfather, Peter Cooper. In 1972, it was transferred to this Beaux-Arts mansion (1898), built by wealthy industrialist **Andrew Carnegie** (1835-1919). Surrounded by a wrought-iron fence and an inviting garden, the chateau-style residence once contained 64 rooms on six stories. Today, only the ground, first and second floors feature exhibit galleries, while the third and fourth floors are given over to office space, the library, and various reference centers dedicated to the study and preservation of design trends. Affiliated with the Smithsonian Institution in 1968, the museum re-opened as the National Museum of Design in 1976.

Evocative of the turn-of-the-century design tastes, the exquisite interior is noteworthy for its rich **oak panelling**, in particular in the entrance hall and staircase. Exhibits change regularly (about 12 a year), each focusing on a particular aspect of design or a type of decorative or functional object, and displaying a selection of objects from the permanent collection. Highlight of the collection are 50,000 original **prints** and **drawings**, ranging from works by 15C Italian master Andrea Mantegna to Americans Frederic Church and Winslow Homer, and 20C Italian Surrealist painter Giorgio de Chirico. The museum's rich holdings also include delicate textiles dating from the 3C BC; decorative arts including silver, bronze and wrought-iron metalwork; examples of jewelry and goldsmith's work; wallpaper samples; bandboxes; porcelain, glass and earthenware; furniture; woodwork; and hardware (18C and 19C Chinese birdcages and splendid clocks).

Located on the third floor, the library includes a picture reference section and archives of color, pattern, textiles, symbols and interior design.

EL MUSEO DEL BARRIO

1230 Fifth Ave. ● *6 train to 103rd St. Map p 2. The museum is closed for renovations and will reopen in February 1994 with a 25th anniversary exhibit. For visiting hours* ☎831-7272.

Housed in the left wing of an imposing U-shaped building fronting Fifth Avenue, this small museum (1969) serves as the leading cultural center for "El Barrio," the Hispanic—predominantly Puerto Rican—community of Spanish Harlem *(p 100)*. Devoted to the arts and culture of Puerto Rico and other Latin American countries, the museum presents changing displays of Caribbean artifacts and contemporary painting and sculpture, as well as a permanent exhibit of hand-carved statuettes, known as **Santos de Palo** (saints). The museum plays an active role in the Puerto Rican community, sponsoring lectures and various workshops.

★ FORBES MAGAZINE GALLERIES

Time: 1 hour. 62 Fifth Avenue. ● *4, 5, 6 train to 14th St. Map p 80. Open Tue–Wed & Fri–Sat 10am–4pm. Closed holidays.* ♿ ☎206-5548.

Housed in the ground floor galleries of the Forbes Building, home of the well-known business bi-weekly, an eclectic collection gathered by publisher Malcolm Forbes and his sons has been on view since 1985. Best known for the beautiful series of Fabergé pieces, the galleries also feature a grand ensemble of antique toy boats; thousands of toy soldiers arranged in scenes dramatizing historic events; fine art, ranging from Gilbert Stuart to George Bellows; and American presidential letters and manuscripts.

Highlighting the collection of over 300 objets d'art created by jeweler and goldsmith Peter Carl Fabergé are the **Imperial Easter Eggs★**, produced by Fabergé workshops for the Russian royal family between 1885 and 1916. The museum owns 12 of the 45 such eggs known to exist today. Gold, silver, precious stones and enameling decorate these exquisite fantasies, of which several conceal hidden surprises: note the mechanical bird that emerges and sings when a certain orange is rotated (Orange Tree Egg); the bejeweled replica of the royal coronation coach (Coronation Egg); and the chanticleer that appears on the hour crowing and flapping its wings (Chanticleer Egg).

★★★ THE FRICK COLLECTION

Time: 1 1/2 hours. 1 E. 70th St. ● 6 train to 68th St. Map p 92.

One of the world's most distinguished small museums, the Frick Collection, displayed in a luxurious private mansion, constitutes an exceptional trove of Old Masters, furnishings and decorative arts acquired by a single collector over a period of 40 years.

The Benefactor. – A Pittsburgh coke and steel industrialist, **Henry Clay Frick** (1849-1919) began collecting works of art on his first trip to Europe, which he took in company of his friend, Andrew Mellon, primary benefactor for the National Gallery of Art *(see Michelin Green Guide to Washington DC)*. First concentrating on 18C English paintings, Frick later ventured into sculpture, in particular bronzes, then prints and drawings, enamels, furniture, porcelain and rugs. In 1913, he commissioned this 40-room mansion, designed by Carrère and Hastings (also responsible for the NEW YORK PUBLIC LIBRARY) and erected on the site of the former Lennox Library, to display his holdings. Frick bequeathed the mansion and the collection to a Board of Trustees, with a mandate to transform it into a museum after his death. Following a renovation and extension project undertaken by John Russell Pope, the residence reopened as a museum in 1935. Today, the rich collection contains works ranging from the 14C to the 19C.

VISIT

Open Tue–Sat 10am–6pm, Sun 1–6pm. Closed holidays. $3. ☂. Sunday afternoon concerts (5pm) given throughout the year; children under 10 not admitted; tickets available by mail only, Concert Dept. The Frick Collection, 1 E. 70th St, New York, NY 10021. Wednesday afternoon illustrated lectures (5:30pm) are free. For schedule ☎288-0700. Works of art may occasionally be relocated or removed from exhibit.

Entrance Hall. – A bust of Henry Clay Frick (1922) by Malvina Hoffman is displayed in a niche on the right of the marble-floored hall.

Boucher Room. – Reminiscent of an 18C boudoir, with its intimate and refined atmosphere, this room contains eight paintings by French rococo painter Boucher (1703-1770), commissioned by Louis XV's favorite consort, Madame de Pompadour, in 1752, representing the Arts and Sciences. Among the 18C French furniture are pieces by Carlin and Riesener.

Anteroom. – This room features Hans Memling's *Portrait of a Man* (c.1470), the Flemish artist's earliest known portrait with a landscape background.

Dining Room. – The spacious room, decorated with English 18C paintings in delicate colors, includes portraits by Hogarth, Romney and Reynolds, and a masterpiece by Gainsborough, *The Mall in St James's Park*. Also of note are the 18C English silver-gilt wine coolers and the Chinese porcelain, in particular the pair of cobalt blue vases adorning the mantelpiece.

West Vestibule. – Here are displayed the series of the *Four Seasons* (Boucher, 1755), also commissioned by Madame de Pompadour as overdoors for her residence. Delicate Chinese porcelain ginger jars sit atop the splendid marquetry desk by the workshop of André-Charles Boulle.

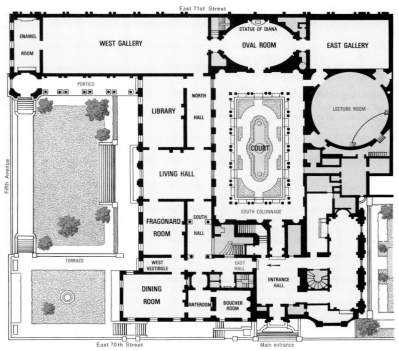

© The Frick Collection, New York, photograph Richard Bryant/Arcaid London

Fragonard Room

Fragonard Room. – The room is named for the eleven decorative paintings by Jean-Honoré Fragonard (1732-1806), a work of inimitable grace that is a hymn to love. Four of the large panels were commissioned by Madame du Barry, a mistress of Louis XV. They recount the various stages of a romantic encounter: *The Pursuit*, *The Meeting*, *The Lover Crowned* and *Love Letters*. Exquisite furnishings add to the total effect: sofas and armchairs covered in Beauvais tapestry after designs by Boucher and Oudry; a Louis XVI commode by La Croix; two delicate tripod tables, one covered in lapis lazuli and the other in Sèvres porcelain plaques; and a marble bust of the *Contesse du Cayla* (1777) by Houdon, on the mantle.

South Hall. – Highlights among the furniture include the Louis XVI drop-front secretary and chest of drawers crafted for Queen Marie-Antoinette by Jean-Henri Riesener. Among the paintings, note Boucher's portrait of his wife and two rare works by 17C Dutch master Vermeer, one of which, *Officer and Laughing Girl*, is remarkable for its radiant luminosity. At the foot of the stairs is a 30-day Louis XV calendar clock, which also contains a barometer. Note also the Aeolian pipe organ and its elaborate marble and gilded screen, installed in 1914.

Living Hall. – Furnished with a desk by André-Charles Boulle and a pair of marquetry cabinets in the style of this famous 17C French cabinetmaker, this room displays 16C masterpieces. The Venetian school is represented by Giovanni Bellini's *St Francis in the Desert* set against a finely rendered landscape, and by two Titian portraits, one depicting the sensual features of a young man in a red cap and the other of *Pietro Aretino*. The commanding figure of *St Jerome* as Cardinal, by El Greco, represents the Spanish school. Typical of the best of the German school, two celebrated portraits by Hans Holbein the Younger depict Sir Thomas More and Thomas Cromwell.

Library. – Dominated by a portrait of Henry Clay Frick (1943, John Johansen) over the mantle, this wood-paneled room houses an array of art books, fiction and volumes of poetry. Enlivening the stately decor are lovely pieces of Chinese porcelain; several small Italian and French bronzes of the 16C and 17C; and the terra-cotta bust of the Swedish miniature painter, Peter Adolf Hall, executed by French sculptor Boizot in 1775. Among the series of English paintings of the 18C and 19C, note in particular John Constable's *Salisbury Cathedral from the Bishop's Garden*.

North Hall. – Above the superb blue marble Louis XVI table hangs Ingres' renowned portrait of the *Comtesse d'Haussonville*, granddaughter of Madame de Staël who hosted a powerful literary and political salon in Paris in the late 18C. The marble bust by Houdon represents the Marquis de Miromesnil, minister of Justice under Louis XVI. The remaining works range from the newly acquired *The Portal of Valenciennes* by Antoine Watteau to Monet's *Vétheuil in Winter*. Chardin's *Still Life with Plums* represents the collection's only still life work.

West Gallery. – In this room, decorated with 16C Italian furniture and Persian carpets, are portraits and landscapes of the Dutch, French, Spanish and British schools. Among the portraits notice *Lodovico Capponi*, a page in the court of Duke Cosimo I de Medici, by 16C Florentine artist Bronzino; an El Greco of the Italian period *(Vincenzo Anastagi)*; works by Frans Hals; three splendid Rembrandts of great intensity of expression *(Self-Portrait, Nicolaes Ruts* and *Polish Rider)*; two famous works by Van Dyck: the Antwerp painter of still life Frans Snyders, and his wife, Margareta; and *Philip IV of Spain*, by Velázquez. Other well-known pieces include *The Forge* by Goya and two large allegorical paintings by Veronese.

Particularly noteworthy among the landscapes are van Ruisdael's *Landscape with a Footbridge*, Hobbema's *Village with Water Mill Among Trees* and *The Harbor of Dieppe* by Turner. A 17C work by Étienne de la Tour, *The Education of the Virgin*, formerly attributed to his father Georges, also deserves attention.

Enamel Room. – Several Italian Primitives and Renaissance works form an appropriate backdrop to the splendid collection of Limoges painted enamels of the 16C and 17C in intense blues and greens. Paintings of interest include *St Simon the Apostle* by Piero della Francesca, *Madonna and Child with Sts Lawrence and Julian* by Gentile da Fabriano and *The Coronation of the Virgin* by Veneziano.

Oval Room. – A life-size terra-cotta figure of *Diana the Huntress* by 18C French sculptor Jean-Antoine Houdon graces this gallery. It is a version of a statue executed for the Duke of Saxe-Gotha and acquired by the Russian Empress, Catherine the Great. Portraits by Gainsborough and Van Dyck gaze down at the statue.

East Gallery. – This room presents a fine assortment of paintings from different schools and periods. Claude Lorrain's dramatic *Sermon on the Mount* dominates the gallery. Other works on display include Greuze's genre painting *The Wool Winder*, *Quay at Amsterdam*, by Jacob van Ruisdael, in which the sail of the boat on the left seems to capture all the light; a portrait by Jacques Louis David of *Countess Daru*, the wife of Napoleon's Quartermaster General; and Degas' *The Rehearsal*. Four portraits by Whistler, including the striking *Mrs. Frederick R. Leyland*, three by Goya and two by Van Dyck complete the collection.

Garden Court. – One of the most delightful parts of the museum, the court provides a cool haven in summertime thanks to its marble floor, fountain and pool, tropical plants and flowers. Originally used as a carriage court, the space was redesigned by John Russell Pope during the 1935 renovation. From the south colonnade you can view the entire court and the statue of *Diana*, by Houdon, in the Oval Room beyond. Among the works of sculpture, note the 15C bronze *Angel* by Jean Barbet.

★ GRACIE MANSION

Time: 1 hour. East End Ave at 88th St. ● 4, 5, 6 train to 86th St. Map p 3. Visit by guided tour (1hr) only, mid-Mar–mid-Nov Wed 10am–3pm. $3. Reservations required. ♿ ☏570-4751.

Located in the northern section of Carl Schurz Park *(p 94)*, a sliver of greenery bordering the East River, this 1799 country manor houses the official residence of the mayor of New York. The Federal style mansion, painted in buff yellow and white trim and adorned with green shutters, bears the name of Archibald Gracie, a merchant who entertained many dignitaries here, including Alexander Hamilton and John Quincy Adams. After passing through several hands, the house was eventually acquired by the city in 1896, falling into neglect until the MUSEUM OF THE CITY OF NEW YORK took it over in 1924. In 1942, it became the official home of the mayor. The current restoration by the Gracie Mansion Conservancy—created under the administration of former mayor Edward Koch—features a striking marbelized entry floor and fine Federal and Empire style furnishings; some personal belongings of the current mayor's family are also on view.

★★ SOLOMON R. GUGGENHEIM MUSEUM

Time: 2 hours. 1071 Fifth Ave. ● 4, 5, 6 train to 86th St. Map p 93.

This spiraling concrete monument to modernism, located on Fifth Avenue between 88th and 89th Streets, is among the most original and widely recognized structures in the US. Visited more than any other building designed by Frank Lloyd Wright, it is as much a work of art as the sculptures and paintings it contains.

Benefactors. – **Solomon R. Guggenheim** (1861-1949) came from a family of German-Swiss immigrants who made a vast fortune in the 19C mining precious metals. Long a supporter of the arts, he and his wife, Irene Rothschild, originally collected Old Masters. In the early 20C, they began concentrating on non-representational, or "non-objective" works—especially those by Kandinsky, Mondrian and Moholy-Nagy—at the urging of their artistic advisor, Hilla Rebay. In 1937, the Solomon R. Guggenheim Foundation was established to encourage art and art education. Six years later, Rebay commissioned Frank Lloyd Wright to design a permanent home for Guggenheim's collection. Unfortunately, Guggenheim died before he ever saw his museum, finally begun in 1956. However, the foundation continues to support the museum holdings. These were enlarged in 1963 with 75 Impressionist and post-Impressionist paintings given to the museum by **Justin K. Thannhauser**, an art dealer who helped pioneer the Modern Movement. In 1975, Solomon's niece, Peggy Guggenheim, also left a collection of Dada and Surrealist works—still housed in her Venetian palazzo on the Grand Canal—to the foundation. In 1992, the Museum opened a downtown branch in SoHo *(p 76)*. Plans are underway for an additional branch in Salzburg, Austria, making this a truly international museum of contemporary art.

"My Pantheon". – The father of modern American architecture, **Frank Lloyd Wright** (1867-1959) revolutionized the field in the early 20C with his natural, organic designs based on geometric forms. Best known for his work with the Chicago school, he was an outspoken critic of New York architecture. The Guggenheim Museum (1956-1959) was his only major commission in the city. Calling it "My Pantheon," after the domed Roman monument, Wright considered the idiosyncratic building, based on a complex trigonometric spiral, his crowning achievement. From the start, however, the museum was controversial. It clashed with its surroundings, was a nightmare to construct and—with its interior ramp and sloping walls—proved a difficult place to both view and display art. As a result, there have been many alterations: most recently, the 1992 renovation by Gwathmey Siegel & Assocs. added a 10-story annex and restored much of Wright's original design.

The Central Park side of Fifth Avenue offers a good view of the entire museum, dominated by a four-tiered spiraling cone, or "nautilus." The smaller, round wing, or "monitor" stands to the left, with the new limestone tower just behind. Inset metal circles in the sidewalk paving echo the circle motif of the building and continue on the travertine floor inside.

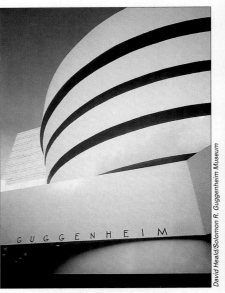

David Heald/Solomon R. Guggenheim Museum

Solomon R. Guggenheim Museum

VISIT

Open Fri–Wed 10am–8pm. Closed Thanksgiving Day & Dec 25. $7. ✗ ᘿ ☏ *423-3500.*

Few public spaces in New York rival the drama of the main gallery, encircled by the famous spiraling ramp. Depending on the current show, you can start your visit at the top or bottom; either way, it will be a journey of discovery as Wright's kaleidoscopic composition of rounded forms, repeated in the railings, furnishings and elevator banks, unfolds and changes at every level. More than 1/4 mile long, the ramp now opens on four levels to the new annex galleries. Additional galleries are found on the top three floors of the monitor building, lit by plate glass windows offering tantalizing views of the museum's exterior and of CENTRAL PARK. Outside, off the fifth floor, is a terrace garden featuring the David Smith sculpture, *Cubi xxvii.*

Collections. – The Guggenheim Foundation's holdings comprise more than 6,000 paintings, sculptures and works on paper. The core collection includes 195 works by Kandinsky—the largest assemblage in the US—and more than 75 pieces by Klee. Chagall, Delaunay, Dubuffet, Mondrian and the Cubists Léger and Gris are featured as well. Acquired in 1990, the Panza di Biumo collection has amplified the holdings with more than 300 contemporary pieces, primarily from the 1960s and 1970s, by such Minimalists as Carl André, Dan Flavin and Robert Morris.

A selection from the **Thannhauser collection**, located on the second floor of the monitor building, is the only permanent display. The earliest work is a pre-Impressionist landscape by Pissaro, *Les Coteaux de l'Hermitage à Pontoise* (c. 1867). There are also canvases by Renoir *(Woman with a Parrot)* and Manet *(Before the Mirror, La Comtesse Albassi)*, and Van Gogh *(The Viaduct, Mountains at Saint-Rémy)* and Toulouse-Lautrec *(Au Salon)*. You will also find still lives by Cézanne and small sculptures by Degas and Maillol. Picasso is especially well represented, with early works *(The End of the Road, Le Moulin de la Galette)* and the 1931 painting, *The Craft Jug and Fruit Bowl.*

The museum also offers continuously changing shows in the main gallery and adjacent annex, and in the Guggenheim's SoHo gallery *(p 76)*.

★ INTERNATIONAL CENTER OF PHOTOGRAPHY

Time: 1 hour. 1130 Fifth Ave. ●*6 train to 96th St. Map p 3. Open Tue–Sun 11am–6pm (Tue 8pm). Closed holidays. $4.* ☏*860-1783. Branch at 1133 Ave of the Americas.* ●*any train to 42nd St. Open Tue–Sun 11am–6pm (Tue 8pm). Closed holidays. $4.* ᘿ ☏*768-4682.*

Located in an elegant, brick, Georgian Revival townhouse, the ICP exhibits major works by 19C and 20C photographers and photojournalists. Distinguished by seven œil-de-bœuf windows just below the roof line, the building once housed the headquarters of the National Audubon Society. It was acquired by the ICP and opened to the public in 1974. Today, the rich collection comprises over 12,500 original prints, shown on a rotating basis here and at the center's midtown branch *(1133 Ave of the Americas)*. In addition, the center offers audiovisual presentations and educational programs, and operates a well-stocked bookshop.

INTREPID SEA-AIR-SPACE MUSEUM

Time: 1 hour. Pier 86 at W. 46th St and 12th Ave. ●*take any train to 42nd St, then the M42 or M34 bus to the 42nd St Pier. Map p 3. Open Memorial Day–Labor Day daily 10am–5pm. Rest of the year Wed–Sun 10am–5pm. Closed Jan 1, Thanksgiving Day & Dec 25. $7. Guided tours (30min) available.* ✗ ⅙ ☏245-0072.

MUSEUMS

Berthed at a pier in the Hudson River is the aircraft carrier *Intrepid*, a veteran of World War II and the Vietnam war, and recovery vessel on two occasions for Mercury and Gemini space missions. Decommissioned in the 1970s, the *Intrepid* now serves as a floating museum, dedicated to the technology and history of sea, air and space warfare.

The main attraction is the supercarrier itself, a veritable floating city, and its maze of corridors, enormous decks, high island bridges and slender bow flaring out above the waterline. On the hangar deck, exhibits offer insight into the navy, aviation, the *Intrepid* and space technology. On the flight deck, aircraft appearing ready for flight on a moment's notice may be viewed close-up. Accompanying the exhibits in the Pioneers Hall are multimedia presentations, including a film *(17min)* on the day-to-day operations on board a carrier at sea, and a dramatic audio-visual recounting *(12min)* of the events that occurred Thanksgiving Day 1944, when the ship was hit by two kamikaze attacks. The Technologies Hall contains displays on jumbo jets, rockets and complex weaponry.

Admission to the *Intrepid* includes a tour of the **USS Growler**, a 1958 guided missile submarine now decommissioned and open to the public *(last tour 5:30pm)*. Also on view are the **USS Edson**, the 946th and last example of the United States Navy's all-gun destroyers; the famous lightship, **Nantucket**; and the **A-12 Blackbird**, the largest and fastest single seat plane ever flown.

JAPAN HOUSE

333 E. 47th St. ●*any train to Grand Central Terminal. Map p 48. Open for special exhibits. For schedule & visiting hours* ☏752-3015.

This black, low-rise building, located a short walking distance from the UNITED NATIONS, houses the headquarters of the Japan Society, a cultural and educational organization. Designed in contemporary Japanese style, the interior contains a bamboo pool, exhibit gallery, auditorium, library, language center, conference rooms and garden, all of which blend together gracefully to create a simple and tranquil effect. Exhibits of Japanese art, films, music and dance are presented on a temporary basis *(call ahead for schedule)*.

★ THE JEWISH MUSEUM

Time: 1 hour. 1109 Fifth Ave. ● *4, 5, 6 train to 86th St. Map p 3. Open Sun–Thu 11am–5:45pm (Tue 8pm). Closed Jewish holidays. $6.* ⅙ ☏423-3230.

Founded in 1904, this unique repository of Judaica offers insight into Jewish history, life and culture, through historical and literary materials, ceremonial objects and Zionist memorabilia. Paintings and sculpture by Jewish and Israeli artists illustrate and reflect Jewish life throughout the centuries.

First housed in the library of the Jewish Theological Seminary *(3080 Broadway)*, the museum moved into this ornate, French Renaissance mansion (1908) in 1947, when its owners, Felix and Frieda Warburg, donated it to the seminary. A new wing, added by architect Kevin Roche in 1992, doubles the exhibit space.

Comprising over 27,000 pieces, the collection features a wealth of ceremonial objects, including the blue mosaic upper section of the Ark wall from a 16C Persian synagogue, rare Hanukkah lamps, a pair of ornate 17C silver Rimonim (used to decorate the Torah), a wood-carved Torah Ark from the 12C and velvet-bound prayer books. The museum also houses contemporary art, textiles (including elaborate wedding shawls), archaeological artifacts from the Holy Land and Hebrew coins and medals.

The museum houses the National Jewish Archives of Broadcasting, dedicated to Jewish contributions to television and radio. In addition to its permanent collection, the museum offers a program of rotating exhibits, special events, films, lectures and children's programs.

LOWER EAST SIDE TENEMENT MUSEUM

Time: 1/2 hour. 97 Orchard St. ●*F train to Delancey St or B, D train to Grand St. Map p 73. Open Tue–Fri 11am–4pm, Sun 10am–5pm. $3. Walking tours every Sunday (2hrs) $12.* ⅙ ☏431-0233.

Located in a 6-story tenement (1863) in the midst of bustling ORCHARD STREET, this museum features a series of changing exhibits and programs focusing on all facets of the immigrant experience. A detailed exhibit depicts the lives of various families in a typical tenement, while a video and photo murals further chronicle the lifestyle of Lower East Side dwellers. The museum also offers an ambitious schedule of walking tours, slide shows and living histories.

For recorded information on current events and activities in the city: music, dance, street fairs, festivals, etc, call Parks and Recreation Information ☏*360-1333.*

★★★ THE METROPOLITAN MUSEUM OF ART

Fifth Ave at 82nd St. ● *4, 5, 6 train to 86th St. Map p 93.*

A world-renowned institution, the Metropolitan Museum of Art houses a veritable encyclopedia of the arts covering 5,000 years, from prehistory to the 20C. Richly endowed and supported, the "Met" has grown to be the largest museum in the Western hemisphere, attracting over 5 million visitors yearly.

Historical Notes. – Founded on April 13, 1870 by members of New York's Union League Club, the museum first opened in the former Dodsworth's Dancing Academy, on 681 Fifth Avenue, in 1872. The first gift to the museum was a Roman sarcophagus. Soon thereafter, General di Cesnola, a former consul in Cyprus, sold the trustees his collection of over 6,000 antiquities (mainly Cypriot glass and stone objects). In 1877, Catherine L. Wolfe donated 143 paintings, representing the Dutch and Flemish schools. Since then, the collection has grown considerably, either from purchases or from bequests and gifts of wealthy benefactors, including the Astor, Morgan, Rockefeller, Marquand, Hearn, Altman, Bache, Lehman and Wrightsman families. Today, the museum owns over 3 million objects, a fourth of which is currently displayed in the Met's 236 galleries.

The Building. – In 1880, the museum moved to its present location. Designed by Jacob Wrey Mould and **Calvert Vaux**, the landscape artist who collaborated with Olmsted in the creation of CENTRAL PARK, the Gothic-style, red brick edifice stood on land belonging to the City of New York. It still forms part of the present building (only the western facade is visible from the Lehman Wing).

The monumental Beaux-Arts facade facing Fifth Avenue, built in gray Indiana limestone, was designed by Richard Morris Hunt and completed in 1902, although the sculptural decoration has never been finished. The southwest wing was added in 1888, while the north and south side wings, designed by McKim, Mead and White, were completed in 1911 and 1913 respectively. The privately endowed Thomas J. Watson Library (designed by Brown, Lawford & Forbes), founded in 1881, was finished in 1965. On the occasion of the museum's centennial celebrations in 1970, a comprehensive architectural plan was devised to bring the entire museum to physical completion. This master plan included a series of new wings: the Robert Lehman Wing (1975), the Temple of Dendur in the Sackler Wing (1978), the American Wing (1980), the Michael C. Rockefeller Wing (1982), the Lila Acheson Wallace Wing (1987) and the Henry R. Kravis Wing (1991), all of which were designed by the architectural firm of Roche, Dinkeloo and Assocs. Connecting the main building and the Lila Acheson Wallace wing, the Carroll and Milton Petrie European sculpture court, opened in 1990, provides a skylit, sun-drenched area dotted with benches, greenery and statuary.

Principal sections of the museum. – We have organized the museum's 19 departments into 15 selected headings. *See plan p 121.*

Collection highlights are indicated in green boxes in the order of the visit.

VISIT

Open Tue–Sun 9:30am–5:15pm (Fri & Sat 8:45pm). Closed Jan 1, Thanksgiving Day & Dec 25. Suggested contribution $6. Same day admission to The Cloisters (p 101). ✗ & ☎535-7710. Owing to budgetary restrictions the museum has alternating gallery hours on Tue, Wed & Thu. Call ahead for schedule ☎879-5500.

The main entrance of the Met is on Fifth Avenue, across from 82nd Street. You will enter the Great Hall around which are located various services: checkrooms, information desk, art book and gift shops. Recorded tours of the collections and special exhibits are available for rent at a desk in the Great Hall and near special exhibit areas. Audio-guides are available for certain departments and temporary exhibits. Certain galleries may be closed (inquire at the information desk in the Great Hall) and specific works of art may be exhibited in locations other than those indicated here.

Beyond the Greek and Roman galleries, at the far left of the building, in the south wing, are a cafeteria and restaurant.

In addition to special exhibits and concerts, the museum offers a comprehensive program of classes, gallery tours, lectures, courses and films through its Ruth and Harold D. Uris Center for Education (ground floor).

We suggest you begin your visit at the Visitor Information Area in the Uris Center (ground floor). Large scale floor plans, an exhibit gallery, wall displays and a slide program shown continuously in the Orientation Theater provide information on the museum, its collections, programs and special exhibits.

Consult the legend on the inside front cover for an explanation of symbols and colors appearing on maps throughout this guide.

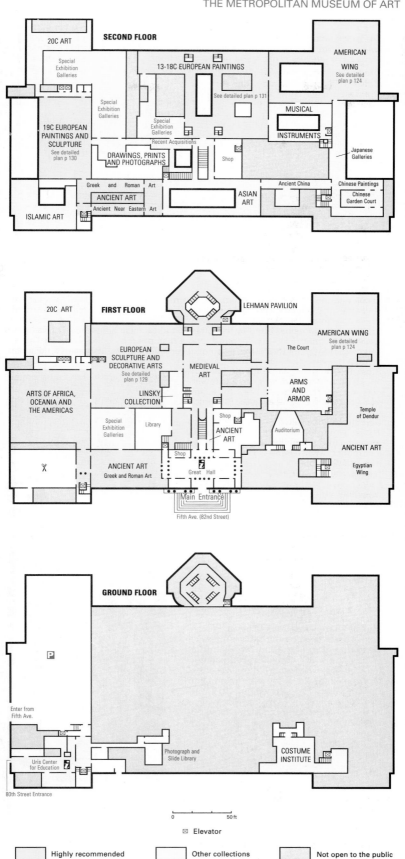

SECOND FLOOR

20C ART

Special Exhibition Galleries

Special Exhibition Galleries

13-18C EUROPEAN PAINTINGS

See detailed plan p 131

AMERICAN WING
See detailed plan p 124

MUSICAL INSTRUMENTS

19C EUROPEAN PAINTINGS AND SCULPTURE
See detailed plan p 130

Special Exhibition Galleries

Recent Acquisitions

DRAWINGS, PRINTS AND PHOTOGRAPHS

Shop

Japanese Galleries

Greek and Roman Art

ANCIENT ART

Ancient Near Eastern Art

Ancient China

Chinese Paintings

ISLAMIC ART

ASIAN ART

Chinese Garden Court

FIRST FLOOR

20C ART

LEHMAN PAVILION

AMERICAN WING
See detailed plan p 124

The Court

EUROPEAN SCULPTURE AND DECORATIVE ARTS
See detailed plan p 129

MEDIEVAL ART

ARMS AND ARMOR

Temple of Dendur

ARTS OF AFRICA, OCEANIA AND THE AMERICAS

LINSKY COLLECTION

Library

Special Exhibition Galleries

Shop

ANCIENT ART

Auditorium

ANCIENT ART

Egyptian Wing

ANCIENT ART
Greek and Roman Art

Shop

Great Hall

Main Entrance
Fifth Ave. (82nd Street)

GROUND FLOOR

P

Enter from Fifth Ave.

Photograph and Slide Library

COSTUME INSTITUTE

Uris Center for Education

80th Street Entrance

0   50 ft

⊠ Elevator

Highly recommended   Other collections   Not open to the public

MUSEUMS

★★★ AMERICAN WING   4 1/2 hours. Plan p 124.

The museum's comprehensive collection of American art traces the history of this country, from the colonial period through the early 20C. This world-class assemblage of Americana is displayed on the three floors of the American Wing, which contains period rooms, decorative art galleries and a section devoted to paintings and sculpture.

- Tiffany stained-glass windows
- Sullivan staircases
- Saint-Gaudens and LaFarge mantelpiece
- Facade of the United States Bank
- Tea urn (Paul Revere)
- Tea service (attributed to Christian Wiltberger)
- Art glass (Tiffany)
- Six-shell mahogany desk and bookcase (Newport)
- High chest of drawers (Boston)
- *Lady With Her Pets* (Hathaway)
- Toy animals (William Schimmel)
- Shakers' Retiring Room
- Bookcase and desk (Baltimore)
- Sideboard
- *George Washington* (Stuart)
- *View from Mount Holyoke, Massachusetts, after a Thunderstorm – The Oxbow* (Cole)
- *The Rocky Mountains* (Bierstadt)
- *The Aegean Sea* (Church)
- *Washington Crossing the Delaware* (Leutze)
- *Andrew Jackson* (Powers)
- *Prisoners From the Front* (Homer)
- *The Gulf Stream* (Homer)
- *Northeaster* (Homer)
- *Max Schmidt in a Single Scull* (Eakins)
- *The Bronco Buster* (Remington)
- *Madame X* (Sargent)

The Court

Located to the rear of the museum, the enormous, glass-walled garden court presents the works of well-known American artists and architects in a pleasant, landscaped setting. The various pieces, reflecting a wide range of styles, include a multitude of pieces designed by the Tiffany Studios, including several **stained-glass windows [A]** and the Islamic-inspired loggia fashioned by Louis Comfort Tiffany *(p 123)* for his Oyster Bay home; a pair of decorative cast-iron **staircases [B]** designed in 1893 by Louis Sullivan for the Chicago Stock Exchange Building (demolished in 1972); Frank Lloyd Wright's triptych window made for a children's playhouse; and an imposing marble **mantelpiece [C]**, which once graced the Fifth Avenue home of Cornelius Vanderbilt.

The selection of 19C and 20C sculptures arranged throughout the garden illustrates a number of stylistic trends in the development of American sculpture. The earlier pieces, dating primarily from the 1850s, reflect a period when American artists traveling abroad were inspired by the antique statuary of Italy and the ideals of the classical world. Note, in particular, George Grey Barnard's *Struggle of the Two Natures of Man*.

Following the Civil War, Augustus Saint-Gaudens, returning from his studies in Italy and Paris, exerted a strong influence on American sculptors through his numerous large-scale memorials and symbolic figures. The *Diana* covered in gilded copper gracing the center of the court is an example of his work.

Equally famous was Daniel Chester French, who is best remembered for his impressive *Seated Lincoln* in the Lincoln Memorial (Washington DC). French is represented here by replicas in marble of two of his works, on the balcony overlooking the Court *(gallery 201)*: the enigmatic *Mourning Victory* and the Milmore Memorial.

At the north end of the court, the **facade [D]** of the United States Bank (Wall Street branch) has been installed. Erected in 1824 in the Federal style, the building was designed by Martin E. Thompson and constructed of Tuckahoe marble from quarries in Westchester County, New York.

Ascend the stairs to the balcony level.

Pewter, Silver, Glass, Ceramics. – *Galleries 201, 202, 203.* Major designs and stylistic trends in American pewter, silver, glass and ceramics are illustrated by exhibits on the balcony overlooking the Court.

The Metropolitan Museum of Art, gift of Ruth and Frank Stanton

Stained-glass window *Grapevine* by Tiffany Studios

In the 17C and 18C, pewter—a metal composed principally of tin with small amounts of lead and antimony—was transformed into a wide range of household and ceremonial items. In gallery 202, note the tankard made by John Will (18C); a typical example of the popular drinking vessel of the period, this piece is prized for its delicate floral engraving. Displayed in the second wall case is one of several works by the patriot-silversmith, Paul Revere, owned by the museum: a large tankard topped with a pineapple finial. A **tea urn** fashioned by Paul Revere (1791) is also shown in this gallery.

Especially interesting is the close relationship between silver fashions of the period and furniture design trends: the simple, pear-shaped contours of the 18C teapot made by Peter van Dyck recall the gracefully curved cabriole leg characteristic of the Queen Anne style; the eagle, adapted from the Great Seal of the United States, was a popular motif during the early years of the new Republic: eagle finials complement the refined engraving of the four-piece **tea service** (1799) attributed to Christian Wiltberger, and said to have been a wedding present to Eleanor Custis on the occasion of her marriage to Lawrence Lewis, a nephew of George Washington.

Elaborate Rococo Revival tea services are reminiscent of the richness of the intricately carved Chippendale pieces. The exquisite one-of-a-kind pieces by Tiffany and Company—the Adams gold vase, encrusted with pearls and semiprecious stones, and the Magnolia vase (1893) covered with gold, enamels and opals—are hallmarks of America's "gilded age" of railroad kings, coal barons and finance tycoons.

In gallery 203, the section reserved for glass, the first group of cases features hand blown, cut, engraved and pressed glass. Craftsmen working in the traditional methods to create fine glassware, produced the hand cut and engraved compote ordered by Mrs Lincoln for the White House in 1861.

There are numerous examples of pressed glass, an American innovation that revolutionized the glass industry in the early 19C. Pressed into pattern molds mechanically rather than by hand, this type of glassware could be produced rapidly and at a low cost in a wide range of forms and patterns: a clear glass compote made in Pittsburgh in the 1860s illustrates the popular Thumbprint pattern.

Nearby an exhibit focuses on blown-molded glass: the glass blown into a mold is embossed with a pattern, then removed from the mold and blown into a larger shape. Other wall cases illustrate late-19C American art glass, a type of ornamental opaque glass that featured shaded coloring, a rich texture and an elegant shape.

The highlight of the collection, however, is the beautiful iridescent **glass work** by **Louis Comfort Tiffany**, son of the founder of the famous jewelry store (p 36). A proponent of the Art Nouveau movement, Tiffany was one of the most influential innovators of his day. His vases and lamps, distinguished by a luminous quality of colors and sensuous grace of form, are considered masterpieces of American decorative art.

Among the remaining exhibits note the selection of American ceramics and pottery: pitchers and statuettes of Parian ware, a white porcelain so named because it resembles the marble quarried on the Greek island of Paros; stoneware jugs decorated in cobalt blue; and a variety of items in Rockingham, an earthenware glazed a streaked brown color.

Interior Decoration

Beyond the facade of the United States Bank, a series of period rooms and decorative arts galleries illustrate the development of stylistic trends from the 17C to 20C. Although strongly marked by the English tradition, American decoration was also influenced by continental styles.

To visit the period rooms and decorative arts galleries in chronological order, begin on the 3rd floor. Take elevator E2 from the 1st floor.

Early Colonial Period (1630-1730). – *3rd floor; galleries 301-312.* Located past the gallery of 17C furniture, the sparsely decorated 1674 Hart Room *(gallery 303)*, from Ipswich Massachusetts, features a huge fireplace, plaster walls, exposed hand-hewn beams, a low ceiling and tiny casement windows, all typical of the period. In gallery 305, the Newington Room contains decoratively painted furniture typical to the settlements of the Connecticut Valley. The Meetinghouse Gallery *(gallery 309)* presents examples of 17C and early-18C furnishings, which often recall the European styles brought over by the first settlers. The roof trusses of this gallery are inspired by those found in the Old Ship Meetinghouse in Hingham, Massachusetts (1681).

Gallery 310, a room from the John Hewlett House (1740-1760) on Long Island, illustrates both a classical influence—in the fluted pilasters and heavy cornice—and the survival of the Dutch tradition, with the Biblical fireplace tiles and the large cupboard. Contrasting with the somber, modestly furnished Hart Room *(above)* of an earlier date is the spacious John Wentworth Room (1695) from Portsmouth, New Hampshire *(gallery 312)*. This room marks the transition into the 18C with double-hung sash windows, a large mantelpiece, and pine paneling framing the fireplace and covering an entire wall. The easy chair and high chest of drawers, decorated with veneers and japanning (an imitation of lacquer-ware), are among the new forms of furniture to appear.

Take elevator E1 to the 2nd floor then follow the stairway to the Old Wing. Begin in gallery 210.

Late Colonial Period (1730-1790). – *2nd floor; galleries 209-215.* During this period, the interiors—particularly in the wealthy seaport cities of Boston, Newport, New York, Philadelphia and Baltimore—became increasingly elegant as mahogany replaced maple and walnut. The gracefully curved cabriole legs first gained popularity, then were supplanted by the heavily carved rococo designs of the English

AMERICAN WING

THIRD FLOOR

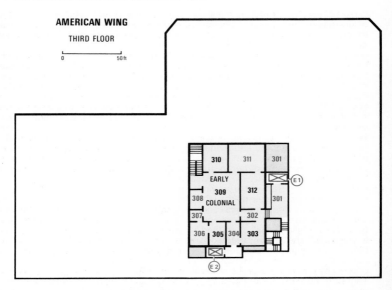

SECOND FLOOR

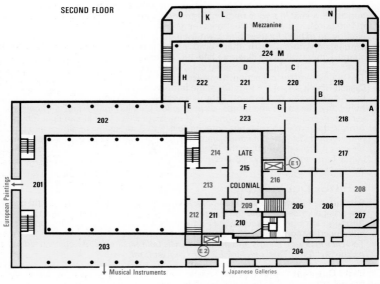

FIRST FLOOR

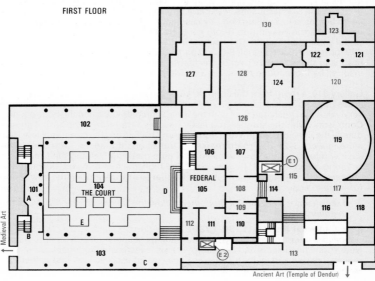

cabinetmaker, Thomas Chippendale. Although regional differences in style prevailed, the homes in cosmopolitan cities were generally characterized by a taste for refined decoration and comfort, while simple styles interpreted by local artisans continued to persist in rural areas.

The Pennsylvania German Room *(gallery 210)* attests to the colorful folk art traditions of the German immigrants, who adorned their furniture and household items with brilliantly painted geometric and floral patterns and animal figures. The chest painted with red and white tulips, unicorns and doves was probably a dower chest. Nearby, the Powel Room *(gallery 211),* a parlor from the home (1766) of the last colonial mayor of Philadelphia, contains rich mahogany furniture, set off against the most striking feature of this room, the handpainted Chinese wallpaper.

The largest reconstitution on this floor is the 1792 Alexandria Ballroom *(gallery 215)* from Gadsby's Tavern in Alexandria, Virginia. The two chimneys, the musician's gallery, the Queen Anne and Chippendale chairs, and the brass chandeliers reflected in the old mirrors transport us to another era: it was here that George Washington attended his last birthday ball in 1798.

Continue into the New Wing (galleries 204-208).

The handpainted English wallpapers in the Van Rensselaer hall *(gallery 206),* from Albany, New York, depict scenic landscape panels surrounded by a flourish of scrolls and rococo designs. In the Marmion Room *(gallery 207),* from Virginia, handpainted landscapes, fruit-filled cornucopia and urns topped with flowers cover the wooden wall panels; the cornice, pilasters and bottom panels are painted to simulate marble.

Galleries 204 and 205 highlight regional differences in furniture styles and fashions. In gallery 204, note the stately six-shell mahogany **desk and bookcase** made in Newport (1760-1790), the Boston-made japanned **high chest of drawers** (1730-1760), and the cabinetwork of the tall case clocks, which came into vogue in the 18C.

Galleries 217-224 and the mezzanine level highlight American paintings and sculpture *(see p 126 for descriptions).*

From gallery 205 take the staircase down to the 1st floor; begin in gallery 116.

Folk Decoration. – The folk traditions of the untrained artisan and craftsman developed simultaneously with the high-style decorative arts, from the colonial period through the 19C. Working primarily in rural areas, the folk artist painted portraits, such as **Lady With Her Pets** (Rufus Hathaway, 1790), flat in appearance and lacking perspective, and carved and decorated useful items for the home and farm.

The galleries in this section contain scrimshaw dating from the whaling era, and tiny gaily painted **animals** made by William Schimmel, an itinerant craftsman who carved toy animals in exchange for his room and board. Dating from the same era is the neat, airy and sparsely furnished **Retiring Room** *(gallery 118)* of the Shakers, a religious sect that reached its peak in America in the 19C. The pure lines and superb craftsmanship of the chairs, tables and cupboards they made, mirror the order and harmony that guided the lives of the members of this sect. Stenciling, a decorative technique, which uses precut stencils and paint, was used to embellish the furnishings, floors and walls of many homes.

In gallery 119, John Vanderlyn's panorama, painted between 1816 and 1819, transports the viewer to the gardens outside the palace of Versailles in the 19C.

Federal Period (1790-1820). – This section features a series of period rooms of the Federal period, the decades of economic expansion following the Revolution. The light and delicate lines of the neoclassical style predominated, as exemplified in the work of Scottish architect-designers James and Robert Adam. Inspired by Roman art and architecture, the Adam brothers had an important impact on the furniture and building designs of their day in England, and ultimately in America.

In furniture, forms were lighter than those of the colonial period, and carving was subdued in favor of veneers, inlay and marquetry. Painted glass panels adorn the 1811 **bookcase and desk** *(gallery 105)* and the imposing **sideboard** (1795-1815) in the Baltimore Room *(gallery 106).*

Elaborately carved and gilded looking glasses, and decorative shelf clocks made principally by New England clockmakers, add a light note to the restrained classical interiors. Architecturally, the influence of the Adam brothers is seen in the use of classical motifs (urns, swags), slender pilasters and colonnettes, delicately adorned fireplace mantels and pastel tones. The overall effect is of understated elegance as in the 1811 Benkard Room *(gallery 107)* and the 1805 Haverhill Room *(gallery 111).* The 1810 **Richmond Room** *(gallery 110)* is unusual for the period because of its heavy moldings, mahogany woodwork and the massive proportions of its doorways. Furnishings made by the New York cabinetmakers, Duncan Phyfe and Charles Honore Lannuier, are set off by the scenic wallpaper in muted colors, depicting the grand monuments of Paris.

The Revival Styles (1820-1870). – The neoclassical style, which predominated during the early 19C, gave way in later decades to a succession of revival styles: Gothic, Rococo, Renaissance, Louis XVI and Egyptian. Inspiration varied, giving rise to furniture fashions ranging from the elegant, refined Greek Revival forms of Duncan Phyfe *(gallery 121)* to the rich, heavily ornamental designs of John Henry Belter *(gallery 122).*

Especially grand were the elaborate furnishings, architectural detailing and decoration of the Renaissance Revival style *(gallery 124).* The adjacent gallery features a stairhall designed in 1884 by the architectural firm of McKim, Mead and White for a house in Buffalo, New York.

In gallery 127, the contemporary style of the early 20C is exemplified by the living room from the Francis Little House (1912-1914) designed by Frank Lloyd Wright *(p 117)*. Decorated in warm earth tones and looking out on Central Park, the well-proportioned interior forms a harmonious extension of the outdoors.

Painting and Sculpture

The approximately 400 works on display from the museum's collection are arranged chronologically, constituting a general survey of American art from the colonial period to the early 20C.

Begin in gallery 217.

18C to mid-19C. – *Galleries 217-221, 223.* In the 18C, a number of foreign-born and native portrait painters predominated in America. Born in Scotland, John Smibert *(Mrs Francis Brinley and Her Son Francis)* studied in Italy and settled in Boston in 1729, opening the era of professional painting in the colonies. Particularly well known were John Singleton Copley, who painted prominent personalities of his day, and Gilbert Stuart, best known for his portraits of **George Washington [A]**.

By the late 18C Americans were traveling abroad to study with their fellow countryman, Benjamin West, in London. West, a leader of the neoclassical movement, painted allegorical canvases *(The Triumph of Love, gallery 218)*, drawing his subjects mainly from history and mythology. The grand manner and scale he favored inspired his student, John Trumbull, to paint large historical canvases. In *The Sortie Made by the Garrison of Gibraltar (gallery 218),* Trumbull dramatizes an event that occurred during the siege of the English fortress by the French and Spanish.

Gallery 219 features portrait painting, which began in the early 19C and reached its peak in the hands of the Romantic painters, Thomas Sully *(Mother and Son)* and Samuel F.B. Morse *(The Muse)*, the latter better known as the inventor of the telegraph. In the meantime, other artists were turning their attention to genre scenes. George Caleb Bingham (**Fur Traders Descending the Missouri, B**) transported the viewer further west to a land familiar to few.

Landscape painting also flourished. The huge, lyrical canvases of the Hudson River school, America's first school of landscape painting, depicted the grandeur and beauty of a vast, still largely unspoiled American continent. The best-known artists of the school were Thomas Cole, with **View from Mount Holyoke [C]** *(gallery 220)*, Asher B. Durand with *The Beeches,* Albert Bierstadt with **The Rocky Mountains [D]** *(gallery 221),* and Frederic E. Church with **The Aegean Sea [E]** *(gallery 223)*.

In the mid-19C, pride in the nation's history and great geographical and economic expansion inspired Emanuel Leutze to paint **Washington Crossing the Delaware [F]** *(gallery 223)* recounting that historical moment when, on Christmas night, 1776, Washington made a surprise attack on the Hessians. At the far end of gallery 223 is Hiram Powers' marble bust of **Andrew Jackson [G]**.

Mid-19C to 20C. – *Galleries 222, 224 and Mezzanine.* Distinctly American in temperament were **Winslow Homer**, **Frederic Remington** and **Thomas Eakins**. Homer's experience as an illustrator is reflected in his early paintings, which depict the events of the time, such as the Civil War scene, **Prisoners from the Front [H]**. Gallery 224 contains works by Frederic Remington who immortalized the cowboy, scout, Indian, and cavalry of the Old West, and the vanishing frontier, in his action-filled bronzes (late 19C). Also in gallery 224 are several small works by Albert Pinkham Ryder.

Take the stairs straight ahead down to the Mezzanine.

The dramatically elegant **Madame X [O]** was created by fashionable portrait painter John Singer Sargent, who was trained in Paris and influenced by the portraits of Velázquez.

In his later paintings, Homer found inspiration in the powerful forces of the sea, and his vigorous interpretations made him a master of naturalism, as evidenced in **The Gulf Stream [K]** and **Northeaster [L]**. Eakins, a contemporary of Homer, shared the latter's direct manner but preferred to paint people: *The Thinker: Portrait of Louis Kenton* reveals the influence of Velázquez, while *The Writing Master* reveals a familiarity with Rembrandt's technique. Predating Impressionism, his scenes of sports of the day are of interest for their brightly illuminated out-of-doors setting: **Max Schmidt in a Single Scull [N]**.

In the late 19C other American painters began to adopt the style of the Impressionists: the quick unbroken brushstrokes, uneven paint surfaces and bright colors that characterized the canvases of William Merritt Chase *(At the Seaside)* and Childe Hassam *(Winter in Union Square)* clearly show the influence of the French artists.

Many American painters spent a considerable part of their lives abroad, including Mary Cassatt *(Portrait of a Young Girl),* a student of Degas and the only American to become a prominent member of the Impressionist group; and James McNeill Whistler *(Arrangement in Flesh Colour and Black: Portrait of Theodore Duret)* who spent much of his career in England.

Also located on the mezzanine level is the Henry R. Luce Center for the Study of American Art, which presents, in chronological order, fine art and decorative art objects that are currently not on display. An elaborate computer network (AWARE—American Wing Art Research) allows access to over 10,000 catalogued objects.

Sights described in this guide are rated:

★★★   *Highly recommended*

★★   *Recommended*

★   *Interesting*

★★★ ANCIENT ART

This section includes the Egyptian Wing, Greek and Roman Art and Ancient Near Eastern Art.

Egyptian Wing *(1st floor) 3 hours*

Displayed in a series of galleries north of the Great Hall, this large collection, ranging from the Predynastic period (prior to 3100 BC) to the Coptic period (AD 641), includes over 35,000 objects reflecting Egyptian civilization, one of the earliest in the history of man.

The life and customs of the ancient Egyptians were closely bound to religion. They believed that death was only a transition on the journey from this life to the eternal world, and built temples and tombs as dwelling places for the spirits of the dead. Most Egyptian art comes from these temples and tombs, which were constructed to house not only the remains of the deceased, but also the many objects needed to ensure life in the next world.

> *We suggest you visit the galleries chronologically by beginning on the right side as you enter the Wing. The door jambs between galleries identify the time period.*

Orientation Area. – *Gallery 1.* Comprehensive descriptions, a time line and a wall map, along with predynastic objects, sculptures and a stone sarcophagus, introduce the visitor to the civilization of ancient Egypt. Enter the mastaba (an Arabic designation for an above-ground tomb) and chapel of Pernebi, the burial site of a dignitary of the Fifth dynasty court at Memphis.

Dynasties 1-18. – *Galleries 2-15.* Presented in gallery 2 are examples of reliefs, sculpture, architecture and everyday objects from the First through the Tenth dynasties (3100-2040 BC), and reliefs from the famous Cheops Pyramid (Fourth dynasty). The two stone figures of a bound prisoner kneeling down (Fifth dynasty) are portrayed with slanted eyes and deep facial furrows to indicate they are foreigners. Figures such as these were placed in the royal temples of the Old Kingdom to symbolize the king's control over disorder. Also from the Fifth dynasty are wood and stone statues of officials.

The Sixth dynasty was followed by a period of political strife. After two centuries of instability, a Theban king, Nebhepetra Mentuhotpe, reunited Egypt and established the golden age known as the **Middle Kingdom**. The objects in galleries 3-5 belonged to him, his family and the officials who served him. Outstanding is the group of **models** from the 11th dynasty tomb of Mekutra, chancellor of Mentuhotpe. These small painted models showing workers in the bakery, the brewery and the slaughterhouse, among others, present a fascinating picture of daily activities in ancient Egypt. The boats lining the back wall, and the colorful wooden figures in the Procession of Bearers also come from his tomb.

In galleries 6 and 7, note the massive red granite offering table used in the funerary temple of Amenemhat I, and the Stela of Montuwosre, a stone tablet that has retained much of its original paint and is engraved with hieroglyphs describing Montuwosre's career as a king's steward.

Objects exhibited in gallery 8 illustrate the high standards reached by artisans of the Middle Kingdom, especially in portraiture and jewelry. A superb group of **12th dynasty royal portraits** includes the small but delicately carved representation of Senwosret III as a sphinx, and the highly expressive face of the same king in red quartzite. Displayed just beyond are the **royal jewels** of Princess Sithathoryunet excavated from her tomb at Lahun. Note the girdle of amethyst beads and gold spacers shaped like leopard heads, which were designed to tinkle rhythmically as the princess walked. The gold pectoral of Senwosret II, a gift from her father, is inlaid with a myriad of tiny pieces of semiprecious stones; at the center of the design, a kneeling god supports the king's cartouche.

Displayed in gallery 12, the monumental **statues of Queen Hatshepsut** (early 18th dynasty) from her funerary complex at Deir el Bahri, portray the queen in a variety of poses: the colossal red granite kneeling statues show Hatshepsut in a rigid pose as a male, wearing the white crown of Upper Egypt or the nemes headdress; in sharp contrast is the graceful seated figure in white limestone, which presents her without a beard as a ruler possessing more feminine qualities.

The funerary mask of Hatnofer *(gallery 13)*, covered in gold foil, is also from the early 18th dynasty. The same fine workmanship is evident in the fragile gold sandals and falcon-headed collars *(gallery 14)*, which served as funerary adornments to three royal wives.

The last group of artifacts in this section *(gallery 15)* represents the reign of Amenhotpe III. These works are of interest for the high quality of their sculptural detail. Note, in particular, the superbly preserved rendition, in faience, of Amenhotpe III as a sphinx. The four diorite statues in the center of the room represent Sekhmet, the lion-headed goddess of the desert and destruction, and the powerful protectress of the pharaoh.

Dynasties 18-30. – *Galleries 16-24, 26, 29.* This section covers the Amarna, Ramesside and Late periods from 1379 to 330 BC. Reliefs, sculpture and funerary art from the reign of Akhenaton, who moved the capital of Egypt from Thebes to Amarna, and other 18th dynasty kings (Tutankhamun, Ay and Haremhab) are arranged in galleries 16-18. In gallery 17, royal statuary includes a head of the boy king Tutankhamun and a head of the god Amun. Also displayed here is a rare find: the materials from the embalming of Tutankhamun and the remains of the banquet held at the closing of his tomb. In a separate glass case, together with objects from a royal tomb in the Valley of the Kings, is an alabaster canopic jar with a lid carved in the form of a portrait head.

Entering gallery 18, note the central statue of General Haremhab, who was later crowned king of Egypt. The enormous basalt sarcophagus of Harkhebit, incised with his name and titles in hieroglyphs, dates from 664 to 525 BC. In the hallway, the limestone statue of Yuny, and the pair statue of Yuny and his wife provide insight into the garments and jewelry of the period. The funerary papyrus intended to assist the deceased in passing through the next world and the granite doorjamb of Ramesses II are also of this period.

Gallery 19, to the left, is devoted to the Ramesside period, named for the succession of 19th and 20th dynasty pharaohs named Ramesses. Representations of two kings of the period include a kneeling statue of Sety I and the head of Amenmesse. The stela of Ptahmose bears four prayers and a representation of Ptahmose.

In gallery 20, note especially among the museum's extensive holdings from dynasties 21 through 25, a tiny gold statuette of Amun holding the Ankh—symbol for life—and the group of magnificently painted ornamented coffins of the 21st dynasty, which includes the inner and outer coffins of Henettawy, Tabakmut and Menkheperra. The mummy, cartonnage and coffins of Kharushere all date from the second half of the 22nd dynasty.

Among the bronze and faience temple sculptures and small objects of the period in gallery 22, notice a bronze figure of Osiris with golden inlay and two decorative faience bottles inscribed with prayers for a happy new year. Along one wall, funerary material includes delicate gold foil mummy amulets and faience shawabtys, miniature servants intended to perform menial tasks for the deceased in the afterlife, and a choice assortment of scarabs and bijoux.

Gallery 23 focuses on objects from the 30th dynasty (380-342 BC), including Prince Wennefer's massive sarcophagus granite relief from the temples of the Delta and the magnificent "Metternich Stela."

Occupying the entire gallery 25 is the **Temple of Dendur**, dating from the early Roman period (time of Augustus), around 15 BC. The temple was a gift from the Egyptian government in the 1960s in recognition of American assistance in saving the temples of Nubia, including Abu Simbel, from being submerged by the lake created by the Aswan Dam.

Ptolemaic Period; Roman-Coptic Periods (30 BC-641 AD). – *Galleries 26-29, 31, 32.* Of special interest are galleries 26 and 29, which have been set aside for the museum's rich collection of color facsimiles of tomb and temple paintings. Galleries 27 and 28 display stone sarcophagi, mummies and two long papyri (excerpts from a "Book of the Dead") ranging in time from Alexander's conquest of Egypt (332 BC) to the death of Cleopatra (30 BC).

Gallery 31 contains a collection of Roman art from the time of Augustus (30-1 BC) to 4C AD; note here the remarkable **Fayum Portraits**, eight portrait-panels painted in wax in 2C AD. Also shown in this section is a group of about 40 excellent pieces of Coptic Art (Egyptian Christian period, 2C-641 AD) including a wide range of ceremonial, traditional and ritual objects as well as pieces hailing from monastic communities.

Greek and Roman Art   *(1st and 2nd floors) 1 hour*
On the 1st floor there are nine galleries south of the Great Hall and one gallery north of the main staircase; on the 2nd floor there are four galleries south of the Great Hall balcony.

Located on the first floor, the large collection of Cypriot antiquities and Cycladic objects illustrates the variety of art created by these early centers of civilization. The collection traces the evolution of Greek and Roman pottery and sculpture, and also includes examples of Etruscan art (bronze chariot from the 6C).

The **Greek and Roman Treasury** *(north of the main staircase)* displays the museum's collection of ancient Greek and Roman gold and silver plate, with a focus on table ware and ceremonial vessels. Note especially the gold libation bowl (3-4C BC) embellished with circles of acorns and beechnuts, and the archaic silver jugs and ladles (Greek, 6C BC).

The Geometric period in Greece produced works with pure and simplified lines, such as the bronze statuette of a horse (1C BC-1C AD). The search for form, especially in the portrayal of the human body (Kouros, 7C BC), dominates in the grave monuments and reliefs from the Archaic period.

The Classical period produced sculptures showing greater freedom; these are often represented by Roman copies of the Greek original. The Hellenistic period developed greater diversity and realism, as can be seen by the portrayal of age in the *Peasant Woman* (2C BC).

The evolution of pottery followed a similar pattern when the geometric designs of the early period were superseded by human forms and scenes portraying mythological subjects of everyday life *(2nd floor galleries)*. The black and red figure techniques are both represented. The outstanding **Euphronios Krater**, dating from about 515 BC, is displayed in gallery IV. This red-figured calyx-krater—signed by both the potter, Euxitheos, and the painter, Euphronios—depicts on one side the body of Sarpedon, son of Zeus, being lifted by Sleep and Death, and on the other, an arming scene.

The first gallery next to the Great Hall contains an interesting collection of sarcophagi, and a group of portrait busts typical of the realism of expression of the later Roman period. Adorning the walls is a series of wall paintings from a villa at Boscoreale near Pompeii, which was buried by the eruption of Vesuvius in AD 79. The paintings recall traditional theatrical scenery and prominently employ the characteristic Pompeian red. In the southeast corner of the Great Hall before entering the gallery, the bedroom (cubiculum) from the same villa has been embellished by a 2C mosaic floor, which probably originated from a bath near Rome.

Ancient Near Eastern Art *(2nd floor) 1 hour*

The collections of this department cover a vast region of southwestern Asia, reaching from Turkey to Afghanistan and the Indus Valley, and from the Caucasus Mountains in the north to the Arabian peninsula in the south. On view are sculptures, pottery and metalwork dating from the sixth millennium BC to the beginning of Islam, with particular emphasis on the Sumerian and Assyrian civilizations of Mesopotamia and the prehistoric, Achaemenian and Sasanian civilizations of Iran. Highlighting this section is a group of 20 large stone panels from the palace of Ashurnasirpal II, King of Assyria from 883 to 859 BC. Low relief carvings depict the king (holding a bow and bowl), bird-headed and human-headed deities, and the sacred tree, symbolizing fertility, while inscriptions extol the king and the accomplishments of his reign. Located nearby, the two enormous, five-legged, winged creatures once adorned the palace entranceways. Note also the finely carved ivories (8C BC), excavated at Nimrud, Iraq.

The glazed lion panels originally graced the Ishtar Gate (6C BC), built in Babylon by Nebuchadnezzar II. Additional objects on view include the cylinder and stamp seals from Mesopotamia; stone sculptures from Sumeria; a group of bronze artifacts (8-7C BC) from cemetery sites at Luristan; and painted pottery (5000-4000 BC), silver and mercury gilded drinking horns (rhytons) and vessels (8C BC-6C AD) from Iran.

★★★ EUROPEAN SCULPTURE AND DECORATIVE ARTS
(1st floor) 3 hours

This is one of the museum's largest departments, comprising over 60,000 works of art ranging from the Renaissance to the early 20C. Pieces include sculpture, furniture, ceramics, woodwork, glass, metalwork and textiles, with an emphasis on French and English furniture and French and German porcelain, exhibited in exquisitely re-created period rooms.

Northern Renaissance and Italian Galleries. – *Galleries 1-5, 8-10.* These galleries include the interior of a chapel faced with marquetry paneling, modeled after the one in the French Chateau de la Bastie d'Urfé (1550); the Elizabethan "Nelson Room" from the Star Hotel Great Yarmouth (Norfolk); and a paneled room with ceramic stove from Flims in Switzerland. In the center of gallery 2 stands a monumental table inlaid with alabaster and semiprecious stones; it was designed by the architect Jacopo Barozzi da Vignola for the Farnese Palace in Rome, in the 16C. A small vestibule provides an entrance to the rococo bedroom *(gallery 9)* from the Sagredo Palace in Venice (early 18C). Faience on display includes Italian maiolica from Urbino, Gubbio and Deruta (16C) as well as later productions of the Delft and French workshops.

English Galleries. – *Galleries 14-20.* To follow the development of English decorative arts from 1660 to 1840, begin in gallery 19. A staircase from Cassiobury Park, Hertfordshire, by Gibbons, represents the decorative arts of the 17C *(gallery 19)*, while the rococo style of the mid-18C is reflected in the stucco decoration of a dining room from Kirtlington Park, Oxfordshire, now arranged as a drawing room *(gallery 20)*.

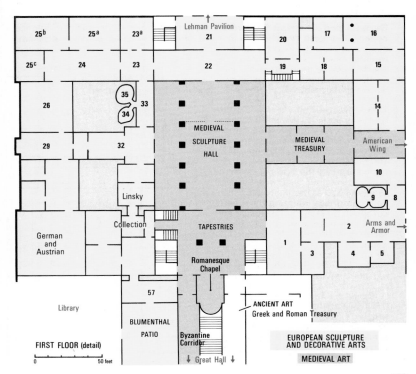

FIRST FLOOR (detail)

0 — 50 feet

The Tapestry Room *(gallery 17)*, formerly at Croome Court, Warwickshire, was designed by Robert Adam (1728-1792), who gave his name to the Adamesque style. The crimson wall coverings and upholstery, ordered by Lord Coventry, were made at the Gobelins factory and designed by François Boucher. Also designed by Adam is the refined dining room *(gallery 16)* from Lansdowne House, London. Pastel colors, pilasters, niches for ancient statues, and "Pompeian" stucco decoration stand in delicate contrast to the deep tones of the mahogany table and chairs. The Lamerie silver and an elaborate chandelier complete the arrangement. Galleries 15 and 18 present a varied collection of 18C English decorative arts; French objects produced during that same period are displayed in galleries 21 and 22.

French Galleries. – *Galleries 23-29 and 32-35*. These galleries of 18C period rooms and settings present a full and rich panorama of the French decorative arts. The introductory gallery *(33)* contains a Paris shopfront of 1775. Embellished with pilasters and fancifully carved garlands, this charming boutique facade is typical of the Louis XVI style. In its windows are displayed outstanding examples of Paris silver. Branching off of the gallery are two elegant small rooms *(galleries 34, 35)*. The rococo boudoir from the Hôtel de Crillon is graced with pieces of furniture from the Chateau of St-Cloud, including a daybed made for Marie-Antoinette. The Bordeaux Room is a delicately paneled circular salon decorated and furnished in the neoclassical style.

Hung in the Louis XV room *(gallery 23)* is a replica of the famous *Portrait of Louis XV as a Young Boy* painted by Rigaud and hanging at Versailles. Among the porcelain in the Sèvres Alcove Gallery is a unique vase in the form of a ship and pieces in the delicate turquoise-blue for which Sèvres was famous. Beyond the alcove is a graceful room *(gallery 23a)* from the Hôtel Lauzun, in Paris, the setting for an exquisite collection of French furniture inlaid with Sèvres porcelain plaques. Masterpieces by the cabinetmakers Carlin, Weisweiler and Bernard II van Risenburgh (B.V.R.B.) are also displayed. The bronze and marble clock in the form of a black woman is by André Furet, watchmaker to Louis XVI; when one of the figure's earrings is pulled, the hours and minutes appear as numbers in her eyes.

Four 18C rooms open into the Louis XVI gallery *(24)*, furnished with Japanese lacquered furniture. The white and gold paneled salon *(gallery 25a)* from the Hôtel de Varengeville contains magnificent Louis XV furniture, particularly the king's own desk from his study at Versailles. In the room from the Palais Paar in Vienna *(gallery 25b)*, a late rococo room in blue and gold tones, are exquisite pieces of furniture, among them a writing table by Van Risenburgh and a rock-crystal chandelier. The neoclassical, oak-paneled reception room *(gallery 25c)* from the Hôtel de Cabris in Grasse still retains the original gilding on the paneling. Among the treasures in the room is a *nécessaire de voyage,* a collapsible table used for traveling, dressing and eating. The Hôtel de Tessé room *(gallery 26)* with its gray and gold neoclassical paneling was the grand salon of the Comtesse de Tessé's residence. The room displays a rare 17C Savonnerie carpet and furniture made for Marie-Antoinette by Jean-Henry Riesener.

The final two galleries highlight art from the reigns of Louis XIII and Louis XIV. The Louis XIV style state bedchamber displays a set of hangings embroidered with allegories of the Seasons and the Elements; several pieces of furniture by André-Charles Boulle, appointed cabinetmaker to the king in 1672; and a monumental carved chimneypiece after designs by Jean le Pautre.

German and Austrian Galleries. – Ceramics on display include 18C faience pottery, enameled Zwischengold glass (1730) from Bohemia, and a large assemblage of Meissen stoneware and porcelain. The floral garden room furniture was commissioned by Prince Bishop Adam Friedrich von Seinsheim for his Franck-enstein Pavilion at Schloß Seehof near Bamberg, Germany.

★ **The Jack and Belle Linsky Collection.** – Opened in 1984, these galleries present the private collection compiled by the Linskys over a period of 40 years. Approximately 375 works of art are displayed in seven rooms designed to create the intimate setting of a private residence. Praised for its beauty as well as its quality, the collection comprises paintings by early European masters, Renaissance and Baroque bronzes, European porcelains, 18C French furniture, jewelry and fine examples of goldsmith's work.

Among the paintings representing the Italian, Flemish, French, Dutch and German schools, note the *Madonna and Child* by the Venetian, Carlo Crivelli (15C), and the earliest dated work (1597) by Rubens, a portrait painted on copper of an architect or geographer. The expressive bronzes include *Monk-Scribe on a Dragon* (12C) and Antico's *Satyr* (16C). Exhibited in a late-18C period room are an 18C commode by

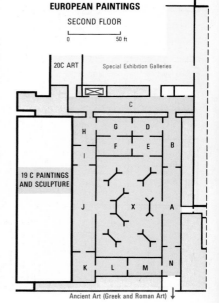

EUROPEAN PAINTINGS

SECOND FLOOR

0   50 ft

20C ART   Special Exhibition Galleries

C

H   G   D

F   E   B

I

19 C PAINTINGS
AND SCULPTURE

J   X   A

K   L   M   N

Ancient Art (Greek and Roman Art) ↓

David Roentgen and a writing table inlaid with exquisite marquetry crafted by Jean-François Oeben for Mme de Pompadour. Over 200 rococo porcelain figures, from the factories of Meissen and Chantilly, dot the various rooms. Equally noteworty are the porcelain figures depicting Russian national types made at the Imperial Porcelain Manufactory in St Petersburg (late 18C).

Blumenthal Patio (Vélez Blanco). – Reconstructed in the museum in 1964, this Renaissance patio comes from the castle of Vélez Blanco in Spain. The white marble galleries and the fine bas-relief decoration by Lombard sculptors, as well as the capitals, arches and balustrades bearing Italian Renaissance motifs, reflect typical Mediterranean architecture. The Latin inscription beneath the cornice gives the name of the owner, Pedro Fajardo, and the dates of construction (1506-1515). Gallery 57, adjacent to the Blumenthal Patio, displays examples of Italian bronze statuettes by the masters of this art from the 15C to 18C (Bellano, Riccio, Antico, Giovanni Bologna, Vittoria).

★★★ **13-18C EUROPEAN PAINTINGS**   *(2nd floor) 4 hours. Plan below. Recorded tours of the galleries are available. If you set out to see a particular school of art, call ahead to find out whether the gallery is open (☎879-5500).*

This department occupies some 40 galleries, presenting over 3,000 works of art from the 12C to the 19C. The strength of the collection lies in Italian, Flemish, French and Dutch works, although the museum also owns paintings by English and Spanish masters. The works are arranged by national schools in chronological order.

- *The Epiphany*
  (Giotto or his workshop)
- *The Journey of the Magi*
  (Sassetta)
- *Man and Woman at a Casement*
  (Fra Filippo Lippi)
- *The Last Communion of St Jerome*
  (Botticelli)
- *Pietà* (Crivelli)
- *Madonna and Child* (Bellini)
- *Venus and the Lute Player* (Titian)
- *Young Woman with a Water Jug*
  (Vermeer)

- *Aristotle with a Bust of Homer*
  (Rembrandt)
- *Penitent Magdalen* (La Tour)
- *Mezzetin* (Watteau)
- *The Crucifixion and The Last Judgment*
  (Jan van Eyck)
- *Francesco d'Este* (Van der Weyden)
- *The Rest on the Flight into Egypt* (David)
- *The Harvesters* (Bruegel the Elder)
- *Venus and Adonis* (Rubens)
- *View of Toledo* (El Greco)
- *Juan de Pareja* (Velázquez)

Italian Galleries   *Galleries 1-4b, 5-9, 22, 30*

Primitives and 15C. – *Galleries 3, 4, 4a, 4b, 5, 6.* Often painted on wood, these works usually represent religious scenes with gilded backgrounds. However, works by the Florentine, Giotto, or the Sienese, Sassetta, mark the re-introduction of perspective and volume.

In gallery 3, **The Epiphany**, by Giotto or his workshop, brings together the Angel appearing to the Shepherds, the Nativity and the Adoration of the Magi. Like Giotto, Sassetta is especially important for his careful treatment of landscape and human approach to his subjects, as exemplified in **The Journey of the Magi**. Works by Sassetta, Giovanni di Paolo *(Madonna and Child with Saints)* and Segna di Buonaventura *(Saint John the Evangelist)* illustrate the Sienese school.

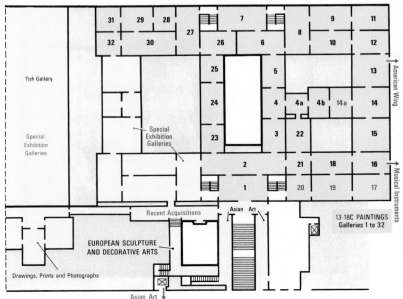

Gallery 4 is devoted to 15C secular painting. Above the *cassone* (marriage chest) ornamented with a battle scene, hangs a Fra Filippo Lippi painting of a **Man and Woman at a Casement**; the portrait of a woman, nearby, may be the work of Giovanni di Francesco. Also represented is the Florentine, Ghirlandaio *(Francesco Sassetti and His Son Teodoro)*; note the contrast between the firm features of the man and the soft features of his son.

In gallery 4a, the ceiling of a Sienese palace, painted by Pinturicchio (1454-1513), has been remounted. Note the allegorical and mythological scenes *(Triumphs* after Petrarch, the *Three Graces* and the *Judgment of Paris)*. Also on display are 15C secular paintings from Florence and Siena. Galleries 4b and 6 highlight the Florentine school, represented by Botticelli's masterpiece, **The Last Communion of St Jerome** *(4b)*, and the glazed terra-cotta sculpture *Madonna and Child with Scroll (4b)* by Luca Della Robbia. Note the exquisite *Birth of the Virgin (6)* in a classical setting, attributed to the Master of the Barberini Panels.

Among the Northern Italian paintings displayed in gallery 5 is a **Pietà** from an altarpiece by the Venetian, Carlo Crivelli, a **Madonna and Child** by Jacobo Bellini, Cosimo Tura's *Flight into Egypt,* and Mantegna's *The Adoration of the Shepherds.*

Renaissance (16C). – *Galleries 7, 8, 9.* The Met's high Renaissance paintings are dominated by the Venetian school, which is characterized by vivid colors, large foreground figures and backgrounds that often depict real landscapes.

Decorative canvases by Tintoretto *(The Miracle of the Loaves and Fishes)* and Titian **(Venus and the Lute Player)** are hung in gallery 8. Also of interest is Titian's large portrait of Filippo Archinto, Archbishop of Milan, and Lorenzo Lotto's *Venus and Cupid.*

Highlighting the religious paintings in gallery 7 is Raphael's *Madonna and Child Enthroned with the Young Baptist and Saints Peter, Catherine, Cecilia and Paul.* Note *The Agony in the Garden,* a small panel from the predella of an altarpiece, which Raphael completed in 1505 for a convent at Perugia.

Gallery 9 displays works by comparatively minor artists, including the soberly executed portrait by Moretto da Brescia, *The Entombment,* and Solario's *Salome with the Head of Saint John the Baptist.* The large canvas of *Saints Peter, Martha, Mary Magdalen, and Leonard* is by Correggio, the leading painter of Parma.

17C. – *Gallery 30.* Among the works exhibited in this gallery are Caravaggio's *The Musicians* with their sensuous and effeminate features, *The Coronation of the Virgin* by Annibale Caracci, and *Charity* by his pupil, Reni.

18C. – *Galleries 1, 2 and 22.* Gallery 1 is devoted to the 18C Venetian master, Giovanni Battista Tiepolo. His canvases, painted in luminous colors, depict scenes filled with turbulent movement. In gallery 2 hang two paintings of the same period by Pannini illustrating the monuments of Rome, *Ancient Rome* and *Modern Rome;* note Michelangelo's sculpture *Moses* in the center of the latter painting.

Gallery 22 exhibits an additional work by Tiepolo *(A Dance in* the *Country)* and contains two other great Venetians at the height of 18C Baroque style: Francesco Guardi with his views of Venice and Pietro Longhi, whose intimate scenes, drawn with minute care, depict the daily life of the Venetian nobility.

The Metropolitan Museum of Art, Henry G. Marquand Collection

Young Woman with a Water Jug by Johannes Vermeer

Dutch Galleries *Galleries 12-15*

The collection concentrates on works from the 17C, the "golden age" of Dutch painting. The Met owns 33 works by **Rembrandt** covering all phases of his career. Using light with great ingenuity, the painter gave careful attention to the hands, jewels, collars and cuffs of his subjects.

In gallery 12, note the lively activity in Jan Steen's *Merry Company on a Terrace*. Also on display are the later Dutch paintings showing serene interior scenes, seascapes and landscapes with vast skies. A masterpiece by Vermeer, **Young Woman with a Water Jug**, bathed in a soft light, immediately attracts the eye *(illustration p 132)*. The Met owns five Vermeers, more than any other museum in the world. Note also the graceful and refined figures in *Curiosity* by Ter Borch. In gallery 13 hangs one of Rembrandt's earlier portraits, *Man in Oriental Costume (The Noble Slav)*, dating from the 1630s. The high point of this collection, Rembrandt's celebrated **Aristotle with a Bust of Homer**, is a symbol of philosophic reflection. This imaginary portrait was signed and dated 1653.

In gallery 14, Rembrandt's later works, including a self-portrait and portraits of his fellow citizens, reveal the painter's deep psychological insight. Not to be overlooked is his *Toilet of Bathsheba*, notable for its uncompromising realism. The vivacious and colorful group portraits by Frans Hals record a different aspect of the life of the burghers as in *Merrymakers at Shrovetide* and *Young Man and Woman in an Inn*.

French Galleries

Galleries 10, 11, 18, 21. Currently, gallery 11 exhibits works by Dutch artists.

17C. – *Gallery 10*. An impressive **Penitent Magdalen** by Georges de la Tour illustrates the restraint and strength of expression of the French school. Nicolas Poussin is represented by *The Rape of the Sabine Women*. In *View of La Cresenza*, Claude Lorrain created a classical type of landscape combined with subtle luminosity. His *Trojan Women Setting Fire to their Fleet* depicts a passage from Virgil's *Aeneid*.

18C. – *Galleries 18, 21*. In gallery 18, the *Self-Portrait with Two Pupils* by Adélaïde Labille-Guiard has been interpreted as the artist's feminist reaction to the practice of limiting the number of women who could become members of the French Royal Academy. *The Silver Tureen* by Chardin moves by its frank simplicity, while *Broken Eggs* by Greuze reflects the artist's Italian training and the influence of Dutch genre painting on his style.

Gallery 21 traces the development of the art of the portraitist, from the polished figures by Drouais *(Madame Favart)* to the sober works of Duplessis *(Madame de Saint-Maurice)*. Along the walls hangs a succession of "fêtes galantes," which were popular during the reign of Louis XV. Among them are the tender and sad **Mezzetin**—a character from the *Commedia dell'Arte*—a small but celebrated work by Watteau, and the *Dispatch of the Messenger*, a pastoral scene by Boucher. Refined genre paintings by Fragonard are also exhibited, including the lively sketch, *Italian Family*, and *The Stolen Kiss*.

English Galleries *Galleries 2, 16*

In these galleries are hung a number of 18C portraits brilliantly executed in fresh colors, but somewhat superficial in their charm. Gallery 2 presents works by Thomas Gainsborough *(Mrs Grace Dalrymple Elliott)* and Sir Joshua Reynolds *(Hon. Henry Fane with His Guardians* and *Colonel George Coussmater)*.

Flemish and German Galleries *Galleries 23-28*

15C. – *Gallery 23*. Depicting sacred subjects and portraits almost exclusively, the 15C Flemish works are characterized by a taste for the picturesque and familiar details. Jan van Eyck is represented by **The Crucifixion** and **The Last Judgment**. These dramatic scenes may have been designed as side panels of a triptych, whose central panel has disappeared. Set on a luminous landscape, *The Annunciation* is also attributed to Jan van Eyck. *Portrait of a Carthusian* was painted by his contemporary, Petrus Christus.

The works by Rogier van der Weyden *(Christ Appearing to His Mother* and **Francesco d'Este)** and the *Portrait of a Man* by Hugo van der Goes reveal a different style in Flemish art. This gallery also contains several portraits by Memling, including *Tommaso Portinari and His Wife*.

15-16C. – *Galleries 24-26*. Gallery 24 contains religious works by Gerard David, including *The Nativity with Donors and Saints Jerome and Vincent: The Annunciation* (part of a polyptych from a church near Genoa), the *Crucifixion*, and **The Rest on the Flight into Egypt**. A *Virgin and Child* by Jan Gossart called Mabuse is also of interest.

The theme of the Adoration of the Magi is treated by the Flemish painters, Quentin Massys, Hieronymus Bosch and Joos Van Ghent. Also note *The Annunciation* by Van der Weyden, formerly attributed to Memling, which is set in the room of the Virgin; the figures occupy most of the foreground and the tunic of the angel Gabriel with its fine gold embroidery is especially striking.

The German school is represented in gallery 25 by Dürer's *Salvator Mundi, Saint John on Patmos* by Baldung and portraits of German and English personalities by Hans Holbein.

Gallery 26 is of special interest with several works by Lucas Cranach the Elder *(The Judgment of Paris, The Martyrdom of St Barbara, Samson and Delilah)* and a masterpiece by Bruegel the Elder, **The Harvesters**.

17C. – *Galleries 27, 28*. These two galleries present Rubens and his circle. Notice Rubens's flamboyant **Venus and Adonis** and several portraits by Van Dyck, who served as an assistant to Rubens and went on to become one of the leading 17C Flemish painters.

Spanish Galleries *Galleries 2, 29-32*

The Spanish character—grave, mystic and passionate—is expressed in the works of great Spanish masters such as El Greco, Goya, Velázquez, Murillo and Ribera. Gallery 29 contains the works of El Greco, including the portrait of *Cardinal Guevara, Grand Inquisitor* and his superb **View of Toledo**. Also displayed is Velázquez's *Supper at Emmaus*.

Among other works by Velázquez in gallery 31 note the *Portrait of Philip IV, King of Spain*, and the outstanding portrait of **Juan de Pareja**, Velázquez's assistant and traveling companion. This masterpiece, an example of the artist's mature style, is astounding for its vitality and lifelike appearance.

★★★ 19C EUROPEAN PAINTINGS AND SCULPTURE
(2nd floor) 2 1/2 hours. Plan p 130.

The galleries in this section of the museum have been given letter designations in this guide in order to facilitate locations of major works.

The collection of 19C European paintings and sculpture, one of the museum's great strengths, is displayed in the 14 André Meyer galleries on the second floor of the Michael C. Rockefeller Wing. The works on display provide an overall view of the 19C, from the academic, conservative works of the French Salon to the avant-garde canvases of the Impressionists and post-Impressionists.

The museum recently re-organized its collection, following the acquisition of the Walter H. Annenberg Collection.

• *The Death of Socrates* (David)	• *Terrace at Sainte-Adresse* (Monet)
• *Madame Leblanc* (Ingres)	• *La Grenouillère* (Monet)
• *Grand Canal Venice* (Turner)	• *Madame Charpentier and Her Children* (Renoir*)*
• *Abduction of Rebecca* (Delacroix)	
• *Majas on a Balcony* (Goya)	• *Sunflowers* (Van Gogh)
• *Woman with a Parrot* (Courbet)	• *Cypresses* (Van Gogh)
• *Boating* (Manet)	• *Mont Sainte-Victoire* (Cézanne)
• *Autumn Landscape with a Flock of Turkeys* (Millet)	• *14-year old Little Dancer* (Degas)
• *Hand of God* (Rodin)	• *Woman with Chrysanthemums* (Degas)

Neoclassicism, Romanticism, Realism. – *Galleries N, A, B*. The neoclassical school (early 19C), inspired by the art of ancient Greece and Rome, is represented by David's stoical and severe **The Death of Socrates**. David's follower Ingres was a master of the elegant pure line, as evidenced in the portraits of *Monsieur Leblanc* and **Madame Leblanc**. The graceful *Portrait of a Young Woman, Mlle Charlotte du Val d'Ognes*, formerly attributed to David, may have been painted by another of his followers.

In **Grand Canal, Venice**, as well as in his later work, *Whale Ship*, the English painter, Joseph Turner, places great emphasis on light and color in a manner that anticipates Impressionism.

In a more romantic vein are Delacroix's **Abduction of Rebecca**, inspired by Sir Walter Scott's novel *Ivanhoe*, and a copy of Goya's flamboyant **Majas on a Balcony**. Goya won recognition for his portraits of children *(Manuel Osorio)* and Spanish nobility and dignitaries *(Don Sebastián Martínez y Pérez)*.

Rebelling against the established conventions of the academic painters, Courbet executed his hunting scenes, landscapes and pictures of the sea with vigorous realism. Represented without mythological pretext, his nudes, including **Woman with a Parrot**, caused quite a stir at the time.

The Barbizon School, Millet, The Salon. – *Galleries D, E, F, G, H*. Reacting against the idealized rendering of classical landscape painting, the members of the Barbizon school painted directly from nature (Théodore Rousseau: *Forest in Winter at Sunset*; Daubigny: *Apple Blossom*).

Corot's feathery gray-green landscapes were much in favor during his lifetime; today many prefer his human figures *(Woman Reading Sybille)*, with their simplicity of expression and attitude.

Among the painters showing their devotion to the Dutch school, Millet is known for his somber landscapes extolling the life of the peasant: **Autumn Landscape with a Flock of Turkeys**.

Adjacent areas contain works in the established academic tradition, as upheld by the Paris Salon of the French Academy. A variety of exotic, romantic, mythological, idyllic and historical subjects are treated. Note Bastien-Lepage's *Joan of Arc* and Ernest Meissonier's *Friedland*.

The large canvas by Rosa Bonheur, *The Horse Fair,* a masterpiece in its time, was purchased by Cornelius Vanderbilt and presented to the museum in 1887.

Sculpture Gallery. – *Gallery J*. Inspired by ancient frescoes, allegorical in content, Puvis de Chavanne's mural panels celebrate such virtues as family and country *(Cider and the River)*. Among the marble sculptures by Carpeaux, is the monumental, dramatic composition *Ugolino and His Sons*. Highlighting the collection are works in marble, bronze and terra-cotta by **Rodin**. Rodin's fascination with the hands as a means of expression can be seen in his **Hand of God** and the models of hands in a glass case nearby. Impressed by the powerful figures of Michelangelo, Rodin created his large-size bronze representations of *Adam and Eve*. Also of interest are the busts of *Countess Anne de Noailles* (called "Madame X"), *St John the Baptist* and *Balzac*.

Impressionists, Post-Impressionists. – *Gallery X*. Manet, a precursor of Impressionism, was greatly indebted to Spanish masters. Among the numerous works by Manet are: *The Spanish Singer, Woman With a Parrot* and the somber *Dead Christ, with Angels*. His later association with the Impressionists is seen in *Boating*.

Impressionism took its name from a canvas painted by Claude Monet, *Impression: Soleil Levant (not in the museum's collection)*. Painting outdoors, the members of the group sought to render visual transitory impressions gathered from nature and everyday life, and to capture the fleeting effects of light by juxtaposing pure tones of color. Among the large number of landscapes by Monet in the collection, note the cheerful **Terrace at Sainte-Adresse**, the luminous **La Grenouillère** with its rippling waters, the graceful *Poplars*, and the dramatic rendering of the cliffs and sea at Etretat. The *Rouen Cathedral* is perceived in blazing midday sun, whereas *The Houses of Parliament* are veiled in a mist, which tends to dissolve all solid forms. *The Bridge Over a Pool of Water Lilies* is one of a series of views of this subject which Monet painted.

Renoir's delicate palette is revealed in his landscapes *(In the Meadow)* and most notably in his portraits of graceful young women *(By the Seashore)*. The intimate family portrait of **Madame Charpentier and Her Children** was exhibited at the Paris Salon in 1879, and marked the beginning of Renoir's success as an artist.

Van Gogh's personal expression is shown in portraits, landscapes and still lives. In his *Irises*, **Sunflowers** and **Cypresses**, swirling lines and vehement brush strokes are used to express intense emotion. The works on display by Cézanne represent all facets of his art, encompassing classical and modern concepts. Note his luminous landscapes, including the *Gulf of Marseilles Seen from l'Estaque* and **Mont Sainte-Victoire**; his almost geometrical paintings of still life, suggesting the first hints of cubism; and his figures *(The Cardplayers, Madame Cézanne in a Red Dress)*.

Study for a Sunday Afternoon on the Island of La Grande Jatte (Seurat) and *View of the Port of Marseilles* (Signac) acquaint the viewer with the pointillist technique developed by these two artists.

Among the post-Impressionists are Toulouse-Lautrec, who portrayed the dissolute, sometimes dark, sides of Parisian life *(The Sofa),* and Gauguin who depicted the beauty of the South Seas with bold colors and statuesque figures *(la Orana Maria)*.

Degas. – *Galleries K, L, M*. Exhibited in three galleries are works in several media, demonstrating Degas's interest in the study of body movement. Degas portrayed ballet dancers in a variety of poses in paintings *(The Dance Class, The Rehearsal of the Ballet on the Stage)*, pastels *(Dancers Practicing at the Bar)* and in bronze (the statuette of a **14-year old Little Dancer**). The small bronzes in the glass case echo the movements of the dancers depicted on the canvases. Scenes painted from everyday life include *A Woman Ironing* and **Woman with Chrysanthemums**.

The collection of bronze horses bears witness to Degas's admiration for the energy and grace of horses in motion.

★★ LEHMAN PAVILION *(1st floor) 1 hour*

Considered one of the finest private art collections in the US, the Robert Lehman Collection was compiled by financier Philip Lehman and his son, Robert. Ringing a central garden court, a series of seven period rooms and galleries, designed to recreate the atmosphere of a private home, house the collection of some 3,000 works of art.

Shown in rotating exhibits, the collection is most famous for its Italian paintings of the 14C and 15C, including works by Sassetta *(St Anthony in the Wilderness)*, di Paolo *(Expulsion from Paradise)*, Botticelli *(Annunciation)*, Bellini *(Madonna and Child)* and Crivelli *(Madonna and Child)*.

Representing the Northern Renaissance are Petrus Christus *(St Eligius)*, Gerard David, Memling and Cranach the Elder. Works by Rembrandt, El Greco *(Christ Carrying the Cross)* and Goya exemplify the 18-19C Dutch and Spanish schools. French masterpieces of the 19C and 20C include Ingres' *Portrait of the Princesse de Broglie* and Renoir's *Young Girl Bathing*.

In addition to the art work, the period rooms contain magnificent examples of the decorative arts, including tapestries, furniture, Venetian glass, bronzes and enamels. Displayed on the lower level, the rich collection of drawings includes works by Dürer and Rembrandt, as well as some 200 Venetian drawings (18C).

★★ MEDIEVAL ART *(1st floor) 1 1/2 hours*

Tracing the development of art from the fall of Rome (4C) to the Renaissance (16C), the museum's extensive collection in Medieval art comprises more than 4,000 works from the early Christian, Byzantine, Migration, Romanesque and Gothic periods. Among the treasures not to be missed are some exquisite pieces of Byzantine silver, Romanesque and Gothic metalwork, and Gothic stained glass and tapestries. *Additional Medieval art objects are exhibited in the Cloisters (p 101).*

Located on the left side of the main staircase, before entering the Medieval art galleries, the **Early Christian and Byzantine Corridor** features the Second Cyprus Treasure (7C), ivories and enamels representative of Byzantine art. Among the fine examples of metalwork from the Early Medieval period, note the chip-carved silver-gilt and niello pieces from the Vermand Treasure (northern France). Pass through an Italian Romanesque, marble portal from San Gemini, in Umbria, to the main hall. Located to the right, under the staircase, a re-created **chapel** displays Romanesque carvings.

Medieval Tapestry Hall. – Hung along the walls of this small hall is an ensemble of **tapestries**, dating from the 14C to the early 16C, woven principally in the workshops of Flanders (Arras, Brussels and Tournai). At that time, the tapestries were as practical as they were ornamental, serving to temper drafts and dampness. The Annunciation, begun early in the 15C, is related to a painting by Melchior Broederlam, a court painter in Burgundy. An interesting series of tapestries, commissioned by Charles the Bold, Duke of Burgundy, depicts the arming of Hector during the Trojan War.

Dating from the late Gothic period, large panels of stained glass from Cologne, Germany, and England fill two walls of the gallery.

Medieval Sculpture Hall. – This large hall was built to evoke the ambience of a church, with a nave separated from the side aisles by massive columns. Stretching between two columns, a splendid Baroque, wrought-iron **choir screen** rises almost the full height of the hall. Begun in 1668 for the Cathedral of Valladolid, in Spain, it was completed in 1764. At Christmas, the museum exhibits a magnificent tree and an 18C Neapolitan Nativity scene in front of the choir screen.

A large collection of sculpture and bas-reliefs, mainly from Burgundy, Italy and Germany, traces the development of Gothic sculpture from the 13C to the 16C. Note especially the 15C Burgundian Virgin and Child from Poligny, France. Also on display is a rare group of panels representing Baptism, Marriage and Extreme Unction.

Medieval Treasury. – In addition to portable shrines, reliquary caskets and sacramental objects, the Treasury also contains two fine sculptural groups (early 16C) of the Entombment and Pietà, from the Périgord region of France.

The wall and central glass cases display an assemblage of precious objects, including an Ottonian ivory situla (holy water bucket); a 13C Limoges enamel shrine decorated with scenes from the life of Christ in coppergilt; the silver reliquary head of St Yrieix (13C, Limousin), which once held fragments of his skull; and a processional cross covered in silver (12C, Spanish). The richness of the collection of Romanesque and Gothic enamels rivals that of the French ivories of the 13C to 15C, which includes a rosary with beads in the form of skulls.

Before leaving the hall *(on the right)* note an unusual German saddle of bone housed in a glass case. The decoration, in low relief, depicts scenes of courtly love.

★★ ARTS OF AFRICA, OCEANIA AND THE AMERICAS
(1st floor) 1 1/2 hours

The galleries displaying primitive art are located in south wing of the museum, named in honor of Nelson Rockefeller's son, Michael, who died while on an expedition to the island of New Guinea in 1961. The core of the collection encompasses approximately 3,500 works of art donated to the museum by Nelson Rockefeller in the late 1970s. The department now owns about 8,000 objects spanning a period of 3,000 years. Among the most impressive objects on display are the towering memorial poles *(mbis)* and attractively decorated shields of the Asmat of Irian Jaya (Western New Guinea) collected by Michael Rockefeller.

The galleries are divided into three sections representing the three major divisions of the collection: Africa, Oceania and the Americas.

Africa. – Sculpture, primarily ritualistic masks and figures carved in wood, dominates the art of Africa, which is essentially religious. The first gallery contains a collection of monumental sculpture by the Dogon of Mali. Note the 7ft-high elongated male figure standing with arms raised and a wooden container featuring the head and tail of a horse, which was used to hold sacrificial meat during ceremonies celebrating the myth of creation.

Adapting animal traits to headdresses and masks, the Bamana people created antelope headdresses with extremely slender vertical lines, as well as ferocious-looking Senufo helmet masks incorporating the jaws and teeth of a crocodile, the horns of an antelope and the tusks of the warthog. To the rear, among the Bamana figures, note a Mother and Child sculpture, one of several in the collection.

The adjacent exhibit area displays figures, masks and the chief's ceremonial stool carved by the Buli Master; the small ivories and wooden figures from Zaire, notably an ivory mask from the Lega people, are also of interest. The serene Fang reliquary head was carved to protect a box that contained the skulls of honored ancestors.

Highlighting this area is a collection of dark brass items—plaques, animals, figures and heads—from the royal court of Benin. Dating from the 16C to 19C, the heads are adorned with caps and chokers of the type still worn by the king today. A precious **ivory mask**, a royal ornament also from Benin, is displayed in a separate case. Carved into the hair of the mask are mudfish, symbolic of wealth and royalty, and faces that represent the Portuguese merchants who arrived in Nigeria in the 15C. When leaving this section, on the right, pause to admire the naturalistic double headdress of the Ekoi people of Nigeria and the wooden mask (from a triple mask) carved by the Ibibio people.

Oceania. – A masterfully carved tall drum from the Austral Islands and a ceremonial **shield** inlaid with shells (Solomon Islands) reflect the ornamental as well as utilitarian purpose most objects served in cultures from the Pacific Islands. The first gallery presents objects from New Guinea, including elaborately decorated shields, masks, fence posts, ceremonial boards and slit-gongs (drums); paintings etched on sheets of bark, recreating the roof of a ceremonial house, are displayed overhead.

A long, spacious glass-walled hall has as its focal point a remarkable group of nine delicately carved **poles** *(mbis)*, ranging up to 20ft in height. These Asmat *mbis* serve as a centerpiece for the other objects arranged in this hall: carvings with intricate openwork from New Ireland, figures sculpted from fern wood, a standing slit-gong from New Hebrides and a 25ft-long crocodile effigy from Papua New Guinea.

Americas. – The first gallery houses the Treasury, where exhibits of gold ornaments, vessels and masks from South and Central America include a pair of Mochica shell and stone mosaic ear spools (3-6C); a pendant (Colombia, 13-16C) in the form of a figure wearing an elaborate headdress; and a boldly painted Paracas **funerary mask** (Peru, 3-1C BC; *illustration below*). Also from Peru are the luxurious yellow and blue feathers (late 7-8C) hanging on the far right wall, a group of silver vessels and ancient Peruvian pottery.

The Metropolitan Museum of Art, gift of Alice K. Bache

Gold Funerary Mask (Peru)

The adjacent gallery features the arts of Mesoamerica. Here, note especially the Mayan **seated figure** (6C), one of the few extant three-dimensional Mayan pieces in wood. Cases mounted along the wall contain "smiling figures" (7-8C) from Vera Cruz, characterized by their broad faces and wide grins; and ornamented stone objects (yokes, palmas, hachas) associated with the ancient ritual ball game. The superb relief carving of the Maya is exemplified by a stone stele from Mexico. A refined jade mask illustrates the artistry of the ancient Olmec civilization (1200-400 BC) of Mexico.

★ **ARMS AND ARMOR** *(1st floor) 1 hour*

Displayed in ten recently renovated galleries, this encyclopedic collection comprises over 14,000 arms, designed mainly for display rather than for actual military use. Surrounding a vast central hall, the western galleries feature European arms—including rare pieces commissioned by various kings and rulers—while the eastern galleries focus on articles from China, Japan, India, Turkey and Iran.

Dominating the vast hall is a striking display of parade armor, replete with suits of armor and horses, designed by Wolfgang Grosschedel and Kunz Lochner in the 16C. Surrounding glass cases display finely chiseled and embossed arms while colorful flags and banners hang overhead.

Arms and armor predating the 16C include pieces from the Crusades, a helmet said to be Joan of Arc's and a group of shields for battle and tournament. Among the most arresting pieces of the collection are the parade helmet of François I, by renowned Milanese armorer Filippo Negroli; the embossed shield (1555) designed by Étienne Delaune for Henry II of France; and the three quarter armor of Anne de Montmorency, High Constable under the same king.

Arms of tempered steel, predominantly made in Toledo, Spain, include daggers, swords and rapiers, halberds, lances and pikes; especially handsome is the sword with the chiseled cup hilt, which belonged to the Marquis of Spinola (16C). Among the firearms, note the pair of flintlock pistols (1786) belonging to Empress Catherine the Great. A double-barreled pistol (c. 1540) by Peter Peck of Munich made for Emperor Charles V is one of the earliest in existence.

A small gallery on the north side displays firearms from Europe and America. The eastern galleries present articles from the Far and Near East ranging from small arrowheads to elaborate suits of armor. Of particular interest are the late-15C helmet from Iran, which adopts the shape of a turban, and various sabers and their scabbards intricately decorated with inlaid emeralds, diamonds and other precious stones. Highlighting the Japanese collection is a medieval *yoroi* (14C), or armor, composed of a leather cuirass and a four-sided skirt.

MUSEUMS

★ ASIAN ART
(2nd floor; also accessible by elevator or stairway in the Egyptian Wing) 1 hour

Winding their way around the main stairway and the balcony above the Great Hall, the Asian art galleries trace the development of Chinese, Japanese, Korean, Indian and Southeast Asian art, from the third millennium BC to the present, through ceramics, metalwork, paintings and sculptures, bronzes, jades and textiles.

The centerpiece of the collection is the **Garden Court★**, a reproduction of a Ming dynasty courtyard and scholar's study in Soochow, China. Set apart from the mainstream of museum traffic, and meticulously landscaped with Chinese plantings, the court re-creates a setting similar to that in which Chinese artists and intellectuals once worked. The principal features of the courtyard are best viewed from the irregular stone steps: the moonviewing terrace facing the garden entrance, the half pavilion to the left and the walkway opposite, and the south wall with its latticed windows and formal rock arrangement. Branching off on either side of the courtyard are galleries of Chinese paintings. Rotating exhibits span four dynasties—Sung (960-1279), Yuan (1279-1368), Ming (1368-1644), Ching (1644-1911)—as well as the modern era, and illustrate a wide range of subject matter from landscapes and flower paintings to Buddhist and Taoist themes.

Highlighting a gallery to the north of the Great Hall, a huge mural from Shansi in northern China (14C) depicting Buddha and his assembly forms a magnificent background to the monumental collection of Chinese Buddhist sculpture of the 5C and 6C. Ancient Chinese art is displayed in a series of galleries beginning to the left of the wall mural. Spanning the period from the Neolithic (early second millennium BC) through the T'ang dynasty (10C AD), these galleries include jades, ceramics, bronze ritual vessels and tomb art.

The galleries dedicated to **Japanese Art** feature changing exhibits of paintings, sculpture, lacquer, woodblock prints and Edo period scrolls from the museum's collection—note the superb irises in *Yatsuhashi* by Ogata Korin. This section also includes the central altar from a 12C temple; a shoin-style meditation room modeled on a room in the Onjo-ji temple (17C) outside Kyoto; and *Water Stone*, a sculpture by Isamu Noguchi *(p 160).*

★ COSTUME INSTITUTE *(ground floor) 1 hour*

This center for costume research and study was created in 1937, with a view to collecting and preserving costumes past and present. Today, the 40,000-article collection of western and regional garbs includes costumes from five continents, ranging from the elegant wardrobes of ancient royalty to chic fashions by the most distinguished contemporary American and French couturiers. *Changing exhibits run from mid-December to mid-April and mid-June to the Sunday before Labor Day; the galleries are closed the remainder of the year.*

★ ISLAMIC ART *(2nd floor) 1 hour*

This section traces the development of Islamic art, beginning with the founding of Muslim religion in the 7C and ending in the early 19C. Encompassing works from various geographical regions, including Mesopotamia, Persia, Morocco, Egypt, Syria and India, the collection is particularly known for its displays of glass- and metalwork, miniatures and classical carpets.

In the first gallery, a map and descriptive text introduce the visitor to the diversity and range of Islamic culture. The opulence of an 18C Syrian house is reflected in the richly paneled reception room decorated with an ornamented ceiling, painted and gilded walls, a marbled fountain and a magnificent marble floor. Gallery 2, devoted to the museum's excavations in Nishapur, a thriving Persian city (9-12C), contains rare wall paintings and a collection of objects in metal, stone, glass and ceramics; some are engraved with inscriptions and the famous arabesque motifs.

Presented in chronological order, the objects on display gain in refinement as the centuries unfold. In gallery 5, admire the colorful tile panels and the intricate wood- and metalwork from the Mamluk period. The early 16C wood ceiling hails from Moorish Spain. A pair of Egyptian doors (14C) bearing a kaleidoscopic pattern carved in wood and ivory illustrate the Muslim mastery of intricate design.

Further displays include ivory carvings, artfully painted ceramic bowls, decorated glass mosque lamps, bottles and jugs from Iran, and jade vessels and jewelry from 17C India. In gallery 4c note the **mihrab** (1354; prayer niche indicating the direction of Mecca), an exquisite 11ft-high mosaic from Isfahan, composed of glazed ceramic tiles in geometric and floral patterns and inscriptions from the Koran.

Painting, which found a lively expression in the illustration of manuscripts, is represented by the delicate art of **miniatures** as practiced in Persia, India and Ottoman Turkey. Highlighting the collection is an ensemble of miniatures depicting episodes from the great Persian literary work known as the "Shah Nameh" or "Book of Kings" *(gallery 6).*

An array of sumptuous carpets *(galleries 7 and 8)* attests to the importance of carpet weaving brought to perfection in the workshops of Egypt, Persia, Turkey and India. Also in gallery 8, note the gilded Ottoman helmet and a rare Ottoman Court prayer rug from the late 16C.

★ MUSICAL INSTRUMENTS *(2nd floor) 1 hour*
Audio equipment ($3.75) enables the visitor to hear the instruments play period music (available at Acoustic Guides Desk, 1st floor).

This section presents an original and rare collection of more than 4,000 musical instruments from all periods and all parts of the world. The western galleries focus on European instruments, including the oldest extant piano (1720); three Stradivarius violins, crafted by the famous violin maker of Cremona; two classical guitars belonging to Andres Segovia made out of rosewood, spruce and mahogany; and an outstanding series of keyboard instruments decorated with marquetry, sculpture and paintings, including the spinet made in 1540 in Venice for the Duchess of Urbino. Other interesting instruments include a Flemish double virginal of the 16C decorated with musical scenes; lutes, zithers and guitars from the 17C; and wind instruments made of shell, bone, goatskin and Meissen porcelain. The eastern galleries highlight instruments from the Near and Far East, the Americas and Africa, including seldom-seen pieces such as an Indonesian sesando, a type of zither made out of palm leaves; an Indian mayuri, or bowed sitar; and a Shaman rattle from the Queen Charlotte Islands, off the west coast of Canada. Often selected for their role in society as well as for their tonal qualities, most of them are in working order and are used for occasional concerts.

★ **20C ART** *(Lila Acheson Wallace Wing) 1 1/2 hours*

Devoted to art forms from 1900 to the present, the Lila Acheson Wallace Wing displays over 8,000 paintings, sculptures, works on paper and decorative arts on its three floors and in the skylit sculpture court on the mezzanine level. Located on top of the wing, the **rooftop garden★** offers a superb setting for contemporary sculpture, including Rodin's *Burghers of Calais*, while affording splendid **views** of Manhattan's midtown and uptown skylines *(open May through November)*.

The museum's holdings encompass works by European artists such as Bonnard, Matisse and Picasso *(Gertrude Stein)*, including the Berggruen collection of 90 works by Paul Klee, donated in 1984. However, the strength of the collection lies in American art, in particular works by the Group of Eight, Abstract Expressionists and Minimalists artists.

Among the early 20C paintings are Marsden Hartley's *Portrait of a German Officer* and Georgia O'Keeffe's *Cow's Skull: Red, White and Blue*. In the post-World War II period, New York developed as the center of the contemporary art world and witnessed the development of Abstract Expressionism with such artists as Jackson Pollock *(Autumn Rhythm)*, Willem de Kooning *(Easter Monday)* and Mark Rothko *(Untitled Number 13)*. More recent works by Roy Lichtenstein *(Stepping Out)*, James Rosenquist *(House of Fire)*, David Hockney, Clyfford Still, Frank Stella, Ellsworth Kelly and other important American and European painters continue the survey of 20C art through the 1970s and into the 1990s. Sculptural works include creations by Archipenko, Giacometti, Pevsner, Smith and Noguchi.

DRAWINGS, PRINTS AND PHOTOGRAPHS *(2nd floor) 1 hour*
At the top of the main staircase, to the left. Presented in the form of temporary exhibits; check on schedules at information desk.

Drawings. – The collection of over 4,000 works focuses on Italian and French artists from the 15C to 19C, including Michelangelo, Pietro da Cortona, Romanino di Brescia, Poussin, David and Delacroix. The Dutch and Spanish schools are also represented with drawings by Rubens, Rembrandt and Goya. Highlights of the collection include a nude male figure by Raphael, the *Redemption of the World* by Veronese and the *Garden of Love* by Rubens.

Prints and Photographs. – The collection of prints highlights various techniques, including woodcuts, lithographs and other forms of engraving, with a focus on 15C German, 18C Italian and 19C French images. Among the most memorable early works are: *Battle of the Ten Naked Men* by Antonio Pollaiuolo; *Bacchanal with a Wine Vat* by Andrea Mantegna; *The Four Horsemen of the Apocalypse* by Albrecht Dürer; *Summer*, after Pieter Bruegel; *Time, Apollo and the Seasons* by Claude Lorrain; and Rembrandt's *Faust in His Study* and *Christ Preaching*.

The 18C artists represented include Englishman Hogarth, Roman Piranesi, Frenchman Fragonard and Spaniard Goya. Particularly noteworthy among 19C works are Daumier's *Rue Transnonain* and Toulouse-Lautrec's *Aristide Bruant*.

Forming the core of museum's holdings in photography is a large collection of Alfred Stieglitz photographs, acquired between 1928 and 1949.

★ MUSEUM FOR AFRICAN ART

Time: 1 hour. 593 Broadway. ●N, R train to Prince St or A, C, E train to Spring St. Map p 80. Open Wed–Sun 11am–6pm (Fri & Sat 8pm). Closed Jan 1 & Dec 25. $3. Guided tour (1hr) Sat & Sun 2pm. & ☎966-1313.

This small but active museum is one of only two in the US devoted exclusively to African art. While there is a limited permanent collection for study, the focus is on broad-based changing exhibits featuring both contemporary and historical pieces, including painting, sculpture, textiles and masks.

Since opening as the Center for African Art in 1984, the museum has mounted more than 16 major traveling shows exploring Africa's artistic traditions and cultural heritage. In 1993, the center moved from the Upper East Side to new quarters in SOHO, where three galleries create an intimate environment. Architect Maya Lin, best known for the Vietnam Veterans Memorial in Washington DC, designed the museum interior to represent Africa, using vibrant yellows, deep blue greens and earthy grays. A colorful shop in the lobby offers traditional crafts, including pottery, clothes, baskets and jewelry from villages across the African continent; each item bears a tag providing information on the people who made it and its significance in African culture. The museum also offers music, dance and performance art programs on Friday evenings. Additional programs explore African film, television, music, theater and storytelling.

MUSEUM OF AMERICAN FOLK ART

Time: 1 hour. 2 Lincoln Square. ● *1, 9 train to 66th St. Map p 89. Open Tue–Sun 11:30am–7:30pm. Closed holidays.* ᵭ ☏ *977-7298.*

This small museum was founded in 1961 as an urban venue for folk art and is dedicated to the presentation and preservation of the folk heritage of the Americas. The artists represented are mainly self-taught, and the objects are functional and, for the most part, hand-made. The museum is quartered across from LINCOLN CENTER, in the northwest corner of a towering condominium building. Three major exhibits a year in addition to several traveling exhibits and special programs are presented in three galleries radiating from the central lobby. The permanent collection spans two centuries and includes furniture, paintings, sculpture, decorative and everyday objects. Selections from the collection on permanent display include two 19C weather vanes, several painted and decorated objects reflecting early American crafts, and an exquisite quilt.

★★ MUSEUM OF THE CITY OF NEW YORK

Time: 1 1/2 hours. Fifth Ave at 103rd St. ● *6 train to 103rd St. Map p 2. Sights. Open Wed–Sat 10am–5pm, Sun 1–5pm. Closed holidays. Suggested contribution $5.* ᵭ ☏ *534-1672.*

Founded in 1923 as America's first institution dedicated to the history of a city, this museum chronicles the changing face of New York from a modest Dutch trading post to a thriving, international metropolis. Originally housed in the Gracie Mansion *(p 117)*, it moved to the present Georgian Revival building fronting Central Park in 1929. The museum's rich collections span three centuries of New York memorabilia, decorative arts, furnishings, silver, prints and paintings.

Basement. – The Volunteer Fire Gallery depicts the history of fire fighting through prints, texts and artifacts, including a horse-drawn double decker Big Six model. The adjacent hall and small gallery feature temporary exhibits. The *Big Apple Video*, highlighting the development of New York and its people through sound and image, provides an excellent introduction to the city *(presented daily in the auditorium every half hour).*

First Floor. – *Main entrance.* A lofty rotunda, dominated by a graceful, spiraling staircase, bisects two long galleries displaying a series of rotating exhibits. The information desk and museum shop are located to the left of the entranceway.

Second Floor. – Six **period alcoves** ranging from a traditional Dutch living room (17C) to a turn-of-the-century drawing room contain appropriate furnishings and costumes reflecting the evolution of New York interiors. Highlighting the gallery, the luminous stained-glass window was crafted by Richard Morris Hunt. Examples of three centuries of **silver** including a gold Tiffany tea service (1897) and monogrammed Dutch tankards are displayed in the New York Silver collection. Parlor furnishings found in various galleries include a cabinet-bookcase given to songstress Jenny Lind, containing seven volumes of Audubon's *Birds of America.* Other galleries present the marine and cartographic history of New York through maps, charts, model ships and carved figureheads.

Third Floor. – The Toy Gallery features a delightful selection of playthings from the museum's collection of over 6,000 items. Arrayed thematically, the objects range from plush teddy bears to intricate mechanical banks. The exquisite series of **doll houses★** includes the rare 1769 Ann Anthony Pavilion noted for its "shadow box" style and primitive wax figures. Other elaborately crafted houses reflect the predominant domestic styles at various periods. The Stettheimer House re-creates a 1920s New York brownstone complete with celebrity figurines and artwork by Marcel Duchamp and other avant-garde artists.
Lining the main hall's walls, portraits of famous New Yorkers provide a pictorial history of the changing fashions in the city.

Fifth Floor. – Two ornate rooms from John D. Rockefeller's 1860s residence—formerly located on the site of the Museum of Modern Art's sculpture garden *(p 141)*—reflect the opulent tastes of the late Victorian era. The master bedroom features heavy damask furnishings and forest green walls hung with gilt framed paintings from Rockefeller's private collection. The American Renaissance-style dressing room contains inlaid pearl rosewood furnishings by master woodworker George Schasty. Note also the two Childe Hassam paintings hanging above the ebonized Steinway piano in the Flagler alcove.

★★★ THE MUSEUM OF MODERN ART

Time: 3 hours. 11 W. 53rd St. Garden entrance at 14 W. 54th St. ● *E, F train to 53rd St. Map p 33.*

One of the world's preeminent cultural institutions, the Museum of Modern Art (MOMA) offers an unparalleled overview of the modern visual arts. The rich collection includes not only painting, drawing and sculpture, but also photography, decorative, graphic and industrial art, architectural plans and models, video, and the most comprehensive film archive in the US.

Historical Notes. – The founding of the museum dates back to 1929, when three private benefactresses—Abby Aldrich Rockefeller, Lillie P. Bliss and Mary Quinn Sullivan—launched a campaign to promote the modern arts in the US. The first show, of the then little-known post-Impressionists, opened in temporary quarters that fall. Over the next decade, founding director **Alfred H. Barr Jr** shaped the museum's philosophy, which emphasizes ideas as much as objects, and introduced the novel concept of a multi-departmental museum of art. Among Barr's pioneering exhibits were shows of photography, design and architecture, which at the time were not acknowledged as legitimate art forms.

The Building. – Now much altered, the original 1939 marble-and-glass museum building by Philip Goodwin and Edward Durell Stone was one of the first examples of the International Style in the US. (The term "International Style" came from Barr's groundbreaking 1932 show, "Modern Architecture: International Exhibition," organized by Philip Johnson and Henry Russell Hitchcock.) The sculpture garden and east wing are 1964 additions by Philip Johnson. A 1979 renovation by Cesar Pelli more than doubled the gallery space, and added the glass-faced Garden Hall and a 44-story residential tower to the west.

The Collections. – From an initial 1931 bequest by Lillie P. Bliss of 235 works—including key paintings by Cézanne, Gauguin, Seurat and Redon—the museum's holdings have grown to encompass more than 100,000 pieces. There are six divisions: painting and sculpture (major artists from the 1880s to the present); drawings (Dada, Surrealist, school of Paris, Russian avant-garde and American artists); prints and illustrated books (bibliographic arts and printmaking, including the graphic arts of Picasso); photography (masters from the 1840s to the present, including Atget, Stieglitz, Cartier-Bresson, Weston and Friedlander); architecture and design (architectural models, posters, decorative arts and transportation); and film and video (silent, experimental, animated, documentary, feature films and stills from around the world).

VISIT

Open Thu–Tue 11am–6pm (Thu 9pm). Closed Dec 25. $7.50. ✗ ఈ ☎*708-9400.*

Two theaters are located on the lower level, while the bookstore, information desk, Garden Café, video gallery and temporary exhibits are on the first floor, which opens onto the Abby Aldrich Rockefeller **Sculpture Garden** *(free concerts are given Jul & Aug every Fri & Sat 7pm).* This marble-paved sanctuary, one of Manhattan's loveliest outdoor spaces, serves as a gallery for works by some of the world's most widely recognized sculptors, including Rodin's *Monument to Balzac* (1898), Henry Moore's *Group: Large Torso: Arch,* Gaston Lachaise's *Standing Woman* and Picasso's *She Goat,* whose belly is made of a basket.

The upper floors house temporary shows, painting and sculpture (second and third floors), photography (second floor), prints and illustrated books (third floor), and architecture and design (fourth floor). Selections from the permanent collection are presented in roughly chronological order. The following description offers an overview of some of the major schools and movements represented.

Post-Impressionism. – This term refers to several movements that emerged in Europe between about 1880 and 1905 in reaction to French Impressionism. Defining color through the interplay of reflecting light, the Impressionists sought to create a naturalistic "impression" of their subject (Claude Monet's *Waterlilies,* 1899-1926) instead of a literal rendering. By contrast, the post-Impressionists, including Paul Cézanne, Vincent Van Gogh *(The Starry Night)* and Henri de Toulouse-Lautrec, emphasized form, rendered through simplified shapes and expressive line; many also embraced symbolism and religious themes. Pierre Bonnard, Paul Gauguin and Édouard Vuillard, members of the Nabis, a group of French painters who favored flat areas of pure color, are also considered post-Impressionists, as is the Pointillist painter, Georges-Pierre Seurat *(Evening at Honfleur),* known for expressing form with small dots of color.

The Museum of Modern Art, New York, Lillie P. Bliss Bequest

Les Demoiselles d'Avignon by Pablo Picasso (oil on canvas 8' x 7' 8")

THE MUSEUM OF MODERN ART

Fauvism. – When a group of painters, including Henri Matisse *(The Red Studio)*, André Derain *(Bathers)* and Maurice de Vlaminck *(Autumn)*, mounted a show of dazzling canvases splashed with impulsive brush strokes of color at the 1905 Salon d'Automne in Paris, the critic Louis Vauxcelles was so stunned by the violent appearance of the works that he called the artists "les fauves," or wild beasts. While the movement lasted only until 1907, its characteristic bold, spontaneous compositions, in which form was analyzed through color, had a strong impact on the development of European Expressionism.

Cubism. – Pablo Picasso and Georges Braque pioneered this influential modern movement in 20C painting and sculpture, which was a radical departure from traditional Western art. In an effort to understand the problems of spatial construction, the artists reduced their subjects to apparently abstract geometrics, in which solids became transparent and convex planes concave. The two primary sources of this approach—African sculpture and the later paintings of Cézanne—were first combined in Picasso's 1907 work, *Les Demoiselles d'Avignon (illustration p 141)*. The fractured planes in works by Braque, as in *Man with a Guitar* (1911), show a characteristic emphasis on the relationship of shapes rather than on the shapes themselves. Cubism influenced many other early 20C artists, including Juan Gris *(The Breakfast)*, Fernand Léger *(The City)* and the American, Stuart Davis, and is considered the forerunner for abstract painting. Marc Chagall's works *(I and the Village)*, influenced by Cubist proportions, Fauve colors and Russian folktales, exude a highly individualistic style. Cubism was also expressed in such sculptures as Picasso's *Glass of Absinthe* and *Woman's Head*.

Expressionism. – This emotional approach, which held that art was valid only if it sprung from the artist's "inner necessity," was dominant in Germany from about 1905 to 1925. Following on the heels of Symbolists Edvard Munch *(The Storm)* and Gustav Klimt *(Hope II)*, and influenced in part by Medieval woodcuts and African tribal art, expressionist works embraced distorted forms, violent stylization and harsh color combinations in an effort to reject the "superficiality" of naturalism. At the core of the movement was Die Brücke, a group of Dresden artists formed in 1905 and led by Ernst Kirchner *(Street Berlin)*, and a group of Munich Expressionists known as Der Blaue Reiter, including Wassily Kandinsky *(No. 201)* and Paul Klee *(Actor's Mask)*, founded in 1911. One of the major and most individualistic Expressionists was the Austrian painter, Oskar Kokoschka, known for his powerful portraits and self-portraits.

Futurism. – The poet F.T. Marinetti founded this Italian art movement in 1909 declaring that "the splendor of the world has been enriched with a new form of beauty, the beauty of speed." Futurists demanded that all aspects of art and culture, including film, architecture, music and literature, shed the numbing confines of tradition and embrace the dynamism of modern technology. The tense, turbulent energy of Futurism is clearly evident in Umberto Boccioni's paintings *(The City Rises*, 1910) and sculptures *(Development of a Bottle in Space* and *Unique Forms of Continuity in Space)*, and in Giacomo Balla's *Swifts: Paths of Movement + Dynamic Sequences* (1913).

Abstract Art: Suprematism, Constructivism and De Stijl. – Pure abstract, or nonrepresentational art—in which the basic elements of color, line and form express reality through abstract suggestions originating in the mind—emerged in Russia before World War I. Around 1914, Kandinsky produced what are thought to be the first paintings with no references to recognizable objects or situations. In 1918, Kasimir Malevich unveiled his famous Suprematist series, including *White on White*, in which pictorial references are reduced to basic geometric shapes. Such works were meant as a fundamentally "honest" art seen to embody the spirit of a new socialist society.

Following the same ideal, sculptors Naum Gabo, Antoine Pevsner and Vladimir Tatlin founded the Russian Constructivist movement (1917-1920), creating highly structural sculptures in wood, glass, metal and plastic that symbolized a new industrialized era. Their work, along with the paintings, graphics and photographs of Alexander Rodchenko, influenced the Bauhaus in Germany and the De Stijl movement in Holland. The latter group, formed in 1917, included such painters as Piet Mondrian *(Broadway Boogie Woogie)*, whose graphic compositions in primary colors and gray and black attempted to express reality through a harmonious order of lines and rectangles.

Dada and Surrealism. – Lasting from 1915 to about 1923, the protest movement of Dada was an indictment of the bourgeois values and the senseless brutality of World War I. The nihilist members, including both Americans and Europeans, rejected all established values, creating instead a "non-art" meant to shock and provoke (the word "dada," meaning hobby horse, was picked at random from a dictionary). A typical Dada collage was made of randomly torn paper bits, ripped from ads and catalogues; a sculpture might be made of a snow shovel or toilet bowl. Jean Arp, Marcel Duchamp *(The Passage from Virgin to Bride)* and Francis Picabia were exponents of Dada, which also attracted the German, Kurt Schwitters, and American expatriate Man Ray. In Paris, this trend toward absurdity helped spawn Surrealism in the 1920s. There were two schools of Surrealist painting: one group, including Joan Miró *(Hirondelle/Amour)* and Max Ernst, painted with symbols and hallucinatory images; the other, including René Magritte *(The False Mirror)*, Paul Delvaux and Salvador Dali *(The Persistence of Memory)*, employed realistic images, although in dislocated, dreamlike and often macabre compositions. Among the more violent surrealist sculptures is Alberto Giacometti's *Woman with her Throat Cut*.

MUSEUMS

Neue Sachlichkeit. – This term, meaning "new objectivity," coined in Germany in 1923, referred to a trend among such artists as George Grosz, Otto Dix and Max Beckmann toward distorted compositions that were meant as scathing comments on the spiritual emptiness of German society and the effects of war. These works featured dark, disturbing images as in Beckmann's triptych, *Departure* (1933).

Mexican Mural Renaissance. – Painters Diego Rivera, David Alfaro Siqueiros and José Clemente Orozco were the founders of this movement, which, lasting from about the 1920s to the 1940s, glorified the working man and the Mexican Revolution. Sharing an affinity for pre-Columbian art, the three are known for their monumental murals, often street and genre scenes, that dealt with the issues of human suffering and social protest.

Naive Art. – Characterized by a non-academic, almost innocent appearance, naive—or primitive—art is typified by the direct and simple images of painters as diverse as Henri Rousseau and Grandma Moses. While naive painters do not adhere to a particular movement, their fresh, ingenuous approach has been increasingly influential both here and abroad since the early 20C.

American Regionalist and Figurative Painters. – The best-known members of the conservative Regionalist movement, associated with the 1930s Depression, are Thomas Hart Benton and Grant Wood, whose realistically rendered, folksy paintings celebrated life in small-town America as a deliberate grass-roots reaction to the sophisticated art of the previous decades. Edward Hopper *(House by the Railroad)* and Andrew Wyeth rank among the leading figurative painters, known for realistic, often melancholy, renderings of American scenes and moody landscapes like Wyeth's *Christina's World* (1948).

Abstract Expressionism. – Emerging in the 1940s, this American movement was largely non-representational. Styles varied considerably, but all eschewed traditional values and emphasized spontaneous, emotional expression. Typical was Action Painting, in which the artist dripped paint onto the canvas, as in the rhythmic designs of Jackson Pollock *(One)*, or slashed it on with a brush, as in the turbulent compositions of Willem de Kooning *(Woman, I)*; more calligraphic were Franz Kline's boldly marked works *(Chiefs)*. The term Color Field was used to describe such Abstract Expressionists as Mark Rothko and Barnett Newman, whose lyrical canvases explored the effects of large planes of color. Robert Motherwell, a pioneer of Abstract Expressionism, created bold monochromatic compositions that combined planar explorations with the aggressive slashes of Action Painting.

Pop Art. – Celebrating the images of mass media and popular culture, this light-spirited movement emerged in Britain and America in the mid-1950s and lasted to the early 1960s. Adherents included Andy Warhol *(Gold Marilyn Monroe)*, Roy Lichtenstein *(Girl with Ball)*, Jim Dine, David Hockney, Claes Oldenburg, Robert Rauschenberg and Jasper Johns *(Flag)*. Their work consisted predominantly of outsized icons of everyday objects, represented by collage, air-brush and commercial printing techniques, and soft blow-up sculptures.

Conceptual Art. – Emphasizing idea over craftsmanship, conceptual movements, including performance art and site-specific installations, emerged in the 1960s and are still strong today. The process of execution (as in releasing kites into the air) is the art, rather than a static, finished product. A similar attitude defines Minimal art, particularly sculpture by such artists as Tony Smith and Andre Judd, meant to be experimented in environmental and spatial terms. The Minimalist painters Joseph Stella, Kenneth Noland and Ellsworth Kelly, in turn, used simple shapes and colors in an effort to find expression through medium rather than image.

Recent Trends. – With the 1980s came reactionary trends to the preceding decades, including Neo-Expressionism, which patently rejected the quiet restraint of Minimalism. The term Neo-Expressionist has been applied to such artists as German painters Georg Baselitz and Markus Lupertz and the American, David Salle. While they work independently, their art is all provocative and highly charged, often displaying sexual, and sometimes vulgar, imagery.
Among photography's leading figures of the period is Robert Mapplethorpe, whose graphically sexual images also challenged the conventional view of what is and is not art. The Graffitists were also a prominent counterculture group in the 1980s, creating a body of work inspired by subway graffiti. Noted graffitists are Keith Haring, whose "canvases" included chalkboards and vinyl tarpaulins, and Jean-Michel Basquiat. More recently there has been a move to Neo-Abstraction, a new form of non-representational art. Going beyond the surface treatments of earlier abstract art, members of this movement, including Elizabeth Murray *(Popeye)* and Robert Morris *(Untitled 1982)*, seek new ways to explore the true meaning of abstraction. To keep visitors abreast of the latest trends, the Project Series presents rotating exhibits of artists on the cutting edge.

We welcome your assistance in the never-ending task of updating the texts and maps in this guide. Send us your comments and suggestions:

Michelin Travel Publications
Michelin Tire Corporation
PO Box 19001
Greenville, SC 29602-9001

★ MUSEUM OF TELEVISION AND RADIO

Time: 1 hour. 25 W. 52nd St. ● E, F train to 53rd St or 6 train to 51st St. Map p 33. Open Tue–Sun noon– 6pm (Thu 8pm). Closed holidays. Suggested contribution $5. Guided tours (1hr) available. ♿ ☎621-6800.

Created by CBS chairman William S. Paley with a view to preserving an increasingly popular aspect of 20C American culture—radio and television—, this museum (1975) is the first of its kind in the world. Originally located on East 52nd Street, the museum moved to its new location in 1991. Designed by John Burgee and Philip Johnson, the 17-story structure sheathed in limestone houses several theaters, screening rooms, individual listening/viewing consoles, three public galleries and an extensive library with a computerized card-catalog *(4th floor)*.
The museum's collection comprises tapes of over 50,000 radio and television programs and commercials, which visitors can request and listen to or view in the consoles. Major public events from war reportage to presidential elections are represented as well as dramatic and comedy productions from the previous 70 years of broadcasting. The museum also mounts programs on changing themes in its theaters and screening rooms.

NATIONAL ACADEMY OF DESIGN

Time: 1 hour. 1083 Fifth Ave. ● 4, 5, 6 train to 86th St. Map p 93. Open Wed–Sun noon–5pm (Fri 8pm). Closed holidays. $3.50. ♿ ☎369-4880.

Established in the early 19C to provide New York City with an art school and to hold exhibits of contemporary painting, sculpture, engraving and architecture, the National Academy has earned its place among the city's venerable cultural institutions. Located in a small, rounded townhouse, the Academy has, since its inception, amassed one of the country's finest collections of American art.
The first floor features a charming, wood-paneled bookshop that leads into a marble entrance foyer dominated by a gracefully sweeping staircase. The statue of *Diana* is by Anna Huntington Hyatt, the wife of Archer M. Huntington who acquired the building in 1902 and turned it over to the Academy in 1940. The second and third floors are devoted to temporary shows from the permanent collection and traveling exhibits. The practice of requiring candidates for membership to present a portrait of themselves and a representative example of their work, led to the growth of the Academy's rich holdings of 19C and 20C American art, and brought to the collection the works of such famous members as Winslow Homer, John Singer Sargent, Augustus Saint-Gaudens, Isabel Bishop and Thomas Eakins.
Through its School of Fine Arts, the National Academy offers programs in drawing, painting, sculpture and graphics.

★★ THE NEW-YORK HISTORICAL SOCIETY

170 Central Park West. ● B, C train to 81st St or 1, 9 train to 79th St. Map p 89. Owing to budgetary restrictions, the exhibit galleries are not scheduled to reopen before fall 1994. The library is open to the public Wed–Fri 10am–5pm. ☎873-3400. The collection of architectural drawings, prints and photographs (3rd floor) is open by appointment only.

Housed in an austere, neoclassical edifice (1908) fronting CENTRAL PARK, the Society was chartered in 1804 with a view to collecting and preserving the history of the United States. Three centuries of Americana are displayed on the four floors of the museum, New York City's oldest, which also includes a renowned research library.

First Floor. – Selections from the permanent collection are displayed in the two main galleries. The auditorium features special programs emphasizing the contributions of American history to contemporary culture.

Second and Third Floors. – The second floor's showpiece is the spectacular collection of Tiffany glass, lamps, shades and stands. More than 150 pieces in a multitude of colors, textures and patterns reflect the diversity of styles produced by the New York-based Tiffany Studios *(p 123)*. A selection of ornithologist John J. Audubon's original watercolors for the "Birds of America" (painted while he traveled throughout North America) is also on display. The Luman Reed Gallery, a re-creation of an early 19C New York private gallery, features presidential portraits by Asher B. Durand and the grandiose *Course of the Empire* by Thomas Cole, principal founder of the Hudson River school. The research library, which houses a rare manuscript of the Federalist Papers, is also located on this floor.
The third floor displays a collection of toys, mechanical banks and *millefiori* paperweights.

Fourth Floor. – The exhibits on this floor capture the scope and spirit of 18C and 19C American arts and crafts. The Bryan Gallery's red moiré walls exhibit works of art (14C-19C) collected by Thomas Jefferson Bryan over the course of 20 years. Selections from the Hudson River school collection include Frederic Church's monumental *Cayambe* and Thomas Cole's *View on Catskill Creek, New York*, capturing the eerie light of an autumn afternoon. Eastman Johnson's *Old Kentucky Home* and Thomas Crawford's 1856 sculpture, *The Indian*, reflect the richness of America's cultural landscape. Over 40 portraits, including Rembrandt Peale's *Stephen Decatur*, span the styles of American portraiture. Serving pieces by 18C New York silversmith Myer Myers and a two-part, Federal style desk, designed by Charles Pierre L'Enfant *(p 63)* and used by the first US Congress (1789), are among the most prominent holdings in the decorative arts collection.

THE NEW MUSEUM OF CONTEMPORARY ART

Time: 1/2 hour. 583 Broadway. ●6 train to Spring St or N, R train to Prince St. Map p 80. Open Wed–Sun noon–6pm (Sat 8pm). Closed holidays. $3.50. ఉ. ☎219-1355.

Founded in 1977, this museum is an international forum for contemporary artists—many unknown or unrecognized—whose work deals with popular culture, the environment, feminism, the media, politics, and controversial health issues such as AIDS. While there are no permanent exhibits, the museum mounts some 15 to 20 temporary shows a year, including eye-catching (and often ear-catching) installations in the streetfront window. Many invite visitor participation and are often designed to provoke.

NEW YORK CITY FIRE MUSEUM

Time: 1 hour. 278 Spring St. ● 1, 9 train to W. Houston St or C, E train to Spring St. Map p 80. Open Tue–Sat 10am–4pm. Closed holidays. Suggested contribution $3. ఉ. ☎691-1303.

Located in a 1904 firehouse, this colorful museum displays the most comprehensive collection of fire-related art and artifacts in the US, from the mid-18C to present time. The collection includes an intriguing array of badges, buckets, pump wagons, fire sleighs, trumpets, helmets and fire insurance marks. Also featured are a fire hydrant (the first in New York was installed in 1818) and a sliding pole (invented in Chicago in 1858). Among the most unusual exhibits is a dog that served between 1929 and 1939 as an honorary member of Company 203 in Brooklyn, sliding down poles, climbing ladders and locating trapped victims in burning buildings; now stuffed, he resides behind glass.

★ OLD MERCHANT'S HOUSE

Time: 1/2 hour. 29 E. 4th St. ●6 train to Astor Place. Map p 84. Open Mon–Thu 1–4pm, Sun 1–4pm. Closed holidays & Aug. $3. ☎777-1089.

Erected in 1832 by Joseph Brewster as one of six identical row houses, this red brick townhouse with its Greek Revival doorway was sold in 1835 to Seabury Tredwell, a prosperous merchant. The house remained in the Tredwell family for nearly one hundred years. It is the only 19C house in Manhattan to survive intact with its original furniture and family memorabilia. Today renovated into a museum, the house is a characteristic period piece, illustrating the lifestyle of an affluent 19C family. Just up the street, at no. 37, is another Greek Revival house, built for Samuel Tredwell Skidmore. Unfortunately, this structure has not been restored and is in a dilapidated state.

★★ PIERPONT-MORGAN LIBRARY

Time: 1 1/2 hours. 29 E. 36th St. ● 4, 5, 6 train to 33rd St. Map p 32.

A cultural treasure trove, this venerable institution houses an outstanding collection of rare books, manuscripts, drawings, prints and works of art assembled by **J. Pierpont Morgan** (1837-1913), an inveterate collector whose interest in art, literature and history resulted in an unusually broad and varied accumulation of objects.

The Buildings. – In 1902, Morgan commissioned the firm of McKim, Mead and White to erect a permanent home for his collection to be accessible to the public following his death. The Italian Renaissance style main building *(33 36th St)* was completed in 1906 after several tempestuous tugs-of-war between Morgan and Charles McKim. The annex on the corner of Madison Avenue was added by Morgan's son in 1928. Both edifices house a museum and a research library filled with rare and exemplary items attesting to the development of Western civilizations. The annex is connected to a large brownstone building on the corner of Madison Avenue and 37th Street—the younger Morgan's former residence—by a glass enclosed court, dotted with chairs and tables. The brownstone now contains the museum's book shop.

Visit

Open Tue–Sat 10:30am–5pm, Sun 1–5pm. Closed holidays. Suggested contribution $5. ఉ. ☎685-0610.

The marble polychrome vestibule leads to the main hall used for rotating exhibits *(on the left)* and a reading room open to accredited scholars *(on the right)*. A cloister area, also reserved for temporary exhibits, allows passage to the 1906 building.

The West Room. – The opulence of Mr Morgan's former study is enhanced by a painted and carved wood **ceiling** (16C), red damask hangings, 15C-17C stained-glass windows and massive black wood furniture. Paintings and statuettes, enamels and metalwork of the Middle Ages and the Renaissance blend harmoniously with the decor. Above the marble mantel attributed to 15C Florentine sculptor Desiderio da Settignano is a portrait of Morgan by Frank Holl. Among the works of art, note Tintoretto's *Portrait of a Moor* (1570), *Madonna and Saints Adoring the Child* by Perugino, the wedding portraits of Martin Luther and his wife by the workshop of the 16C German artist, Lucas Cranach the Elder, and a small portrait attributed to the François Clouet school of painting.

A colorful, Renaissance-inspired **rotunda** adorned with lunettes, mosaic panels and free-standing lapis lazuli columns connects the West Room to the Library.

The East Room/Library. – Lined with three-tiered floor-to-ceiling bookshelves, this solemn room contains rotating displays from Morgan's world-acclaimed collection of illuminated Medieval and Renaissance manuscripts, dating back to the 5C; thousands of letters and autographed manuscripts; a superb collection of gilded and bejeweled book bindings; thousands of drawings by such artists as Dürer, Rembrandt and Rubens; and a wide selection of music manuscripts including scores by Mozart, Beethoven, Haydn and Mahler.

On permanent display is one of the Library's three **Gutenberg Bibles** (mid-15C). Works of art embellishing the room include a 16C Flemish tapestry, representing the Triumph of Avarice, hanging above the marble fireplace. The carved ceiling sports a series of lunettes and painted spandrels featuring the signs of the zodiac.

★ THE STUDIO MUSEUM IN HARLEM

Time: 1 hour. **144 W. 125th St.** ● *2 train to 125th St. Map p 2. Open Wed–Fri 10am–5pm, weekends 1–6pm. Closed holidays. $3.* ☏*864-4500.*

Established in 1968 to provide studio space for African-American artists, this small museum has expanded and grown into a major cultural center and now mounts about eight temporary shows a year. Selections from the permanent collection of 1,400 works by prominent and emerging artists of the African diaspora (African, African-American and Caribbean origins)—including Romare Bearden, Alvin Loving, Faith Ringgold and Betye Saar—are on view about once every 18 months. Jewelry, crafts and books fill the ground-floor gift shop.

★★ WHITNEY MUSEUM OF AMERICAN ART

Time: 1 1/2 hours. **945 Madison Ave.** ● *6 train to 77th St. Map p 93. Open Wed & Fri–Sun 11am–6pm, Thu 1–8pm. Closed holidays. $6.* ✗ & ☏*570-3676. The museum operates a branch in midtown Manhattan, in the Philip Morris Building (p 46).*

Dedicated to the advancement of contemporary artists, this museum holds one of the world's foremost collections of 20C American art, housed in a stark, granite building designed by Marcel Breuer and Hamilton Smith. Rising above a sunken sculpture garden in a series of inverted stairs, the cantilevered edifice (1966) represents a striking example of the Brutalism style of architecture. A controversial proposal by Michael Graves to add a new wing that would provide additional exhibit and office space, has been temporarily put on hold.

Founded in 1931, the museum grew out of the Greenwich Village studio *(p 80)* of sculptress and art collector **Gertrude Vanderbilt Whitney** (1875-1942). After founding the Whitney Studio Club, Gertrude began acquiring works by living American artists, creating the core of today's collection of over 10,000 works by such painters as Hopper, de Kooning, Kelly, Gorky, Prendergast, Demuth and Motherwell, and sculptors such as Calder, Nevelson, Noguchi and David Smith. The museum moved to the current building, its third home, in 1966. From its inception, the museum has provided a unique venue for American artists and played a special role in the development of contemporary art. Rotating selections from the permanent collection are displayed year-round.

A special feature, in the entrance foyer, is Alexander Calder's miniature **Circus** with its dozens of performers and animals; a film showing Calder's last complete circus performance supplements the exhibit. The museum's frequently changing exhibit programs have been known to explore daring, innovative and often times controversial topics.

The Film and Video department presents works by independent American film and video artists. The museum is also known for its series of invitational Biennials, held since 1932, which attempt to offer to the public a representative cross-section of the current American art scene.

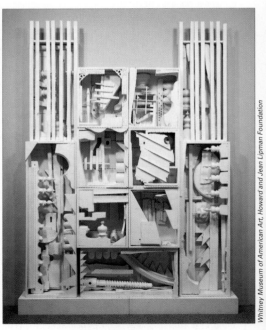

Whitney Museum of American Art, Howard and Jean Lipman Foundation

Dawn's Wedding Chapel II (1959) by Louise Nevelson

The Bronx

Area: 41 square miles
Population: 1,203,800

The only New York borough located on the mainland, the Bronx was named after Jonas Bronck, a Danish émigré, who arrived here in June 1639. The borough developed in the late 1800s around the village of Morrisania [AZ], which now forms the section of the Bronx around Third Avenue and 161st Street. Two members of the Morris family, for whom the village was named, were prominent during the Revolutionary period: Lewis Morris, a signer of the Declaration of Independence, and Governor Morris, penman of the US Constitution. The Bronx was a part of Westchester County until 1898, when it was incorporated into New York City.

Today, the Bronx has over 1.2 million inhabitants. The number of Central and Eastern European residents has steadily declined, while the borough has experienced a new influx of blacks and Hispanic immigrants. The southern part of the borough is mainly inhabited by lower income groups; more prosperous sections are found to the north. To the east lies the largest park in New York City, Pelham Bay Park *(p 149)*, with its popular sandy beach, Orchard Beach. The borough is linked to Manhattan by 12 bridges and 6 subway tunnels.

SIGHTS *Map p 148*

*** **The Bronx Zoo.** – *Bronx River Parkway at Fordham Rd. ● 2, 5 trains to Pelham Parkway to reach the Bronxdale entrance of the zoo. Open Apr–Oct daily 10am–5pm (Sat & Sun 5:30pm). Rest of the year daily 10am–4:30pm. $5.75 (Wed free), $2.50 off-season. ✕ ✆ ☎718/367-1010.* Covering 265 acres of woodland, this popular zoo is located in Bronx Park, a vast expanse of land laid out in the late 19C on both banks of the Bronx River. Over 4,000 animals of more than 700 species roam in indoor and outdoor exhibit areas, which are often separated from visitor pathways only by a moat.

Visit. – *For a good overview of the zoo, we recommend taking the Zoo Shuttle (Apr–Oct Mon–Fri 10am–4:30pm, weekends & holidays 10am–5pm; $1.50), a tractor train that tours the entire zoo, or the Skyfari aerial tramway (same hours as Safari Tour), which offers expansive views of the site. Visitors may also stroll through the zoo at their leisure (see map p 148).*

Snow leopard

Bill Meng/New York Zoological Society

The Bengali Express monorail *(May–Oct Mon–Fri 10am–4:30pm, weekends & holidays 10am–5pm; $1.50)* passes through 38 acres of hilly, wooded land on its journey into **Wild Asia**, which is home to Siberian tigers, Asian elephants and Indian rhinoceroses among others. The indoor exhibit at **Jungleworld** *(Apr–Oct Mon–Fri 10am–5pm, weekends & holidays 10am–5:30pm; rest of the year daily 10am–4:30pm; closed last 2 weeks in Feb)* recreates a South Asian rain forest where birds, like Bali mynah, fly free among proboscis monkeys, black leopards and Indian gharials. Other areas of interest include **Baboon Reserve**, the Ethiopian setting for two troops of gelada baboons; the Reptile House; the DeJur Aviary and the Aquatic Bird House; the World of Darkness *(night animals, May–Oct Mon–Fri 10am–5pm, weekends & holidays 10am–5:30pm; rest of the year daily 10am–4:30pm; wildlife exhibit in winter, weather permitting);* and the World of Birds, where hundreds of exotic birds can be observed in natural surroundings. Among the animals not to be missed are the American bison (Bison Range), and on the **Rare Animals Range**, the Mongolian wild horses and the Pere David deer, which have the feet of a cow, the neck of a camel, the tail of a donkey and deer antlers.

Covering over 3 acres of marsh, prairie and wooded land, the **Children's Zoo** *(Apr–Oct Mon–Fri 10am–5pm, weekends & holidays 10am–5:30pm; $1.50)* features more than 100 animals shown in re-creations of their natural habitats: marsh, forest, desert, woodland edge and domestic settings. Various thematic exhibits encouraging active participation educate children on the habitats and traits of various animals.

★★ **The New York Botanical Garden.** – *200th St and Southern Blvd. ●D or 4 trains to Bedford Park Blvd; walk east to Main Garden Gate on Southern Blvd. Open Apr–Oct Tue–Sun 10am–6pm. Rest of the year Tue–Sun 10am–4pm. Open all Monday holidays. Closed Jan 1, Dec 25. $3. ✕ ᒧ ☎718/817-8700.* Located directly to the north of the zoo, this 250-acre garden (1891) encompasses thousands of flower-

ing trees, shrubs and plants that reach their peak in spring and early summer. Favorite attractions include the rose garden, the rhododendron valley, the demonstration gardens, the rock garden, the 40-acre virgin forest, the native plant garden and the Enid A. Haupt Conservatory, which is closed for renovation until summer 1995. The Museum Building *(open Tue, Wed, Thu noon–6pm, Sat noon–4pm; closed holiday weekends)* houses the library, the herbarium with dried plant specimens and fossils, the auditorium and the gift shop. A restaurant occupies the old Snuff Mill, an 18C stone building overlooking the Bronx River.

★★ **Enid A. Haupt Conservatory.** – *Closed for renovation. Scheduled to reopen summer 1995.* The Conservatory, a glass pavilion built in 1901 and modeled after the crystal palaces of the 19C, was restored in 1978 and named for Enid A. Haupt whose gift to the garden made the restoration possible.

The entrance to the conservatory opens onto the Palm Court with its 90ft central dome and collection of lush, tropical plants. By exploring the 11 galleries, visitors will discover a variety of plant environments with flora from around the world: tropical container plants, a fern jungle, orangerie, deserts of the Old and New World displaying a variety of cacti and succulents, and special collections that include carnivorous plants and rare orchids. Six seasonal floral displays are scheduled annually.

In House 1, designed especially for children, visitors can attempt to identify the vegetables, fruits and grains being raised with the products stocked on the "grocery store" shelves located nearby.

ADDITIONAL SIGHTS *Map pp 150-151*

★ **Yankee Stadium.** – [AZ] *161st St and River Ave. ● 4 or D, C trains to 161st St.* This famous baseball stadium, affectionately referred to by lovers of the sport as "the house that Babe Ruth built," was erected in 1923 by brewery magnate Colonel Jacob Ruppert for the team he owned (the Yankees). The stadium's first years were the heyday of Babe Ruth—"the Babe"—one of the outstanding athletes of all times. Babe Ruth hit 60 home runs in 1927, still the American record in the Major Leagues for a 154-game season. When he died in 1948, 100,000 fans came out to pay their respects. A bronze plaque commemorates past Yankee greats: Babe Ruth, Lou Gehrig, Edward Grant Barrow, Joe Di Maggio and Mickey Mantle.

The 57,545-seat stadium underwent a massive remodeling program between 1974 and 1975 and now features sets of escalators serving the upper tiers of the grandstands, an unobstructed view of the playing field and an electronically controlled scoreboard.

Valentine–Varian House [BY D]. – *3266 Bainbridge Ave at E. 208th St. ● D train to 205th St, or 4 train to Mosholu Parkway. Open Sat 10am–4pm, Sun 1–5pm. Closed holidays. $2. ☎718/881-8900.* This fieldstone house originally stood on the opposite side of the street, on land acquired in 1758 by Isaac Valentine. The scene of many skirmishes during the Revolution, the area was purchased in 1791 by Isaac Varian, a prosperous farmer whose son later became the 63rd mayor of the city of New York.

Situated on its present site since 1965, the house now contains the **Museum of Bronx History**, featuring a fine collection of prints, lithographs and photographs.

Poe Cottage [AY B]. – *E. Kingsbridge Rd and Grand Concourse. ● D or 4 train to Kingsbridge Rd. Open Sat 10am–4pm, Sun 1-5pm. Closed holidays. $2. ☎718/881-8900.* From 1846 to 1849, this little wooden house (1812) was the home of author Edgar Allan Poe (1809-1849), who wrote *Annabel Lee*, *The Bells, Ulalume* and *Eureka* during his stay here.

Poe moved to this cottage away from the noise and congestion of New York City in the hope of saving his wife Virginia Clemm from tuberculosis; however, she died in 1847. The author died two years later in Baltimore, while on a return trip to the cottage from Virginia. The cottage was moved across the street in 1913 and transformed into a museum in 1917. Today, the restored house contains displays of memorabilia and manuscripts, and an audio-visual slide show *(20min)*.

★ **Van Cortlandt House Museum** [AX A]. – *On Broadway behind visitor center for Van Cortlandt Park. ● 1 train to Van Cortlandt Park. Open Tue–Fri 10am–3pm, weekends 11am–4pm. Closed holidays. $2. ☎718/543-3344.* Built in 1748, this colonial plantation house has been admirably preserved by the city and the National Society of Colonial Dames. It is believed that George Washington used the house as headquarters before making his triumphant entry into New York in November 1783.

The manor, appointed with furnishings in the colonial style, reflects a refinement and style of living typical of the 18C and 19C New York gentry. Among the nine rooms open to the public, note the Dutch room, the kitchen and the nursery, which contains one of America's oldest doll houses.

Bronx Community College [AY]. – *University Ave & W. 181st St. ● 4 train to Burnside Ave.* Founded in 1891 as the Bronx campus of New York University, this institution, now occupied by the Bronx Community College, is made up of 18 buildings lining the banks of the Harlem River.

★ **Hall of Fame for Great Americans** [C]. – *Hall of Fame Terrace at W. 181st St. Open daily 10am–5pm. ✗ ☎718/220-6450.* Completed by Stanford White in 1900, this Beaux-Arts complex, the first American Pantheon, consists of an outdoor colonnade, 630ft in length, surrounding three buildings. This unique sculpture museum honors Americans outstanding in many fields. Candidates, chosen at least 25 years after their death, are selected by an electoral committee in each of the following categories: arts, sciences, humanities, government, and business and labor. Elections were temporarily suspended in 1979, but since then the structure has undergone restoration and plans are underway to reinstate the election process.

The 102 selected honorees include: Harriet Beecher Stowe, George Washington Carver, Edgar Allan Poe *(above)*, Walt Whitman, John James Audubon *(p 144)*, Susan B. Anthony, the Wright Brothers, Henry Wadsworth Longfellow, Washington Irving *(p 168)*, and presidents Ulysses S. Grant, Thomas Jefferson and Abraham Lincoln.

Pelham Bay Park [CXCY]. – *● 6 train to Pelham Bay Park.* The largest park in the city offers a variety of outdoor activities including golfing, hiking, cycling, tennis, horseback riding, ball playing and fishing. Providing a welcome refuge for swimmers on hot summer days, the popular **Orchard Beach** features one mile of sandy shore.

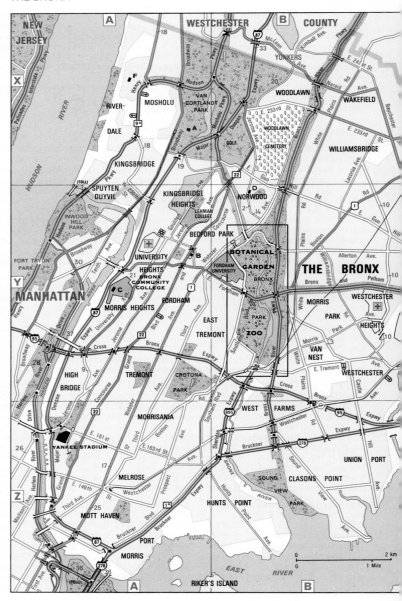

★ **Bartow-Pell Mansion [CY E]**. – *Open Wed, Sat, Sun noon–4pm. Closed holidays & last 3 weeks in Aug. $2.* ♿ ☎ *718/885-1461.* The history of this site dates back to 1654 when Thomas Pell purchased the land from the Siwanoy Indians. Robert Bartow, a descendent of Pell's, erected the Classic Revival stone mansion overlooking Long Island Sound between 1836 and 1842. The elegant interior contains Greek Revival detailing, including a freestanding elliptical staircase and furnishings in the American Empire style.

Wave Hill [AX F]. – *625 W. 252nd St.* ● *1, 9 train to 231st St, then bus 7, 10 or 24 to 252nd St. Open May 15–Oct 15 Tue–Sun 9am–5:30pm (Wed dusk). Rest of the year Tue–Sun 9am–4:30pm. Closed Jan 1, Dec 25. Free (weekends $4). Guided tours of garden & greenhouse Sun 2:15pm.* ✗♿ ☎ *718/549-3200.* Opened to the public in 1965, this enchanting 28-acre estate comprises award-winning gardens and greenhouses, rolling meadows and lush woodlands, overlooking the Hudson River. The 18 acres of landscaped gardens contain over 3,000 species of plants and a variety of trees.

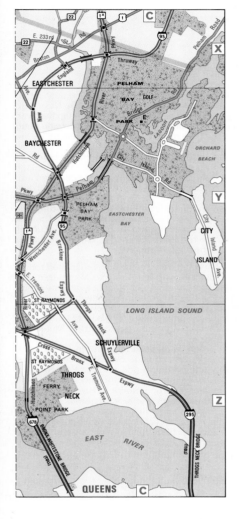

Also on the premises is an 1843 mansion, the former home of such celebrities as Mark Twain, Teddy Roosevelt and Arturo Toscanini. The building was restored in the 1960s, along with another edifice constructed in 1905. Today, the estate focuses on nature appreciation and education, offering programs in landscape design, horticulture, land management and the arts.

Sights described in this guide are rated:

★★★   *Highly recommended*

★★   *Recommended*

★   *Interesting*

Brooklyn

Area: 71 square miles
Population: 2,300,700

Situated on the western tip of Long Island *(p 171)*, Brooklyn extends from the East River to Coney Island and from the Narrows to Jamaica Bay. Brooklyn is New York's most populous borough.

A Long and Rich Past. – Brooklyn was founded in 1636 by Dutch settlers who called it Breuckelen ("broken land") after a small town near Utrecht. The present borough of Brooklyn was made up of six small towns. One of the original settlements was founded on Wallabout Bay, near the area where the Brooklyn Navy Yard was located until 1966. Gradually, the settlements spread westward along the river. By the late 18C, regular ferry service to Manhattan was established, allowing Long Island farmers to cross the river and sell their produce in lower Manhattan. By the early 19C, Brooklyn had become a pleasant residential area. Many prosperous New Yorkers established their homes here and commuted into Manhattan for work.

In 1834, Brooklyn became an incorporated city with about 30,000 inhabitants. It developed into an important industrial and trading center and was integrated into New York City in 1898, after absorbing a number of villages whose names still designate various sections of the borough.

By 1883, the BROOKLYN BRIDGE formed the first direct link with Manhattan; the Williamsburg Bridge followed in 1903, and the Manhattan Bridge in 1909. The first subway connection dates from 1905. More recently, the Brooklyn-Battery Tunnel, completed in 1950, and the VERRAZANO-NARROWS BRIDGE, opened in 1965, have further facilitated travel between Brooklyn and the other boroughs.

A Special World. – Although Brooklyn can hardly be considered isolated today, with the almost half a million Brooklynites who commute to Manhattan, the borough has retained its distinctive personality as vividly described by Betty Smith in her book *A Tree Grows in Brooklyn (1943)*. Furthermore, a number of writers have enjoyed living here, especially in the Brooklyn Heights area *(below)*, including Walt Whitman (who wrote for the now defunct *Brooklyn Daily Eagle* in 1846), Herman Melville, John Dos Passos, Thomas Wolfe, Truman Capote, Arthur Miller and Norman Mailer.

A visitor passing through Brooklyn is first impressed by its huge size, and its labyrinth of streets and avenues lined with neat, straight rows of houses. A closer look, however, reveals a great variety of neighborhoods, such as Park Slope, a choice residential neighborhood; Brooklyn Heights, a charming enclave that is still the refuge of a few "old families"; Williamsburg, containing Hassidic Jewish, Hispanic and Italian communities; Flatbush, with fine private homes and lively commercial streets; Bensonhurst, a predominantly Italian section; and Bedford-Stuyvesant, an area where a substantial proportion of Brooklyn's black population resides. The borough's ethnic makeup includes black, Italian, Jewish, Greek, Middle Eastern, Scandinavian, South American and Polish groups as well as a sizable Caribbean population.

★★ BROOKLYN HEIGHTS *Map p 153*

Heavily fortified during the Revolution, Brooklyn Heights was the site of General Washington's headquarters during the Battle of Long Island.

In the mid-19C this section of Brooklyn developed into a choice residential area, owing largely to its proximity to the city. Yet Brooklyn Heights enjoys a distinct identity, with a serenity often likened to that of a small countrified town. Its narrow, tree-shaded streets are lined with brownstones and town houses that represent almost every style of 19C American architecture.

Walking Tour
Time: 2hrs. Distance: 2.8mi. Begin at Monroe Place. ● *2, 3 train to Clark Street.*

Leaving the subway station, walk toward Monroe Place. At the corner of Clark and Henry Streets stands the Hotel St George, once the largest hotel in New York City. Most of the building has been converted into coops and luxury apartments, while an unrenovated section facing Henry Street still functions as a hotel. *Turn into Monroe Place.* At **46 Monroe Place**, a brick and brownstone Greek Revival dwelling, note the decorative wrought-iron basket urns set on stone pedestals. The pineapple topping the baskets was a symbol of hospitality during the shipping era.

Turn right at Pierrepont St and continue to the corner of Henry St.

82 Pierrepont Street represents a splendid example of Richardsonian Romanesque, with its bulky massing, rough unfinished masonry surfaces, rounded arches and low relief carving. Built in 1890 as a private residence, it was later enlarged and has recently been converted into apartments.

Turning into Willow Street, you will note **nos. 155, 157** and **159**, three Federal style houses with handsomely detailed entranceways. A skylight in the pavement in front of no. 157 allows daylight to filter down into a tunnel which connects no. 159

to **no. 151**, formerly a stable and now an apartment. Farther up the street, on the opposite side, **nos. 108-112** represent a picturesque example of the Queen Anne style, with their great variety of building materials and blend of elements of the Romanesque, Gothic and Renaissance styles.

Continue on Willow St and turn right on Orange St.

At no. 75 Orange Street stands the **Plymouth Church of the Pilgrims** *(open Sept–Jun Sun–Fri 9am–5pm; Jul–Aug Tue–Fri 9am–5pm)*. The first Congregational Church in Brooklyn, this simple brick meeting house dating from 1846 served for 40 years as the pulpit for Henry Ward Beecher, who is well remembered for his anti-slavery efforts and other progressive sentiments. President Lincoln worshipped here on two occasions in 1860, and many eminent authors and statesmen have spoken here over the years. In Hillis Hall, the fellowship hall, note the large stained-glass windows by Tiffany.

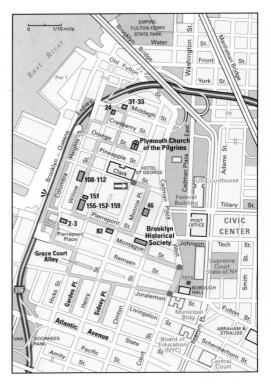

> *Backtrack to Hicks St and continue two blocks farther north; turn left onto Middagh St.*

Several Federal-style clapboard houses, built in the 1820s, line the street. Among the best preserved are the double frame house at **nos. 31-33** and the charming dwelling at **no. 24**.

> *Take Willow St to Cranberry St and continue toward the East River to the Brooklyn Heights Esplanade.*

Overlooking the harbor, the esplanade offers magnificent **views★★★** of the FINANCIAL DISTRICT; the view is especially impressive in the early evening when the lights glimmer across the river. Behind the terrace lies a series of houses with lovely private gardens.

> *Walk the length of the esplanade; turn left onto Montague St and left onto Pierrepont Place.*

Note **2** and **3 Pierrepont Place**, two of the most elegant brownstones in New York.

> *Return to Montague St and continue on Montague Terrace; turn left onto Remsen St and right into Hicks St.*

Off to the left is **Grace Court Alley**, a picturesque mews that was the stable alley for the fine homes on Remsen Street.

> *Continue along Hicks St and turn left onto Joralemon St.*

The intersection of Hicks and Joralemon Streets was the location of the country home of Philip Livingston, a signer of the Declaration of Independence. It is reported that on August 29, 1776, General Washington met at Livingston's home with his chiefs of staff to plan the evacuation of his army. Several pretty, tree-lined streets branch off of Joralemon Street, such as **Garden Place** and **Sidney Place**.

> *Continue east on Joralemon St to Court St.*

The Civic Center area presents a contrast to the residential section, with its massive public buildings, such as Borough Hall, the former Brooklyn City Hall and the massive Richardsonian Romanesque central post office. Farther down Fulton Street is Brooklyn's "downtown," including the famous department store Abraham & Strauss.

> *Continue on Montague St, the commercial heart of Brooklyn Heights. One block down, turn right on Clinton St and continue to the next corner.*

The Brooklyn Historical Society. – *128 Pierrepont St.* This organization is the primary source of material related to the history of Brooklyn. It contains a large collection of books, documents and artifacts on the borough, features special exhibits, educational programs, concerts and walking tours, and houses the borough's only history museum.

Brooklyn's History Museum. – *Open Tue–Sat 10am–5pm. $2.50.* ♿ *☎718/624-0890.* Using five symbols that represent Brooklyn (the Brooklyn Bridge, Brooklyn Navy Yard, Brooklyn Dodgers, Brooklynites and Coney Island), the museum retraces the history of the borough and the diversity of its people.

We suggest ending the tour with a leisurely stroll on **Atlantic Avenue** at the foot of Brooklyn Heights. Exotic restaurants, food stores and antique shops line the avenue, the commercial center for the neighboring Middle Eastern community.

PROSPECT PARK AND VICINITY   Map p 155

★ **Prospect Park.** – ● *2, 3 train to Grand Army Plaza. For recorded information on current events in the park ☎718/788-0055.* Once part of an estate belonging to the Litchfield family, the 526-acre tract of land was purchased by the city in piecemeal fashion between 1859 and 1869. Encompassing rolling meadows and wooded bluffs, streams, brooks and a lake, the park was designed by Frederick Law Olmsted and Calvert Vaux (architects of CENTRAL PARK) in 1860. A network of paths and road-ways winds through the park linking its various sections.
The main entrance of the park is at Grand Army Plaza, a majestic oval plaza embel-lished with a monument to President Kennedy and a triumphal arch dedicated to the Civil War dead.

Boathouse Visitor Center. – ● *D or S to Prospect Park. Open May–Oct weekends noon–5pm.* ✗ ♿. The former boathouse (1905), modeled after a 16C Venetian build-ing, has been restored and serves as the park information center. It is also the departure point for tours conducted by the Urban Park Rangers.

Lefferts Homestead. – ● *D or S to Prospect Park. Open May–Dec weekends noon–4pm.* ♿. A graceful gambrel roof crowns this 18C colonial farmhouse, which was moved to the park in 1918. The interior contains period furniture and handcarved paneling.

★★ **Brooklyn Botanic Garden.** – *1000 Washington Ave.* ● *2, 3 train to Eastern Parkway. Open Apr–Sept Tue–Fri 8am–6pm, weekends 10am–6pm. Rest of the year Tue–Fri 8am–4:30pm, weekends 10am–4:30pm.* ✗ ♿ *☎718/622-4433.* Located to the east of Prospect Park and to the south of the Brooklyn Museum *(below)*, this out-standing botanical garden contains a great variety of vegetation. The 52-acre garden is a refreshing oasis that invites visitors to explore its Japanese Garden, Shake-speare Garden, Children's Garden and Conservatory.
The 4-building **Conservatory** complex *(open Apr–Sept Tue–Sun 10am–5pm; rest of the year Tue–Sun 10am–4pm)* houses numerous varieties of flora. Not to be missed are the rose garden, the rows of cherry trees, the herb garden and the garden for the blind (Fragrance Garden).

Brooklyn Public Library. – ● *2, 3 train to Eastern Parkway or D train to 107th Ave. Open Tue–Thu 9am–8pm, Fri–Sat 10am–6pm, Sun 1–5pm. Closed mid-Jun–mid-Sept on Sundays.* ♿ *☎718/780-7700.* Occupying a triangular plot, this monumental building was completed in 1941. The main library contains about 1,600,000 volumes nearly all of which can be borrowed; 58 library branches are located throughout the borough.

Park Slope. – Situated just west of Prospect Park, this is one of the most desirable residential areas in Brooklyn. Rows of handsome town houses, punctuated by church spires, line the wide, shaded streets, presenting a picture of the borough as it existed in the 19C. The architectural style is typical of the period between the Civil War and World War I.

Montauk Club. – *Northeast corner of Lincoln Place and 8th Ave.* This brownstone and brick mansion was constructed in 1891 in a style reminiscent of a Venetian palace. Of particular interest are the friezes, which depict historic scenes associated with the Montauk Indians.

★★ **BROOKLYN MUSEUM**   *3hrs. Map p 155. 200 Eastern Parkway.* ● *2, 3 train to Eastern Parkway. Open Wed–Sun 10am–5pm. Closed Jan 1, Thanksgiving Day, Dec 25. $4. Guided tours (1hr) available.* ✗ ♿ *☎718/638-5000.*

Housed in a monumental Beaux-Arts building designed by McKim, Mead and White, the Brooklyn Museum displays a rich collection of over 1,500,000 arti-facts, ranging from Egyptian antiquities to contemporary American art. Begun in 1895, the building was never completed to its original specifications. Various elements, such as the central facade, with its pediment and peristyle, and the east wing were added in the early 1900s, but by 1934, the architectural firm canceled its contract and work on the building came to a halt. In 1986, the museum hired archi-tects Arata Isozaki and James Stewart Polshek to complete the structure while redesigning, expanding and improving the existing gallery space. The most impor-tant result of that effort is the newly refurbished West Wing, in particular the contemporary art gallery, on the fifth floor.

First Floor. – Devoted to the primitive arts, this floor presents an eclectic collection of artifacts compiled, for the most part, by curator Stewart Culin in the early part of the century. The African gallery displays handsome wooden statuettes, masks and ceremonial shields, and witch doctors' wands. Art from the Americas ranges from pre-Colombian jewelry and textiles (note the Paracas textile from 100 BC), and pot-tery from Peru and Mexico, to magnificent totem poles from the Haida Indians on the Northwest Coast. Oceanic art includes sculptures, musical instruments and headdresses from Papua New Guinea, New Zealand and the Solomon Islands.

...yptian collection, one
...ged in two sections: one traces
...on from 1350 BC to the end of the Ptolemaic

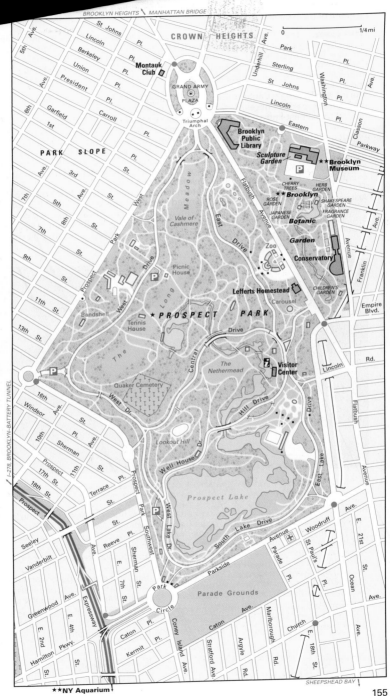

CROWN HEIGHTS

0   1/4 mi

St Johns
Lincoln Pl.
Berkeley Pl.
Union Pl.
President Pl.
Montauk Club
GRAND ARMY PLAZA
Triumphal Arch
Garfield
Carroll
1st
Pl.

PARK SLOPE
3rd
5th
7th
8th
9th
11th St.
13th St.

Sterling
St Johns
Lincoln
Eastern
Parkway

Brooklyn Public Library
Sculpture Garden
★★ Brooklyn Museum
CHERRY TREES
HERB GARDEN
ROSE GARDEN
★★ Brooklyn
SHAKESPEARE GARDEN
FRAGRANCE GARDEN
JAPANESE GARDEN
Botanic
Garden
Conservatory

Zoo

★ PROSPECT PARK

Meadow
Vale of Cashmere
Picnic House
Long Meadow
Bandshell
Tennis House
The

Lefferts Homestead
Carousel
CHILDREN'S GARDEN

Empire Blvd.

Drive

Central Drive

Quaker Cemetery
The Nethermead
Visitor Center
Lincoln Rd.

Lookout Hill
Well House Dr.
Hill Drive

16th
Windsor Ave.
St.
10th Pl. Ave.
Sherman
Prospect
17th St. 11th St.
18th St.
Prospect
Terrace Pl.

Prospect Lake
South Lake Drive

Seeley
Vanderbilt
Reeve Pl.
Sherman St.
E. 7th St.
Woodruff
Parade Pl.
St Paul's Pl.
E. 21st St.
Ocean Ave.

Greenwood Ave.
E. 4th St.
Caton Pl.
Kermit Pl.
Hamilton Pkwy.
E. 2nd St.

Park Circle
Coney Island Ave.
Parade Grounds
Parkside
Caton Ave.
Stratford Rd.
Argyle Rd.
Marlborough Rd.
Church Ave.
E. 18th St.
Ocean Ave.

★★ NY Aquarium

155

A Storm in the Rocky Mountains, Mt. Rosalie by Albert Bierstadt

The Brooklyn Museum

Bellows. In the section devoted to the Hudson River school note especially the large canvases by Bierstadt: *A Storm in the Rocky Mountains, Mt. Rosalie* (1866); Cole: *The Pic-Nic*; and Durand: *First Harvest in the Wilderness*. The Lowenthal Bequest has increased the museum's holdings of modern American paintings and sculptures, with 31 works by such well-known artists as Georgia O'Keeffe, Max Weber, Marsden Hartley and Stuart Davis.

Housed in the newly renovated West Wing, the gallery of contemporary art showcases 80 works created after World War II by American and European artists, including paintings by Joseph Kosuth, Philip Pearlstein, Mark Rothko and Pat Steir.

Throughout the years, the museum has gathered an important and fascinating collection of architectural ornaments salvaged from demolished buildings, displayed in the **sculpture garden** *(behind the main building beside the parking area).*

*Admission prices and hours quoted in this guide were accurate
at the time of publication.*

AROUND BROOKLYN   *Map pp 158-159*

★ **Shore Parkway** [ACZ]. – This pleasant drive follows the coast from Bay Ridge all the way to QUEENS and KENNEDY AIRPORT, affording successive views of the Verrazano-Narrows Bridge and STATEN ISLAND, the Rockaways and Jamaica Bay.
On bright sunny days, when superb views extend across the glittering water, Shore Parkway offers a refreshing respite from the bustle of Manhattan.

★★ **Verrazano-Narrows Bridge** [AZ]. – *Toll-bridge: $6.00 per car paid only on westbound crossing.* ● *R train to 95th St–Fourth Ave.* The spider web silhouette of the Verrazano-Narrows Bridge, the longest suspension bridge in the US, links Brooklyn to STATEN ISLAND above the Narrows (the entrance to New York Harbor). The bridge bears the name of the Italian explorer, **Giovanni da Verrazano**, a Florentine merchant in the service of French King François I, who discovered the site of New York in 1524. At the Brooklyn entrance to the bridge stands a monument composed in part of stones from the castle of Verrazano in Tuscany, and from the beach of Dieppe, the French port from which the pilot sailed.
The Triborough Bridge and Tunnel Authority began work on the bridge in January 1959. The project cost $305,000,000. On November 21, 1964, the bridge was inaugurated in the presence of Governor Nelson Rockefeller and the bridge's engineer, O.H. Amman, who also designed the GEORGE WASHINGTON BRIDGE.

A Few Figures. – The bridge has a total length of 6,690ft. The main span between the towers (rising 690ft above water) extends 4,260ft. The main cables have a diameter of 3ft. The bridge, which is high enough to allow the largest ocean liner to pass, has two levels of traffic (six lanes each) but no sidewalk for pedestrians.

Coney Island [ABZ]. – ● *B, N, F, O, M or D trains.* Located to the south of Brooklyn and bathed by the Atlantic Ocean, this beach resort and amusement area attracted over 1,000,000 people on busy summer Sundays in the 1900s. Today Coney Island is no longer the safe attraction it was at the height of its popularity.

From Rabbits to Frock Coats to Bikinis. – In Dutch times, this sandy island was inhabited only by rabbits, who left it their name (*Konijn Eiland* meant Rabbit Island). This title was soon transformed into its rough English "sound-alike," Coney Island.
In the 1830s the broad beaches lining the island began attracting well-to-do city dwellers. Coney Island developed into a fashionable resort and became the site of elegant hotels, hippodromes and casinos. Fifty years later, the resort became a popular amusement area and the clientele changed. The first roller coasters appeared in 1884, followed some years later by a merry-go-round and a huge Ferris wheel (George W.G. Ferris built the first one for the Chicago World's Fair in 1893).

The Resort. – The great attraction of Coney Island was its amusement parks, where scenic railways, loop-the-loops roller coasters and Ferris wheels competed with phantom trains, interplanetary rockets, merry-go-rounds and shooting galleries. For many years the star attraction was the **parachute jump**, still standing but now defunct, erected during the World's Fair of 1939-1940; the lover of thrills could drop in a chair, which was attached to a parachute and guided by cables.
Coney Island's heyday lasted into the 1940s. Then, through the 1950s, the crowds diminished and, owing to a lack of prosperity, the area began to decline. Buildings grew shabby and were allowed to deteriorate, while restaurants and other establishments were permanently closed. Today all but a small section of the once-gigantic amusement area has fallen into disuse. For many New Yorkers and out-of-towners, however, a stroll on Coney Island's boardwalk, the 3.5mi stretch of sandy beach and ocean water, the hot-dog and cotton candy stands and a handful of attractions still remain a pleasant diversion on a warm summer day.

★★ **The New York Aquarium** [BZ]. – *W. 8th St and Surf Ave.* ● *F or D trains to W. 8th St–New York Aquarium. Open daily 10am–5pm. $5.75.* ✗ & ☎ *718/265-FISH.* Opened in 1896, the New York Aquarium has been located at the corner of the Boardwalk and West 8th Street since its move from the Battery (*p 66*) in 1957. In large outdoor pools, whales, seals, sea lions, dolphins and New York's only Pacific walrus go through their paces. Not to be missed are the penguin colony and a 90,000-gallon shark tank holding five types of free-swimming and bottom-dwelling sharks, including stingrays.
The indoor aquariums, some decorated with live corals, exhibit more than 10,000 specimens and 300 different species from the world over, including Pacific reef fish, primitive fish, piranhas, chambered nautilus, clownfish and anemones. Of special interest are the Hudson River exhibit; an exhibit on native sea life; and the African Rift Lake and Red Sea exhibits, home to species found only in those two bodies of water. The aquarium was the first to exhibit and breed beluga whales in captivity.
Discovery Cove, a 20,000sq ft educational center opened in 1989, features 65 exhibits including a 400-gallon wave tank showing subtidal, intertidal and upper tidal zones; a reproduction of a living coral reef where jewel-like small fish dart among anemones and barnacles; and a New England lobster boat in its own salt water dock. The summer of 1992 witnessed the opening of the Sea Cliffs exhibit, a 300ft-long rocky coast habitat for walruses, harbor seals, sea otters and fur seals.
In summer and fall: dolphin and sea lion shows; in winter and spring: beluga whales join the sea lions.

Brooklyn Children's Museum [BX M]. – *145 Brooklyn Ave at corner of St Mark's Ave.* ● *3 train to Kingston Ave; walk one block west on Eastern Parkway and turn right onto Brooklyn Ave; continue 6 blocks north to St Mark's Ave. Open Wed–Fri 2–5pm, weekends & during school holidays noon–5pm. Closed Jan 1, Thanksgiving Day, Dec 25. $3.* & ☎ *718/735-4400.* Founded in 1899 in Brower Park, this institution was one of the first museums designed especially for children. Painted with bright,

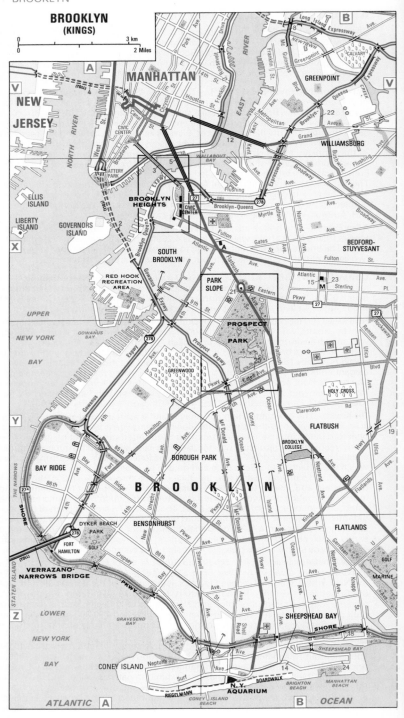

BROOKLYN
(KINGS)

bold colors, the 4-story building has housed the museum since 1977. Interactive, "hands-on" exhibits cover the areas of cultural and natural history, the sciences and the performing arts. The museum invites active participation, offers family workshops and presents special performances year-round.

Brooklyn Academy of Music [BX A]. – *30 Lafayette Ave. Events are listed in local newspapers.* Since it first opened in this imposing Beaux-Arts building in 1908, the Brooklyn Academy of Music has hosted a number of luminaries. It was here that Stanley recounted to the public the details of his meeting with Livingstone and that Enrico Caruso gave his last performance. Other well-known names associated with the Academy include Arturo Toscanini, Isadora Duncan and Sarah Bernhardt. One of the city's foremost cultural centers, the BAM offers a varied and innovative program of dance, theater, music and lectures.

BRIDGES AND TUNNELS

MANHATTAN

QUEENS

Unless otherwise indicated, all telephone numbers given in this guide are in the 212 calling area. The area code for Brooklyn, Queens, Staten Island and the Bronx is 718.

Queens

Area: 113 square miles
Population: 1,951,600

Named after Catherine of Bra-
ganza, the wife of Charles II of
England (1630-1685), Queens is
the largest borough of New York
City. Situated on Long Island, east
of BROOKLYN, it extends from the
East River in the north to Jamaica
Bay in the south. A cluster of factories in the Long Island City area,
where artists have renovated lofts
into studio and living spaces,
gives way to more residential sec-
tions to the southeast, such as Forest Hills and Jamaica. The borough also contains
the area's two major airports (John F. Kennedy and LaGuardia). Once the site of two
World's Fairs, in 1939 and 1965, Queens today draws sports fans to its Aqueduct
Race Track [CZ], Shea Stadium [BX] and USTA National Tennis Center [BY].

SIGHTS   Map pp 162-163
*Due to the distances between sights and their remote locations, it is advisable to
visit Queens by car.*

Jamaica Bay Wildlife Refuge [CZ]. – ● *A train to Broad Channel. From the subway station, take Noel Rd to Cross Bay Blvd and turn right (.8mi). Visitor center on
the left. Open daily 8:30am–5pm. Guided tours (1–3hrs) available.* ☎ *718/318-
4340.* Located just south of JFK Airport, this peaceful wildlife refuge is a major
migratory haven for birds, attracting a wide variety of waterfowl, land and shore
birds. It forms part of the Gateway National Recreation Area, one of the nation's
largest urban parks.

A self-guided **nature trail★** through the marshes affords pleasant views of the
Manhattan skyline, to the west *(distance: 1.8mi; time: 1 1/2hrs; request free permit
at the visitor center).*

Farther south on Cross Bay Boulevard, beachfront communities dot the five miles
of **Rockaway Beach★** *(access from ● A, C and H trains at stations between 25th and
116th Sts).* On sunny days, New Yorkers stroll up and down the wide boardwalk,
enjoying the fine breezes and ocean views.

★ **American Museum of the Moving Image [AX M1].** – *35th Ave and 36th St in
Astoria.* ● *R or G trains to Steinway St. Walk south on Steinway St and turn right on
35th Ave. Open Tue–Sun noon–4pm (weekends 6pm). $5.* ☎ *718/784-0077.*
Located on the former site of the Astoria Film Studios, this unique museum is
devoted to the history, technology and art of film media, including motion pictures,
television and video. The collection encompasses works by video artists Nam June
Paik and Red Grooms; costumes, props and memorabilia from the television and
film industries; and clips from movies, videos and advertisements. Screenings from
the film collection are presented on a rotating basis throughout the year.

★ **Isamu Noguchi Garden Museum [AX M2].** – *32-37 Vernon Blvd.* ● *N train to
Broadway. Sat & Sun shuttle bus service from Manhattan, call museum for schedule. Open Apr–Nov Wed & weekends 11am–6pm. $4. Guided tour (1hr) 2pm.* ☎
☎ *718/ 204-7088.* Conflicting and harmonious relationships between nature and the
man-made are a recurrent theme in the sculpture of **Isamu Noguchi** (1904-1988), the
renowned Japanese-American artist whose works include public spaces (Detroit's
Hart Plaza), playgrounds (Atlanta's Playscapes), gardens, fountains and theater sets.
Noguchi designed and installed this museum in his former studio quarters in 1985.

Shigeo Anzai/Isamu Noguchi Foundation

Isamu Noguchi Garden Museum

Over 250 works of art are on display in 12 indoor galleries, while several carved stone pieces adorn the tranquil outdoor sculpture garden, dotted with Japanese black pine trees. A video presentation *(50min)* on the artist's life is shown continuously throughout the day *(first floor)*.

Jamaica Arts Center [CZ E]. – *161-04 Jamaica Ave.* ● *E or F trains to Parsons Blvd then 053 or 054 bus to 161st St. Open Mon–Sat 9am–5pm. Gallery open Tue–Sat 9am–5pm.* & ☎*718/658-7400.* Founded in 1972, this center operates as a community cultural center, offering educational programs, exhibits, workshops and classes in the performing and visual arts.

Reformed Church of Newtown [BY]. – *85-15 Broadway, Elmhurst.* ● *R or G trains to Grand Ave-Newtown. Open Tue–Sun 10am–5pm. Closed holidays.* In 1731, this church was organized as a congregation of the Dutch Reformed Church. It was entirely rebuilt in the Greek Revival style in 1831.

Flushing [CX]. – A small settlement named Vlissingen was established on this site in 1643; the Dutch name was eventually transformed into Flushing. The town soon became associated with the **Quakers**, or Society of Friends. Believers in a simple way of life, tolerance towards others, and pacifism, the Quakers were often persecuted. John Bowne, an Englishman who settled in Flushing, allowed Quakers to hold meetings in his home. His arrest for permitting the Quakers to meet in his home (and ultimate acquittal) helped establish religious freedom in America. Flushing still has one of the oldest **Friends' Meeting Houses** in America *(on Northern Blvd near Linden Pl)*. At 137-15 Northern Boulevard stands the old Flushing **Town Hall**, a Romanesque style building (1862), which has been restored to its original appearance.

Bowne House [CX A]. – *37-01 Bowne St.* ● *7 train to Main St. Visit by guided tour (1hr) only, Tue & weekends 2:30–4:30pm. Closed mid-Dec–mid-Jan. $2.* & ☎*718/359-0528.* The oldest structure in Queens, this house (1661) was inhabited by nine successive generations of the Bowne family, including John Bowne *(above)*. The house contains a collection of 17C and 18C furniture as well as pewter, paintings and documents, all of which belonged to the Bowne family.

Kingsland House [CX D]. – *143-35 37th Ave. Open Tue & weekends 2:30–4:30pm. $2. Guided tours available.* ☎*718/939-0647.* Erected in c.1785, this 3-story edifice presents a mix of Dutch and English traditions; note in particular the divided front door and central chimney. The former farmhouse now serves as the headquarters of the Queens Historical Society and houses the local history museum.

Flushing Meadow Park [BC Y]. – Once a swamp favored by ducks and then a sanitary landfill, this 1,275-acre park was developed in the 1930s to accommodate New York's first World's Fair (1939). Designs for the park included the creation of **Meadow Lake**, measuring 3/4mi in length, and the **New York City Building**, which housed the United Nations General Assembly *(p 48)* between 1946 and 1949 and now contains the spacious galleries of the Queens Museum, as well as a skating rink.
In 1964-1965, the park was the site of New York's second World's Fair. Vestiges of this event include the **Hall of Science [B]**, recently renovated and expanded with its museum of science and technology, and the 140ft high **Unisphere [C]**.
To the north of Flushing Meadow Park, **Shea Stadium [BX]** also dates from the 1964-1965 World's Fair. Home of the New York Mets baseball team, it can hold 55,000 to 60,000 spectators.

Queens Museum of Art [BY M3]. – *In the New York City Building.* ● *7 train to Willets Point–Shea Stadium. Open Tue–Fri 10am–5pm (Jun–Aug Tue 8pm), weekends noon–5pm. Closed Jan 1, Thanksgiving Day, Dec 25. $3.* & ☎*718/592-5555.* Conceived as an arts center for the borough of Queens, the museum was renovated and its exhibit space expanded for temporary shows. On display are installations on artist Keith Haring and on the history of the New York City Building *(above)*. The huge scale model of New York City, which presents a detailed panorama of the five boroughs, is under renovation until 1994.

Queens County Farm Museum. – *73-50 Little Neck Parkway in Floral Park. Take Long Island Expressway to Exit 32. Continue south on Little Neck Parkway (10 blocks to museum entrance).* ● *E, F train to Q-Gardens, then Q46 bus to Little Neck Parkway. Open May–Sept Thu & weekends noon–5pm. Rest of the year weekends only.* & ☎*718/347-3276.* This 47-acre tract of nature trails, fields and farm buildings provides a refreshing change from the bustle of the city. The 18C Flemish-style farmhouse *(currently under restoration)*, replete with its original furniture, and the greenhouses, barns, sheds and petting zoo provide visitors, especially children, with an informative glimpse of Queens County's agrarian origins.

John F. Kennedy International Airport [CZ]. – *For access see p 180.* One of the busiest airports in the world, Kennedy International Airport covers 4,900 acres in the southeast corner of Queens, along Jamaica Bay, an area the size of Manhattan Island from midtown to the Battery. Construction, begun in 1942 on the site of the Idlewild Beach golf course, was placed under the jurisdiction of the Port Authority of New York and New Jersey in 1947. Opened as the New York International Airport at Idlewild a year later, the airport was renamed in 1963 to honor the late president. The Kennedy air cargo center, the busiest in the US, handles approximately 35 percent of all the nation's air imports and exports.

International Arrivals Building. – An arched pavilion forms the center of this 2,000ft-long building (Skidmore, Owings & Merrill), which houses the arrival hall and, in its wings, a number of airline terminals. Adjacent to the building, the 11-story air traffic control tower rises to 321ft, making it the tallest such tower in North America.

QUEENS

★ **TWA International Terminal.** – Evoking a huge bird with outspread wings, this soaring structure (1962) is a masterpiece of the architect Eero Saarinen (p 40). The building is composed of four intersecting vaults rising from four load-bearing points.

LaGuardia Airport [BX]. – *For access see p 180*. Located in close proximity to Manhattan (8mi from midtown), this major airport bordering on Flushing and Bowery bays was established in 1939 and named after **Fiorello H. La Guardia**, mayor of the city from 1934 to 1945. Affectionately known as "the little flower," Mayor La Guardia was himself a pilot and recognized the importance of air travel to New York. Despite its relatively small size, which is one ninth of Kennedy's, LaGuardia is capable of handling the bulk of the area's domestic flights.

BRIDGES AND TUNNELS

MANHATTAN

Over the great bridge, with the sunlight through the girders making a constant flicker upon the moving cars, with the city rising up across the river in white heaps and sugar lumps all built with a wish out of non-olfactory money. The city seen from the Queensboro Bridge is always the city seen for the first time, in its first wild promise of all the mystery and the beauty in the world.

F. Scott Fitzgerald, *The Great Gatsby*, 1926

Staten Island

Area: 60 square miles
Population: 379,000

The fifth borough of New York City, Staten Island is still a relatively rural area, often referred to as "the forgotten borough." Most of the island is flat, although it boasts the highest point on the Atlantic coast south of Maine—Todt Hill (410ft above sea level). Formed by the terminal moraine of a Quaternary glacier, the island measures about 14mi long and 8mi wide. White sandy beaches run along the southeastern shore. Still fairly uncrowded, the best known are South Beach and the Gateway National Recreation Area, which includes Great Kills Park and Miller Field.

Named after the Dutch States General, Staten Island acquired its alternate name in honor of the Duke of Richmond, son of Charles II, king of England. Today, Staten Island is primarily a bedroom community. Its population includes the descendants of several old families who have lived there since the 18C.

SIGHTS   *Map p 165*
To visit the sights described below, visitors may take buses from the ferry terminal at St George or, in some cases, the Staten Island Rapid Transit (map p 165).

★ **Staten Island Ferry.** – *Departs St George Ferry Terminal to Whitehall Terminal in Manhattan. In service 24hrs/day. Passengers only. Round-trip 50 cents. ⚐ ☎718/ 390-5253.* Any visit to New York should include a trip on the Staten Island Ferry. On the windy voyage, the ferry skirts the Statue of Liberty, affording magnificent **views★★★** of Manhattan and the bay. The ferry runs night and day, transporting some 21 million passengers a year. It is interesting to recall that this ferry was the start of "Commodore" Vanderbilt's fortune *(p 46).*

St George [BY]. – Facing lower Manhattan across the bay, this small town is surrounded by attractive suburban homes and gardens. In the waters near St George quarantine was imposed on ships arriving from overseas in the 1850s. St George has been the seat of the county and borough government since 1920.

Staten Island Institute of Arts and Sciences [BY M]. – *75 Stuyvesant Place. From the Staten Island ferry terminal walk one block west to Wall St. Turn left on Wall St and walk one block to the museum at Stuyvesant Place. Open Mon–Sat 9am–5pm, Sun 1–5pm. Closed holidays. $2.50. ⚐ ☎718/727-1135.* Founded in 1881, Staten Island's oldest cultural institution features a variety of exhibits illustrating the history, geology, flora and fauna of the island as well as frequent shows of painting, sculpture, graphics, furniture and photography.

Snug Harbor Cultural Center [BY B]. – *1000 Richmond Terrace. From St George Ferry take S40 bus. Open dawn to dusk. Closed Jan 1, Thanksgiving Day, Dec 25. For program information ☎718/448-2500.* Founded in 1833 as the first maritime hospital and retired sailors' home in the US, the 80-acre park and its 28 buildings are being restored and converted to a center for the visual and performing arts. Architectural treasures include a row of Greek Revival buildings overlooking the Kill van Kull.

Home to several arts organizations, the Staten Island Botanical Garden and the Staten Island Children's Museum, Snug Harbor also offers concerts, art shows and special events year-round.

Staten Island Children's Museum. – *1000 Richmond Terrace. From the Staten Island ferry terminal take the S40 bus to Snug Harbor. Follow signs to the museum. Open Tue–Sun noon–5pm. Closed holidays. $3. ⚐ ☎718/273-2060.* Interactive exhibits, creative workshops and field trips encourage children to learn by doing. Most activities are designed for children between the ages of 2 and 12.

Staten Island Zoo [BY]. – *614 Broadway. From Staten Island ferry terminal take S48 bus to Forest Ave and Broadway. Turn left on Broadway and walk 2 1/2 blocks to the zoo. Open daily 10am–4:45pm. Closed Jan 1, Thanksgiving Day, Dec 25. $3 (Wed pm free). ⚐ ☎718/442-3100.* Located in Barrett Park, this small zoo, opened in 1936, is especially known for its comprehensive collection of snakes and reptiles.

★ **Jacques Marchais Center of Tibetan Art** [BZ E]. – *338 Lighthouse Ave. From Staten Island ferry terminal take S74 bus to Lighthouse Ave. Turn right and walk up the hill. Open Apr–Nov Wed–Sun 1–5pm. Closed holidays. $3. Guided tours (1hr) available. ☎718/987-3478.* Laid out on Lighthouse Hill in enchanting terraced gardens, the center displays a rare collection of art covering the culture, religion and mythology of Tibet, Nepal, China, Mongolia and India. The museum buildings were constructed to resemble a small Buddhist mountain temple. Highlights of the museum include an authentic 3-tiered Buddhist altar and a large Tibetan *thangka*, or scroll painting, depicting the Green Tara, goddess of universal compassion. The *thangka*, which was painted in the 17C, has been painstakingly restored by Tibetan artist Pema Wangyal using only traditional techniques and materials.

High Rock Park Education Center [BY F]. – *200 Nevada Ave. From the Staten Island ferry terminal take S54 bus to Rockland Ave, then walk 3 blocks; turn right on Nevada Ave. Open daily 9am–5pm.* ⚐ *718/667-2165.* Marking the center of the island, a large tract of forest with a varied topography and a wide range of flora and fauna provides an attractive spot for hiking. The center offers a self-guided tour, conducts special environmental educational programs and workshops, and holds a variety of cultural programs.

★ **Historic Richmond Town [BZ].** – *441 Clarke Ave. From Richmond Rd turn on St Patrick's Place, then right on Clarke Ave; or take S74 bus from Staten Island ferry terminal. Open Apr–Dec Wed–Sun 1–5pm. Rest of the year Wed–Fri 1–5pm. Closed Jan 1, Thanksgiving Day, Dec 25. $4.* ⚐ *718/351-1611. Tickets may be purchased at the visitor orientation center in the Third County Court House.* Located in one of the earliest settlements on Staten Island and the island's geographic center, this historic village traces the evolution of community life in Richmond Town from the 17C to 19C through a variety of buildings, furniture, gardens and implements. The village comprises 29 structures, including private dwellings, craft shops, a schoolhouse and municipal buildings, which have been restored and opened to the public. Staff members dressed in period costumes reenact everyday chores and, occasionally, artisans demonstrate the crafts of yesteryear.

Visitor Orientation Center. – The imposing Greek Revival structure containing the center was the third **County Court House** (1837) to be built between the 18C and early 20C when Richmond Town was the seat of county government.

Staten Island Historical Society Museum. – Some parts of the attractive red brick building date back to the middle of the 19C when it served as the office of the county clerk and the Surrogates Court. Changing exhibits and documents relate the history of the island.

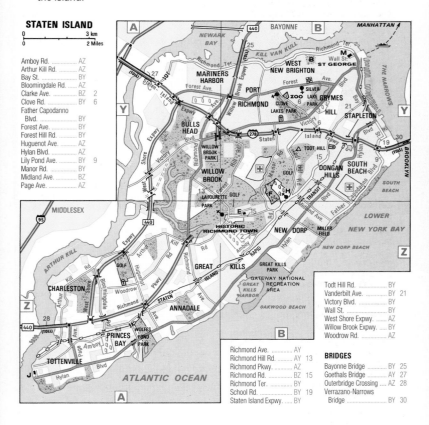

STATEN ISLAND

0   3 km
0   2 Miles

Stephens-Black House. – Facing the visitor center, this building was the residence of the Stephen D. Stephens family who operated the adjoining general store until 1870. Today the house is decorated with furnishings of the mid-19C and the store is stocked with goods that would have been sold around the time of the Civil War.
The **Print Shop** and the **Tinsmith Shop** *(located on either side of the Stephens-Black House)* are original structures that were moved to this site in the 1960s. They are furnished to represent shops of their trades and offer seasonal demonstrations of the crafts of printing and tin work.

The dolls, games and toys on display on the upper floors of the **Bennett House** are nostalgic reminders of the joys of childhood in days gone by.
Located across Richmond Road, the Dutch Colonial **Guyon-Lake-Tysen House** was erected in the mid-18C; the interior furnishings reflect this time period. Domestic skills such as spinning and weaving are demonstrated seasonally.

Treasure House. – A tannery was established here at the beginning of the 18C. A century later, the house's owner discovered $7,000 in gold hidden in a wall *(closed; restoration in progress)*.

Voorlezer House. – Built at the end of the 17C, this building served as a church and schoolhouse (reputedly the oldest elementary school in the US), as well as a residence for the church clerk *(voorlezer)*.

Moravian Cemetery [BY H].

– This peaceful, garden-like cemetery is affiliated with the Moravian church located at the entrance. Adorned with a columned portico, the white church was constructed in 1845 by the Vanderbilt family, one of whose ancestors belonged to the sect in the 17C. The original church, a Dutch Colonial style structure erected in 1763, now serves as the cemetery office.

The Moravian denomination, founded in the 15C as an evangelical communion in Bohemia (Moravia), accepted Protestantism in the 17C. Ascetic in its beliefs, the church adhered to strict observance of the teachings of the Bible.

Conference House [AZ J].

– *7455 Hylan Blvd. From the Staten Island ferry terminal, take the Rapid Transit to Tottenville. Exit onto Bentley St and turn right onto Hopping Ave, then left onto Amboy Rd, then right on Satterlee; continue to Hylan Blvd. Open mid-Mar–mid-Dec Wed–Sun 1–4pm. Closed Thanksgiving Day. $2. Guided tours (45min) available.* ☎718/984-6046. Situated at the southwestern tip of Staten Island, Conference House is named after the negotiations between the British and Americans, including John Adams and Benjamin Franklin, which took place here on September 11, 1776 after the Battle of Long Island in a futile attempt to end the emerging Revolutionary War.

The 17C fieldstone manor house has been restored and now contains a historic museum. The interior, furnished with 18C pieces interprets the life and times of Colonel Christopher Billtop, the house's original owner.

The waterfront vantage point affords splendid views across the river and the bay to New Jersey.

Consult pp 177-186 for details on annual events, shopping, recreation and additional practical information.

Beyond the City Limits

The fame and glitter of New York City have somewhat obscured the attractions of its outskirts. Nevertheless, not even the passing tourist should neglect the charms of the country air, hills and forests, islands and beaches, forts and historic mansions, which abound in this region. New Yorkers are aware of these advantages, as is evidenced in the grand estates and more modest homes on Long Island and in Westchester. About one-fourth of the people who work in Manhattan live in the suburbs.

Long prized by weekend vacationers, this area is also extremely well equipped for longer trips, with an extensive network of roads and parkways, hotels, motels and other recreational facilities; opportunities abound for tennis, golf, boating and sailing, horseback riding (from foxhunting to dude ranches), fishing, skiing and freshwater and ocean swimming.

This section presents three basic excursion trips that provide a pleasant change from the hustle and bustle of Manhattan. There are many other possibilities for longer trips: Niagara Falls, the Catskills or the Adirondacks, Albany and Saratoga in New York State; the Berkshires and Old Sturbridge Village in Massachusetts, or New Haven and Old Mystic Seaport in Connecticut to mention but a few *(consult the Michelin Green Guide to New England)*.

★★★ THE HUDSON RIVER VALLEY

Time: 3 days. Map p 168.

Originating high in the Adirondacks, the Hudson flows 315mi to the sea. Navigable as far as Albany, it is linked to the Great Lakes by the Erie Canal, once a busy waterway between Albany and Buffalo. On its journey south to New York City, the majestic Hudson flows between rocky crags and wooded peaks, a romantic and even grandiose setting. The river has often been celebrated in literature and art, especially by the painters of the Hudson River school *(p 26)*, whose best-known representatives were Thomas Cole, Albert Bierstadt and Frederic Edwin Church.

EXCURSION *175mi round-trip*

This trip covers only the southern part of the Hudson River Valley, which is best seen in the fall, when Indian summer gilds the forests lining the river banks. If you have only one day available, we recommend driving north on the east bank in the morning and returning on the west bank in the afternoon. US Route 9, heading north, and US Route 9W, for the return, afford occasional views of the river.

> *Leave Manhattan via the Henry Hudson Parkway, which leads into the Saw Mill River Parkway. Exit Executive Blvd; continue to its end at North Broadway; turn left, then right on Odell Ave, then left on Warburton Ave and continue for 1.3mi. After Yonkers, exit from the Saw Mill River Parkway at Ashford Ave–Dobbs Ferry. Follow Ashford Ave west, then turn right on Broadway (Rte 9). Beyond Irvington, a road to the left, W. Sunnyside Lane, winds along a valley to Sunnyside, on the banks of the Hudson.*

The Hudson River Museum of Westchester. – *511 Warburton Ave, Yonkers. Open Wed–Sat 10am–5pm (Fri 9pm), Sun noon–5pm. Call ahead for holiday hours. $3, planetarium $4.* ✗ & ☎*914/963-4550.* This stone mansion on the banks of the Hudson was built for local financier John Trevor in 1876. Late Victorian in style, the house features Eastlake interiors, including four rooms that have been restored to depict the lifestyle of an upperclass 19C family.

A modern wing, added in 1969, displays changing exhibits of art, history, and science. In the **Andrus Planetarium**, shows on the planets are presented using the museum's Zeiss M015 star machine.

Lyndhurst

East facade, Lyndhurst

★ **Sunnyside.** – *Open Mar–Dec Wed–Mon 10am–5pm. Rest of the year weekends 10am–5pm. Closed Jan 1, Thanksgiving Day, Dec 25. $6. Guided tours (1hr 30min) available.* & ☎914/631-8200. *"Passport" ticket for Sunnyside, Lyndhurst, Philipsburg and Van Cortlandt entitles holder to 20% discount on admission fees to all sites.* Located on the east bank of the Hudson River, Sunnyside was the home of the author-humorist and scholar, **Washington Irving** (1783-1859), who purchased the cottage in 1835. Author of *Diedrich Knickerbocker's History of New York* and chronicler of Rip van Winkle and Sleepy Hollow, Irving lived here intermittently for the last 25 years of his life, transforming the original stone cottage into what he called his "snuggery." Today a museum, the mansion displays furniture and memorabilia tracing Irving's life. Landscaped in the romantic style favored during the mid-19C, the surrounding 20-acre grounds offer splendid views of the Hudson.

★ **Lyndhurst.** – *On Rte 9 in Tarrytown, .5mi north of Sunnyside. Open May–Oct Tue–Sun 10am–4:15pm. Rest of the year Tue–Sun 10am–3:30pm. $6. Guided tours (45min) available.* & ☎914/631-0046. Perched on a wooded bluff above the Hudson River is the picturesque Lyndhurst mansion, resembling from the distance a baronial castle on the Rhine. Originally a 2-story villa designed in 1838 by Alexander Jackson Davis for William Paulding, a former mayor of New York City, the house was enlarged by Davis for the subsequent owner, George Merritt, in 1865. In 1880, the 67-acre estate and its mansion were acquired by the financier and railroad tycoon, Jay Gould. Lyndhurst remained in the family until the death of Gould's daughter, the Duchess of Talleyrand-Périgord, in 1961. The house is an outstanding expression of the Gothic Revival style applied to domestic architecture. An array of peaks, pinnacles, porches and turrets embellish the exterior, accenting the mansion's irregular shape. In the interior, the Gothic mood dominates, exemplified by ribbed and vaulted ceilings, pointed arches, stained-glass windows and imposing Gothic furnishings. In the dining room, note the simulated marble colonnettes and leather wall coverings popular in the 19C. Many other examples of marbleization and simulated masonry can be found throughout the house.

★ **Philipsburg Manor.** – *On Rte 9. Same hours and admission as Sunnyside. Guided tours (1hr 30min) available.* & ☎914/631-8200. This stone mansion appears as it did in the early 18C, when it was an important gristmill trading site along the Hudson River. Begun in the 1680s by the Philipse family, the manor is outfitted with period furnishings. Also on the property are an operational water-powered gristmill, a 200ft-long oak dam, and a large mid-18C barn, inhabited by oxen, sheep and cows.

> *Continue northward on US 9, passing through Ossining, site of the Ossining Correctional Facility formerly known as Sing Sing prison. Take the Croton Point Ave Exit. Turn right, then right again on South Riverside Ave.*

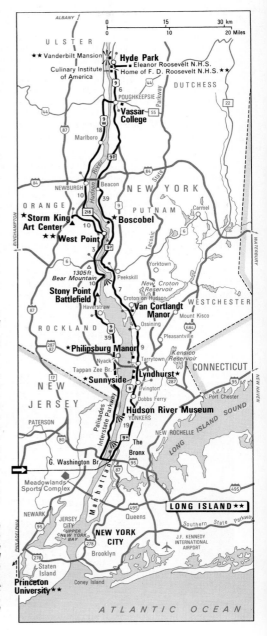

Van Cortlandt Manor. – *Off Rte 9. Open Mar–Dec Wed–Mon 10am–5pm. $6. Guided tours (1hr 30min) available.* ๕ ☎*914/631-8200.* Home to the Van Cortlandt family for 260 years, the manor house has been restored to its appearance during the Revolutionary War period, when it was owned by Pierre Van Cortlandt, patriot and the first lieutenant-governor of New York State, who presided over 86,000 acres. It is believed that the manor has been visited by such notable personalities as Benjamin Franklin, the Marquis de Lafayette, Count de Rochambeau and John Jay. The house contains original family furnishings, paintings and pewter. Located on the property, the ferry house, ferry house kitchen, fields and gardens evoke 18C life in the Hudson Valley.

Continue on Rte 9 North to Peekskill then bear left onto Rte 6/202 West; at Bear Mountain Bridge follow Rte 9D North.

This drive offers beautiful views of the river and the New Jersey Palisades as the road dips into the valley and then rises into the hills.

★ **Boscobel.** – *Rte 9D, 4mi north of the junction with Rte 403. Open Apr–Oct Wed– Mon 9:30am–5pm. Rest of the year Wed–Mon 9:30am–4pm. Closed Jan–Feb, Thanksgiving Day, Dec 25. $5. Grounds only $2. Guided tours available.* ☎*914/265- 3638.* Set back from the road and overlooking the Hudson River, Boscobel, a handsome example of Federal domestic architecture, was conceived by States Morris Dyckman (1755-1806) in 1804 and completed after his death by his wife, Elizabeth. In the 1950s the property on which Boscobel originally stood was sold and the mansion was almost destroyed. Preservationists acquired the building and moved it piece by piece to Garrison where it was reconstructed on grounds high above the Hudson. Rebuilt and refurbished, Boscobel opened to the public in 1961.
The overall appearance is one of elegance and refinement. The recessed central portion of the facade, with its slender columns and carved trim, contrasts with the otherwise unadorned exterior. The restored interior features graceful arches, fireplaces adorned with classical motifs, delicately carved woodwork and a freestanding central staircase lit by a tall Palladian window. Furnishings reflecting the Federal period include Dyckman family possessions; note in particular the sideboards—a popular Federal piece—in the dining room.

Follow Rte 9D North into Rte 9 North to Poughkeepsie, seat of Vassar College. From Rte 9 head east on Rte 44/55 then turn right onto Raymond Ave (Rte 376).

Vassar College. – *Raymond Ave.* Vassar is one of the best-known private liberal arts colleges in the US. Founded as a women's college in 1861, it became coeducational in 1969 and now has 2,250 students of which 42 percent are men. The buildings reflect traditional American and European styles, as well as modern trends in architecture: notice Ferry House (Marcel Breuer) and Noyes House (Eero Saarinen), dormitories erected in 1951 and 1958 respectively. The library, expanded in 1976, houses 700,000 volumes.

Continue on Rte 9 to Hyde Park.

Before entering the village of Hyde Park note, on the left, the 150-acre campus of **The Culinary Institute of America**, an educational institution that prepares men and women for careers in the food service industries. It is possible to dine in the four student-staffed restaurants *(reservations required* ☎*914/471-6608).*

Hyde Park. – *Located 6mi north of Poughkeepsie on Rte 9.* Once a resort for wealthy New York families, Hyde Park gained renown during Franklin D. Roosevelt's presidency as what he referred to as his "summer White House."

★★ **Home of Franklin D. Roosevelt National Historic Site.** – *Open Apr–Oct daily 9am–5pm. Rest of the year Thu–Mon 9am–5pm. Closed Jan 1, Thanksgiving Day, Dec 25. $4. Guided tours available.* ๕ ☎*914/229-9115.* Today a National Historic Site, the estate was acquired by Franklin Delano Roosevelt's father in 1867; FDR was born here in 1882. The mansion dates back to the early 19C, but has since been remodeled and enlarged. Following severe fire damage in the early 1980s, the house was extensively refurbished.
Memorabilia of the late president (1882-1945) and his family will be found in the house, library and museum. Exhibits trace the life and career of FDR and his wife Eleanor, a prominent international figure in her own right.
In the rose garden, a simple monument of white Vermont marble marks the final resting place of Franklin and Eleanor Roosevelt.

Eleanor Roosevelt National Historic Site. – *Rte 9G. Visit by guided tour (45min) only, May–Oct daily 9am–5pm. Rest of the year weekends 9am–5pm. Closed Jan–Feb, Thanksgiving Day, Dec 25.* ๕ ☎*914/229-9115.* A 20min film on the life of Eleanor Roosevelt is shown in the playhouse where the guided tour of the grounds begins. The Roosevelts often came to this tranquil natural setting on the Fall Kill for family outings and picnics. A stone cottage was built on the property in 1925 and a year later, a factory workshop was erected to house an experimental business operated by Eleanor Roosevelt (1884-1962) and her friends. After the business folded in the mid-1930s, the building was remodeled and eventually became Eleanor's beloved Val-Kill cottage, named for the stream that flowed close by.
Val-Kill was the only place Mrs Roosevelt ever considered truly to be her own home and after the president's death, it was there she chose to spend her remaining years working, entertaining her friends, and receiving foreign dignitaries.

★★ **Vanderbilt Mansion.** – *2mi north of FDR National Historic Site. Open Apr–Oct daily 9am–5pm. Rest of the year Wed–Mon 9am–5pm. Closed Jan 1, Thanksgiving Day, Dec 25. $2. Guided tours available.* ๕ ☎*914/229-9115.* Located just north of the FDR mansion, this sumptuous Beaux-Arts residence was erected by McKim, Mead and White between 1896 and 1898 for Frederick W. Vanderbilt and his wife, Louise. Now a National Historic Site, it bears witness to a bygone age of opulence. Before the Vanderbilts bought the property in the early 19C, it belonged to famed botanist Dr Hosack *(p 37)*. He and other earlier owners of the estate were exceedingly interested in the landscape; as a result, the grounds represent one of the greatest intact surviving examples of the romantic style of landscape architecture in the US. The interior contains a collection of furniture of 16C-17C design and works of art.

Walking trails along the river, below the mansion, afford scenic **views** to the north and the south.

Return to Poughkeepsie, cross the Hudson and continue on Rte 9W.

★ **Storm King Art Center.** – *Take Rte 9W to the Cornwall Hospital Exit, then bear left onto Rte 107; at the intersection turn right and follow Rte 32 North over the bridge, turning left immediately after the bridge onto Orr's Mill Rd. Sculpture Park open Apr–Nov daily 11am–5:30pm. Indoor exhibits open May–Oct daily 11am–5:30pm. $5.* ☏914/534-3190. This unique outdoor museum of contemporary sculpture covers 200 acres of meadow, hillsides, forest, lawns and terraces. Large-scale works by such artists as Alexander Calder *(The Arch)*, Mark di Suvero, Alexander Liberman *(Iliad)*, Henry Moore, Louise Nevelson, Isamu Noguchi *(Momo Taro)* and David Smith, are installed on the grounds, most of them in settings that have been specially landscaped for the sculpture. Changing exhibits of paintings, graphics and smaller sculptures from the center's collection are presented in the Normandy-style museum building (1935), formerly a private residence on the property.

★★ **West Point.** – *10mi southeast of Storm King Art Center on Rte 218 South.* Overlooking the Hudson River, West Point is renowned as the site of the United States Military Academy.

The Military Tradition. – A military outpost dominating the Hudson in the early 18C, West Point became, during the late 1700s, a training school for artillerists and engineers, under the tenure of General Henry Knox, who was also serving as secretary of War.

It was not until 1802, however, that the US Military Academy, the oldest of the nation's service academies, was established by Congress, and West Point selected as its site.

In the Academy's first year, five officers trained and instructed the ten students; there are now more than 4,200 men and women cadets. Among its graduates,

West Point counts Generals MacArthur (1903), Patton (1909) and Eisenhower (1915); astronauts Borman (1950), Aldrin (1951), Collins and White (1952), and Scott (1954); and General Schwartzkopf (1956).

The Buildings. – In the **visitor information center**, films and exhibits introduce visitors to the history and sights of West Point and the life of a cadet *(open daily 9am–4:45pm; closed Jan 1, Thanksgiving Day, Dec 25; guided tours Apr–Oct every 20min, Nov–Mar daily 11am & 1pm; $4;* ⚇ ☏914/938-2638).

The chapels, monuments and museum are open to the public. The **museum** *(open daily 10:30am–4:15pm; closed Jan 1, Thanksgiving Day, Dec 25;* ⚇), housed in a wing of the former indoor riding ring (Thayer Hall), features Napoleon's sword, Goering's jewel-encrusted marshal's baton, and a collection of arms, which traces the development of automatic weapons from the Civil War to the present. Other buildings of interest include the **Cadet Chapel** *(open daily 8am–4:15pm; closed Jan 1, Thanksgiving Day, Dec 25;* ⚇), an example of the "military Gothic" style, built in 1910; 18C **Fort Putnam** *(open Jun–Oct Thu–Mon 11am–3pm)*, partially restored in 1907 and completed in 1976; the Battle Monument, commemorating victims of the Civil War; and Trophy Point. Among the Revolutionary War relics at Trophy Point are links of the great chain, which was strung across the Hudson River to prevent British ships from navigating it.

The Parades. – *From early September until November, and from mid-March through May, the famous reviews are held; they are known for their precision of movement and the particular stance of the cadets. For schedules* ☏914/938-2638.

Continuing south on Route 9W, you will pass **Bear Mountain**, the highest point (1,305ft) in Palisades Interstate Park.

Stony Point Battlefield. – *Park Rd, off of Rte 9W. Open mid-Apr–Oct Wed–Sat 10am–5pm, Sun 1–5pm.* ⚇ ☏914/786-2521. This battlefield marks the site of the former British fortified position at Kings Ferry, a vital link in the American east-west line of communication. Stony Point was stormed by General Wayne's troops in July 1779. Signs indicate where the fiercest fighting—often hand to hand—took place. The battlefield area is now a state park with a **museum** *(open mid-Apr–Oct Wed– Sat 10am–4:30pm, Sun 1–4:30pm)* and picnic places affording fine views over the Hudson. A commemoration of the battle is held in mid-July with simulations of 18C battle strategies. The oldest lighthouse on the Hudson River is also located on the grounds.

Continue the drive south on **Palisades Interstate Parkway**—offering superb **views**★★ of Yonkers, the Bronx and Manhattan—to the George Washington Bridge, which leads back to Manhattan.

★★ LONG ISLAND

Time: 2 days. Map pp 172-173.

Covering an area of 1,723sq mi, Long Island has a population of approximately 6,878,300 and measures 125mi long and 20mi at its widest point. Although Long Island is often misleadingly said to include only Nassau and Suffolk counties, it actually comprises 4 counties: the other two are Queens (Queens County) and Brooklyn (Kings County), boroughs of New York City.

Owing to its proximity to the city, the western part of the island has developed into a suburban area while the eastern part has remained more rural. As wealthy landowners from the city began erecting residences on the North Shore, the latter became known as the "Gold Coast." The South Shore, with its miles of white sandy beaches, developed into a vacation and resort spot for New Yorkers. Long Island includes numerous attractions: small quiet lanes, rustic villages, a countryside flecked with golf courses and tennis courts, wildlife refuges and palatial "Gold Coast" mansions.

The economy is quite diversified, encompassing light manufacturing, service industries and agriculture. Suffolk County is the largest producer of agricultural products in the state of New York, and a number of farms are engaged in truck farming (fruits and vegetables) and dairy and livestock farming. Ducklings and potatoes are noted area products. Wineries produce Long Island wines from grapes grown in vineyards covering hundreds of acres on the North and South Forks. Seafood is particularly abundant on the eastern end of the island: oysters, clams, scallops and lobsters have a well-deserved reputation. Commercial and chartered deep-sea fishing boats leave daily from South Shore communities and Montauk Point.

NORTH SHORE

Facing Long Island Sound, the North Shore features rocky necks and beaches, thick woodlands, hilly coves, bays, inlets and steep bluffs; the northern peninsula, extending 25mi, culminates at Orient Point.

★★ **Stony Brook.** – *Open Wed–Sat 10am–5pm, Sun noon–5pm. Closed Jan 1, Thanksgiving Day, Dec 24–25. $6. ♿ ☎516/751-0066.* A typical Federal-style village of 18C and 19C America, Stony Brook contains a number of reconstructed buildings in a charming rural setting. Situated within this idyllic hamlet founded in the 1930s is **The Museums at Stony Brook**, a complex that now comprises history, art and carriage museums as well as several period buildings (including a blacksmith shop, schoolhouse and barn).

★★ **Carriage Museum.** – An exceptional collection of horse-drawn carriages is presented in thematic displays, which relate the impact of private transportation on American life. The collection includes sporting rigs, pleasure vehicles, farm and trade wagons, sleighs, children's vehicles, coaches, fire fighting equipment, an elaborately decorated omnibus and a Gypsy wagon.

Art Museum. – The **paintings and drawings**★ of **William Sidney Mount** (1807-1868) and other 19C and 20C artists are presented in changing exhibits. Mount settled at Stony Brook where he painted anecdotal records of his rural surroundings. Among the works owned by the museum, the best-known include *Farmer Whetting his Scythe*, *Dancing on the Barn Floor* and *The Banjo Players*.

History Museum. – This museum features displays of antique decoys and **miniature period rooms**, as well as temporary exhibits drawn from the museum's collections and those of other institutions.

★ **Sunken Meadow State Park.** – *Open year-round. $4/car. ⚹ ♿ ☎516/269-4333.* Bordering the Long Island Sound, this park offers a wide range of recreational facilities including golfing (27 holes), bathing, picnicking, nature trails and bike paths. Sunken Meadow refers to the large, fine sand beach lining the sound.

★ **Sands Point Preserve.** – *95 Middleneck Rd, Port Washington. Open mid-Mar– mid-Nov Tue–Sun 10am–5pm. ☎516/883-1612.* Set in this 226-acre park and preserve—one of the last remaining estates of the "Gold Coast"—is **Falaise**★, a Normandy-style manor house (1923), home of the late Capt Harry F. Guggenheim. A courtyard leads to the mansion, embellished with an arcaded loggia overlooking the sound. A collection of 16C and 17C French and Spanish artifacts is displayed in the interior *(visit by 1hr guided tour only, Wed–Sun noon–3:30pm; no children under 10 admitted; $4).*

★ **Vanderbilt Museum.** – *Little Neck Rd, Centerport. Open Tue–Sun noon–4pm. Closed Jan 1, Thanksgiving Day, Dec 25. $5. Guided tours (1hr) available. ⚹*

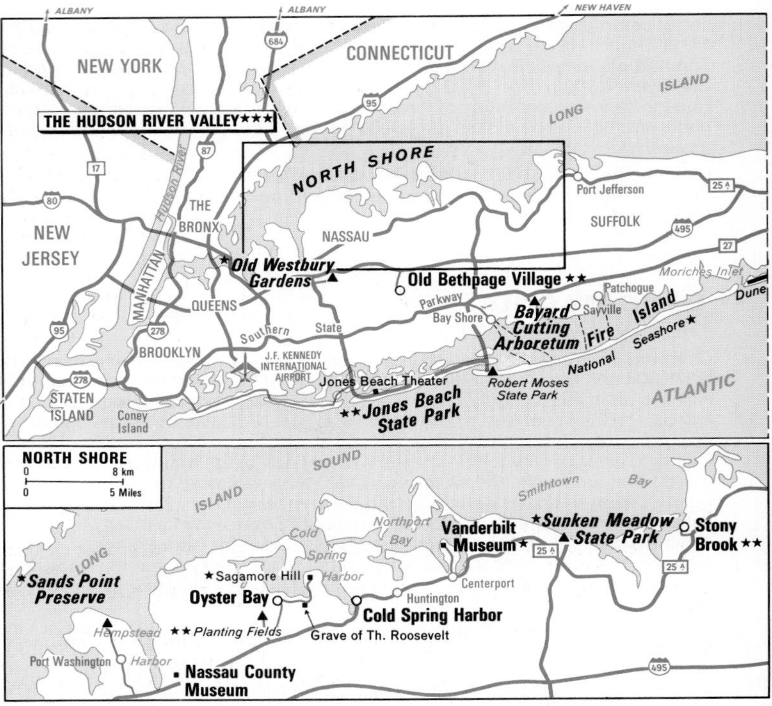

☎516/262-7800. This museum, once the country estate of William K. Vanderbilt Jr, great-grandson of "The Commodore" *(p 46)*, is set on a 43-acre site overlooking Northport Harbor.

The collections gathered by William during his travels include ship models, arms and weaponry, birds and artifacts, many of which are on display in the **Maritime Museum**. The Vanderbilt natural history collections are on view in the house's Habitat wing. Also on the grounds is the **Vanderbilt Planetarium**, which presents a variety of shows. *The Planetarium offers astronomy sky shows throughout the year. For schedule ☎516/262-STAR.*

Cold Spring Harbor. – From 1836 to 1862, the Cold Spring Harbor whaling fleet of nine ships sailed to every navigable ocean in search of whale oil and bone. The commanders of these vessels came from established whaling centers such as New Bedford and Sag Harbor *(p 174)*.

★ **The Whaling Museum.** – *Open Memorial Day–Labor Day daily 11am–5pm. Rest of the year Tue–Sun 11am–5pm. Closed Jan 1, Thanksgiving Day, Dec 25. $2. Guided tours (40min) available. ♿ ☎516/367-3418.* Dedicated to the preservation of the town's history as a whaling port, this museum features several outstanding exhibits, including a fully equipped whaleboat, looking just as it did aboard the whaling brig *Daisy* on her 1912 voyage out of New Bedford. Located nearby, the detailed diorama of Cold Spring Harbor represents village houses, whaling company buildings and wharves as they appeared in the 1840s, the heyday of the whaling industry. Other permanent exhibits chronicle Long Island's illustrious whaling history, and allow visitors to listen to the song of the humpback whale and marvel at the size of an orca (or killer whale) skull.

Dispersed throughout the museum are examples of whalecraft: harpoons, navigational instruments, whaleship models, old prints and maps. Note especially the extensive collection of scrimshaw (carving of ivory tusks or whale jawbones and teeth) demonstrating practically every form of the whaleman's folk art.

Nassau County Museum of Fine Art. – *In Roslyn Harbor. Take Rte 25A East, cross the Roslyn Viaduct and turn left on Museum Dr. Open Tue–Sun 11am–5pm. Closed holidays. $3. Guided tours (1hr) Wed & Sat 2pm. ✗ ♿ ☎516/484-9337.* The museum is headquartered on the grounds of a turn-of-the-century estate built for Lloyd Bryce, the paymaster general of New York, and acquired in 1919 by Childs Frick, the son of Henry Clay Frick *(p 115)*. Changing art exhibits covering all periods are presented in the brick Georgian Revival mansion, which has been converted into eight galleries. The attractively landscaped lawns, ponds and gardens, covering 145 acres, offer an ideal outdoor setting for various sculpture shows. Programs of dance, concerts and lectures are also offered.

Oyster Bay. – Vacation spot, port for pleasure craft and suburban residential town, Oyster Bay has nearly 7,000 inhabitants. In Young's Cemetery lies the grave of **Theodore Roosevelt** *(p 85)*.

★★ **Planting Fields.** – *Planting Fields Rd, Oyster Bay. Open daily 9am–5pm. Closed Dec 25. $3/car. No admission charged Labor Day–Apr Mon–Fri. ♿ ☎516/922-9200.* Formerly the private estate of the financier, William Robertson Coe, the 409 acres

of planting fields contain 160 acres that have been developed as an arboretum; the remaining land has been kept as a natural habitat. The plant collections include over 600 rhododendrons and azalea species *(blooming period: mid-Apr–May);* the Synoptic Garden, comprising approximately 5 acres of selected ornamental shrubs for Long Island gardens; the camelia collection, the oldest and largest of its kind under glass *(blooming period: Feb–Mar);* and greenhouses filled with orchids, hibiscus, begonias and cacti. Amidst these landscaped gardens and spacious lawns stands Coe Hall, a fine example of the Tudor Revival style *(1hr guided tours Apr–Labor Day 1:30–3:30pm; $2).*

★ Sagamore Hill National Historic Site. – *Cove Neck Rd. Open daily 9:30am–5pm. Closed Jan 1, Thanksgiving Day, Dec 25. $2. Guided tours (1hr) available.* ♿ ☎516/922-4447. Located east of the village of Oyster Bay, this gracious mansion is maintained as it was during Theodore Roosevelt's presidency (1901-1909). In the **Old Orchard Museum**, exhibits and a biographical film *(20min)* trace Mr Roosevelt's public and private life.

Raynham Hall. – *20 W. Main St. Open Tue–Sun 1–5pm. Closed Jan 1, Thanksgiving Day, Dec 25. $2.* ♿ ☎516/922-6808. This old farmhouse played an important role during the American Revolution. It was the home of Samuel Townsend whose son, Robert, was Washington's chief intelligence agent in New York City. The interior contains period furniture and memorabilia dating from the 1770s through the 1870s.

SOUTH SHORE

The shoreline fronts the Atlantic Ocean and also faces the Great South Bay.

★★ Jones Beach State Park. – A series of sandy beaches, 6.5mi long, make up this bathing resort, with its double exposure to the ocean and bay. Jones Beach includes the well-known **Jones Beach Theater**, a nautical stadium, heated pools, sports fields and play areas. The Water Tower, modeled after the bell tower of St Mark's Church in Venice, rises above a freshwater well.

★★ Old Bethpage Restoration Village. – *Round Swamp Rd. Open Mar–Dec Wed–Sun 10am–5pm. Rest of the year Wed–Sun 10am–4pm. Closed Jan 1, Thanksgiving Day, Dec 25. $5. Guided tours available.* ✗ ☎516/542-4425. Nestled in a 200-acre valley, Old Bethpage is an active farm community that recreates a pre-Civil War American village. More than 25 historic buildings reflecting the architectural heritage of Long Island, have been moved to the site of the former Powell Farm. Strolling leisurely through the village you will see the blacksmith hammering at his anvil, the cobbler making shoes, the tailor sewing and the farmers working their fields. Depending on the time of the year, sheep shearing, candlemaking and other seasonal activities may also be observed.

★★ The Hamptons. – Dominating a 35mi stretch of Long Island's South Shore, the Hamptons comprises a chain of vacation colonies, beginning at Westhampton Beach, which rims Shinnecock Bay, and ending at Amagansett.

Westhampton Beach. – Formerly a seafaring community, Westhampton is a lively resort where New Yorkers—among them musicians, writers and artists—like to spend their weekends or take up summer residence. The annual Westhampton Beach Outdoor Art Show takes place in early August.

A drive along Dune Road, on the narrow barrier beach, leads past numerous houses exemplifying a variety of styles, from the New England home, brown-shingled and trimmed with white, to the bungalow. A 15mi-long beach extends from Moriches Inlet to Shinnecock Inlet. *Note: sections of Dune Rd are extremely narrow and may be impassable following a rain storm.*

Southampton. – This famous resort is the largest of the Hampton communities and the home of superb estates. On Jobs Lane stands the **Parrish Art Museum**, which focuses on American art of the 19C and 20C, with major holdings of works by William Merrit Chase and Fairfield Porter. Changing exhibits and selections from the permanent collection are presented regularly. *Open mid-Jun–mid-Sept Thu–Tue 10am–5pm (Sun 1–5pm). Rest of the year Thu–Mon 10am–5pm (Sun 1–5pm). $2. Guided tours (1hr) available.* ♿ ☎516/283-2118.

East Hampton. – This town's quaint charm has long attracted writers and artists. The **Main Street** is lined on both sides by magnificent elm trees. The village green, featuring a central pond flanked by fine old houses, gives East Hampton the appearance of an English country town.

★ Old Westbury Gardens. – *Old Westbury Rd. Open May–mid-Dec Wed–Mon 10am–5pm. Gardens $5, house $3. Guided tours (1hr 30min) available.* ♿ ☎516/333-0048. Occupying grounds formerly belonging to John S. Phipps, sportsman and financier, this 80-acre estate contains woods, meadows, lakes and formal gardens. Set in an 18C park, the stately Georgian Revival mansion has been preserved as it was during the family's occupancy, in the early 20C. The interior features antique furnishings, paintings by Thomas Gainsborough and John Singer Sargent, gilded mirrors and objets d'art.

Bayard Cutting Arboretum. – *Rte 27A. Open Apr–Oct Wed–Sun 10am–5pm (rest of the year 4pm). Closed Jan 1, Thanksgiving Day, Dec 25. $3/car.* ☎*516/581-1002.* Started in 1887 by William Cutting in accordance with plans by Frederick Law Olmsted *(p 87),* the Arboretum covers 690 acres of woodlands and planted areas. Many of the specimens in the Pinetum date back to the original planting of fir, spruce, pine and other evergreens. Rhododendrons and azaleas *(blooming period: May-June)* border the walks and drives; wild flowers are also featured.

Fire Island. – Measuring 32mi long and .5mi to less than 200yds wide, the island boasts over 1,400 acres of **National Seashore★**. The island, which has no roads for automobile traffic, emanates an air of relaxed informality. Sections of the island are frequented by the gay community.
Ferry service connects Patchogue, Sayville and Bay Shore to the Fire Island communities and the main developed areas of the National Seashore—Watch Hill and Sailors Haven. *Ferry to Watch Hill from Patchogue departs Jun–Sept 10:15am–3:05pm (6 trips daily). Off-season 2 trips daily. No service Nov–mid-May. 25min one-way. $5/one-way. For schedule* ☎*516/289-4810.*
National Seashore programs at Watch Hill and Sailors Haven feature interpretive walks and special events. Facilities at both areas include a guarded swimming beach, snack bar and marina.

Robert Moses State Park. – The western part of Fire Island is named for Robert Moses, the former superintendent of Long Island parks. Its dunes are a refuge for waterfowl. The Atlantic coast is excellent for surf casting (a method of fishing in which bait is tossed into the ocean at a site where waves break on a beach).

Montauk. – Located on the easternmost tip of Long Island and encompassing a 10mi strip of natural woodlands, stark cliffs, dunes and white beaches jutting into the ocean, Montauk is a favorite center for sports fishermen (deep-sea fishing). Built in 1795, the Montauk Lighthouse, rising at the tip of the peninsula, is located in Montauk State Park.

Sag Harbor. – This sea town with its docks, deepwater harbor nestled in a sheltered cove and **Custom House**—the first custom house established in New York State *(open Jul–Aug Tue–Sun 10am–5pm; Jun & Sept–Oct weekends & holidays 10am–5pm; $1.50; guided tours available;* ♿ ☎*516/941-9444)*—was named port of entry for the United States by George Washington. With its fine colonial homes, Sag Harbor still preserves the nostalgic flavor of yesteryear.
Stop at the **Sag Harbor Whaling Museum** *(open May–Sept Mon–Sat 10am–5pm; Sun & holidays 1–5pm; $3;* ♿ ☎*516/725-0770),* a Greek Revival edifice. The interior, designed as a whaling captain's home, features exhibits on the whaling days.

★★ PRINCETON UNIVERSITY

Time: 1 day. Map p 175.

Situated in the central part of New Jersey, in a small residential town, Princeton University is one of the nation's prominent Ivy League schools. Despite the widespread development of office and research complexes in the area, the town of Princeton remains a desirable place to live.

Access. – *110mi round-trip. A bus line connects Princeton to New York: information at the Port Authority Bus Terminal (p 180). If you drive, leave Manhattan via the Lincoln Tunnel and take the New Jersey Turnpike south to Exit 9; turn right and cross the Lawrence River; take Rte 1 toward Penns-Neck; turn right at sign Princeton-Hightstown. Princeton can also be reached by train (New Jersey Transit) from Penn Station (p 180).*

Historical Notes. – In 1746, a small group of Presbyterian ministers decided to found a college for the middle American colonies, and named it the College of New Jersey. First established at Elizabeth, and then at Newark, it moved to the present site in 1756, after the completion of Nassau Hall *(p 175).* At that time, Nassau Hall was the largest educational building in North America and could accommodate the entire college.
During the Revolution, the college served as barracks and hospitals, successively, for British and American troops. Its capture by Washington on January 3, 1777 marked the end of the Battle of Princeton and a victory for the colonists. In 1783, the college housed the Continental Congress for six months, and the final treaty of peace was signed here. On its 150th anniversary, the College of New Jersey (already called Princeton College) became Princeton University.
Since the 18C, Princeton has been noted for its teaching in political science and its programs of scientific research (the first chair of chemistry in the United States was created here in 1795). Since Woodrow Wilson's presidency of the university, from 1902 to 1910, Princeton has emphasized individual research and small seminars. An honor system prevails for examinations.
The university has a full-time faculty of about 680 and about 6,300 students; 42 percent of the undergraduates hold scholarships or receive special loans. Formerly all-male, Princeton became coeducational in 1969, and women now make up over one-third of the undergraduate population.

VISIT

Free guide service is offered by the students year-round; it is preferable to request a visit three days in advance. Information available at the Orange Key Guide Service, Maclean House ☎609/258-3603.

The 135 buildings of the university are scattered over the 600-acre campus. Only the most important ones are described below.

Nassau Hall. – Named for the Nassau dynasty of Orange, which reigned in England at the time of the founding of the college, this majestic edifice now serves as an administration building. Around Nassau Hall stretches the shady green campus.

Harvey S. Firestone Library. – Containing approximately 5,000,000 volumes, the library also provides 850 individual carrels for students, and lecture rooms for 12 different disciplines.

Chapel. – This small chapel can accommodate a congregation of 2,000. Of note in the interior is a 16C wooden pulpit from the north of France.

Art Museum. – *Open Tue–Sat 10am–5pm, Sun 1–5pm. Closed holidays. ♿ ☎609/258-3788.* The university's art museum is particularly strong in Italian and Northern Renaissance and Baroque paintings; prints and drawings and photographs, which are exhibited on a rotating basis; and Ancient, Far Eastern and pre-Columbian works, displayed on the lower level. Impressionist and 20C French paintings from the Henry and Rose Pearlman Foundation are on long-term loan to the museum.

Woodrow Wilson School. – This noted school of public administration and international affairs was created in 1930.

James Forrestal Research Campus. – Located to the east of Princeton proper, beyond Lake Carnegie, this campus was opened in 1951 for research in applied mathematics, physics and chemistry. It houses the Plasma Physics Laboratory, the university's center for fusion research.

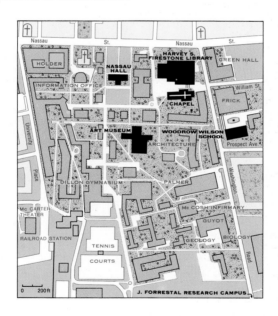

Practical Information

Hiroyuki Matsumoto/First Light

CALENDAR OF EVENTS

Listed below is a selection of the most popular annual events; some dates may vary each year. For more detailed information consult *The New York Times* (Sunday edition), *The New Yorker, The Village Voice* or contact the New York Convention & Visitors Bureau ☎ 397-8222.

Date	Event, *Location*	☎

January–February

mid-Jan	**New York National Boat Show**, *Jacob K. Javits Center*	216-2000
late Jan	**Chinese New Year Celebrations**, *Chinatown (p 72)*	373-1800
all Feb	**Black History Month** *(various locations throughout the city)*	722-9534
mid-Feb	**Empire State Building Run Up**	860-4455

March

early	**Art Expo New York**, *Jacob K. Javits Center*	800/331-5706
mid	**New York Flower Show**, *Pier 92, W. 51st St & Hudson River*	757-0915
17	**St Patrick's Day Parade**, *Fifth Ave from 44th to 86th Sts (p 35)*	
late Mar–early May	**Ringling Brothers, Barnum & Bailey Circus**, *Madison Square Garden*	465-6000
Mar–June	**Biennial Exhibit** (1995), *Whitney Museum of American Art (p 146)*	570-3676

April–May

	Easter Show, *Radio City Music Hall (p 39)*	247-4777
	Easter Sunday Parade, *Fifth Ave (p 35)*	
early Apr	**Greater New York Orchid Show**, *Winter Garden, World Financial Center*	945-0505
mid-Apr	**Rockefeller Center Flower Show**	632-3975
	Macy's Spring Flower Show, *ground floor, Macy's (p 183)*	560-4495
	Spring Flower Show, *New York Botanical Garden, Bronx*	718/817-8700
mid-May	**Arts in Bloom**, *Brooklyn Botanic Garden*	718/622-4433
	Ninth Avenue International Food Festival, *Ninth Ave (37th to 57th Sts)*	581-7029
late May	**You Gotta Have Park**, *Central Park*	315-0385
	Memorial Day Celebration, *South Street Seaport*	669-9400
late May–early June	**Washington Square Outdoors Art Festival** *(p 79)*	982-6255

June

all month	**Free opera performances**, *Great Lawn, Central Park*	362-6000
	Cool Jazz at the Central Park Zoo, *Sea lion pool*	861-6030
early–mid	**Rose Garden Tours**, *New York Botanical Garden, Bronx*	718/817-8700
mid	**Puerto Rican Day Parade**, *Fifth Ave*	
mid–late	**JVC Jazz Festival**, *Carnegie Hall and other venues*	787-2020
June–mid-Jul	**New York Philharmonic Summer Parks Concerts** *(various locations throughout the city)*	875-5709
June–Aug	**Central Park SummerStage**, *Rumsey Playfield*	360-2777

July–August–September

all July	**Serious Fun**, *Alice Tully Hall, Lincoln Center*	875-5400
4 July	**Macy's Fireworks Celebration**, *Hudson River (Chambers to 14th Sts)*	560-4495
	Salute to New York City, *New York Philharmonic, Great Lawn, Central Park*	875-5709
Jul–Aug	**Shakespeare in Central Park**, *Delacorte Theater*	861-PAPP
	Summer Pier Concerts, *South Street Seaport*	669-9430
	Summergarden Concerts, *The Museum of Modern Art (p 140)*	708-9480
	Mostly Mozart Festival, *Lincoln Center*	875-5400
	Music on the Boardwalk, *Coney Island, Brooklyn*	718/625-0080
all Aug	**Lincoln Center Out-of-Doors**	875-5400
early Aug	**Classical Jazz**, *Alice Tully Hall, Lincoln Center*	875-5400
late Aug–mid-Sept	**US Open Tennis Tournament**, *USTA National Tennis Center, Flushing Meadows, Queens*	718/271-5100
early Sept	**Washington Square Outdoors Art Festival** *(p 79)*	982-6255
mid-Sept	**Feast of San Gennaro**, *Mulberry St, Little Italy (p 74)*	226-9546
late Sept	**Race for Mayor's Cup**, *New York Harbor*	669-9400

October

early–mid	**New York Film Festival**, *Lincoln Center*	875-5050
mid	**Columbus Day Parade**, *Fifth Ave from 44th to 86th Sts*	249-9923
31	**Halloween Parade**, *Greenwich Village*	758-5519

November–December

mid-Nov	**New York City Marathon**, *Verrazano-Narrows Bridge to Central Park*	860-4455
	Virginia Slims Tennis Tournament, *Madison Square Garden*	465-6741
late-Nov	**Macy's Thanksgiving Day Parade**, *Central Park West to Herald Square*	290-4495
Nov–Jan	**Christmas Spectacular**, *Radio City Music Hall (p 39)*	632-4000
early Dec	**Lighting of Christmas Tree**, *Rockefeller Center*	698-8676
31 Dec	**New Year's Eve Countdown**, *Times Square (p 54)*	

PLANNING YOUR TRIP

Visitors can contact the New York Convention & Visitors Bureau (2 Columbus Circle, New York, NY 10019 ☎397-8222) to obtain information on points of interest, seasonal events, accommodations, dining facilities and sightseeing. The New York Convention & Visitors Bureau also publishes the annually updated *Big Apple Guide*, which is available free of charge. Foreign visitors can request additional tourist information from the nearest US Embassy or Consulate in their countries of residence.

When to Visit. – Spring is a brief and generally unpredictable season. Sunny days (42°–62°F) can give way to snow showers (not uncommon in April). In the summer, temperatures may rise into the 90s and humidity can be high, especially in July and August. However, all buildings and many buses and subway cars are air-conditioned. A favored season to visit New York is the fall. Warm temperatures (47°–68°F), the clear transparency of the air and the brilliant colors of the trees, especially the reds and oranges of the maples, are typical of this season. Although quite cold in winter (often around 32°F), New York's climate is fairly dry. Heavy snowfall is unusual.

Legal Holidays. – Most banks, government offices, public buildings and schools are closed on the following holidays:

New Year's Day	January 1
Martin Luther King's Birthday	3rd Monday in January
President's Day	3rd Monday in February
Memorial Day	Last Monday in May
Independence Day	July 4
Labor Day	1st Monday in September
Columbus Day	2nd Monday in October
Veteran's Day	November 11
Thanksgiving Day	Last Thursday in November
Christmas Day	December 25

Entry Formalities and Insurance for Foreigners. – Citizens of countries participating in the Visa Waiver Pilot Program (VWPP) are no longer required to obtain a visa to enter the United States for visits of 90 days or less. For a list of countries participating in the VWPP, contact the nearest US Embassy. Upon entry, all travelers to the US must present a valid passport and a round-trip transportation ticket. In some instances, a visa is required. Vaccinations are generally not necessary. Visitors are advised to obtain information on entry regulations from the US Embassy or Consulate before traveling. Great Britain: 5 Upper Grosvenor St, London W1A 2JB ☎1/499-3443; Germany: 5300 Bonn 2, Deichmanns Aue ☎228/3391; Australia: Moonah Place, Canberra ACT2600 ☎6/270.5000.

Visitors should check with their insurance companies to ascertain if their medical insurance covers doctor's visits, medication and hospitalization in the US.

Accommodations. – New York City boasts nearly 65,000 hotel rooms offering accommodation to fit every taste and budget. The most luxurious hotels are located in fashionable midtown, in the vicinity of Fifth, Park and Madison Avenues, while other moderately priced hotels can be found in the theater district. Visitors who favor a less bustling neighborhood in midtown may prefer the Murray Hill and Gramercy Park areas, or Central Park South, which faces the park. In the midtown and Upper East Side sections, many apartment hotels offer suites and apartments that are fully furnished and include daily maid and multilingual concierge services. In addition, visitors will find hotel chains such as Best Western, Days Inn, Holiday Inn, Novotel and Quality Inn scattered throughout midtown. The New York Convention & Visitors Bureau (☎397-8222) publishes a **listing of hotels** in all price ranges that gives location, telephone number, fax number, rates and amenities. This publication is available free of charge.

Hotel rates range from $250 and up a night in the deluxe category to $100–250 for a superior hotel. Moderately priced accommodations run between $60–90. Many hotels offer packages that include lodging, breakfast, sightseeing tours, restaurant or theater bookings at significant savings. Advance reservations are recommended throughout the year. Reservations at discount rates can be made through Express Hotel Reservations. The service is free (Mon–Fri 10am–7pm; ☎800/356-1123). Furnished apartments are available for daily, weekly or monthly stays through The American Property Exchange ☎800/ 747-7784.

Offering an alternative to hotels, **bed & breakfast** lodging can be found in private homes (with or without host) ranging in comfort from moderate to luxurious. Amenities offered include complimentary breakfast, private bath, kitchen facilities and maid service. Prices range from $60–95/night double occupancy to $95–300/night, depending on choice of accommodation. Weekly and monthly rates are available. In some cases, a minimum stay of two nights is required. Major credit cards are accepted. For free reservation service contact: City Lights Bed & Breakfast, PO Box 20355, Cherokee Station, New York, NY 10028 ☎737-7049; Urban Ventures, Inc, 38 W. 32nd St, Suite 1412, New York, NY 10001 ☎594-5650.

Budget accommodation for tourists and students is offered at Malibu Studios Hotel, 2688 Broadway ($35/night; weekly rates available; ☎222-2954) and International House, 500 Riverside Dr ($25/night; weekly rates available; ☎316-8495). The International American **Youth Hostel** (891 Amsterdam Ave) is located in a historic landmark building. Rooms are dormitory-style; amenities include cafeteria, laundromat, garden and meeting rooms ($22/night; $60/night for private room with advance reservation; ☎ 932-2300). The Vanderbilt **YMCA** is located at 224 E. 47th St ☎755-2410. The West Side YMCA (5 W. 63rd St; ☎787-4400) also offers a health club and restaurant. Rooms are $42/night and reservations are suggested, especially during the summer months (May–Sept).

GETTING THERE

By Air. – Most transatlantic flights arrive and depart from **John F. Kennedy International Airport** (JFK) located in Queens, 15mi (allow 1hr driving time) from midtown Manhattan. Also in Queens but only 8mi from midtown Manhattan (allow 30min driving time) is **LaGuardia Airport** (LGA), which is serviced by most domestic and North American air carriers. International and domestic air carriers offer service to **Newark International Airport** in New Jersey, located 16mi (allow 45min driving time) from midtown Manhattan.

For reservations, tickets and flight information for all three airports, contact the individual airline.

Airline	Downtown Location	Reservation ☎
Air Canada	15 W. 50th St (Fifth & Sixth Aves)	800/779-3000
Alitalia	666 Fifth Ave (at 53rd St)	800/223-5730
American Airlines	18 W. 49th St (Fifth & Sixth Aves)	800/227-2537
British Airways	530 Fifth Ave (at 44th St)	800/247-9297
Continental	1384 Broadway (at 38th St)	800/525-0280
Delta	1384 Broadway (at 38th St)	800/221-1212
Air France	120 W. 56th St (Sixth & Seventh Aves)	800/237-2747
Finnair	11 E. 39th St (Madison & Fifth Aves)	800/950-5000
Iberia	509 Madison Ave (at 53rd St)	800/772-4642
JAL	655 Fifth Ave (at 52nd St)	800/525-3663
KLM	437 Madison Ave (at 48th St)	800/777-5553
Lufthansa	750 Lexington Ave (59th & 60th Sts)	800/645-3880
Northwest	299 Park Ave (at 49th St)	800/225-2525
SAS	1384 Broadway (at 38th St)	800/221-2350
Swissair	608 Fifth Ave (at 49th St)	800/221-4750
USAir	1384 Broadway (at 38th St)	800/428-4322
United	260 Madison Ave (38th & 39th Sts)	800/633-8825
Varig	630 Fifth Ave (50th & 51st Sts)	800/468-2744

Airport Transportation. – Buses, taxis and limousines provide service from all three area airports to the five boroughs. Driving times can vary, especially during rush hour traffic (7–9am and 4:30–6pm).
Carey Airport Express Coach Bus service (☎718/632-0500) operates between midtown Manhattan and JFK ($11–12.50 one-way) and LaGuardia ($8.50–10 one-way) airports. Buses run seven days/week every 30min to major points in midtown Manhattan: Grand Central Railroad Terminal, Port Authority Bus Terminal and several midtown hotels. Service is also offered between JFK and LaGuardia airports (6am–midnight; $9.50; allow 1hr).
Shared minibus transportation to any location in New York City, including major hotels between 23rd & 63rd Sts, is provided by **Gray Line Air Shuttle**. One-way fares from midtown Manhattan: JFK ($15), LaGuardia ($12) and Newark ($17). Buses operate seven days/week 6am–7pm (midtown to the airports) and 6am–11pm (airports to midtown). Inbound passengers can obtain shuttle information from the ground transportation desk at all airline terminals. To arrange hotel pick-up, contact the hotel's front desk or call ☎757-6840 or 800/451-0455.
Bus transportation to Newark airport is offered by: **NJ Transit #300 Airport Express Bus** from the Port Authority Bus Terminal, 42nd St & Eighth Ave (24hrs/day; every 15min; $7 one-way; $12 round-trip), and **Olympia Trails Airport Express Bus** (daily 6am–midnight; every 20min; $7 one-way; $12 round-trip) from Pennsylvania Railroad Station, Grand Central Railroad Terminal and One World Trade Center.
Helicopter service connecting JFK with the 34th St East Heliport ($65 one-way) is provided by National Helicopter (☎800/645-3494).
Taxis offer quick transportation from the three area airports. Taxi dispatchers direct travelers to taxicabs. The average taxi fare is $20–25 from JFK, $15–20 from LaGuardia and $30 from Newark. Bridge and tunnel tolls are extra. It is advisable to accept rides from uniformed Ground Transportation agents only, as unauthorized drivers may overcharge passengers.
Chauffeur-driven cars are operated by Carey Limousine Service (☎ 800/336-4646) at fixed rates between JFK ($70), LaGuardia ($55) and midtown Manhattan.
For additional information on transportation to all area airports, contact the Port Authority of New York & New Jersey, One World Trade Center, New York, NY 10048 ☎800/AIR-RIDE.

By Train. – New York City's two main railroad stations are located in midtown Manhattan: **Pennsylvania Railroad Station** (AMTRAK) 31st & 33rd Sts at Seventh & Eighth Aves, Information ☎582-6875 or 800/872-7245; **Grand Central Railroad Terminal** (Metro-North) 42nd St & Park Ave, Information ☎532-4900. Amtrak and the Long Island Railroad (Information ☎718/217-5477) trains arrive and depart from Pennsylvania Railroad Station only. Commuter trains service both railroad terminals. PATH rail lines (Information ☎435-7000) connect Manhattan with many cities in New Jersey.

By Bus. – The Port Authority Bus Terminal (42nd St & Eighth Ave; ☎564-8484), the city's main bus terminal, is used by long-distance and commuter services. From here buses to the area's three major airports leave regularly. Airline ticket counters are located on the main floor of the building. For bus schedules: Greyhound ☎800/231-2222, Peter Pan ☎800/237-8747.

By Car. – *Map p 17.* New York is situated at the crossroads of several major highways: New York Thruway (I-287 and I-87) and New England Thruway (I-95) from the north, Bergen Passaic Expressway (I-80) from the west and New Jersey Turnpike (I-95) from the south.

GETTING AROUND TOWN

Public Transportation. – The subway system is a popular means of transportation in New York City, carrying 3.3 million passengers daily. Riding one of the more than 3,700 public buses that service the island of Manhattan and the boroughs is, however, a more interesting way of experiencing the city. In Manhattan, buses run north and south (uptown and downtown) on most avenues, and east and west (cross-town) on principal cross-town streets. Tourists who wish to avoid the frenzied pace of the city are well advised to leave the streets and transportation systems of the city to New Yorkers during **rush hours** (7–9am and 4:30–6pm).

Subway. – *Map pp 6-9.* The subway is operated by the New York City Transit Authority. Although the system runs 24hrs, seven days/week, some routes do not operate at all times. Subway entrances are indicated on the street level by globes: a green globe indicates that the entrance is staffed 24hrs/day, while a red globe signals restricted operating hours. Colored decals outside each station display subway route numbers or letters indicating which trains stop at the station. The cost of a ride is $1.25 regardless of distance traveled, to be paid for with tokens, which can be purchased at booths located in every station. Transfers are free where subway lines intersect. Senior citizens can ride for half-fare upon presentation of identification or by obtaining a half-fare card from the NYC Department for the Aging (☎577-0819). Handicapped persons are also eligible for half-fare cards (☎240-4131). Signs are displayed in the station indicating the direction of trains "Uptown," "Downtown" or "Brooklyn-bound." Local trains stop at every station; express trains, however, do not. Electronic signs on the side of the subway car list the name of the line, route, point of origin and destination. Subway maps are posted in each train.

Trains generally run every 2–10 minutes during rush hours, every 10–15 minutes during the day, and every 20 minutes between midnight and 5am. During off-peak hours, especially after midnight, it is advisable to ride with a group of passengers or in the car occupied by the train's conductor (usually located in the middle of the train).

City Buses. – More than 200 bus routes service Manhattan and the other boroughs. Bus fare is $1.25 (exact change or subway token is required). Transfers between buses are free and good for one hour (request transfer ticket when boarding). Electronic signs at the front of each bus indicate number, route and destination. Bus stops are generally located at street corners and designated by a sign bearing the bus emblem and route number. Most stops display a "guide-a-ride" map. Many buses are equipped with wheelchair lifts. Buses generally stop every two to three blocks; the rider can signal the driver to stop by pushing the tape strip located above the windows.

Subway and bus maps can be obtained free of charge from the information booth in the Port Authority Bus Terminal, Grand Central Railroad Terminal, at change booths in any subway station, or from the New York Convention & Visitors Bureau. For schedule information ☎718/330-1234 (daily 6am–9pm).

Ferries. – The Staten Island Ferry *(p 164)* connects Manhattan with Staten Island (departs Whitehall terminal 24hrs/day; passengers only; 50 cents round-trip; ☎806-6940). Another ferry services Hoboken, New Jersey (departs from World Financial Center Mon–Fri 6:50am–11pm; $4 one-way; ☎908/463-3779). Roosevelt Island *(p 107)* is accessible by aerial tram (departs 60th St & Second Ave; daily 6–2am; every 15min; from 4:30–7pm every 7min; $1.40 one-way; ☎832-4543).

Taxi. – The city's fleet of yellow taxicabs consists of nearly 12,000 licensed vehicles, which are authorized to pick up street hails. Taxi stands are located at most Manhattan hotels, transportation terminals and entertainment centers. One fare covers up to a maximum of four passengers. Fares start at $1.50 for the first 1/5mi and increase by 25 cents each 1/5mi. An additional 20 cents/min is charged for waiting time; a 50 cents surcharge is added 8pm–6am.

To report lost property ☎840-4734; be sure to give taxi identification number displayed on the dashboard and on the receipt.

On Foot. – The best way to explore Manhattan and its neighborhoods is on foot. Visitors are encouraged to use common sense, stay alert and avoid deserted streets and park areas after dark. New York City's streets are laid out in a grid pattern. Streets run east-west and avenues run north-south. Generally even-numbered streets are eastbound, odd-numbered streets are westbound. In lower Manhattan (downtown) most streets have names rather than numbers.

Renting a Car. – Major automobile rental companies have offices in various parts of Manhattan, the boroughs and at the three New York City area airports. Reservations are accepted through the toll-free service with a major credit card. Most rental companies offer seasonal discounts and accept membership privileges.

Company	Midtown Location	Reservation ☎
Avis	217 E. 43rd St (Second & Third Aves)	800/831-2847
Budget	225 E. 43rd St (corner of Second Ave)	800/527-0700
Hertz	310 E. 48th St (First & Second Aves)	800/654-3131
National	142 E. 31st St (Third & Lexington Aves)	800/227-7368

Many limousine and executive car service companies offer transport within the city and to the boroughs, or will customize an itinerary for a day to suit any visitor's needs (average $60/hr). For a listing of companies consult the official *Big Apple Guide (p 179).*

Driving in Manhattan. – Visitors to New York City are well advised to get around the city without the use of an automobile. To find street parking is difficult, especially on weekdays, and garage fees are high. A parking tax of 14% is added; credit cards are generally not accepted. It is recommended to leave the vehicle in the garage of the hotel. Below is a partial list of 24hr parking garages and gas stations.

24hr parking

Chelnik Parking	345 South End Ave (near World Trade Center)	321-2316
Rockefeller Center Garage	50 W. 49th St (Fifth & Sixth Aves)	698-8530
919 Third Avenue Garage	229 E. 55th St (Second & Third Aves)	753-2972
Meyers Parking	141 W. 43rd St (Sixth & Seventh Aves)	221-8948

24hr gas stations

Amoco	153 Seventh Ave (at 19th St)	989-0022
Gulf Oil	E. 23rd St & East River Dr	686-4546
Hess Oil	502 W. 45th St (at Tenth Ave)	245-6594
Texaco	722 First Ave (at 92nd St)	722-2222

Address Locator. – To locate any address on a particular avenue, take the address number, cancel the last digit, divide the remainder by two, then add or subtract the key number indicated below. The resulting number will give you the cross street located nearest to the building on the avenue. For example: to find the cross street of 500 Fifth Ave, drop the last digit, divide by two, then add 18 (50/2=25; 25+18=43); the cross street near 500 Fifth Ave is 43rd St.

Aves A, B, C, D	+3	Seventh Ave: above 110th	+20
First Ave	+3	Eighth Ave	+10
Second Ave	+3	Ninth Ave	+13
Third Ave	+10	Tenth Ave	+14
Fourth Ave	+8	Amsterdam Ave	+60
Fifth Ave:		Broadway: 23rd-192nd St	-30
below 200	+13	Columbus Ave	+60
201-400	+16	Lexington Ave	+22
401-600	+18	Madison Ave	+26
601-775	+20	Park Ave	+35
776-1286 (do not divide by 2)	-18	Central Park West (divide by 10)	+60
1287-1500	+45	Riverside Dr: below 165th St	+72
Ave of the Americas	-12	(divide by 10)	
Seventh Ave: below 110th	+12	West End Ave	+60

GENERAL INFORMATION

The **New York Convention & Visitors Bureau**, located at 2 Columbus Circle, is open Mon–Fri 9am–6pm, weekends & holidays 10am–6pm ☎ 397-8222. A multilingual staff is available to answer questions, give helpful hints and hand out maps and brochures, including the official *Big Apple Guide*.

The **Times Square Visitor & Transit Information Center** is located at 42nd St & Seventh Ave (open daily 10am–7pm). Its multilingual staff provides the tourist with subway and bus maps and offers information on hotels, restaurants, shopping, theaters, events, museums and sightseeing.

The New York Borough President's Office offers a unique service (free) called **Big Apple Greeter**. Volunteer guides, ranging from students to professionals, take out-of-towners on 2- to 4-hour tours of neighborhoods. Particular emphasis is placed on matching interests and language requirements of visitors and guides. It is recommended to make requests at least two weeks in advance: Big Apple Greeter, Manhattan Borough President's Office, 1 Centre St, New York, NY 10007 ☎ 669-8159.

Time Zone. – New York City is located in the Eastern Standard Time (EST) zone, which is five hours ahead of Greenwich Mean Time. Daylight Saving Time is observed from the first Sunday in April (clocks are advanced 1 hour) to the last Sunday in October.

Business hours. – Business hours for most offices are Mon–Fri 9am–5pm. Banking institutions are generally open 9am–3pm and some offer Saturday service (9am–noon). Certain transit locations (Pennsylvania Railroad Station, Grand Central Railroad Terminal) have extended hours. Most retail stores and specialty shops are open Mon–Fri 10am–6pm (Thu 9pm), Sat 10am–6pm, Sun noon–6pm. Small, convenient neighborhood stores—offering everything from the daily necessities to take-out food and flowers—usually stay open past 10pm.

Post Offices. – The main post office (Eighth Ave & W. 33rd St) is open 24hrs/day. The Grand Central Railraod Terminal post office at Lexington Ave & 45th St operates Mon–Fri 8am–9pm, Sat 9am–1pm. Branch offices are located in all five boroughs; for location and phone numbers check the Blue Pages of the phone directory under US Government.
Some sample rates for first-class mail: letter 29 cents (1oz), postcard 19 cents; international letter 50 cents (1/2 oz), postcard 40 cents. **Express mail** for domestic and international destinations with overnight delivery is accepted at all locations. For additional information, contact the US Postal Customer Assistance Center ☎ 967-8585.

Telephone/Telegrams. – A local telephone call is 25 cents. To call long-distance, dial 1+area code+number. To place an international call, dial 011+country code+area code+number or ask the operator by dialing 0 for assistance. Most hotels place a surcharge on calls made from a hotel room.

To send a **telegram or money transfer** contact Western Union ☎800/325-6000 (24hrs). The cost for the service can be charged to a telephone number or a major credit card. The midtown location for Western Union is at 1414 Broadway & 40th St (open Mon–Fri 7am–midnight, weekends 8am–midnight).

The Press. – The city's leading newspaper, *The New York Times,* has a daily circulation of 1.2 million. The Sunday edition (circulation 1.8 million) features special sections on Arts & Entertainment and Travel. Other daily papers are *Daily News* and *New York Newsday.* The *New York Post* is published weekdays only. Daily newspapers from around the US—*The Washington Post, USA Today, Miami Herald* and *Los Angeles Times*—and from overseas are sold at newsstands throughout the city. Weekly publications—*New York Magazine, The New Yorker* and *The Village Voice*—feature articles, reviews, and provide informative listings on events in and around town. *City Guide* and *Where New York* (available free at hotels and restaurants) are handy guides to shopping, restaurants, entertainment and nightlife.

Disabled Visitors. – Most public buildings, city buses, attractions, churches, hotels and restaurants provide wheelchair access. Disabled persons travel at half-fare on the New York Transit System (☎240-4131). A guide to the city's cultural institutions, *Access for All,* is available free of charge from Hospital Audiences, Inc, 220 W. 42nd Street, New York, NY 10036 ☎575-7676.

MONEY

Banks and Foreign Exchanges. – Most banking institutions are located in midtown or the Financial District. Traveler's checks are accepted at all commercial banks. Chemical Bank offers currency exchange at all Manhattan branches.
Thomas Cook Foreign Exchange Service provides two midtown locations: 41 E. 42nd St (Mon–Fri 9am–5pm, Sat 10am–3pm; ☎883-0400) and 630 Fifth Ave (Mon–Fri 9am–5pm; ☎757-6915). The airport branches offer extended hours: in the International Arrival Building at JFK airport (daily 8am–9pm; ☎718/656-8444) and the Delta Terminal at LaGuardia airport (daily 9am–6pm; ☎718/533-0784). Chequepoint Foreign Exchange locations are: 22 Central Park South between Fifth & Sixth Aves (Mon–Fri 8am–8pm, Sat 9am–9pm, Sun 10am–7pm; ☎750-2400) and 1568 Broadway at 47th St (Mon–Fri 8am–9pm, Sat 8am–10pm, Sun 9am–7:30pm; ☎869-6281). The American Express office (374 Park Ave & 53rd St; ☎421-8240) provides a full range of travel services and offers foreign currency exchange. Members of American Express may cash personal checks up to $200.

Credit Cards. – Most banks are members of the network of Automatic Teller Machines (ATM's) allowing visitors from around the world access to cash withdrawals using bank cards and major credit cards. Visitors are advised to check with the bank in their country to obtain a listing of participating banks and details on transaction fees. MasterCard/Eurocard offers its members emergency aid service at all Thomas Cook offices.

Taxes and Tips. – New York City sales tax is 8.25%. In addition, New York City levies a 6% hotel occupancy tax plus $2 per night; for rooms costing more than $100, another 5% New York State hotel occupancy tax is charged. Since hotel rates do not reflect the taxes, travelers should be aware of these added charges.
Tips or service charges are not added to restaurant bills; it is customary to add 15–20%. Taxis drivers are generally tipped 15%, hotel bellhops $1 per bag, hotel doormen $1 per taxi and hotel maids $2 per day of occupancy.

SHOPPING

The Big Apple is a veritable shopper's paradise—everything from the functional to the bizarre lies within easy reach. Numerous fashionable stores are located on Fifth (between 47th & 57th Sts) and Madison Avenues, where window-shopping is a favored pastime. Trendy boutiques and galleries can be found in SoHo. New York City is also home to the nation's fashion industry, located in the Garment District on Seventh Avenue, south of 40th Street. The New York Convention & Visitors Bureau publishes a **guide to shopping**, which lists establishments by subjects. Below is a selection of department and specialty stores.

Department Stores

Barneys New York (midtown)	Madison Ave & 61st St	826-8900
Henri Bendel	712 Fifth Avenue	247-1100
Bergdorf Goodman *(p 36)*	754 Fifth Ave	753-7500
Bloomingdale's *(p 94)*	1000 Third Ave	705-2000
Galeries Lafayette *(p 41)*	10 E. 57th St	355-0022
Lord & Taylor *(p 32)*	424 Fifth Ave	391-3344
Macy's	151 W. 34th St	695-4400
Saks Fifth Avenue *(p 34)*	611 Fifth Ave	753-4000

Book Stores

A & S Book Co.	304 W. 40th St	695-4897
Comic books, sports & movie memorabilia		
Brentano's Bookstore *(p 34)*	597 Fifth Ave	826-2450
Books, foreign language section		
New York Bound Bookshop	50 Rockefeller Plaza	245-8503
Out-of-print books, maps, photographs, prints		
Rizzoli Bookstore *(p 42)*	31 W. 57th St	759-2424
Books, foreign language section		
Traveller's Bookstore	22 W. 52nd St	664-0995
Travel guides & maps		

Specialty Shops

Dean & DeLuca *(p 76)* *Gourmet food*	560 Broadway	431-8350
FAO Schwarz *(p 36)* *Children's toys, video games*	767 Fifth Ave	644-9400
Fortunoff *(p 36)* *Jewelry, silver, tabletop accessories*	681 Fifth Ave	758-6660
Silver Palate *Gourmet take-out, cookbooks*	274 Columbus Ave	799-6340
Steuben *(p 36)* *Crystal*	715 Fifth Ave	752-1441
Tiffany & Co *(p 36)* *Jewelry, crystal, china, silver*	727 Fifth Ave	755-8000
Zabar's *(p 95)* *Gourmet food*	2245 Broadway	787-2000

Take time to browse through the city's various **flea markets**: Antique flea market (26th St & Avenue of the Americas; Sat & Sun 9am–5pm; ☎243-5343); SoHo Antiques Fair and Collectibles Market (Broadway & Grand St; Sat & Sun 9am–5pm; ☎682-2000). Weekend flea markets are held at 76th St & Columbus Ave (Sun) and Charles St & Greenwich Ave (Sat). For the food lover, a farmer's market (Greenmarket) takes place (Wed & Sat) in Union Square *(p 109)*. Over one hundred international galleries of distinctive antiques, jewelry, oriental porcelains and other objets d'art are located in the Manhattan Art & Antiques Center (1050 Second Ave, ☎355-4400; *p 41*).

Museum shops. – Looking for an unusual gift? Visit the city's numerous museum gift shops where items on sale are fashioned after pieces from the permanent collection and special exhibits—jewelry, sculptures, scarves, stationery, prints, posters and art books. Listed below is a selection of the city's most noteworthy museum gift shops:

American Craft Museum	40 W. 53rd St	956-6047
American Museum of Natural History	Central Park West & 81st St	769-5100
The Brooklyn Museum	200 Eastern Parkway	718/638-5000
Cooper-Hewitt National Museum of Design	2 E. 91st St	860-6868
The Frick Collection	1 E. 70th St	288-0700
Solomon R. Guggenheim Museum	1071 Fifth Ave	423-3615
International Center of Photography	1133 Ave of the Americas	768-4680
The Metropolitan Museum of Art	Fifth Ave & 82nd St	535-7710
Museum for African Art	593 Broadway	966-1313
Museum of the City of New York	Fifth Ave & 103rd St	534-1672
The Museum of Modern Art	11 W. 53rd St	708-9669
Pierpont Morgan Library	29 E. 36th St	685-0610
South Street Seaport	12 Fulton St	669-9455
The Studio Museum in Harlem	144 W. 125th St	864-0014
Whitney Museum of American Art	945 Madison Ave	570-3676

SIGHTSEEING

For visitors with little time at their disposal, we recommend the two- or four-day itineraries described on pp 10-13. A great number of tour operators offer a variety of excursions: sightseeing tours, double-decker bus tours, helicopter rides, guided walking tours, escorted museum tours, cruises around the island of Manhattan and harbor dinner cruises. The New York Convention & Visitors Bureau publishes a listing, *Big Apple Sightseeing Services*, which is available free of charge.

Company	☎	Services
Circle Line Sightseeing Yachts	563-3200	Cruises around the island of Manhattan *(p 12)*. Daily Harbor Lights cruise (7–9pm).
Gray Line	397-2600	Sightseeing tours by bus *(p 10)*, boat and helicopter
Island Helicopter Sightseeing	683-4575	Helicopter rides (day & night)
Liberty Helicopter Tours	465-8905	Helicopter rides (day & night)
New York Double-Decker Tours	967-6008	All-day pass for guided bus tour of mid- & downtown neighborhoods
World Yacht	630-8100	Dinner cruise with live music & dancing (7–10pm)

New York for Children. – Tailored exclusively to children, museums such as the Children's Museum of Manhattan and the Brooklyn Children's Museum *(p 157)* offer year-round programs designed to educate and entertain the young. Other museums, including the American Museum of Natural History and the South Street Seaport provide sections of interest to children. Libraries and performance centers throughout the city organize children's programs during the summer months (May–Sept). Various theaters, such as the *Marionette Theater* (Central Park ☎988-9093), offer entertainment for young and old. The city's many parks and zoos also appeal to children. Nature walks, fishing, playgrounds and beaches at Coney Island *(p 157)* and Orchard Beach *(p 149)* are just a short subway ride away. Kids can ride the roller coasters at Astroland Amusement Park at Coney Island.

The *New York Family* magazine (free), distributed in establishments catering to children, publishes a monthly calendar of events. For a copy ☎914/381-7474. For a listing of events, visitors can obtain the flyer, *New York for Kids,* from the New York Convention & Visitors Bureau *(p 179)*.

ENTERTAINMENT

Visitors and New Yorkers alike can find excitement in the city year-round: spring brings performances by visiting theatrical companies from around the world; summer offers colorful street fairs, ethnic festivals and performances in the city's parks; during the fall and winter the curtain rises at the city's cultural institutions. No visit to New York City is complete without experiencing a Broadway show *(listing of theaters p 53)*. Many museums and libraries feature musical evenings, lectures or film shows. In addition, the boroughs are home to various cultural centers. For a more detailed listing of events, consult *The New York Times* (Sunday edition) Arts and Leisure Guide, *Where New York* or the Calendar of Events *(p 178)*.

Lincoln Center for the Performing Arts (Broadway & 64th St) is home to several performance companies. The season runs from mid-September through mid-May. Season subscriptions often make it difficult to obtain tickets, and performances can be sold out before tickets become available for public sale. Tickets for performances at Avery Fisher and Alice Tully halls can be obtained through Lincoln Center Charge (☎721-6500). For all other performances at Lincoln Center, contact the box office. A service charge of $3.75/ticket is added; tickets will be held at the box office for pick-up or mailed. Major credit cards are accepted. Tickets for some performances can also be obtained through Ticketmaster: ☎307-4100 (Fine Arts) and 307-7171 (Concerts).

Lincoln Center *(p 95)*	Concerts, opera and ballet	Box Office
Alice Tully Hall	Concerts by the Chamber Music Society of Lincoln Center & visiting artists	875-5050
Avery Fisher Hall	Concerts by the New York Philharmonic & visiting artists	875-5030
Metropolitan Opera House	Opera & American Ballet Theater performances	362-6000
New York State Theater	Opera & New York City Ballet performances	870-5570

Listed below is a selection of additional venues where theater and dance productions, and philharmonic and pop concerts are given:

Apollo Theatre *(p 100)*	253 W. 125th St	749-5838
Beacon Theatre	2124 Broadway	496-7070
Carnegie Hall & Weill Recital Hall *(p 42)*	156 W. 57th St	247-7800
City Center	131 W. 55th St	581-1212
Joyce Theater *(p 107)*	175 Eighth Ave	242-0800
Madison Square Garden	Seventh Ave (31st & 33rd Sts)	465-6741
Merkin Concert Hall	129 W. 67th St	362-8719
Radio City Music Hall *(p 39)*	1260 Avenue of the Americas	247-4777
Symphony Space	95th St & Broadway	864-5400
Town Hall	123 W. 43rd St	840-2824

Tickets to Broadway Shows. – Visitors can call the Broadway Show Line (☎563-2929) to obtain a complete listing of shows and to order tickets. A word of advice: some popular shows are sold out for months; it is recommended to purchase tickets early. Full-price tickets can be ordered through Ticketmaster (☎307-4100) and Telecharge (☎239-6200 or 800/233-3123). A service charge of $4–7.50 is added to the ticket price; major credit cards are accepted. However, selection of seats is uncertain. To reserve the seat of your choice, contact the theater box office directly (mail or phone). Licensed ticket agencies sometimes have tickets available when the box office is sold out; expect to pay a substantial service fee (up to 33%). For a listing of agencies, consult the Yellow Pages of the telephone directory. Sometimes the hotel concierge may be able to help secure tickets for a performance.

Discount tickets (25%–50%) are sold on the day of the performance to Broadway, Off-Broadway, Lincoln Center and other performing arts events at TKTS booths. Tickets are usually plentiful for less popular shows; the choice of seats, however, is often limited.

Times Square Theater Center (Broadway & 47th St; ☎768-1818)
evening performance tickets (Mon–Sat 3–8pm)
matinee performance tickets (Wed & Sat 10am–2pm)
matinee & evening performance tickets (Sun noon–8pm)

Lower Manhattan Theater Center (Two World Trade Center; mezzanine; ☎768-1818)
evening performance tickets (Mon–Fri 11am–5:30pm; Sat 11:30am–3:30pm)
matinee & Sunday tickets are sold one day prior to performance (11am–8pm)

Brooklyn TKTS Center (Court & Montague Sts; ☎718/625-5015; *map p 153*)
evening performance tickets (Tue–Fri 11am–5:30pm; Sat 11am–3:30pm)
matinee & Sunday tickets are sold one day prior to performance

Discount tickets for same-day music and dance performances are also available at the Music & Dance Booth (Bryant Park, 42nd St & Avenue of the Americas; ☎382-2323; *map p 32*). Vouchers that are redeemable at the theater box office for two tickets at a 33% discount—**Twofers**—can be obtained free of charge from the Convention & Visitors Bureau *(p 179)*. Tickets for a number of **television shows** that are filmed in New York (Geraldo, Joan Rivers, Donahue, Late Show with David Letterman, Saturday Night Live) are available (free) by writing to CBS (524 W. 57th St, New York, NY 10019) or NBC (30 Rockefeller Plaza, New York, NY 10112).

Nightlife. – A night "out on the town" in New York reflects the cornucopia of cultural events and entertainment the city has to offer, from listening to rock, jazz, western or Latin music in clubs scattered throughout Manhattan to dancing to big band tunes in a supper club in the theater district, from attending the latest

Broadway show to reviewing funky fashions in an East Village or SoHo watering hole. The Oak Room in the Algonquin Hotel, Cafe Carlyle at the Hotel Carlyle and Rainbow & Stars in Rockefeller Plaza are but a few of the many cabarets featuring well-known entertainers.

Restaurants. – From the superb dining experience to the quick bite on the run, the more than 17,000 establishments in New York City can satisfy any visitor and every budget. To experience the ambience of the city, the visitor can savor a hearty meal in a neighborhood bistro, enjoy a freshly baked bagel with cream cheese—a New York institution—in one of the numerous coffee shops lining the avenues, or pick up a salty pretzel with mustard from a street vendor. The city's international flavor is reflected in the variety of its restaurants: authentic Chinese cuisine in Chinatown *(p 72)*; Italian pasta and breads in Little Italy *(p 73)*; upscale continental restaurants in midtown and downtown; ethnic fare in the East Village *(p 84)*; American as well as nouvelle cuisine in Greenwich Village *(p 77)*, SoHo *(p 75)* and Tribeca *(p 107)*. Some landmark New York favorites include: Carnegie Deli, Grand Central Oyster Bar, Mamma Leone's, Rainbow Room *(p 39)*, Russian Tea Room *(p 42)*, Sardi's *(p 54)*, Tavern on the Green *(p 90)* and Windows of the World *(p 60)*. Most New Yorkers prefer to go out to dinner after 8pm. Restaurants in and near the theater district offer pre-theater (6–7:45pm) and after-theater dining. Some restaurants may not be open for lunch on Saturday; many establishments are closed all day Sunday. It is wise to reserve in advance for lunch and evening dining.

Spectator Sports. – **Tennis** tournaments are held annually at the West Side Tennis Club (☎718/268-2300) in Forest Hills, Queens, and the USTA National Tennis Center (☎718/ 271-5100) in Flushing Meadows-Corona Park, Queens, site of the US Open Tennis Championships during late-August to mid-September (☎914/ 696-7284).

The season for **thoroughbred racing** extends from early May to late July. There are two race tracks easily reached from downtown Manhattan: Aqueduct Race Track on Rockaway Blvd in Ozone Park, Queens, and Belmont Park (☎718/641-4700) on Hempstead Ave in Elmont, Long Island. Yonkers Raceway (☎914/968-4200) at Central & Yonkers Aves in Yonkers, north of New York City, hosts **harness racing** events year-round.

	Team/Home Games	Season	Schedule & Ticket Info
Football	New York Giants (NFL) Giants Stadium	Sept-Jan	201/935-8222
	New York Jets (NFL) Giants Stadium	Sept-Jan	516/538-7200
Baseball	New York Yankees (AL) Yankee Stadium	Apr-Oct	718/293-6000
	New York Mets (NL) Shea Stadium	Apr-Oct	718/507-8499
Basketball	New York Knickerbockers (NBA) Madison Square Garden	Nov-Apr	465-5867
	New Jersey Nets (NBA) Byrne Meadowlands Arena	Nov-Apr	201/935-8888
Ice Hockey	New York Rangers (NHL) Madison Square Garden	Oct-Apr	465-6040
	New Jersey Devils (NHL) Byrne Meadowlands Arena	Oct-Apr	201/935-6050
	New York Islanders (NHL) Nassau Coliseum	Oct-Apr	516/794-9300

Unless otherwise indicated, all telephone numbers given in this guide are in the 212 calling area. The area code for Brooklyn, Queens, Staten Island and the Bronx is 718. For a listing of emergency and useful telephone numbers, see p 192.

INDEX

Chrysler Building — Building, street or other point of interest
Rockefeller, John D. Jr — Person, historic event or term
Accommodations — Practical information
25, **30**, *110* — Page reference, **principal reference**, *illustration*

Place names outside Manhattan appear with the following abbreviations: the Bronx (Bx), Brooklyn (Bklyn), Staten Island (SI), Hudson River Valley (HRV), Long Island (LI).

Museums within New York City are grouped under the heading Museums. Numbered buildings appear under the name of the street (for 500 Park Avenue, look under Park Avenue).

A

Abstract Expressionism 26
Abyssinian Baptist Church 101
Accommodations 179
Address locator 182
Airport transportation 180
Algonquin Hotel 54
Alice Tully Hall 96
Allen, Woody 27, 91
Alwyn Court Apartments 42
American Standard Building 34
Amman, O.H. 109, 157
Amsterdam Avenue 95
Ansonia Hotel 95
Apartment hotels 95
Apollo Theatre 100
Aqueduct Race Track Queens 160
Armory Show 19, **26**
Art Deco 25
Art Museum at Stony Brook LI 171
Art Students League 42
Ascension, Church of the 82
Ash Can school **26**, 78
Astor, Caroline 30, 31
Astor, John Jacob **31**, 36, 83
Astor, William 30, 31
Astor Place 83
Astoria Hotel 31
Atlantic Avenue Bklyn 154
AT&T Headquarters *see* Sony Plaza
Audubon, John J. **113**, 144
Audubon Terrace 100, **113**
Avenue of the Americas (Sixth Avenue) 39
    No. 1251: 40
Avery Fisher Hall 96, 185

B

Bacall, Lauren 95
Banks & foreign exchanges 183
Barbedienne, Ferdinand 97
Barnard, George Grey 99, **101**, 103
Barnes, Edward Larrabee 25, 40, 41, 113
Barr, Alfred H. Jr 140
Bartholdi, Frédéric-Auguste 55
Bartow-Pell Mansion Bx 150
Basquiat, Jean-Michel 26, 143
Battery Park 66

Battery Park City 60
Bayard Cutting Arboretum LI 174
Bear Mountain HRV 170
Beaux-Arts 24
Bellows, George 26, 86, 114, 156
Benchley, Robert 27, 54
Benton, Thomas Hart 26, 40, 143
Bernstein, Leonard 95
Bierstadt, Albert 26, 126, 156, *156*, 167
Bleecker Street 81
Bloomingdale's 94
Bogardus, James 76
Booth, Edwin 85, 108
Boscobel HRV 169
Bowery, The 74
Bowery Savings Bank 74
Bowery Savings Bank Building 46
Bowling Green 65
Bowne House Queens 161
Bradford, William 18
Brentano's Book Store 34
Breuer, Marcel 146, 169
British Empire Building 38
Broadway 51, 76
Bronx, The 147
Bronx Community College Bx 149
Bronx Zoo Bx 147, *147*
Brooklyn 152
Brooklyn-Battery Tunnel 66
Brooklyn Academy of Music Bklyn 158
Brooklyn Botanic Garden Bklyn 154
Brooklyn Bridge *29,* 68
Brooklyn Heights Bklyn 152
Brooklyn Historical Society Bklyn 153
Brooklyn Public Library Bklyn 154
Brownstones 24
Bryant, William Cullen **34**, 87
Bryant Park 34
Burgee, John 25, 41, 52, 107, 144
Burlington House 40
Burnham, Daniel H. 109
Burr, Aaron **63**, 69, 101

C

Cafes 78
Calder, Alexander 28, 60, 146, 170
Calendar of Events 178
Campbell Funeral Chapel 92
Canal Street 75

Carl Schurz Park 94
Carlyle Hotel 92
Carnegie, Andrew 42, 114
Carnegie Hall 42
Carrère and Hastings 32, 45, 75, 115
Carriage Museum at Stony Brook LI 171
Cast iron 76
Castle Clinton National Monument 66
CBGB Club 83
CBS Building 40
Celanese Building 39
Central Park 87, *87*
Central Park Zoo 88
Century Apartments 95
Chanin, Irwin 46, 95
Chanin Building 46
Channel Gardens 38
Chase, Salmon P. 64
Chase Manhattan Bank 63
Chelsea 107
Chemical Bank 34
Cherry Lane Theater 81
Chinatown 72, *72*
Chinese Exclusion Acts 72
Christopher Street 80
Chrysler Building 47, *47*
Church, Frederic E. 26, 114, 126, 144, 167
Citicorp Center 45
City Development 25
City Hall 69, *70*
City University of New York 34
Civic Center 68
Clemente, Francesco 83
Cleveland, Grover 56
Clinton, De Witt 66
Cloisters, The 101, *104*
Cold Spring Harbor LI 172
Cole, Thomas 26, 126, 144, 156, 167
Collens, Charles 98, 102
Colonnade Row 83
Columbia University 98
Columbus Avenue 95
Columbus Circle 95
Conceptual Art 26
Coney Island Bklyn 157
Conference House SI 166
Consolidated Edison Building 109
Cooper, Peter 83
Cooper Union for the Advancement of Science and Art 83
Corning Glass Building 36
Cotton Club 100
Coward, Noel 95
Cram, Ralph Adams 96
Cram, Goodhue and Ferguson 35
Crédit Lyonnais Building 40

187

Emergency Numbers

Police–Fire–Ambulance **911**
Poison Control Center (24hrs) 764-7667
Kaufman's Pharmacy (24hrs) .... 577 Lexington Ave (at E. 50th St) 755-2266
Dental Emergency Service 679-3966

Area codes

Manhattan **212**
The Bronx, Brooklyn, Queens, Staten Island **718**
New Jersey .... **201 & 908**

Useful Numbers

JFK International Airport 718/656-4520
LaGuardia Airport 718/476-5000
Newark International Airport 201/961-2000
American Express .... 374 Park Ave at E. 53rd St 421-8240
    Lost or stolen traveler's checks (24hrs) 800/221-7282
Baby Sitters Guild 682-0227
Grand Central Railroad Terminal .... E. 42nd St & Park Ave 532-4900
NY Convention & Visitors Bureau .... 2 Columbus Circle 397-8222
NYC Transit Authority 718/330-1234
    Lost or stolen property 718/625-6200
National Helicopter .... E. 34th St & FDR Drive 800/645-3494
Passenger Ship Terminal .... 711 Twelfth Ave at W. 52nd St 466-7974
Pennsylvania Railroad Station
    (AMTRAK) .... W. 31st & 33rd Sts at 7th & 8th Aves 582-6875
Main Post Office (24hrs) .... W. 33rd St & Eighth Ave 967-8585
Port Authority Bus Terminal .... W. 42nd St & Eighth Ave 564-8484
Satellite Airline Terminal .... 100 E. 42nd St 986-0888
Staten Island Ferry .... South Ferry - Whitehall Station 806-6940
Traveler's Aid Services .... 1481 Broadway 944-0013
Time 976-1616
Weather (24hrs) 976-1212

MANUFACTURE FRANÇAISE DES PNEUMATIQUES MICHELIN
Société en commandite par actions au capital de 2 000 000 000 de francs
Place des Carmes-Déchaux – 63 Clermont-Ferrand (France)

R.C.S. Clermont-Fd B 855 200 507

© Michelin et Cie, Propriétaires-Éditeurs 1993

Dépôt légal 9-1993 — ISBN 2-06-155111-4 — ISSN 0763-1383

**No part of this publication may be reproduced in any form
without prior permission of the publisher.**

Printed in the United States of America 09-93-65 by Hart Graphics, Austin, Texas